INTENSIVE PSYCHOTHERAPY FOR PERSISTENT DISSOCIATIVE PROCESSES

The Norton Series on Interpersonal Neurobiology

Louis Cozolino, PhD, Series Editor

Allan N. Schore, PhD, Series Editor, 2007–2014

Daniel J. Siegel, MD, Founding Editor

The field of mental health is in a tremendously exciting period of growth and conceptual reorganization. Independent findings from a variety of scientific endeavors are converging in an interdisciplinary view of the mind and mental well-being. An interpersonal neurobiology of human development enables us to understand that the structure and function of the mind and brain are shaped by experiences, especially those involving emotional relationships.

The Norton Series on Interpersonal Neurobiology provides cutting-edge, multidisciplinary views that further our understanding of the complex neurobiology of the human mind. By drawing on a wide range of traditionally independent fields of research—such as neurobiology, genetics, memory, attachment, complex systems, anthropology, and evolutionary psychology—these texts offer mental health professionals a review and synthesis of scientific findings often inaccessible to clinicians. The books advance our understanding of human experience by finding the unity of knowledge, or consilience, that emerges with the translation of findings from numerous domains of study into a common language and conceptual framework. The series integrates the best of modern science with the healing art of psychotherapy.

A Norton Professional Book

Intensive Psychotherapy for Persistent Dissociative Processes
The Fear of Feeling Real

Richard A. Chefetz

W. W. Norton & Company
New York • London

Note to Readers: Models and/or techniques described in this volume are illustrative or are included for general informational purposes only; neither the publisher nor the author(s) can guarantee the efficacy or appropriateness of any particular recommendation in every circumstance.

For information about permission to reproduce selections from this book, write to Permissions, W. W. Norton & Company, Inc., 500 Fifth Avenue, New York, NY 10110

For information about special discounts for bulk purchases, please contact W. W. Norton Special Sales at specialsales@wwnorton.com or 800-233-4830

Manufacturing by Courier Westford
Book design by Paradigm Graphic Design, Martha Meyer
Production manager: Leeann Graham

Library of Congress Cataloging-in-Publication Data

Chefetz, Richard A., author.
 Intensive psychotherapy for persistent dissociative processes : the fear of feeling real / Richard A. Chefetz. — First edition.
    p. ; cm. — (Norton series on interpersonal neurobiology)
 Includes bibliographical references and index.
 ISBN 978-0-393-70752-6 (hardcover)
 I. Title. II. Series: Norton series on interpersonal neurobiology.
 [DNLM: 1. Dissociative Disorders—therapy. 2. Psychotherapy—methods. WM 173.6]
 RC480.5
 616.89'14—dc23
                        2014042190

W. W. Norton & Company, Inc., 500 Fifth Avenue, New York, N.Y. 10110
            www.wwnorton.com
W. W. Norton & Company Ltd., 15 Carlisle Street, London W1D 3BS

2 3 4 5 6 7 8 9 0

Poem, Longfellow: Public Domain

Waking the Dead Therapist:
"Waking the Dead Therapist," Richard A. Chefetz, *Psychoanalytic Dialogues*, August 11, 2009, Taylor & Francis Ltd.

Life as Performance Art:
This was originally published in *Knowing, Not-Knowing and Sort-of Knowing: Psychoanalysis and the Experience of Uncertainty* by Jean Petrucelli (published by Karnac Books in 2010), and is reprinted with kind permission of Karnac Books

Dedication

Myron "Mike" Chefetz (1924-1971) deserves recognition as a man of extraordinary intellectual curiosity and talent. He was a good father, a good husband, and a good friend. He never got to write his book, and that is a sadness. Though his death was a great loss I still have two special things he gave me that have become an essential part of who I am: he taught me to love ideas and he took me fishing.

Now I've written my book, Pops, and I think you'd like it. I still go fishing, regularly, in many different ways. Thanks for helping to get me started. Wish you were here. Godspeed.

Contents

Preface:
Holding Hope

I HOPE THE READER WILL FIND THE WORDS IN THIS BOOK AND THE EXPERIENCE they create useful in his or her clinical work—and perhaps also in life. There, it's begun: I am hoping. Hope, it seems, is something I do.

The text that follows is not an easy emotional read, not least because the subject matter is almost invariably related to the horrors of severe interpersonal abuse. The people depicted in these pages have not had an easy time of it.[1] Given that it may be challenging, I hope the professional reader is able to take some consolation in clinical distance while retaining a willingness to engage. This book will have other readers, and I want to address them here: If you are reading about you, or a life close to what you've lived, then please take care of yourself to protect what needs to be protected inside you in the service of making the reading tolerable and useful.

How do my patients tolerate these treatments? One woman, after many years of treatment and many crises of suicidal proportion, put it this way as she lingered at the doorway to my office at the end of a session several years ago: "Stop telling me you hope I'll keep myself safe. What is that? I hate it when you say that. Stop telling me you hope. I don't want it. Just keep it away from me."

I replied, "I hear you, Scylla, and it's also true I really do hope you'll keep yourself safe. You are really the only one who can do that."

---

[1] In this text brief vignettes are composites, and written permission was obtained from people for extended case reports of their treatment. Some data has been intentionally distorted to further protect identity without changing the gist of the treatment described.

"Yeah, well I'm sick of you hoping this and hoping that. So just stop it. I don't want any of your hope."

"I suppose you're not quite ready to acknowledge your own hope."

"You're out of your mind."

"Since you don't seem to be ready to have your own hope, would you mind much if I hold on to your hope for you? I'll keep it safe until you're ready to own it. And just in case there's some hope hidden inside you in a place where it's not in danger of being dismissed or destroyed, I'll still hope you might find a way to know about it and not be so frightened of it."

"I still think you're out of your mind." And she left, and came back the next week for her appointment, just as I had hoped.

What's it like to be an adult when childhood was filled with hope that was repeatedly tricked and betrayed? Who would want to hope and be disappointed—tricked and raped again? Such patients have an extra hard time of it in today's managed care world. Some people hope to make a career in one of the helping professions, train arduously for years, and then find their treatments systematically challenged and undermined by insurance companies who seem to serve private interests rather than public ones. Opposite them are people who have been severely abused and seek treatment only to find they are misunderstood. Too often their unconscious need for self-protection gets them labeled with pejorative diagnostic labels or misdiagnosed. Sometimes they finally meet a clinician who doesn't judge them but says they can't treat them because they're not a specialist in trauma treatment. What happens to hope in this kind of context?

I'm hopeful that reading this book will generate resilient hope for people who have minds too governed by persistent dissociative process, leftover emergency strategies from earlier in life that hobble the growth of a child and distort the metamorphosis into conscious adulthood. I also hope that clinicians who read this book will keep treating their challenging patients and not refer them to a specialist for treatment. One doesn't need to be a specialist. One just needs to gather some special knowledge and add it to the important basics without which no special knowledge is particularly useful.

Besides, it's all about the relationship, in the first place and all the way through.

A book writes itself. The author is the shepherd who guides the ideas growing in his mind, foraging for nourishment, sometimes in the most unlikely places. In these pages I attempt to show the reader what it's like to be both patient and therapist in intensive psychotherapy for persistent dissociative process. Please be aware that my patients are truth tellers. Even when they sometimes say things that are off, they are always trying to tell me the truth about something. In that context I don't believe it is an act of kindness, nor one of propriety, to change the language of an intense and miserable discourse on a painful experience like incest or sexual addiction and end up distorting the truth. So I have not dressed things up to be acceptable to more modest ears. At the same time, I have not disclosed anything close to the worst horrors I have heard about. In some cases, I truly do wish I didn't know now what I didn't know then (Chefetz 2006), back in the idyllic early days of my training as a psychotherapist. To be a faithful witness to a person telling the story of unbearable pain there is no turning away, even if we acknowledge the wish to do just that.

This book is divided roughly in half. The first part introduces the reader to dissociative processes, the vicissitudes of self-states, the beginnings of treatment, the politics of emotion, and the underlying neurobiology relevant to these domains. I prefer to access my knowledge of neurobiology when it is salient in my understanding of clinical process and when it changes how I view my patients and what I say to them. The second part constitutes an immersion in difficult and challenging clinical process, in sexual addiction, countertransference-driven impasse, negativity and negative therapeutic reactions, and enactment. Chapters 10, 11, and 12 contain extensive verbatim dialogue from the same case. Chapter 12 is verbatim dialogue with minimal annotation and stands on the commentaries in Chapters 10 and 11.

In the last three chapters I certainly have not shied away from possible controversy. I am hoping this book will be used for teaching purposes. In that spirit I have shown work that is illustrative of the kinds of inevitable impasses that are part and parcel of any intensive psychotherapy. I discuss the flaws in this work and how my patient and I both learned from engaging in the struggle to understand what neither of us understood. It's a risk to show work that is not going well, but the bigger fault would be to hide it or dress it up like it never happens that way. I hope to meet the challenge that my patients must deal with, being real about what happens.

The case reports are unusual in their extent. Several people with whom I've worked as their psychotherapist appear in more than one chapter. The gift of their permission to use material from their treatments is an extraordinary act of kindness and courage. Every one of these people hoped it would make a difference in the lives of other patients. I don't want to go any further without thanking the people with whom I work in psychotherapy, especially the people who allowed me to write clinical examples taken from their hard work. Imagine what it is like to see your life and your pain in print. I hope the explorations in these pages benefit you and speeds your healing. Thank you for the privilege of working with you. Our work together has made me a better clinician and a better person.

Acknowledgments

THERE ARE MANY KINDS OF GIFTS REFLECTED IN THESE PAGES. LOOKING BACK I have been struck by how extraordinarily fortunate I have been to know so many wise and talented people. Some of the gifts that have been given to me were ones of time in reading earlier versions of these chapters. Time is such a special commodity. These readers provided an extraordinary service to me. I appreciate your efforts. Just having some feedback that what I was writing could be read and enjoyed was an enormous gift. Some readers offered important structural suggestions for changing the direction of chapters, and others begged for clarification of the content. I received a lot of spot-on suggestions. I would like to thank these people for reading, as well as commenting: Zeke Reich, Ellen Lacter, Steve Frankel, Sally Wood, Cathy Neuhauser, Eric Tootell, Tiffany Wetzel, Lisa Lewis, Haim Weinberg, Melissa Rooney, Evelyn Schaffer, Christine Volker, Gabriele Case, Katie Polsky, Lisa Charlebois, Martha Gilmore, Melissa Rooney, Melody Kirkham, Lynette Danylchuk, Kimberly Porter, Andrea Rechtin, Kay Goldstein, Janice Foss, Kelly Couacaud, Krissa Jackson, Carissa Mayer, Ava Schlesinger, Gloria Rodberg, Sharon Hoferer, Rick Hohfeler, Don Chiappinelli, Sheila Cahill, and Martin Dorahy. There are other clinicians with whom I have shared regular group interactions, some over many years, and who have simultaneously both put up with and encouraged me to spell out my ideas: Jean Carter, Monica Callahan, Chris Courtois, Eric Shaw, Shelly Itzkowitz, Elizabeth Howell, Karen Hoppenwaser, Marg Hainer, Joe Silvio, Steve Paley, Tybe Diamond, Linda Guerkink, Adina Shapiro, Kathryn Chefetz, and Myrna Frank. Thank you for "mixing it up" with me.

My thanks also goes to Gordon Kirschner, Don Ross, Rich Loewenstein, Rick Kluft, Bethany Brand, Eli and Liora Somer, Joan Turkus, Gloria Rodberg, Sharon Hoferer, Ava Schlesinger, and Mauricio Cortina, for your friendship and support through the years. Thanks to Steve Frankel for your tenacious respect for the meaning of friendship and for being there for me. Philip Bromberg has been inspiring and challenging, encouraging me to write and grow my voice. I am indebted to you, Philip, in many ways. Thank you. I am grateful to Nancy McWilliams for her support and encouragement in this project. I am grateful also to Bob Winer and Sharon Alperovitz for making New Directions, a program in psychoanalytic writing at the Washington Center for Psychoanalysis, a place where I could grow as a writer. Thank you to Joe Lichtenberg and Rosemary Segalla for paving the road for me to immerse myself in self psychology at the Institute of Contemporary Psychotherapy and Psychoanalysis. A special thanks to Wilma Bucci and Bernie Maskitt for their collaboration in studying the discourse of some of my clinical work, as well as challenging me to hone my ideas. And to John Kerr, thank you for your review of seemingly endless iterations of this text. You've made this a much more readable book and taught me much about writing and editing. To my editor at W.W. Norton, Deborah Malmud, thank you for giving me the opportunity to publish with you. Thanks also for your gentle but insistent limit setting on extensions of my publication deadline. And thanks to Sara Peterson, editorial assistant at Norton, who graciously held my hand while I figured out how to do permissions for the text. Most of all, thank you to my wife, Kathryn Chefetz, for both encouraging me to write and tolerating the process as it stole uncountable hours from our time together. I could not do the work I do without the wellspring of your love. Long live the magic that is in the love we have for each other.

INTENSIVE PSYCHOTHERAPY FOR
PERSISTENT DISSOCIATIVE PROCESSES

Chapter 1

A Mind Hiding from Itself

There was a little girl
Who had a little curl
Right in the middle of her forehead;
And when she was good
She was very good indeed,
But when she was bad she was horrid.
—Henry Wadsworth Longfellow

DISSOCIATION IS ABOUT THE SMALL STUFF, ABOUT THE LITTLE CURLS OF experience that are visible if we look, but often go unnoticed in their routine presence. Dissociation is also about certain kinds of clinical engagements where what is barely noticeable dances with what is solidly impenetrable as the dancers following a rhythm that can be both compelling and baffling.

Dissociation is not just a marker for life experience gone poorly. Dissociative process is something we use every day as we unconsciously sort salience in the flow of consciously and unconsciously perceived mental input. Associative process alerts our awareness that something is worth noticing. Dissociation tells us we need not pay any attention. The healthy result of this sorting is a coherent mind.

The problem is that dissociative process gets recruited when association becomes emotionally dangerous and we can't afford to know about our experience. By itself, that's actually not so bad, really. Just think about the utility of keeping stress to a manageable level simply by closing your associative eyes when there's too much to "take in." The problem comes when dissociative process won't turn itself off. Most of us take having a mind of our own for granted. People plagued by dissociative process don't and can't make that assumption. Sometimes the small stuff is also the big stuff.

Contemporary research offers some insight (but only some) into the puzzles of dissociative process gone awry. Infant attachment has taught us a good deal about dissociation in both children and adults (Lyons-Ruth, Dutra, Schuder, and Bianchi 2006; Ogawa, Sroufe, Weinfield, Carlson, and Egelend 1997), and yet there are still plenty of puzzles. Consider that the kind of persistent mental disorganization and difficulty in thinking and perceiving that are part of the dissociative legacy of these early attachment difficulties are really not solutions a person would voluntarily choose. These difficulties in having and using a mind are regularly experienced as entailing a devaluation of self and can bring in their wake poignant experiences of self-shaming (Lansky 1992). We won't really understand what is going on with these kinds of difficulties unless we can feel and sense them from a patient's point of view.

Understanding what really happens in dissociation—or in clinical entities like dissociative identity disorder—will not be achieved by a technical effort to decide once and for all what the neural or psychological basis of dissociation is all about. That will help, but it must be joined by an effort to spell out in clear and straightforward language what the subjective experience of dissociation is like. This kind of empathetic grasp, hard to achieve, is essential to understanding how the subjective experience of dissociation typically influences the course and conduct of a psychotherapeutic inquiry.

On the Threshold of a Handshake

When dissociative processes are overly active in a person's life, they create a burden that is palpable and yet hidden from view. Consider the following scene. On a typically muggy, but rainy and surprisingly dark Tuesday morning in June, after many years of a twice weekly psychoanalytic psychotherapy, Alice and I stood a couple of feet from each other, near the doorway leading out of my office, as I wondered whether she would reach out to shake my hand in our typical ritual of parting. She seemed hesitant. She was probably reconsidering the usual handshake because the time we had just spent together had the feeling of "pulling teeth." The sense of needing to tug and pull things out of Alice never felt right to me, but this was a familiar feature of her treatment. Things felt hidden, things seemed hard to see.

It was as if Alice did everything possible to hide her mind from me—and from herself. Sometimes she seemed to be aware of this hiding. In particular, she would implore me to help her make contact with those parts of her mind that left a visible trail of behaviors she didn't want. For example, there were eating behaviors that had left her morbidly obese. She would report how helpless she felt finding herself stopping to buy a half-gallon of ice cream on the way home after a long day of work. She would feel ashamed if the clerk recognized she had just done that the night before.

Yet if I asked about the details of her experience in not being able to control her actions, she would deflect the conversation. And if on occasion she answered more directly, it was in the form of two-faced replies. On the one hand, she couldn't stop herself from doing what she didn't want to do. She watched in horror as she bought the ice cream. On the other hand, from another vantage point in her mind, she said she knew exactly what she was doing. She said this was normal for people with eating disorders and wondered why I belabored the point.

There were many times when, after saying something, she would promptly edit the text of what she had just spoken to fix a curl that was out of place, intentionally deflecting our attention away from a fragment of dissociative process in her thinking or feeling. There were also times when she told me flat out that she didn't believe dissociative disorders existed and that whatever she was doing in therapy that looked dissociative she did to please me. Then there were the times when she was flabbergasted that she had said something she had completely not intended to say. And there were still other times when she would chastise herself under her breath—"We'll have none of that"—when she was left inexplicably without access to her adult fund of knowledge and felt like a child. Yet she maintained these things were normal, that these were things normal people experienced. Finally there were the relatively rare times she was able to talk with me about different parts of her mind, some of whom felt younger and filled to overflowing with emotion, and some of whom felt older, went to work, and had nothing but disdain for the disruptive experiences of being emotional, especially angry.

Her anger was openly hated. She sometimes experienced her anger as being a discrete self-state, as more or less belonging to a different Alice entirely. Here a clinician might readily think of the different parts of her mind as "self-states" or "isolated subjectivities." Such terms by themselves did not solve the riddle of what was going on. As much as I had the experience of Alice changing perspectives in a contradictory manner that defied logic, she herself did not. When she read this case report prior to publication, for example, she was more than prepared to agree with its accuracy. She went to great lengths to emphasize that in each instance what she had said had the ring of truth to her. She simply did not notice the contradictoriness. For her, the isolation of subjectivities erased from consciousness the markings of conflict between self-states. The juxtaposition of mutually incompatible elements of experience without anxiety was a dissociative phenomenon associated with self-state changes. In the hypnosis literature it was known as trance logic (Orne 1959). The consequence for me was that the "ring of truth" she heard sounded off-key in my ears.

Alice had really been given little choice about this style of living. Alternately aware of self-states and then intensely in denial and disavowal of them, she had forged an unconscious accommodation to her family. She had learned well that her only hope for maintaining attachment was to not be angry, indeed, not to have any feelings or thoughts that contradicted what either of her parents felt or believed. Burying her feelings wouldn't have worked as well if she knew she had done it.

In the end, Alice was overly successful. She was painfully bereft of a regular emotional life. For her, expressing emotion was like a jail-break where pent-up feelings swarmed out of their prison, bursting with energy and flowing in a torrent that continued until they were exhausted. The eruptions left her humiliated. She hated these explosive episodes of feeling.

As a child, Alice's feelings would also burst out at times and make themselves visible, to her dismay. When she was angry in grade school and disrupted the class, her desk was put out in the hallway. She compensated by believing she was special to be allowed to work on her own with the advanced subjects her teacher provided. She was a gifted student. As an adult, she had lost a job and also an important advancement after angry outbursts. She maintained long-term relationships with several people, but under no circumstances could she let herself feel angry with them. Her ban on anger continued the family policy.

In our relationship, anger had to be made welcome somehow. Anger had to find a way into the room without being dismissed. But it seemed that even though anger was not banned by me, Alice would dissociatively do the deed. The same would happen with other unacceptable emotions. She expressed desperation in her wish to feel her feelings. But after feeling the leading edge of an emotion in a session, she would be unable to maintain conscious alertness. I would try to help her stay alert as I would notice her struggling to avoid trance sleep, her eyes rolling up into her head, the lids involuntarily closing.

In talking with Alice, I came to believe that whatever emotion came into the treatment room needed space to blossom. I also believed it had to come on its own without provocation. It took quite some time to learn that this respectful stance was only partly useful. The childhood humiliations attendant on Alice's emotional life in conjunction with her adult wish to have her feelings combined to ensure that the regularly irregular emergence of her feelings came at great risk of her being shamed. The shame then led to periods of unconsciously hiding the very feelings she longed to feel, with her acknowledging only that she felt numb and denying that her feelings were waiting to be claimed somewhere in the dissociative lost luggage department of her mind.

The opposition between her determination to feel her feelings and her scripted need to detach from emotion finally became visible, almost by chance, during a period in the treatment when things were actually flowing quite well. This was about a year before we stood at the office door with me wondering if we would shake hands. In this earlier period Alice had taken the time to point out to me how pleased she was with our work, which was in contrast to how she frequently dismissed its usefulness. She thanked me in the form of a praising email. The next session ended up focusing on her anger. The email set the stage:

> It worked once again. I am basking in the glow of a good
> therapy session. I really appreciate it, and you, when
> things go well. I also think I am starting to remember
> more. But the more I remember, the less bad things seem.
> I can't recall my father hitting me when I was six years
> old, for example. Well, only a couple of times. The worst
> of it came when I was older and would stand up to him.
> Actually just thinking about this creeps me out, so I won't
> write any more on it.

In her own words is a description of how she handles a potential recognition of emotional experience. She is trying to convince herself that she really doesn't have a trauma history: "the more I remember, the less bad things seem." But then she wavers. "I can't recall" turns into "only a couple of times," but just as quickly comes "this creeps me out," so she decides to stop writing. Perhaps she had distracted herself with something while she was at the computer and the distraction left things still half-buried. Her rational, conscious effort to deflect herself away from consciousness of the unpleasant emotion is also clear. Here it is easy to spot because we have a written text. Imagine how quickly this might go by in a conversation, this "little curl" getting readjusted; one moment longer, and nothing would seem out of place.

When Alice was able to work in a traditional, communicative manner, it was a big relief for both of us and the mood was sometimes light-hearted. There would be mutual enjoyment of the jokes and word plays that might occur during a session. She had a brilliant mind and a great sense of humor. So in the context of a somewhat jovial and conversational tone early in the next session after the email, she handed me a set of papers from a mail-order pharmacy so that I could write new prescriptions for her medications. She was changing insurance companies. We continued our friendly banter as I walked over to my desk to write out the prescriptions. As it happened, her clonazepam prescription was last in the pile, and I privately hesitated in writing a mail-order prescription for a three-month supply of several hundred tablets of this standard minor tranquilizer. It would save her money. It was efficient. It was a potential weapon.

She had been admitted to the hospital six months before the scene in my office after sequestering hundreds of pills that she intended to swallow. We never did figure out what was going on, and the treatment team in the hospital was only able to say she was not a current risk for suicide at the time of her discharge. For months afterward, I doled out her medications in smaller amounts, every few weeks. Eventually it became a scene of repeated painful shaming because Alice no longer felt consciously at risk of self-harm. This was not a little curl; it was a great big one. But it had gone back into place, and she needed to have some trust placed in her to function as an adult. We both put out of our minds how potentially lethal she was. A colleague might have said that we were doing the dance of enactment, both our minds partially closed, in the service of maintaining a relationship (Baker, 1997; Bromberg, 2006).

I reminded myself that we had worked on the safety issue as much as we could earlier that year. The treatment had been going well for months. She had already had over 300 clonazepam pills in her possession. Refilling the prescription was routine.

All this private thinking happened in the briefest of moments. I thought again about how challenging it had been to discuss this subject with her in the past. It upset her. That should be avoided. As I had that thought, I started to verbalize my stream of consciousness. I was still thinking in the background about my old worries of her suicidality. With flickering awareness for these last thoughts in one part of my mind, I said, "I am thinking that we really don't need to worry anymore about my giving you a prescription for a large amount of clonazepam?"

If I might have said this in a way that told her I was proud of her for having kept herself safe, perhaps it would have been all right. But in the way I phrased it and used a voice tone that off-handedly asked a question, as if there was still an issue with her safety, it was not okay. She responded, understandably, with an angry outburst of upset: "Why did you have to bring that up, now?! Things have been going so well in therapy. I knew this would happen. I can't believe it. I came into this session feeling good and now I just want to leave. I'm sick of this happening. Why can't you leave well enough alone? Why did you have to bring this up? Why in the world would you do that?"

I handed her the completed prescriptions as I cautiously made my way back from the desk to my chair, opposite the couch where she sat. She was fuming. She had boosted her body to the edge of the couch, ready to stand up and leave, I thought. As if she read my mind she stood and said, "I've had it. I'm leaving. This is worthless. I'm not going to be able to do any work here today. I might as well leave. This is just a waste of time. Why did you do that? Why did you have to bring that up? This is totally predictable. I just can't work with you. That's it. I'm leaving." She was filled with an energy that aimed its vision straight at the door as she began to walk out.

I gently called her name, and then said in a concerned tone, "You know if you leave now, you take these feelings with you and then what? You'll have these feelings and you won't have learned how to cope with them or what to do with them. I don't think that will do you any good. You'll just end up in an angry spiral. You've done that before. It doesn't help. Why don't you stay and I'll help you work on these feelings? They're just feelings, right? You just need to learn to tolerate them. Go ahead, come on. Just sit down and let's work this through."

I could see her wavering. I had started speaking before her hand had reached the doorknob. She paused within reach of the handle, seemingly thinking things over. That by itself was unusual for her when we got into one of these scenes. She often didn't hesitate at all.

There were two sound-dampening doors to get through, or else she would have had much more success in the past at leaving without my being able to utter a word. I spoke to her hesitation, "Come on, it's okay, you and I really are a good team. We can work on this and get through it."

She sat down. I spoke immediately—I probably had one chance to douse the flames. She had been barely tolerant of being angry in my presence. "Alice, I'm really sorry that I brought up the old medication issue. I know it's resolved. I think I must just have started verbalizing my stream of consciousness as we talked. I ought to have just privately reviewed my thoughts about your safety, and said nothing. You're right, it was unnecessary. I'm sorry." She looked taken aback by my apology. She seemed to soften as she accepted the apology, and I took that as an opportunity to try to pursue what happened in a dynamic frame.

"What do you think happened here this morning, Alice? Is this a repeat of an old scene?" She somehow was able to address the question. She confirmed there was an old script. She recalled how when she was younger she would sometimes become very angry. The result was always harsh looks and dismissive language from her parents as if they were saying to her that she was ugly and her feelings disgusting. She was usually told to go to her room on these occasions, and as she got older she didn't wait to be told, she simply went. She had no recollection of what happened in her room, or how long she stayed there. This happened many times during childhood, and it continued during her teenage years. "My parents used to call this my being in an angry snit. I would get stuck in it, and I couldn't get out."

"I don't think of what happened here as an angry snit, Alice. I think of it as you becoming angry when I did something that hurt your feelings. I understand why you were angry with me. I hurt your feelings. I'm glad your anger could be present to say we needed to talk out the feelings. I think that is something pretty new for you, and a good thing." We continued to talk about the details of past scenes of anger and its dismissal by her parents and how each parent had a particular style of humiliating her.

It could not have been more than a couple of minutes before the session was to end when she suddenly changed tracks and shifted into a space where she was looking sad and young and remorseful. I hadn't expected this. She spoke in a submissive tone, eyes somewhat downcast as if ashamed: "I really am sorry. I don't know why I behaved that badly. We have been working so well together lately. I'm so sorry for how badly I behaved." She had been conversational prior to this, but not apologetic, and most certainly not submissively downcast. Her understandable anger had disappeared. She had experienced a state change. What was she playing out?

"Alice, we need to be really careful here. Your apology is unnecessary. I'm the one who hurt you. You didn't do anything wrong. You got angry, upset, and that was after I said something that was over-the-top, hurtful, and not useful. Are you doing guilt here? Is this part of the old scene after your anger comes out?"

I was working hard to reduce the potential for shame. Her face changed again. Her adult presence returned. She looked at me, and we talked. We learned that as a child she would leave the isolation of her room, find her parents, and apologize for her poor behavior and beg their forgiveness. They would accept, and then nothing more was said. She was playing out the script of the old scene.

"We need to be alert to the possibility, Alice, that if you are angry with me, you'll end up somehow repeating the old scene and burying your anger while taking on guilt for something you didn't do. I hurt you. Should you apologize for that? I don't think so. It's hard for you to hold on to and know your anger until it's spent."

She continued in her more adult collaborative state as we tried to sort out what had happened. But the apologetic state of mind that had come over her didn't tolerate my saying there was no need for an apology and, unfortunately, had disappeared as suddenly as it had appeared. This left no opportunity for further exploration of those apologetic feelings. As might have been predictable, the following email arrived later that day. The apologetic self-state's affective charge had made its way into Alice's adult thinking:

I'm sorry I behaved so badly today. You got to see a perfect example of the snit. My father always accused me of
doing this if I didn't get my way. Today I was so excited to
get back to work with you, and when that didn't happen
the way I wanted, I flipped out. I was really angry with
you. But it wasn't your fault. I grossly overreacted and I
apologize. I don't know why I got so angry; I didn't feel
like I had any control.

   When I left your office, I got in my ninety-degree car
and slept for thirty minutes. I definitely was in a different
state of mind. I scared myself. I hope it doesn't happen
again.

   I'll think about it some more.

Alice was again apologizing for her behavior. She seemed to be
ashamed in regard to becoming angry and in regard to changing states,
which to her meant being out of control. Hiding her unacceptable
feelings from herself, as well as from me, and avoiding shame were all
part of what created the recurrent sense of pulling teeth. The little
curls would go back into place, but I would know I had seen them
tousled, and then I would try to get us back from whatever had caused
the dis-order.

   In the next session we reviewed the angry snit scene again. We
looked at the way her anger was powerfully humiliating and how the
script included self-shaming, guilt, and then a lack of resolution of
what happened as the event disappeared in her memory when she fell
asleep in the car. The meaning of her apology in the session had fallen
prey to her typical amnesia for intense emotion. Left untouched, this
kind of forgetting would solidify and become a dense barrier. Her
script was now visible to me.

   It was not easy to be Alice. Confirmation and validation of emotional reality create coherence. That was still unacceptable to her; the
old betrayals by her parents could not yet be known. Too much reality, too soon, threatened to precipitate a crisis as a major self-deceptive

dissociative emotional structure began to crumble in the face of new perceptions. Guilt was acceptable because it fit the shame script of being bad in relation to her parents. If she could not feel guilty about being bad with me, then she might doubt the motivations of her parents in assigning guilt to her. She could rarely tolerate thinking of her parents in critical ways. The old script was used again and again. She had to protect the relationship she still had with her mother, a mother who couldn't even tolerate Alice's most minor criticisms.

The repeated presence or absence of anger was thus critically important in our work. She once described how as a teenager she was at loggerheads with her father, a not unusual experience, as her earlier email has intimated. Indeed, one particular time he was so incensed he hauled off and hit her in the face.

By the time we stood in the doorway wondering about shaking hands, after another "pulling-teeth" session, we had recently learned that she had "never felt so alive as when my father hit me in the face." It had taken close examination for us to realize that what preceded that hit was feeling alive when she was feeling her anger. Her honest anger gave her life, not his punch. Yet her anger still remained hated by her on principle because when she expressed it, she usually experienced a loss. It repeatedly had undone her efforts in trying to have close relationships, advance in her work, and feel related in her family. Coherent and truthful reality was locked in a contest with the self-deceptions woven into family life. It really was not easy to be Alice.

So when we stood on the edge of a handshake, there was the experience of 10 years of working on the politics of emotion in Alice, and in our relationship, which enveloped us as we stood just a foot or two apart. It's really hard to articulate what it felt like to have it all crystallize in me when she didn't shake my hand and then finally said to me, "I feel like I want to hit you in the face." Speech failed me for a moment. Was I at risk of being assaulted? Was her anger finally visiting and just saying hello? She was leaving herself wide open, at risk of a retaliatory response if I didn't get what she was really saying. I had to respect that. The possibilities of how to respond flooded my mind. There were too many options to process quickly.

Her delivery was flat-voiced, and there was an odd, soft expression on her face of tremendous vulnerability. What she was saying seemed to grow out of the frustration she had just experienced over the difficulties in the session. The feeling displayed on her face was of a child who found herself in a situation to which she was worriedly resigned and understood neither how she had gotten there, how she would extricate herself, nor how to change me so I wouldn't frustrate her by not understanding her (again). Her anger was present, but only partially.

I tried to meet her dilemma with a gentle voice and without a nonverbal indication of me feeling threatened (I wasn't) by just making a matter-of-fact statement: "That's a provocative thing to say, especially given that we're just a couple of feet apart. I'm assuming there's actually no risk of me being hit."

"No, I don't think so."

"You're having a lot of feeling."

"Maybe, but I don't know. I just have this sense of wanting to hit you in the face."

"Whether or not you are in touch with those feelings, they sound very alive somewhere and very important. It sounds like your anger is trying to make its way into the session and having a hard time of it. Shall we plan on talking about it?"

She reached up slowly for my hand, and there was a pervasive sadness in the handshake that I don't quite know how to describe. It was not a hand without any life in it, but it was a hand that was strangely pliable, barely holding mine, neither enthusiastic nor engaged, but somehow still present while not really present, making contact but only of a sort. More than anger was there.

This kind of doorknob moment, the times when things come together just as a session draws to a close, are often filled with potential as well as consternation. For Alice, recent sessions had been punctuated by detached renditions of childhood scenes of being hit in the face by her father when she was angry and alive. Now, a handshake with a reserved heart brought this scene only partially to life. Two days later, she not only was attacking the therapy as useless and bereft of anything of value happening, she had also forgotten she said she wanted to hit me in the face. The curl had been put back in place.

Alice is an able teacher about the depth and complexity of conducting a psychodynamically informed inquiry into the mind of a person who banks on the use of dissociative process in the maintenance of psychological equilibrium. Mental processes achieve balance in the face of overwhelming emotional events through the magic of a careful mix of associative and dissociative process. We both need to know and need not to know about our experience if we are to get through the day and through impossible times. Associative and dissociative process respectively link and unlink the elements of experience in an effort to produce a coherent sense of the feeling of what is happening (Damasio 1999). But referential activity, linking the elements of experience so that nonverbal experience can become verbal, can be impaired when dissociative process is activated (Bucci 1997) and this can leave us bereft of a reliable capacity to contextualize experience. No particular theoretical understanding or technique, however, is a substitute for the power of our relationship to provide a safe space in which Alice, and I, learn and grow. Go ask Alice.

Sorting through Dissociative Process

In my local area, I have a reputation as a clinician who works with dissociative disorders, specifically dissociative identity disorder. In what follows, however, I wish to emphasize that although I pay attention to the comings and goings of the dissociatively isolated subjectivities in my patients, my main interest in doing so is to track the affect, the emotionality, and the associated cognitive structures that teach me about what is happening in the mind-body of my patient. I am less interested in the presence of alternate identity for its own sake. I am more interested in identity alteration as a marker telling me that certain grouped parameters of subjectivity, certain unlinked elements of experience, just made an appearance as part of a kind of conglomerate of self-states. I am more interested in the why and how of the event than in the reified packaging of a "who." It is not that I am uninterested in the alteration of identity, quite the contrary. However, my long experience tells me that attention to the moment-to-moment process in my patient pays much larger long-term dividends.

Novelists can reach into their imagination and breathe life into the minds of unforgettable characters. Truly talented writers can go further and bring to life minds that are not quite wholly present to themselves. But a clinician has to do something harder; he or she has to be able to imagine a mind that is not wholly present while dealing with a person who is. When a mind is born and raised on dissociative process, a clinician's attempts to understand that mind often start on shaky ground. What really happens for the person who has a mind that has long been unconsciously intent on hiding from itself and is now becoming more visible? How can we make conscious what by design is a mental stealth technology dedicated to hiding what was intolerably incompatible with conscious awareness?

A central part of ending a mind's wholesale reliance on dissociative process is making those processes conscious in a non-shaming way. In many ways this follows an approach similar to a mentalization-based therapy (Bateman andFonagy 2006) and to the development of affect consciousness that is part and parcel of dialectical behavioral therapy (Linehan 1993). It is critical to appreciate the extent to which shame is generated in knowing about one's own mental disorganization and failure to effectively live a life (Lewis 1987a). I have endeavored to find ways to make talking about dissociative process less toxic and more user-friendly—and patient-friendly—by using everyday language that is as jargon-free as possible. In talking about dissociative process, abstract concepts have their place. That place is not the consulting room.

In trying to map out a straightforward model of dissociative process in this book, I rely heavily on clinical work. Accordingly, before I go any further, I thank my patients for their hard work. This is work that has enabled them to live lives they often felt were impossible to achieve, and it has been responsible for all manner of growth for them, as well as me.

Five years into a twice-weekly psychodynamic psychotherapy one woman described a moment of dissociative experience like this:

I don't like it at all that stuff pops up in my mind and takes me over. I could feel it in my body, I could feel myself wanting to scream NO and I felt like I could vomit. Your voice even frightened me and that scared me too because I knew it was a safe voice, but I didn't know it either and I couldn't tell if I was safe or not; and it was all in a flash after you said my name, and then it was gone, somewhere. I don't know where, and I want to know, but not exactly. What I really need is to stop thinking about this before it happens again.

Are there some signposts to help clinicians understand what they hear when patients try to tell them what they only barely comprehend about what is real inside them or outside? Is there anything reliably orienting, anything typical of such a mind that could provide a way in to at least some kind of tolerable contact, some kind of coherence, or even just less pain? The question is important, and at the same time the experience of one's own mind varies enormously between people who have minds organized around dissociative process. Listen to this conversation, very different in tone from the previous excerpt, transcribed verbatim from a psychotherapy session of a woman, a tradeswoman talking about a tiling job, who has been in once-weekly treatment for about four years:

"You are a talented person!"
"Oh, but I never finish anything!"
"Yeah, but you have the talent."
"Yeah, 'til I get bored with it. You know. It's like for a while I don't do anything. People have said I should start a business and everything. But it wouldn't work, I wouldn't stay with it."
"Do you figure that your shifts in doing it and being bored with it have something to do with your inner world?"
(*She speaks immediately*) "Oh yeah, definitely!" (*Laughs*)
"I notice the hesitation in your response."

(*Laughs*) "I understand it more now than I did years ago. It's like, you know, I didn't know back then. Now I know that my inner world helps me be creative, like different ideas. (*Laughs*) Or, I don't know. You know, I'd be working on a project, and get ready to start finishing it up, and suddenly I'd have no idea on how to do it. Like, (*laughs, then continues sarcastically*) that's good! What am I doing? I never could understand that before. I kind of understand that now."

"Now that you understand it is there anything you can do about it?"

"Sometimes."

"How does that work?"

"It works out pretty good sometimes. You know. It's like sometimes I feel like I'm in control. (*Laughs*) Sometimes, no matter what I try and do and control, whatever, it's just not happening."

"Uhhuh. So do you have any experience where you go someplace and you say: Oh, I don't know anything about this, and you can sort of reach inside yourself and..."

"Yeah, and all these facts and everything come up and it's like an instruction . . . Step 1 . . . Stand up! . . . It's like I hear what I'm supposed to be doing and I start doing it!"

"You hear it in your mind?"

"Uhhmm, yeah."

"Like someone's reading you instructions?"

"Yeah. It's like okay, I get it now. Or, it's like I get this picture of something completed, and I suddenly think to myself: Oh, that's what I'm doing here!?"

"Where did the picture come from?"

"I don't know. It's like one of those lightbulbs coming on, you know, in the cartoons, you know, like to explain it to myself. You know, sometimes stuff like that just pops into my mind, and ..."

"So, you go to a job that has already been started, and you don't know what it's about?"

"No, that's not happened. It's more like I have an unfinished project. And it's like I get there and stare at it and go: Well, I guess I can do this with it. And I guess it's like, well I wonder why this part's done like this if this is what I'm doing? And this and that. And it's like frustrating 'cause I get into all these details of what I could or couldn't do or whatever, and then like three days later I'll go down and go: Oh, I didn't finish that. And I just finish it, just like that. And I go: Well how come now I know how to do it? You know, three days ago I sat there for four hours trying to measure a quarter of an inch and not being able to do it right. It's like sometimes I can't draw a straight line with a ruler, *nailed down*, with something on top of it! It's like sometimes I'm totally inept. The thought of running my circular saw . . . I think sometimes I'm left-handed and sometimes I'm not. I have a left-handed circular saw. And I go to start cutting things sometimes, and it's in my right hand, and it's like I can't figure out, you know, it's like my brain is saying: You're on the wrong side (*laughter*), and it doesn't work. You can't cut things right, you don't do anything right."

Detecting Dissociation

Dissociative experience is mostly subtle to an outside observer. With all the standard media hype about dissociative disorders, it would be easy to be misinformed or misled and think dissociation was outrageously obvious. Some might say: What could be more outrageous than the presence of child and adult alternate personalities switching back and forth in a person? Reading the words of my patients, it is quickly becomes clear that although the obvious and dramatic change from one self-state to another in dissociative identity disorder is what immediately catches our attention, from the patient's perspective the moment-to-moment change in subjective experience is most salient. Unless we are specifically curious about it, this is simply overlooked.

Most of the gifts that understanding dissociative process brings to the general conduct of psychotherapy are in the form of enhancing the ability to listen for those brief moments of dissociation when there is a disruption in the flow of a person's thoughts, bodily feelings, emotions, and actions. One learns to pay closer attention to the discontinuities of experience, to the absence of what ought to be present, the presence of what emerged unexpectedly, the mysterious little curls of experience that are often overlooked.

Those curls are easy to overlook. Consider, for a moment, the work of Mary Main and her colleagues in sorting out their observations of infants whose attachment behavior in the Strange Situation was anomalous. The Strange Situation, for readers unfamiliar with attachment research, involves observation of the behavior of one-year-old toddlers who undergo multiple separations and reunions with their mothers in an unfamiliar play room (Ainsworth, Blehar, Waters, and Wall 1978). In Mary Ainsworth's initial study, to everyone's surprise, it turned out that the children invariably appeared to show one of three distinct patterns: secure, resistant, and avoidant. Subsequent research bore out this finding again and again. However, in further studies some children showed certain peculiarities in their behavior that were only apparent on very close examination of the videotape; peculiarities, moreover, that could not fit anywhere into the overall classification scheme but did not cohere into a fourth or fifth pattern either. Then, too, there were children who were known to come from maltreating home environments who were being classified as having a "secure" attachment strategy. What Main and her colleagues did was look more closely at both anomalous groups of children. Initially they came up with enough of the details of infants whose attachment behavior was unclassifiable to formulate the Type D infant attachment, which they called disorganized/disoriented (Main 1993, 1995; Main and Hesse 1990; Main and Morgan 1996). It then turned out that these same features also demarcated the maltreated infants. What was salient in these children were fleeting behaviors that momentarily revealed, as the name indicates, either disorganization or disorientation. The inference drawn from this fleeting behavior is that the internal working models for attachment behavior are either simultaneously and/or sequentially contradictory in these infants. It is as if the children are simply unable to figure out whether the parent whom they see is safe or dangerous to approach. Accordingly, they cannot organize a consistent behavioral response without momentary breakdowns in what they are doing. This shows up in specific behavioral sequences visible on the video recordings. Children start out moving toward a parent and then freeze in their tracks, stilling. They move toward the returning parent and then drop to a squat and rock. They veer off to hug the technician or the door jamb. These kinds of momentary disruptions are regularly found in maltreated infants and toddlers, and they are prognostically important. Intriguingly, however, this pattern also shows up in the children of mothers who were intensely grieving severe losses at the time of the child's birth (Mauricio Cortina, personal communication, 2009). These children often enough become dissociative adults, in my experience, and yet there is no gross trauma history, their interpersonal trauma is hidden,[1] sometimes via painful neglect. Among other possible outcomes, several longitudinal studies have linked Type D attachment in infants to adult dissociation (Liotti 1999; Lyons-Ruth 2003, 2008; Ogawa et al. 1997). Although it is impossible to enter the mind of a one-year-old (except imaginatively), it is hard to look at the videotapes of disorganized/disoriented toddlers and not notice that at times they appear to be having frankly dissociative moments. They glaze over, freeze, stop what they are doing, seem to lose their orientation, move for very brief periods in an automaton-like manner, insert a momentary aggressive movement like a slap into reaching for a hug, and so on. It appears that early in life they learn to rely on dissociative processes in managing a breakdown in their procedural strategies for maintaining attachment to their caretakers.

This research has important ramifications for a theoretical understanding of dissociation. But the point I want to make here is how difficult it was initially to spot the telltale behaviors of these children, as dramatic as they may sound in my retelling. The reactions that lead to a classification of disorganized/disoriented most often happen lit-

---

[1] Thanks to Elizabeth Howell for raising this important distinction.

erally in seconds and fractions of a second and then disappear. This essentially ephemeral quality made them hard to spot at the beginning. Even in a one-year-old, the little curls are easy to miss.

If we translate the theoretical implications of the foregoing into practical lessons for working psychodynamically with adult dissociative process, at least some of my patients are likely to demonstrate simultaneously and/or sequentially contradictory internal working models of attachment in terms of John Bowlby's original descriptions. At times, the behavioral contradiction is overt, as in Alice wanting to give me a punch, and saying so, while otherwise taking my leave in a relatively demure way. At other times, however, it is anything but overt. As a therapist, I have to be able to tolerate noticing what is contradictory in my patients' behavior toward me or others without letting it slip by or mentally writing it off as an unimportant verbal gaffe or an innocent logical misstatement. I have to listen for simultaneous and sequential contradictory logic, conflicting displays of emotion, and actions that contradict speech. I have to learn to notice the stigmata of fearful or confused expectancies on the face and in the body language of my patients. I have to really look at my patients' faces, the pulsations in their necks, rates and patterns of breathing, eye movements, and more if I am to catch the physiological tags of affective and other experience that are disrupted. Little flickers of muscle movement in a forehead or a crease of consternation or confusion are events not to be missed. Psychological experience roosts on the body.

Disconfirmation

In *The Gathering*, novelist Anne Enright (2007) eloquently goes out of her way in the story to craft the emergence of a small and terrible mystery, something real, but maybe not, and then again . . . At the bottom of the mystery lies an act of disconfirmation of a kind that I have found often puts a seal on dissociative experience and helps render it all the more inaccessible and all the more uninterpretable when it becomes accessible. Part of what I found so moving about this segment of the story was the self-doubt of the little girl turned adult so carefully depicted as her mind struggles with a picture of sorts from when she was eight years old. Clearly embedded in the storyline is the shame that hardens under her aunt Ada's silent, unfeeling gaze, and the darkness into which this child falls as a result. There is the deftness of a process reminiscent of dream work when a narrow lemon sweet makes its appearance.

> I remembered a picture. I don't know what else to call it. It is a picture in my head of Ada standing at the door of the good room at Broadstone.
>
> I am eight.
>
> Ada's eyes are crawling down my shoulder and my back. Her gaze is livid down one side of me; it is like a light: my skin hardens under it and crinkles like a burn. And on the other side of me is the welcoming darkness of Lambert Nugent. I am facing into that darkness and falling. I am holding his penis in my hand.
>
> But it is a very strange picture. It is made up of the words that I say. I think of the "eye" of his penis, and it is pressing against my own eye. I "pull" him and he keels toward me. I "suck" him and from his mouth there protrudes a narrow, lemon sweet.
>
> This comes from a place in my head where words and actions are mangled. It comes from the very beginning of things, and I can not tell if it is true. Or I can not tell if it is real. But I am sickened by the evil of him all the same. . . . The pattern on the wallpaper repeats to nausea, while hot in my grasp, and straight and, even at this remove of years, lovely, Nugent's wordless thing bucks, proud and weeping in my hand.

Aunt Ada is still watching:

> Is she pleased with what she sees? Does this please her?
> When I try to remember, or imagine I remember, look-

ing into Ada's face with Lamb Nugent's come spreading over my hand, I can only conjure a blank, or her face as a blank. At most, there is a word written on Ada's face, and that word is, "Nothing". (Enright 2007, pp. 221–22)

The protagonist cannot tell if the picture is real or true, but she is "sickened by the evil of him all the same." Her doubting feels related to what she eventually experiences as the word written on Ada's face, "Nothing," a word of bold disconfirmation of the injustice of Nugent's role in the scene. In the lack of Ada's reaction, the clarity of her face indicating that she will not act, how can an eight-year-old assign any realness or truth to this possible event?

This is the same kind of storyline I hear in my office from grown women who have been forced into incest by their father at night and then have a pleasant family breakfast the next morning with no mention of the happenings from before dawn. A mother's question: "How did you sleep last night, honey?" is the opening gambit. With nothing more than a father's "I slept like a log last night" as a model of an acceptable reply, how is a daughter to respond to her mother? Incest experiences may have a dreamy depersonalized quality. Was it real? Did it happen? How did Ada react?

Dissociation is mostly not about dissociative disorders. It is about how a mind struggles to cope with the intolerable and unbearable. The child who struggled with a mangled, shame-laden memory captured in strange pictures tells us she doesn't know, now, as an adult, who is looking back on those real-or-not scenes. She can't figure out if she remembers, or is just coming up with something because she is trying to remember. Enright teases out the emergence of the experience of the not clearly knowable, sowing doubt and belief like mingling mists that get lost in each other, indecipherable and yet still visible as "Something" about "Nothing." With this invalidation, this failure to acknowledge, this emotional unresponsiveness or dis-responsiveness of the witness, the dissociative quality of a wound of sexual abuse is made complete. The injury to meaning lies not in the hard fact of the physicality in the deed, nor in the sensations, nor in the impact in being used and discarded, nor in frequent repetition, nor in the banal inconvenience of it all. It is the disconfirmation of the meaning of an experience that banks the fires of shame and casually drops a guillo-tine on tolerable associative process that might make a coherent story. It is one thing to be raped, orally or otherwise. It is another thing altogether when the violence and indignity of that humiliation has a response only in absentia.

Dissociation is not a bad thing; it is part of normal mental processes. It does certain magic tricks for us that are indispensable and mostly invisible. When it's good, it really benefits us. It keeps us from being overwhelmed by what is intolerable as well as what there is really no need to know, the irrelevant. Yet dissociation can be a fortress that can become a prison when it confuses "I don't need to know" with "I can't tolerate knowing right now." The dissociative act of creation is related to the inability of a mind to tolerate the initial experience of what is unbearable. It is then characteristic of the little and implicitly felt but still unknown islands of experience to desperately become connected, even through the oddest, most inadvertent ways. Accurate meaning is missing, but having a "second-best" somewhat unkempt curly narra-tive that "explains it all" reduces the anxiety of the opaque terror and horror still running amok in a mind that is hidden from itself.

It is not that dissociative process totally removes all vestiges of what ought to be linked together. The act of dissociation creates a paradoxical mental structure that becomes a regularly avoided thorn in an otherwise healthy mind. Dissociative process both disrupts the linking potential between two elements of experience that by all rights go together and yet binds seemingly unlinked ends of the experience in relation to each other (Chefetz 2004). We usually don't think of dissociative process as a potentially creative one, but these bindings are some of the little curls that are noticeable if we look. Knowing about dissociative process means understanding that there is more to the structuring of experience than ideational content or linguistic narrative. Somatosensory associa-tions, for example, can lead to a whole realm of understanding experi-ence if we add to the psychoanalytic "tell me what comes to mind" the additional request to "tell me what comes to body."

When there is active dissociative process, ordinarily expectable linkage may not occur between elements of experience such as behavior, affect, sensation, and knowledge (Braun 1988). Freud called attention to this kind of process when he described the defense of isolation of affect (Freud 1909). What is less well appreciated is that we are talking about dissociative processes not only when we talk about isolation of affect but also when we talk about any of the basic mechanisms of defense. Denial, for example, is the dissociation of truth in the face of overwhelming evidence; disavowal, to take another example, may include denial of knowledge or of responsibility for an action or event. These are processes of unlinking; they are dissociative. Dissociation is not so much of a problem until it refuses to give back what it protectively takes: the liveliness of experience, the context and meaning of what happens. When it does this, then it truly is horrid.

The cessation of dissociative unlinking, with repair of binding-disruptions, is often the scene of painful realization. Then the curls don't seem like they were so out of place, after all. You can see this in the words of Anya, whom you'll meet in Chapters 2 and 7, and here was about five years into her treatment when she crafted an acknowledgment of Father's Day of which this excerpt is part:

> In the last several years there have been many times that I have started and stopped running. Every time I have ever started I am always at first shocked about how hard it is to breathe when I run. And then I almost always quit running for the same reason: because I start to have knee pain. Well, after walking quite a bit in the past few weeks and quite a lot more even in the past week I started to jog tonight and I immediately thought, "The breathing thing was about the past." Tonight I ran up two small hills and I was fine. I realize now that any panic or thoughts of anxiousness over the struggle to breathe, that was really about when my father used to choke me. So I am running up a hill tonight and feeling a little winded, but basically I am totally fine and I think, "My thing in the past about

the breathing was actually a memory/thought/feeling/ reaction about when my father used to choke me." And my very next thought, after thinking that neither of my knees were bothering me at all, not even after walking all of those miles this week and then jogging, was, "And the thing about the knee pain—that is/was never about running either. That was about having the weight of a man on my back that was twice my own weight. That was about being on my knees and being raped by my father.

The Three Pillars of Dissociative Process

Isolation, exclusion, and deflection are three signposts one can use to follow dissociative experience in one's own life and the lives of others. Isolation is no more complex than isolation of affect. When emotion is not known, when affect is isolated, the context and meaning of experience is grossly distorted. Emotion is the great contextualizer. Without it, life goes black and white, and although we can appreciate much in the mastery of an Ansel Adams landscape, what is it to be human when sky is not blue and leaves are not green except in memory? We can't figure out what's going on when there is little affective mortar to hold together the meaning of a behavior. Pounding a fist on the arm of a chair could be a declaration of "Now I've had it," the beginning of a rage, or an emphatic expression of affection, as in "My, you are such a gift to me." Without associated affective cues, we just don't know what to make of lived moments. Worse, they don't feel lived; they feel more like the province of the walking dead.

Dissociative exclusion describes a mind's more or less regular efforts to continue sequestration of a particular element of experience. It can be a daunting task to keep dissociative exclusion up to date. Exclusion had been successful for Anya, who initially thought her breathlessness at jogging and her knee pain were related to physical exertion here and now. Exclusion processes are also active in screen memories. On one hand there is a memory. On the other hand, the memory contains more and means more than what is visible in it. Exclusion is about disruptions in experience, places where the normal links have been cut and reglued and the whole reassembled into another shape. When a memory is painful, or shameful, the failure of the scene to resolve with exploration is often a hint that a screen has been erected. Dissociative process gives screen memory some of its stored-up dramatic impact when it is subjected to psychodynamic inquiry.

For example, a woman bitterly recalled a gang rape and worked hard to connect all the elements of her experience. Yet the intense back pain she was experiencing did not resolve. Only after she realized that what was missing in the scene was the presence of her sister, also captive and also raped, did she get relief from her physical pain because we could then explore additional related scenes of abuse. Somatization is a dissociative process (Nijenhuis 2000), I might add, and we pay a steep price when this possibility is overlooked in the medical investigation of chronic pain. Partially successful exclusionary process is also visible in sensory memories that are confused with medical symptoms, like a burning pain in wrists that links to the memory of rope burns from being tied down during sexual abuse (Meares 1999). Vaginal burning, painful intercourse, low back pain, throat pain, loss of appetite, nausea, vomiting, headache, and so on can all represent failures of dissociative exclusion and the intrusion of experience that "just doesn't make sense."

An unconscious process, dissociative exclusion fails most obviously when there is a flashback of a traumatic scene. These are often triggered by unavoidable minor associations, like a flicker of light or an unexpected touch on a shoulder. These elements, which may also involve something about the therapist, are yet one more instance of the odd creativity of dissociation; the triggering element has remained as a cut-off strand of experience from the event, ready to attach to the present in novel ways and bringing with it other strands. Major life events like a miscarriage or the birth of a child may also trigger dissociated memories, say, of an abortion related to rape. Here the connection is more clear. Similarly, a daughter's birthday may trigger a major reaction if it corresponds to an age at which her mother was first incestuously raped. And, yes, the flashback of posttraumatic stress disorder (PTSD) is a dissociative symptom, a failure of exclusion. PTSD criteria read like a short laundry list of dissociative isolative and exclusionary processes (intrusion, numbing, and avoidance).

Although isolation and exclusion are pretty straightforward constructs, deflection has more of the tenor of what has been eloquently described as "weak dissociation," the dissociation that exists only in the reality of the lack of effort to know something that could be known (D. B. Stern 1997). Deflective processes include posttraumatic avoidance as well as the kind of breaking off from exploration described by Alice's email: "Actually just thinking about this creeps me out, so I won't write any more on it." Alice demonstrates how an afflicted person can approach something and veer off just before bumping into it in a manner that might create meaning. The avoidance of meaning is very striking in deflection. I consider it a mark of a strong treatment alliance and much increased emotional strength in my patients when they catch their own deflective process, keep it conscious, and work with it.

In dissociation, the three processes typically work in tandem. Isolation may prevent linking or cause unlinking. Exclusion maintains isolation. Deflection assists exclusion on a psychological level. If these three processes are mapped against the four general lines of cleavage in dissociative experience, to wit, between the realms of behavior, affect, sensation, and knowledge (Braun 1988), there is potentially a lot of explanatory or at least heuristic power at hand. There are many varieties of dissociative experience (R. J. Loewenstein 1991) that can be understood in this manner. Again, this kind of understanding is not the same as an empathic grasp of the patient's particular experience. But it is a useful way of parsing what our patients tell us and guiding our inquiry into the details, so that we can get ever closer to what the individual actually lives through and with.

The Persistence of Dissociation

What's perhaps most troublesome about dissociative process is that it erases its tracks as it does its work. We hide from ourselves that we are hiding. We have amnesia for our amnesia. We don't notice that we don't notice. Moreover, when dissociative process clicks into place, it tends to continue until it's disturbed by new inputs or just rusts into ineffectiveness. It doesn't just stop when the danger is over; it often goes overboard in its efforts. That makes sense because affectivity is much more of a right brain process. Unlike the logical, sequential accuracy of timelines and language that animate left-brain processing, right brains do nonlinear work. What's important to a right brain about trauma is that *it happened*, which to the right brain can mean that it might still be happening. "If it happened once it could happen again, why forget? Why let down my guard? Who cares how old I am, it could happen again, couldn't it? The world has so much craziness and violence in it. Don't you realize it is a dangerous place?" Even if you are six feet tall and weigh 200 pounds, it just may be that the memory of being the 40-pound shrimp of a kid you used to be is still stuck in your right brain, still implicitly reacting to the unlinked feeling in your body of being captured, held, raped, and discarded. It's not that you necessarily remember. It's just that you can't let go of the fear when you haven't yet relieved your right brain of its timeless worry by creating a reconstructed narrative of experience that can be part of an emotionally alive script. We each need an honestly complete personal narrative that includes a past and a present, and includes now being an adult living in a body and with additional resources. The right brain doesn't always get updated on important information when the left brain becomes too disorganized by right brain emotionality every time it tries to put things together (Chefetz 2010).

The persistence of a dissociative reaction after the reason for it is gone is the centerpiece of a compelling first-person account by Katherine Friedman, writing for the *New York Times* Magazine's "Modern Love" column. Friedman captures how dissociation can freeze one's reaction to a moment, even after the moment has passed. Following are some excerpts of her description of what was, and what could have been.

A newly married Katherine Friedman rides with her husband, in a plane, high over the mountains of Mexico, when the sudden quieting of the engines and dipping of the nose of the plane make clear the plane is falling out of the sky quickly. Her life does not flash before her eyes. There seems to her to be no particular wisdom revealed. There is only a kind of dismay that the moments before death might be so routine, so "banal."

She will miss her family, and she anticipates the pain of their grief and feels badly for them. But then the plane stops falling and lands safely. Still there is something odd in her experience going forward. She doesn't feel lucky, as her husband does. She doesn't even feel alive:

> I feel indifferent. . . . I watch everyone around me experi-
> ence what I should be feeling. No, it's worse: I watch them
> and condemn them for the utter uselessness of their joy.
>   I tell myself . . . this feeling will pass. I am still absorb-
> ing the shock. Give it a few days . . .

But nothing changes: "The next day is much the same . . . I am still waiting for the wash of relief, the thrill of feeling reborn, of escaping death." By the time a new plane is sent, and she stands in line at the airport with the other passengers, she is still waiting to feel

> the familiar tingle of anticipation about returning home
> and the surge of anxiety upon boarding the airplane. But
> I feel neither. . . . I am not afraid to fly. In fact, I am not
> afraid of anything. . . .And here I remain—among friends
> and loved ones, at the beginning of my marriage and all
> the fierce entanglements of life. Yet . . . it seems I created
> a break between my former and current selves that isn't
> so easily bridged.
>   At home, I go to the grocery store, rub the dog's belly,
> fold the laundry, return my mother's calls. . . . But
> week after week I am still in that other place, a half step
> removed, wondering when and how I am ever going to
> come back from this.
>   A month after my return, the answer comes in the form

of a phone call summoning me to the emergency room: my father has had a heart attack.

And it is not until I am beside him in the intensive care unit, gripping his hand as he battles his weakened heart for each breath, that I feel my own heart pounding again for the first time since that day. It's all so familiar: the panic, the terror, the threat of imminent loss. . . . My father, laced with wires and unconscious, is pulling me back. (Friedman 2006)

Dissociation is the Magician. Sometimes he comes as a friend who sneaks in through the back door, unnoticed, only a momentary disturbance visible in the smoke from the fireplace as he moves quickly by; things are somehow not the same afterward. Sometimes his visit is for the better, helping us survive by making incoherent what we once thought we saw. But if he overstays his invitation, his spectral curtain may become a kind of shroud. He is then the ghost of the past, too afraid to help us lift the draperies and live, even though he tries. He becomes trapped in his own magic, unable to stop what he has started and unable to tolerate the deadening pain of his creation.

For all the hoopla and controversy about dissociation and trauma and the spectacular symptoms sometimes seen, dissociative process is often only a subtle alteration of conscious perception and memory. Sometimes it is just a numbing that does not go away long after a plane has landed. If a person is lucky enough, they may somehow be pulled back from this kind of deadness. But if the person is unlucky, the escape from deadness may bring a resumption of a misplaced private psychophysiologic hell, like recurrent panic attacks, an occasional signature of forgotten intolerable experience. When it's good . . . but when it's bad!

What really happens in dissociation is subtle on one hand, and profound on the other. Dissociative process unlinks the elements of experience in such a way as to often leave us unaware that anything is broken. Emotion, behavior, knowledge, and somatic experience become detached from awareness, memory of experience may disappear in whole or in part, and a mind can become a stranger to itself, living a life with a sense of being somehow incomplete, less than wholly alive, and sometimes oddly yet profoundly ashamed. Could you be Alice, standing and hesitating to shake my hand and wanting to punch me in the face; or the working craftswoman who one day can't remember how to tile the wall or cut the tiles; or Ms. Friedman, surviving a near plane crash without a sense of joy in the first days of a new marriage; or Anne Enright's fictional heroine looking at Ada and waiting for something more than "Nothing"? It is challenging to discern what is happening in each of these minds to produce these kinds of subjective experiences.

Whether it is via an alteration in the experience of self or other, or of the inner world of the mind, or of the outer world in which we all live, subtle dissociative process operating in tension with our more familiar associative processes can change our subjective experience in ways designed to protect us that nevertheless might end up imprisoning us and limiting the possibilities for living. If our world was always overflowing with traumatic experience, then that would be fine. Fortunately, most of us don't live in that kind of space.

Clinicians of every stripe are burdened with the task of trying to make coherent in their own minds what is incoherent for their patients when dissociative processes are active. In an effort to spell out what I have learned by studying attachment, affect theory, neuroscience, and the fertile soil where psychoanalytic studies mingle with psychotraumatology, I have tried to frame dissociative process in a way that makes it more visible, if only we stop to look for the little curls of experience that can teach us so much. In the next chapter I'll spend more time spelling out what the clinical setting looks like from this perspective and how less subtle forms of dissociation show themselves in different contexts.

Chapter 2

Life as Performance Art:
The Search for Felt Coherence

WHEN SHE WAS A CHILD, ANYA HAD THE UNPOPULAR HABIT OF TAKING perfectly good items that were regularly strewn about her room and throwing them in the closet, her way to "clean up." After a while, the collection was quite impressive, she said. Sometimes she spent several hours sitting quietly on the pile in the closet, door closed, in the dark.

When the pile got to be too much for her mother, Anya was ordered to do something about it. She attended to the command by dutifully taking a new black plastic garbage bag, filling it to the brim with the household goods that had collected in the closet, and dragging the heavy bag out to the curb, where she put it next to the other trash. This prompted a family ritual of her parents rushing to the curb before their possessions were carted off. They regularly retrieved many useful goods that were in the bag. Her father used to say that Anya was "crazy."

It turned out that Anya wasn't crazy. She was not crazy at all. It's just that her manner of communication was embedded in action to an extent that nobody really appreciated, including Anya. Why would anyone put perfectly useful goods in the trash? Who would do such a thing? Why did she sit on the pile of "trash" in the closet for hours? What did she know then that I didn't know now? And, more important, what did she seem to know now in her actions that she didn't really know, then or now?

Enactive Knowing

What Anya was exhibiting as a teenager was a kind of enactive knowing. One can think of this as a variety of performance art, a term

she proposed to me. This way of knowing is often related to unconscious enactment of past experience, in life and in therapy. While
enactment in treatment may be understood as involving countertransference responses and processes of projective identification (Chused
1991; McLaughlin 1991), for clinical situations I prefer a description of enactment that pays proper respect to dissociative processes
(Bromberg 2006). These create the fertile ground in which parts of
experience are buried and then influence whatever grows from that
soil. (Bromberg goes further: Not only enactment but personality as
a whole, according to Bromberg, is formed by the magnetic effects of
dissociative experience on the trajectory of motivation and meaning-
making processes in all of us.)

The isolation of experience, a dissociative process, renders it only
implicitly present. This leaves us blind to the extent to which many
of our actions, thoughts, and feelings are unconsciously guided by
the appraised risk of reexperiencing emotionally invalidating and dis-
confirming scenes involving emotions such as humiliation and toxic
shaming. However, just as not all dissociation is pathological, not
all unwitting action in therapy or life deserves the technical label of
enactment. At least as far as clinical interactions go, I would reserve
the term *enactment* for when the dance (Baker 1997) of isolated experience between the therapist and patient occurs in some kind of meaningful synchrony.

But putting enactment proper to one side for a moment, our topic
here is enactive knowing. (I take up the topic of enactment in Chapters
10, 11, and 12.) The question is this: How do we properly characterize actions that are in important ways unwitting, and whose meaning
escapes the person doing the acting because dissociation is operating
silently beneath the threshold of awareness?

Enactive knowing is a fundamental capacity. In psychotherapy, both
enactive knowing and the repetition of past interactions are based
on the same kinds of implicit, procedural knowledge that everyone
uses and gathers over a lifetime through behavioral experience. There
are many theoretical depictions of this kind of knowledge generally,
many different conceptual roads to exploring its various domains.

Bowlby emphasized internal working models of attachment inclusive of affects, ideas, behavior, and world-view (Bowlby1982). Tomkins was appropriately appreciative of affect scripts (Tomkins 1995). Ryle developed a model for understanding procedural elements of experience through a cognitive-analytic therapy paradigm that made use of the concept of behavioral scripts and expectancies (Ryle 1999). All of these rubrics—behavioral scripts, affect scripts, internal working models—involve enactive knowing. We somehow feel the need to start the script of the scene, and then implicit memory guides how we pick up our cues as we go along. Implicit memory is about action and procedure, whereas explicit memory involves declaration and language. Enactive knowing thus potentially entails a kind of performance art, more or less from the get-go (Chefetz 2010). The following description by Bardy and Motett makes that reasonably clear:

> Enactive knowledge is information gained through perception-action interactions with the environment. Examples include information gained by grasping an object, by hefting a stone, or by walking around an obstacle that occludes our view. It is gained through intuitive movements, of which we often are not aware. Enactive knowledge is inherently multimodal, because motor actions alter the stimulation of multiple perceptual systems. Enactive knowledge is essential in tasks such as driving a car, dancing, playing a musical instrument, modeling objects from clay, performing sports, and so on. Enactive knowledge is neither symbolic nor iconic. It is direct, in the sense that it is natural and intuitive, based on experience and the perceptual consequences of motor acts. (Bardy and Mottet 2006)

This is not pathology; this is business as usual. In so many situations, we "know," we get by, simply by doing. Let's take this a step further. Beyond the implicit dimension in procedural knowledge that is ubiquitous, there can also be a dissociative quality in enactive behavior when the context of the action is detached. That can lend its own perplexities to what Bollas called "the unthought known" (Bollas 1987). Faced with action that does not speak for itself, like Anya putting out the trash, the clinical challenge is how to "smoke out" what isn't thought, but nevertheless regularly leaves tracks in the fresh snowfall on a distressed mind's inner landscape.

What's Under the Hood?

The organization of the human central nervous system contributes to the reality that abnormal conditions disrupt everyday kinds of operations and provoke shifts in function that meet our needs for emergency responses. It would be nice if those emergency responses shut off once the crisis passes, but that doesn't always happen. Such is the case in considering what happens in a traumatic moment like rape that activates persistent dissociative processes.

Our everyday working memory, which is a short-term system, is mediated by a sea horse–shaped bilateral brain organ, the hippocampus, that sits in a group of similar structures just under the cerebrum, the folded structure most people readily identify as our brain. The cerebrum (or neocortex) is a librarian's dream in terms of its capacity to store information; it is an evolutionary advance over the much smaller cortices of other primates, like apes and monkeys. The area beneath the neocortex is appropriately called the subcortical area, and it's in this area that the seahorse rides—the hippocampus. Mediating short-term working memory, spatial relationships, geography, and everyday emotion, the hippocampus loses cell volume in the wake of posttraumatic stress disorder (PTSD), depression, and other mental illnesses. Importantly, it gains cell volume during healing processes (Bremner et al. 2003; Phelps 2004; Schmahl, Vermetten, Elzinga, and Bremner 2003; Vermetten, Schmahl, Lindner, Loewenstein, and Bremner 2006). The hippocampus figures in some scenarios of decline in the elderly. My beloved mother-in-law was slowing down quite a bit at age 92 when she got lost driving her golf cart in her retirement village. Her short-term memory for events became terrible, and she became anxious and confused. It was the end of independent living for her, and it was her hippocampus that betrayed her.

Hippocampal function also decreases with massive stress, while such an event or threat activates another brain organ, the amygdala (Latin for *almond*), which sits just in front of the hippocampus on both sides of the subcortical region known as the limbic system. The amygdala is the warning siren that makes it hard to think or speak, when it goes off (Davis 1998; Ledoux 1995; Metcalfe and Jacobs 1996). Rauch and colleagues (1996) established this by scanning the brains of people reading scripts of their own traumas, as well as neutral scripts, in a population recruited from emergency room patients with various documented traumas. When the personal trauma narrative was read, but not when the neutral scripts were read, the amygdala lit up on the right side. An unexpected corollary finding was that Broca's area, the left-side neocortical region that coordinates the expression of language as speech, lost perfusion (its blood supply decreased dramatically). There was thus a functional loss of speech, an aphasia akin to what can happen in a stroke, temporary but profound. For people who have been raped, the finding offers a new avenue for understanding why some of them were unable to speak or protest during the assault. There was no loss of courage during the rape, just a shift in blood flow! Any rape victim who couldn't verbally protest, couldn't get words out, couldn't scream, needs to know this. There is no shame in speechless terror. There is also no shame in blocking out the experience afterward.

The separation of functions between everyday and emergency routine makes our brains ripe for providing us with dissociative experience. Ordinarily the neocortex can quiet the amygdala by using experience as a teacher, but only if the fear is not overwhelming. Normal orbito-frontal and medial prefrontal cortical regulation of amygdalar activation typically develops during the first two years of life in the context of secure attachment; conversely the degree of regulation is reduced in insecure attachment (Schore 2003). Thus, insecurely attached children and adults are at greater risk for developing the symptoms of PTSD.

There are several lines of neurobiological evidence that make it clear we can hold compelling thoughts in mind without explicitly knowing their provenance. Likewise we can have conflicting thoughts in mind without having any anxiety about it. The wiring of our brains lends itself to this, surprisingly, but it's not really astonishing if you consider the modular nature of the brain regions that must coordinate and knit together perceptions to make an associatively coherent experience. Consider the following interaction between Michael Gazzaniga, the noted expert on split-brain phenomena, and his female patient, V.P., who had undergone the split-brain procedure for epilepsy and who knew and liked Gazzaniga. In one experiment after her surgery, V.P. was shown a movie of a violent murder, but because of her split brain, she consciously experienced the movie as only a flash of light. The region of brain associated with speech was no longer connected to the region that processed the visual information and V.P. could therefore only know the movie as a flash of light. However, after the movie, she still said she felt kind of jumpy. In fact, and oddly, she recognized that she now felt frightened of Dr. Gazzaniga! She had a very definite feeling, implicitly. Quite reasonably, even automatically, she attributed that feeling to what she could perceive, namely, the man right in front of her, explicitly. Her emotionality had been stirred, and she knew there was fear, but she didn't know why, and she couldn't connect her affective experience with its true source (Carter 1999).

A man with loss of both hippocampi (the famous case of H.M.; Squire and Kandel 1999) had the expectable loss of short-term memory and an inability to form new long-term memories. He could remember what he learned for several minutes, but then he could not explicitly recall the new knowledge. One day, his neurologist reported to the patient what he had just learned from the patient's wife: the patient's mother was quite ill. Several minutes later, the neurologist asked the patient how he was. The patient reported that he was fine. After several more minutes of conversation, the patient asked if he could borrow the doctor's telephone. Why? He wanted to call his mother. Why? He didn't know. He just had a strong urge to do it. He wanted to make sure she was okay. He didn't know why he was concerned. Although, like V.P.'s visual dilemma, this man couldn't explicitly name the problem, implicitly he had a "sense" that he needed to do something in regard to his mother. This feeling of "needing to do" is part of the implicit memory system that often guides our intuitive activities, where "I need to do something" just because "I feel like it!"

In patients like V.P. and H.M., some of the wires have been cut, so to speak. What that demonstrates is that knowledge can be present, leading to affect and action, without any understanding of its origins. The question becomes whether we can model dissociative processes in patients with intact neural functioning. Reinders and Nijenhuis and their colleagues (Reinders et al. 2003, 2006) used brain scanning to study the functioning of the cerebral cortex in several individuals with dissociative identity disorder. They compared scans of individuals who had "switched" from one identity to another in an effort to discern what neurological substrate (if any) was operative in the alteration between self-states. They observed that the patterns of activation for each self-state were widely spread across many areas of the brain on both the left and right sides, and that between self-states there were significant noncongruent patterns. Put more technically, each of the different self-states in dissociative identity disorder activated widely disparate areas of brain on both sides of the corpus callosum (the left–right and right–left neural information highway that is physically separated in split-brain patients); this was consistent with the hypothesis of unintegrated experience existing between those self-states. Split-brain experience is not a model for dissociative disorders, but it does teach us about implicit memory and dissociation of some functions. Brain scans in anatomically intact people with dissociative disorders tell us that there can be different patterns of neural activation in different self-states.

So far, this may seem sufficiently perplexing for one day. But it's not nearly the whole picture. Consider, for example, that even in situations of trauma involving only verbal abuse, there is clearly a pattern of delayed neural development. The hippocampus (short-term working memory, spatial orientation), precuneus (executive function), and corpus callosum (left–right and right–left information transfer) all show a developmental lag in children who are ridiculed and bullied, but not physically or sexually abused (Teicher, Samson, Sheu, Polcari, and McGreenery 2010). The emotional impact of abuse is profound: Psychiatric disorders emerge earlier, more frequently, with greater severity; are associated with neurobiological abnormalities; and have more comorbidity and show less response to treatment when an individual was maltreated (Teicher and Samson 2013). Linking together the elements of experience, the formulation of personal narrative, and the work of association in general are impeded in the face of maltreatment. Thus, emotional abuse alone leaves dissociative processes relatively unfettered as they go about pruning even vaguely threatening experience from awareness in an understandable frenzy of self-protection. We have no cogent experimental model for what happens if we combine the effects of emotional, sexual, and physical abuse; we just have our sad clinical experience.

Dissociation: The Engine Generating Performance Art

Experience that is too affectively charged and can neither be assimilated into our existing models of the self-in-the-world, nor accommodated by any ordinary expansion of those models, is bereft of a framework within which it can be understood. Sadistic sexual abuse is one example. Consider the difficuly of assimilating the trauma of rape in comparison to a more a widely and publicly experienced trauma like the events of September 11, 2001. Moments like sadistic rape have impact far in excess of watching the World Trade Center building's collapse and saying out loud or silently: "I don't believe it! I can't believe it!" Let us remember just how shocking, how unimaginable, that event was. For some people it was enough to view the collapse of the buildings to trigger a peri-traumatic dissociation—"Is this happening?"—while for others the unassimilable scene was watching people leap from the towers, sometimes hand in hand together, and fall to their deaths rather than be burned alive. Even now, writing these words catapults me personally into moments of painful reverie, and

I only watched from a television screen. I felt compelled to visit the Pentagon in my hometown and travel to New York to see with my own eyes the aftermath of what had happened.

A patient of mine reported on the experience of his sister, who lived just several blocks from the World Trade Center towers. Two days later, he reported what she had specifically told him about how she was horrified as she stood and watched people jump from the towers. He was upset and concerned for her well-being. Several weeks later, as we sat in session, I asked him how she was doing, concerned about the potential for a posttraumatic reaction. Encouraged to make contact with her, he reported his experience to me with a sense of disbelief. She told him he was mistaken. She never actually saw people jump. She read about it in the newspaper! Dissociative processes had created an alteration of perception and attribution when it was too much to know something. Assimilation and accommodation failed. For victims of sadistic sexual abuse, however, things are much worse. There is no protective distance and certainly no need to travel to the scene of terror afterward to make sure it was real. Where ordinarily the obfuscating fog of depersonalization might offer some respite, dissociation often fails in sadistic abuse. The pain, the deliberately inflicted miserable pain, drags the victim back into his or her body, and it is too often only with unbearable pain and loss of consciousness that there is relief. Only the blessing of amnesia works if it finally comes after depersonalization, derealization, identify confusion, or identity alteration have combined to do what they can to isolate the pain from consciousness.

Our minds seek coherence whenever there are fragments and raw chunks of our lives that are untethered from our personal narratives of living and repeatedly poking at us via things like flashbacks and somatic memories. This unconscious tendency to try and resolve the unfinished narrative lies at the heart of what Freud called the *repetition compulsion* (Freud 1920) and Mardi Horowitz subsequently called the *completion tendency* (Horowitz 1986). Freud's idea that we repeat so as to forgo the possibility of remembering is a clinical concept that you can see being played out by Anya and the story of her sexual addiction (explored in Chapter 7). A current sexually abusive relationship deflected her attention from the earlier abuse from her father. Importantly, she became conscious of the deflection as a preface to stopping the current addictive behavior. However, the underlying motivation that tilts us in the direction of repeating, sometimes in a compelling but still blind manner, is what I want to explore here.

For example, Seth, a middle-aged man, had been plagued by a compulsion to engage in erotic activity with men, didn't understand why, didn't want to behave in this manner, and couldn't seem to help himself. (This quality of not wanting to repeat also appears in Anya's story, and it is a paradoxical element in many compulsive behavioral addictions, as well as in other repetitions of the past.) Seth's sexualized behavior decreased dramatically when he became conscious of sadistic sexual abuse in his childhood and then later in teenage years when he was prostituted by his father. When he started treatment, he was aware of his adult sexual compulsions, but not his childhood abuse. Like Anya, Seth's repetitious behavior eventually yielded to his efforts to control it, but only after he identified the earlier scripts of abuse. The most painful parts of what Seth had to tolerate to gain control of his actions and stop his performance art lay in the discovery that his mother and father were both involved in the abuse. In particular, the depth of his father's control of him became visible suddenly, when at the conclusion of a particularly painful psychotherapy session I suggested he might call or write to me to tell me about urges to repeat, rather than take action. He became visibly frightened, changed self-states, and in the high-pitched voice of a frightened child told me he had to tell his father and couldn't tell me, or he would be punished. We had stumbled on a script in which his father pimped him and then, upon his return home, interrogated him about his experiences as a prostitute. Father was sexually excited by this and would subsequently rape Seth as an assertion of his dominance and authority. This is sadly typical of the depth of painful betrayals that trigger dissociative process residing at the core of repetition. The child is destructively marked as personal property owned by the perpetrator (Shaw 2013). Is it any wonder dissociative process is often so invisible?

The pain of having valued attachment figures at the center of such betrayals was extraordinary. That pain had been intolerable for Seth and Anya. At the core of the repetition was unbearable intense emotion vis-à-vis their mothers and fathers. We are implicitly compelled to resolve the pain of unbearably intense emotion, and the variety that is most problematic is the bitterly painful emotional experience that originates within the attachment bond. Necessarily, that pain becomes subject to dissociative process, to isolation, exclusion, and deflection. Like carbon monoxide, it is tasteless and odorless. It may make us sick rather than kill us, if we are lucky (though some would argue about where the "luck" is in surviving years of repetition of painful experience and profoundly felt failures to end abuse and be safe).

Repetition does distract from memory, as Freud proposed, and it does move efforts at healing toward completion, as Horowitz indicated. At this juncture, it is my understanding that what underlies repetition is a paradox: There is a desperate need to feel unbearable feelings that are not tolerable, and each approach into the realm of the unbearable simultaneously triggers a dissociative disruption of experience. The combination of approach and failure itself constitutes a humiliation and reinforces the feeling of the intolerability of the feelings. This is part of why addiction so often seems accompanied by a cloud of shame, the aura of a failure to feel the unbearable. It is not possible to bear these feelings alone, nor is it possible to bear these feelings when approaching them creates a repetition of a moment of dissociation and a loss of coherence. What was different for Anya and for Seth was that for the first time in their experiences, they had the emotionally alive presence of a safe-enough other person in whom they confided their experience. This other person was willing to feel into the experience of their struggle, not shame them, and model the stable left and right brain function that allowed them to achieve felt coherence without fully activating their dissociative process. Imparted knowledge and learned techniques are of little value without the feeling of being safe enough with another person when being grabbed by the dissociative claws of the repetition compulsion and needing somebody to help you maintain your balance.

The repetition compulsion is maintained by dissociative processes (R. J. Loewenstein 1991), *including isolation, exclusion, deflection, and self-state shifts, etc., that undermine approaching intolerably painful feelings by activating automatic and unconscious escape from the unbearable, and thereby repeats the shaming and humiliation of old wounds in new failed efforts to heal.* Without a safe-enough other, the repetition cannot resolve.

We can clearly understand, from the perspective of infant attachment theory, how unresolved experience, Type D, lacks coherence. The simultaneous or sequential contradictory behavior of the Type D infant reflects an inability to resolve the child's own intense emotion that occurs in response to the unpredictability of the presenting emotional states of the parent. Sroufe first proposed that an additional goal of infant attachment went beyond the proximity-seeking of Bowlby's behavioral model and included a sense of "felt security" (Fonagy, Gergely, Jurist, and Target 2003). I extend this sense of felt security into the narrative realm. We all seek to create an emotionally and linguistically coherent narrative of our lives. We seek felt coherence and relax when things finally do make sense. (Of course, we may be willing to accept incorrect narratives if they can make enough sense and also relieve us of the otherwise intolerable content of experience.)

I see the problem of repetition of trauma as less a compulsion to repeat what is unresolved and more a need to make sense out of disparate elements of experience using the only means available when thinking and feeling are blocked by dissociative process: action. Within action, I include both enactive knowing and the more elaborate kind of therapeutic enactment that takes advantage of the dance of dissociative experience in patient and clinician. Bucci correctly calls the unresolved elements "unlinked" as a way to denote the lack of referential associative process. I believe these elements nevertheless remain bound to each other even in their disrupted condition (Chefetz 2004), influencing behavior. Thus, when meaning making is deprived of access to the channels of explicit knowing and emotionally alive sensing, only action remains as a means of communication. In other words, what we only know implicitly is condemned to be told mostly with action until it can be made explicit and coherent. I have dubbed this tendency to strive for coherence the "coherence principle."

The Coherence Principle

The human mind is organized in such a manner as to establish coherence. There is a primal division of function that is, for our purposes, best understood as the contrast between left-brain, logical, mathematical, linguistic, linear, time-and-space-defined boundaries versus right-brain affective, sensory, motoric, rhythmic, nonlinear operations that, for example, facilitate the dream operations of condensation, displacement, and symbolic substitution. It is a useful shorthand (though a significant oversimplification) to think of left-brain operations as "thinking," and right-brain operations as "feeling."

How do we integrate the linear and nonlinear elements of experience? Our minds live in the routine tension between associative and dissociative processes that determine the creation of coherent meaning for experience. Transfer of information between left and right hemispheres helps sort details of experience for salience and creates symbolic and subsymbolic links that move in complexity from the indexical, through the iconic, and finally discernible in the symbolic realm of spoken language (Keinänen 2006). It is important to note that spoken (but not written) language engages both left- and right-brain processes in a compelling way. Speech requires left-brain logical and expressive organizational activity and right-brain tonal and emphatic nuance. Speech also is supervised and observed for both accuracy and emotive quality, sometimes evoking from the speaker an "I think you might get a better feel for what I am driving at if I say it this way" kind of sentiment.

Have you ever had the experience of (or observed) the development of an inability to speak during a eulogy at a funeral? It is not that the reading of prepared remarks hasn't already happened; it is that speaking them out loud completes the affective linking of a coherent narrative that provides the full context of meaning for our words. Speaking a prepared eulogy for the first time may stop you in your tracks when the emotions flood in with spoken words. Speaking is an action that contributes to coherence. Actually telling the story is a central part of creating coherence (Rynearson 2006). Performing a story is not the same as telling it, even if the meaning is covertly or even overtly conveyed.

Left- and right-brain elements of experience are knitted into a coherent narrative by the left brain's ability to interpret what the right brain's emotionality generates but can't name. The right brain has a very limited capacity to interpret the nature of whatever emotion is being felt! It knows there is intensity, and it knows the behavioral scripts that fit that intensity, but it can't name the feeling (Bermond, Vorst, and Moorman 2006). This conclusion is similar to that reached by researchers into split-brain phenomena (Gazzaniga 1995; Gazzaniga, Bogen, and Sperry 1962). The left brain and right brain come to different conclusions about the meaning of experience and about the action required to resolve a situation. Additionally, our capacity to speak during emotional overload becomes limited when high-intensity emotion somehow provokes the amygdala to cause a reduction of blood flow in the area of the brain that generates expression of thought. Broca's aphasia is a well-known stroke syndrome. Less well known is that we become speechless in fear or intense pleasure, when emotional circuitry is overloaded. Our ability to generate narrative is impaired during highly emotional moments (Rauch et al. 1996).

Neurobiological reality provides additional interesting lessons for clinicians: Massive activation of one hemisphere inhibits activity in the other hemisphere, as a normal response (Bermond et al. 2006). Obsessional adaptations aside, "keeping busy" during an emotionally stressful time decreases arousal and modulates our ability to feel emotion. Action can have an additional function: It may be a distraction from feeling. Moreover, high levels of emotionality can preempt thoughtful approaches to a challenge. Hemispheric overloads thus modulate emotion both ways: When either side of the brain is overloaded, the production of coherent narrative suffers. We can see the influence of hemispheric overload in everyday language: "I'm too upset to think about the details of what needs to happen tomorrow. We'll have to deal with it later!" "I'm sorry I was so blunt. I was so focused on what

I was doing that I forgot my manners!" Both statements suggest an overload in the right hemisphere.

Healthy minds search for coherence. Coherence is most easily achieved in the context of optimal physiological arousal; this occurs in a safe relationship, what Bromberg has artfully called "safe, but not too safe" (Bromberg 2006). We must constantly sort what we perceive, inwardly and outwardly, to achieve coherence. We sort and unconsciously "decide" whether something is a match: "Should I exclude or include this element of experience from this scene?" "Should I associate or dissociate this element of experience?" Most sorting is outside awareness. Thus, coherence is a function that is dependent on the tension between associative and dissociative processes. Maintaining coherence may trump reality testing if it eliminates intolerable anxiety over the meaning of a toxic event. The toxic event might be intrapsychic in nature, or it may be something happening in the world. Either way, achieving felt coherence relieves emotional tension and puts the brakes on enactive repetitions.

A patient with a dissociative disorder (Rachel, whom you will read about in Chapter 8) was in intensive psychotherapy for five years when the valued, stable relationship with her husband ended due to his death from cancer. For more than two years afterward she was sexually promiscuous, for the first time in her life. The behavior resisted any analysis related to the loss of her husband, and there was no ostensible history of sexual abuse. Three years later, however, at the funeral of a beloved family member, she nearly fainted when she looked across the church and saw the person whom she suddenly remembered had severely abused her, emotionally, physically, and sexually, for a number of years in her childhood. With the exploration of this experience in therapy, and the achievement of coherence about her actions, her promiscuity ended rapidly.

Teaching the Left Brain to Dance

The recent emphasis in trauma studies has been on two main areas related to right-brain function: the failure of medial prefrontal cortex to inhibit the emotional emergency centers in the amygdala, and the lowered threshold for adrenaline release secondary to resetting autonomic activity after the hyperarousal of trauma (Schore and Schore, 2008). In plain language,it is as if our minds still feel as though we are about to get hurt (autonomics and failure of extinction for distant memory, see Chapter 6) and we can't reason our way out of that expectancy (prefrontal cortical influence on emotion fails).

A useful heuristic vis-à-vis intense emotional reaction is that left-brain logical, mathematical, and linguistic functions can't control more primitive subcortical mid-brain emotional circuitry and don't understand what the right brain is upset about. The left brain is also clear that if the right brain is so upset, then the left brain will gladly pass up the opportunity to know what is making that right brain so frantic. Left-brain avoidance strategies include, denial, disavowal, minimization, rationalization, disowning, obsessive preoccupation, ritual undoing, staying busy, working until exhausted, and then ignoring the clues that something emotionally charged is going on by simply "not going there"—isolation of affect.

Eventually, for people who rely heavily on these left-brain strategies, avoiding intense emotion becomes a necessity. Overloaded and pent-up emotional strata in the brain create flooding if left-brain distractions suddenly stop. Staying rule-bound is a Shangri-La familiar to some of those people who make a career out of the practice of law or engineering, among other heavily left-brained careers. Often these are people who watch their feet when trying to learn how to dance. Going with the flow of the music is tantamount to losing control, a worry meant to close the door on the possibility of having intense feelings that actually flow! Teaching the left brain to dance is a way of reframing the relational aspect of an intensive psychotherapy where thinking things through goes hand in hand with moving to the music of a life.

In the hard-earned safety of a relationship, the left brain of a person begins to trust that the emotional aliveness in their therapist is something they might consider tolerating and then unconsciously emulate in their own processing of emotion. In the therapist's scrupulous attention to interpersonal boundaries, the right brain gains a tentative confidence that it will not be emotionally assaulted. The right brain develops a sense that if it feels threatened, spoken language is enough to stop the action of the therapist. In the world of interpersonal abuse words have lost their meaning, especially the words of the patient, and the only reliable source of information is through action. "No" has been stripped from the patient's lexicon of available expressions. Protest was brutally squashed. Anger as protest is marked as dangerous—it is not a thought for the survivor of violent childhood abuse. In these situations, the negotiation of the capacity for meaningful and emotionally alive communication in psychotherapy becomes an art form.

Teaching the Right Brain to Read Music

It's troubling to appreciate that the left brain doesn't always understand what disturbs the right brain after traumatic experience. It's as if the left brain knows to be afraid, but doesn't know why, and that only makes things scarier. It's akin to the second fear phenomena described in panic syndromes (Weekes 1969/1990). We become frightened of being frightened and scrupulously avoid attending to our reactions only to become subject to an adrenaline surge bursting through into consciousness as a clue that there is an unresolved emotional disturbance going on. Apparently neither the left nor the right brain has enough experience to read right-brain music and interpret its meaning when overwhelming emotional experience is writing the musical score. The right brain needs left-brain cognitive appraisals of emotional meaning before it can understand what it is emotionally experiencing. The notion of emotional communication being almost all right brain to right brain (Schore 2003) ought to be conceptually expanded. The left-brain interpreter mechanism is bereft of the skills and experience to understand the emotional dimensions of trauma. The right brain has a hard time making inferences about the meaningful drift of associations to "the emotional music" without an accompanying coherent narrative created by the left brain. The somatosensory symphony that is part of traumatic recollecting and remembering must be correctly interpreted and incorporated into a personal narrative. The right brain doesn't know how to read the music when the chaotic composition of traumatic experience is playing in the body with "surround sound" that is wired to muscles, bowel, and so on. Secure parenting, in this view, must include the parent engaging the child in a process where there is active explicit and implicit emotional communication; the parent notices the feelings and then names emotions they can see the child experiencing. This naming process, both behaviorally and affectively, is powerful in shaping the child's behavior and self-image. The Circle of Security Project shows with clarity that Type D, A, and C insecure parenting can evolve to Type B secure parenting when mothers learn to correctly intuit or observe the meaning of behavior in their infant children. Most exciting is that this can actually alter infant attachment patterns as a parent learns these new skills (Marvin et al. 2002). The clinician's role is clear in this situation: provide affective containment that settles autonomic arousal and assist in constructing general and then more specific new narratives that actively name and support left- and right-brain processes to coherently interpret experience, assign affective valences, and fit the newly understood experience into an ever expanding autobiographical narrative. The value of an emotion-focused treatment is robustly clear. If we are trying to teach the left brain to dance, we are also trying to teach the right brain to read music. The functions of the clinician's brain, left and right, must be openly engaged for the patient to feel safe enough to tolerate formerly intolerable disturbances.

What is normal creates unfortunate burdens in trauma, even when the event is only of an exquisitely painful emotional experience. We have noted how overactivation of one hemisphere as compared to the other can interfere with the interpretation of experience and lead to the failure to assimilate or accommodate traumatic experience. The inability to integrate left- and right-brain cognitive-interpretive and emotional-experiential elements leads to a de facto dissociation of intense experience. Nothing need be repressed to remain outside awareness; it simply never gets glued together via association. This is a dissociative process; the ghost of repression need not be conjured here. This is not quite the "weak dissociation" of Don Stern (1997), the failure to know something for lack of effort. This is the disaggregation of Janet (1907) as seen in the failure to link implicit and explicit right- and left-brain functions. This is what Stern called "unformulated experience."

What really happens in dissociation? Associative and inhibitory processes fail. The normal integrative functions of the mind fail. The creation of a complete narrative of interpretable experience does not occur. Experience is incoherent: behavior, affect, sensation, knowledge (Braun 1988) may not be linked together on either a subsymbolic or symbolic level (Bucci and Maskit, 2007). Affect may still be present but is significantly isolated from interpretability and may induce scripted emotional behavior (Bermond et al.2006). Higher cortical brain areas are not prepared to deal with the physiologic disarray of intense affects when cortical inhibition of sympathetic nervous system outflow fails (van der Kolk, MacFarlane, and Weisaeth 1996). We can't interpret our experience, but it intrudes piecemeal, albeit incoherently, almost begging for understanding; so we avoid or withdraw, and with more intensity we get numb, and sometimes we get "triggered" and are gripped with fear that seems to make no conscious sense. We can even alternate from numbness to flooding and from flooding to numbness and not know why! When we search our memory banks, we may only find fragments—evidence that the hippocampus had a great deal of trouble processing whatever was going on. When hippocampal processes go off-line as the amygdala's sirens blare, a quiet little brain organ, the cerebellum, a ball of spaghetti tucked away at the base of the brain, is busy fashioning memories of the bodily positions associated with the emotional content of experience (Manni and Petrosini 2004). (I expand on this in Chapter 5 in a discussion of emotion and dissociative experience.) The bottom line here is that bodily experience, though it may be isolated, adds fuel to the compelling fire that burns inside us to make coherent the fragments of experience that are bereft of personal narrative. This may account for the usefulness of including the body as part of the work that occurs in activating and understanding intense emotion, such as the use of movement as a therapeutic modality (Ogden, Minton, and Pain 2006), for example, dance. When persistent dissociative processes rob us of a coherent understanding of our lives, we repeat, and we use performance art.

To sum up, dissociation is not a banishing act that puts intolerable experience in orbit, completely isolated from reach. Dissociation is a paradoxical binding-disruption where the tag ends of what ought to match can't connect. They are held in close proximity, tethered but outside awareness. These incomplete psychic constructions nevertheless influence behavior and reactivity via implicit processes, including the scripted performance of actions whose ultimate meaning is not apparent. We all seek coherence, both consciously and unconsciously. Both enactive repetition and enactment seek coherence through whatever mode of expression will finally, logically, and emotionally make sense out of what was incoherent, unbearable, and unspeakable. Often this is action, a rudimentary attempt to know by doing. But in the wake of trauma, this can lead to behaviors, often repetitive ones, without the crucial links made to autobiographical knowledge.

An Old Script Being Enacted

My young adult patient, who had sat on piles of household goods as a child, sent me an email on the day before her usual Monday morning session. Short, and not sweet, it was written with each word starting with a capital letter, for emphasis:

> Today Is A Day When It Is Hard To Keep Going. I Literally Got Through The Afternoon By Thinking About A Suicide Plan, Notes, A Sort Of "Make Shift" Will And I Even Picked Up My Room And Packed Another Box; As Though Tidying Up For Departure. But I Will See You Tomorrow Morning Though.—Anya

How would you respond to this? What are the considerations for safety, the patient's need for freedom to have their thoughts and feelings, the need to not let the action get out of hand, and so on? I chose to think about these things but not engage in action. This was the third year of our work, we had been through many suicidal, and parasuicidal crises, and she regularly (but not always) sought out me or another trusted person when she was distressed. Sometimes she retreated to her bed for several days, not showering, not eating, fully withdrawn from all but her beloved cats. She said she would see me the next day, so I put the potential self-harming behaviors on a special shelf in my mind and went on with my day.

The Monday session began with her silence. "There's really nothing to talk about," she soon said. I countered that it seemed as if there was so much to talk about it wasn't exactly clear where to start! "What have you been doing with your time, over the weekend?" I asked, trying to get inside the context of her email message. "You know, Anya, that was quite the email you sent to me yesterday. I'm concerned about what it meant."

"Oh, that, well, I've been puttering around my room, collecting things and putting them in boxes. I've nearly finished, at this point," she said in a tone reminiscent of having gone about the day cleaning all the windows in a house and being nearly done.

"Why are you putting things in boxes?"

"I don't think I'm going to need them, and I don't want my land-lady to be bothered with having to clear out my room if it's a mess. That's too much work for her, and she already does too much for me."

"I don't understand, Anya, why would she be clearing out your room, where are you going?"

"I think it's about time that I just left this place, Dr. Chefetz," she said as if I had totally failed to understand what was going on in her life. "There's nothing for me here, and I don't want to keep on being in pain," she said, as the tears started to run down her cheeks. "I'm just garbage, and it's time to put me out of my misery." She was implicitly on the way to the curb, but not yet in a black plastic bag.

I asked her for more details about what was supposed to happen. She explained that she had not yet quite figured out how to kill herself, but she was working on it. She considered the possibility of hanging herself, as her fiancé had done near the end of her second month of therapy. She was clear that she didn't want to be a burden for anybody, that nobody should be inconvenienced by her death. Her landlady would just put the boxes out on the curb with the other trash when Anya was gone. She would also probably be glad to take care of her cats.

There were times when in a period of relative well-being Anya would work with her sewing machine, making clothes for her cats, dressing them up playfully, like the Cat in the Hat, and so on. Now she was planning her death, in honest detail. She was letting go of beloved relationships. She was taking the organizing steps I had seen in many other patients whose suicides I had interrupted over the years.

"It seems pretty clear that you are planning to kill yourself, and taking care of all the details so you don't put anybody out after you've done yourself in," I said plainly. "That's not okay with me, Anya."

She was reassuring, in her own way. She said, "You know, Dr. Chefetz, with as much work as you've done with me, if I kill myself it has nothing to do with you and that you won't have failed me at all; it will be something I've done completely on my own and you would not have to feel bad at all, would you?"

"Of course I'd feel awful and that I've failed you, Anya."

"But, Dr. Chefetz, that's not logical! It would be me who had done this."

"It doesn't matter what's logical or not. Feelings don't have to be logical, they just are. It's how I feel, Anya. You said earlier that you know I've been really invested in helping *you* in the therapy. I have worked hard, but my investment is in you, not in the therapy, even if that's what we do together. And if you killed yourself, then I would feel a miserable grief, and that I had failed you. Logical or not, that's what I would feel." But my feelings weren't the order of the day; hers were, and I needed to find out more. "What is all this about, Anya, and why might this be happening right now?"

"I really don't know, Dr. Chefetz." She clearly switched self-states and emotionally stepped back from her nearly nonchalant reassurance that I had done all I could for her and could feel guiltless if she killed herself. She spoke with sadness in her voice. "I've been thinking a lot about when I lived back home and how I used to go around the house and collect the things I liked, putting them all over my room, and just sort of letting them accumulate. It used to eventually drive my mother crazy, especially when she could no longer walk in the room because of the clutter." She went on to tell me the story about putting perfectly good things in the trash out at the curb. She reminded me about how her father had once again, on this occasion, repeated the lament he so often used, that she was "crazy!"

"Anya, I want you to know that I get it about the message you tried to send to your parents that they were throwing away a perfectly good daughter along with perfectly good things that were in that big plastic bag. That's why you sat on the heap in your closet, I believe. It was a message. I don't want you to throw yourself away. It would be terribly sad if after having survived the horrors of the emotional abuse, and the sexual and physical abuse, that all these years later you might kill yourself as you finally become conscious of your life. It's one thing to know how you were abused, and how awful that was, but it's another thing to realize in the deepest ways, how little understanding, if any, your parents had about you. Now you appreciate the pain of not really being related to or with them, in any of the ways in which you now value relatedness. I think that in some ways that's a bigger hurt than the grossly abusive things."

Anya had constructed a suicide fantasy that was a match for the way she felt she had been thrown away with "perfectly good stuff" that she had collected in a closet, which she often sat in, and that her parents had retrieved from the curb. It was a way she had attempted to tell them they were throwing away a perfectly good child, their daughter, and that somebody needed to get her out of the trash. She was asking me to notice, and I knew I had to be explicit in naming what was going on.

"If you put yourself in the trash now, literally, then there is no way to get you back," I said. "I'm hoping we can talk about these feelings, and that you won't act on them."

"Tell me it's okay, Dr. Chefetz, that I don't have to do anything this week, that I can just do nothing, and that it's okay, please? Tell me that my job is just staying alive; tell me that's all I have to do. If that's all I have to do, then I think I can make it to the next appointment. I think I can do that. Just tell me it's okay not to do anything else, please?!"

"Yes, Anya, of course, that's the name of what needs to happen right now. That's all that needs to happen. Your job is to just stay alive, and that's good enough. Okay?

"Yes."

"Then, call me if you need to. I'll be here for you."

"I know, Dr. Chefetz. Thank you for helping me."

The next day, in a brief email exchange, Anya reminded me what she had been absentmindedly thinking about, but had forgotten, as had I. A year ago, almost to the day, the daughter of her fiancé had also killed herself by hanging. Another perfectly good daughter had been thrown away. In the only way in which Anya could communicate what was unbearable and isolated (dissociatively held) from her awareness, she told both her own story and the story of a major loss via the implicit process of enactive repetition, performance art. Finally, the action of her story made sense.

This is an updated and expanded version of a chapter originally published in *Knowing, Not-Knowing and Sort-of-Knowing: Psychoanalysis and the Experience of Uncertainty*, edited by Jean Petrucelli (Karnac Books, 2010), and is reprinted with kind permission of Karnac Books.

Chapter 3

Recognizing Dissociative Experience and Self-States

The human being is a guest house
Every morning there is a new arrival

A joy, a depression, a meanness
Some momentary awareness comes as an unexpected visitor

Welcome and entertain them all
Even if they are a crowd of sorrows, who violently sweep your
house
and empty it from its furniture
still, treat each guest honourably.
He may be clearing you out for some new delight.

The dark thought, the shame, the malice,
meet them at the door laughing
and invite them in.

Be grateful for whoever comes,
because each has been sent as a guide from beyond.

—Jelaluddin Balkhi Rumi (1207–1248)

EVERY MORNING FOR SEVERAL WEEKS A MIDDLE-AGED MAN WITHOUT A FULLY developed system of self-states—an "alter" system of dissociative identity disorder (DID), if you will—but with many stigmata of self-state influence and shifts in perspective, has spoken of waking in a miserable emotional space reminiscent of his childhood. He has learned that if he goes to the gym and works out vigorously, then the negativity, nausea, profound sense of physical weakness, and wish to hide from the world fades into the background and he feels prepared for his day as a high-energy professional specializing in motivation. Who would have thought? It turned out that his old experience of waking up in his childhood environment, and then having to deal with an assault on reality that was ongoing in his family, provoked this waking experience of emotional collapse, appeasement, and withdrawal. This was a survival strategy for a child too young to leave home and unable to be present in an emotional vacuum that presented a daily vampirish version of having the life sucked out of him. If I had not already known that he had a dissociative disorder, there would have been a lack of clues hinting in that direction. The single salient clue in his description was the planned state change he negotiated for himself. He had learned to tolerate his child-sized overwhelming upset by putting his adrenalin to work at the gym, where he could burn it off, thereby creating a new context for experience that provoked a shift to a contemporaneous, embodied, adult self-state.

Clinicians new to the world of dissociative experience regularly go through a crisis of trying to understand how to translate what they have read about DID into what they are seeing and hearing in their consultation room that doesn't seem to fit those academic descriptions. There is often an expectation that all people with a dissociative disorder will demonstrate obvious switching behaviors and have separately named self-states like Mary, Samantha, or Aaron. My patient doesn't fit this description, but he has self-state-related experiences. My experience is consistent with that of Richard Kluft's broader experience that only 10 to 15 percent of patients who meet criteria for DID will present in a classic manner (personal communication, 2008) with a fully developed alter system and obvious switching.

The original, seminal contributions to understanding dissociative phenomena (Braun 1984; Kluft 1985; Kluft and Fine 1993; R. J. Loewenstein 1991; Putnam 1989) and complex posttraumatic stress disorder (PTSD)(Herman 1992; Horowitz 1986; Terr 1991; van der Kolk, Hostetler, Herron, and Fisler 1994) have naturalistically given way to a more nuanced literature over time. This has come about through the adoption of perspectives from developmental psychology and behavioral states (Putnam 1997), attachment (IJzendoorn 1995; Lyons-Ruth 2003; Main and Hesse 1990; Solomon and Siegel 2003), and the neurobiology of states of mind (Reinders et al., 2003, 2006; Siegel 1999). There has also been an effort at a synthesizing model of "structural" dissociation (van der Hart, Nijenhuis, and Steele 2006) and a multiple self-state model in relational psychoanalysis (Bromberg 1998, 2006, 2011; Howell 2005, 2010; D. B. Stern 1997). Still, the early observations of Kluft, Braun, Sachs, Fraser, and many others hold true, even if their conclusions have been somewhat reframed (Bowman and Markand 1996; Braun and Sachs 1985; Chu 1998; Frankel and O'hearn 1996; Fraser 2003; Frischholz, Lipman, Braun, and Sachs 1992; Kluft 1983, 1985, 1987, 2000, 2006, 2013; R. J. Loewenstein 1994; Ross, Heber, Norton, Anderson, Anderson, and Barchet 1989; Steele, van der Hart, and Nijenhuis 2001; Turkus and Kahler2006; Watkins and Watkins 1997). We continue in their debt. No matter what one's perspective, the challenge is to figure out how to understand a patient's presentation and engage him or her in exploratory conversation that makes sense about things dissociative that are congenial to conversation.

People with dissociative experience come to us hoping clinicians can help them understand what subjectively plagues them; at the same time clinicians are often struggling to understand the same thing. The fact is that people with dissociative disorders present with subjective experiences that for them are normal, but which for a clinician can easily be discounted as a person being quirky, inattentive, or a space cadet or having a constitutionally bad memory. None of those terms describe the experience of a person, however. When I engage a new patient in a detailed exploration of their subjective experience of just about anything of interest to them, I look for the presence of discontinuities in their attention, sudden changes in state, gaps in memory for ordinary events, and their relative ability or inability to focus their remarks and organize their thoughts. The notion of coherence in the adult attachment interview (IJzendoorn 1995; Main 1993) is highly instructive in terms of appreciating the significance of patterns in the patient's narrative that show interruptions, hesitations, distractions, deflections, and often memory loss for what the question was or even for the first part of a response. These patterns are typical of narratives in Type D attachment.

Often I find that people with unknown but active dissociative processes are mystified by their behavior and inability to consistently be who and how they think they are regarding skills, social ability, work effort, and so on. There are also more elaborate lost-time experiences, feelings of detachment from their physical self (depersonalization) or from the world (derealization), and self-harming or injurious behaviors that include things like cutting and burning, as well as significant over- or undereating. There can be typical addictive behaviors, for example, sexual acting out or substance and alcohol use, and there can be significant compartmentalization of behaviors in the workplace and at home that make spouses incredulous about the glaring inconsistency of competence they observe in their dissociative spouse at work but not at home. Until you've made the effort to keep these kinds of experiences in your clinical mind, it's easy to miss things or not notice their significance (R. J. Loewenstein 1991).

Here is an example of how dissociative experience can be overlooked from an excellent text about negative therapeutic reactions (Seinfeld 2002), a topic I take up later in Chapter 9. Seinfeld's patient, Diane, has told him that when she leaves his office, he ceases to exist. He replies empathically that then she was all alone with her problems.

> I asked her what happened to her relationship with me in her mind between sessions. She looked at me as if I were crazy, and said that she never thought of it. . . . [I said,] It is like I disappear for you when you leave . . .She replied: "Yes, it's like that with everyone and everything. I forget that my son exists. People get angry at me because I forget appointments or don't call them" . . . Laughing, she added, "It's not normal, is it?" (Seinfeld 2002, p. 43)

The circuit breaker-like discontinuities of memory that plague Diane point toward active dissociative process and potential changes in self-state, with state-dependent memory. Seinfeld seems to hold to the view that patients like Diane are schizoid, and this would be in agreement with the view of Winnicott and Guntrip, as we will see later. He also believes that "in working with schizoid patients, it is most important that the clinician overcome the extreme detachment and apathy that can occur in both transference and countertransference." He is quite attuned to the clinical scene. About another patient, Ellen, he observes, "the patient manifested the schizoid defenses of depersonalization and derealization, resulting in a sense of unreality between patient and therapist. The therapist acknowledged the artificiality that is inherent in the therapeutic situation—therapy room appearing like a movie set—and the patient was able to recognize and discuss schizoid defenses" (Seinfeld 2002, p. 115). Seinfeld's empathic stance is admirable, and he readily identifies some relevant processes, which he labels "schizoid." But with the first patient, Diane, her experience is not interpreted by him as an amnesia that could reflect switching phenomena and isolated self-states, nor does he seem to think it's especially important that Diane forgot his query about depersonalization and derealization. As for the second patient, he describes derealization clearly, another hallmark of dissociation, but takes things no further. Seinfeld's book is about negative therapeutic reactions; his model of mind is an object-relational one. He clearly appreciates Fairbairn's work, and like Winnicott and Guntrip, he is knowledgeable and aware, yet he doesn't seem to appreciate the implications of dissociative process and its possible effects on subjective experience, nor the potential for a more elaborate dissociative disorder.

My intent here is to illustrate how otherwise highly skilled clinicians may simply not appreciate dissociative process and its implications. Could they be more effective? Like Seinfeld, I'm intent on increasing coherence in the mind of my patients. My experience is that naming dissociative processes and identifying constellations of experience that fit a multiple self-state model of mind decreases anxiety, greatly increases the feeling of being understood and heard, and often relieves generalized depression and despair reflecting the fatalism that can develop regarding ever being understood. I am not saying

Diane and Ellen had dissociative disorders, but that might have been the case. If these two women did have organized self-states, then not noticing them might eventually stall a treatment or leave large areas of concern unexplored.

For example, a colleague referred a young man with dissociative symptoms to me for further evaluation. Almost as an afterthought, he told me that one of his patient's long-term and incorrigible symptoms was trichotillomania (repetitive hair pulling or twisting). It had never responded to psychotherapy or medication of any stripe. When I asked this young man about it, he became animated in a way that included a kind of playful twinkle in his eye that was nearly hidden by verbalized self-disgust, which he clearly expected me to join. "It's a horrible thing that I do," he said. "I'm really terrible about it, too," he added. "When I do it I really love it, though. It excites me," he blurted out.

"That's kind of interesting," I said. I was immediately aware of the harshness of his self-judgment.

"Most people think it's actually sick or weird."

"I have no idea what it's about, but it's certainly not sick or weird in this office. I think it's interesting that it includes some excitement for you. How does it excite you? What do you find so important about it?" Excitement is often present in addictive behavior and should be explored.

"Nobody has ever asked me that. Well, I'm really not sure, but I can tell you that I just love the way the ends of my hair feel between my fingers. I focus on that and there is a moment when I can feel the ends split and that's what brings on the excitement. After that I somehow relax and it's very pleasant." As I listened and observed him, I had an odd sense of listening to a youngish child telling me about their most favorite private thing in the whole world, the thing that they count on to make them feel good. So I responded in context.

"That's pretty neat that you have a way to make yourself feel good. No wonder it's exciting for you."

"You don't think it's terrible that I'm excited about something so bad?"

"It doesn't seem bad to me. Right now what I understand is that it feels good, it's important to you, and I can appreciate that something like that isn't something you'd want to give up. That just wouldn't make sense to me."

"Nobody ever has thought it's okay for me to do this."

"I think that everybody needs ways in which they can count on feeling good to relieve tension. I suspect this does that for you." As I took in this conversation, I became curious about the potential for his hair twisting habit being a self-hypnotic induction for affect regulation and relaxation. I also couldn't shake the feeling of his child-like enjoyment of it. So I approached the scene as I had others before. I asked a simple question in a very specific way.

"Would it be okay if I asked you a question?"

"Sure."

"I'm going to ask the question, a very simple one, and I'd like you to respond with what comes into your mind and not to edit it. Just tell me about the first thing that comes into your mind, okay?"

"Okay."

"Remember how you told me you get excited about twisting your hair, and you feel the feeling of the ends splitting, and it feels so good? How old do you feel then?" For a moment, his eyes moved in tandem as he looked suddenly up and to the side, and I understood there had been a quick response in his mind. But he didn't go with that. I could hear the rationalization start...

"Well, I suppose . . ."

"Please don't consider what response you think you ought to have, just tell me the response that came immediately into your mind, the response that happened right when I asked you my question and your eyes moved up and to the side, remember?"

"Yes. Well, what I heard in my mind was the number five."

"Okay. What do you make of that?

"I don't like thinking of myself as being so childish when I twist my hair."

"Gee, I don't think of you as childish, and it's also true that it sounds like you feel young, perhaps like a child feels, but that's different than the pejorative term of feeling childish, right? Does child-like feel like a better fit than childish?"

"Yes, it does, and I like it a lot more than childish."

"It sounds to me that for a very long time, perhaps since your childhood, you learned you could really focus on the sensation of the hair twisting and then splitting hairs between your finger tips, and that when you did that you relaxed and it felt good. No wonder you got excited about it. Might that be the case?"

"Yes, it's always been like that, but I've always thought of it as something terrible, not something I did to relax, but that is exactly what happens."

"Would you be interested in learning a way to relax like that very quickly so you have an alternative way to do that without injuring your hair?"

"You can do that? I mean there's a way I could do that?"

"Sure. It seems to me that when you focus your attention on the feelings in your fingertips, as you feel the hair ends split, you are inducing a self-hypnotic state. Why not learn how to do that in a straight-forward way now as an adult?"

"Oh, I think that would be really wonderful."

There were several things I did in this brief interaction that violated the client's expectations derived from the history of standard reactions clinicians had to his story throughout the years. First, I have a model in my mind that all minds are composed of a conglomerate of self-states (clinicians, too), and this freed me up to notice shifts in emotion and what appeared to be potential shifts in subjectivity in my patient, perhaps shifts from one self-state to another. When I heard the story of the mechanism of his hair twisting habits, I noticed the potential for a self-hypnotic induction for naturalistic affect-regulation. I observed that he sounded somewhat excited and child-like in his expressions. I created the hypothesis in my mind that I was observing a state change kindled by absorption into the emotional qualities of the scene. Different self-states often have different core emotional qualities, such as sad, ashamed, happy. I did not see excitement as part of an illness. I heard it as part of a self-regulatory affect script (Tomkins 1995). I was focused on the emotion-regulating potentials in his actions. He was focused on shame and humiliation scripts that were induced by family members and other clinicians who had tried to rid him of this problem when they had no good substitute for it to regulate emotion and help him relieve emotional tension. He really liked learning self-hypnosis.

In fact, people with dissociative disorders are more likely to have hypnotic capacity than are other diagnostic categories, such as mood disorders, anxiety disorders, and schizophrenia (Frischholz et al. 1992). Although many people with persistent dissociative experience are highly hypnotizable, research indicates that high hypnotizability is not a requirement for development of a dissociative disorder (IJzendoorn and Schuengel 1996; Nash, Hulsey, Sexton, Harralson, and Lambert 1993). Still, the presence of high hypnotizability in this population is of paramount importance given the utility of hypnosis for affect regulation and containment (Kluft 1983), fractionated abreaction (Kluft 2013), and psychotherapeutic exploration (Watkins 1971, 1992; Watkins and Watkins 1997). As with all special techniques, thorough knowledge of the limitations of hypnotic technique is recommended (Hammond et al. 1994). I have been well trained in hypnosis and its utility, and I would not wish to work with the dissociative disorders without that knowledge base and attendant skills.

A Delicate and Cautious Approach

People with dissociative disorders have had experiences that have taken them, at some point, beyond being, beyond Winnicottian notions of the need for going-on-being, and catapulted them into Kohutian annihilation, to a place of ongoing nonbeing, as occurs with sustained attacks on linking (Bion 1959). To say people present to us tentatively, like the man with trichotillomania, armed with shame and humiliation scripts, is to grossly understate their dilemma. The inherent perspective in unintegrated self-states from an emotionally obliterating childhood climate is usually cautious, to a fault, and any formulation that omits this point is probably somewhat in error.

An approach to psychotherapy that appreciates dissociative process, compartmentalized function (Holmes, Brown, Manselld, Fearon, Hunter, Frasquilho, and Oakley 2005), and self-states will also be sure to investigate the moment-to-moment subjective experience of not wanting to do something and still doing it, as in the repetition compulsion and addiction. Some people are aware of "getting into a state" and being stuck there for a while. One person told me they knew about their rebellious, irresponsible state, their sad state, and their striving adult state.

> But I have to keep my rebellious state pushed into the background because when it happens I sometimes can't get control back and then I really suffer at work or with friends when everybody gets blown off; it's like those relationships suddenly are of no consequence to me. People get pretty upset with me and can't understand what got into me. I'm not exactly sure either, but I know I can't control this state I get into very well.

Stuffing down food, and the experience of physical detachment from self (being physically present versus depersonalized) while watching this kind of compulsive eating, just like the rebellious state noted above, often exists in tandem with other dissociative states. I conversationally frame the overall constellation as "different ways of being you." The words are important because the phrase acknowledges differences while the context remains an integrative "you"—one person. This phrase, different ways of being you, is easier to digest than terms like self-states or alter personalities, where music from the Twilight Zone (Grams 2008) is conjured. Alter personalities, however important and accurate as a term, can elicit thoughts of being taken over by an intruding self-state or may inadvertently play into the delusion of the separateness of self-states. That kind of metaphorical mishap, or hijacking, doesn't need to happen, and sometimes it doesn't. But when it does, then an avoidable insult is already history.

In the exploration of dissociative process, there must be a specific interest in the qualities of the state(s) in the patient's experience of experience, an interest in how perception and experience shift. We need to explore, note how things might conflict, and be curious about the absence of conflict between states when it seems like it ought to be present. We need to know what resolves the tension between states and what constitutes the perspectives and motivations of a given state. A good exploratory psychotherapy is one where there is curiosity all over the place. This makes for a very fine mesh through which a clinician can sift the content of a session if persistent dissociative experience is to become observable and conscious. It goes far beyond emotional and transferential dimensions. It goes beyond cognitive schemas. It is more than assessing behavioral scripts. It combines all these and in addition looks at the extent to which these experiences are organized and stuck together in relatively enduring patterns that are held distinctly separate and seem not to inform each other. These self-states are the stars in a constellation of what it means to be a person with different ways of being, and there can be variable degrees of integration underlying an intermittently coherent sense of self. It is a painful reality to be aware that being counted on to show up in the morning, and even go to the gym, to get it together, so to speak, is not simply a given.

The focused and openly curious discourse suggested here often grossly violates the general psychoanalytic dictum of not asking questions and allowing the patient the freedom to speak their mind, associatively, so as to let them show (not simply tell) what is in their mind in a way that is not directed by the mind of the therapist. I understand the value of that freedom, and there are times when I cultivate it. It is also true that it may not help someone discover the extent of the dissociative process working in the background of their mind when that process uses obfuscation and deflection as an implicit part of a mostly avoided experience of being mindful.

Dissociative process isn't going to raise its hand and speak up. It has no intention of being recognized. That's the whole point, in a way—to hide. Who would desperately work to get relief from unbearable experience by pulling the plug on that experience and then turn around and point out where the socket and plug are? Maintaining dissociative adaptation through persistent exclusion and deflection is in the service of remaining normal. Much dissociative experience, like depersonalization, feels sufficiently strange that it can leave a person with the sense that they are on the verge of going crazy and being locked up—good reason to veer away. The intellectualization of depersonalization experience can be equally confounding in its own way. One young man, with robust and chronic depersonalization was asked if a particularly adverse event troubled him, and he responded in context: "Well, since I don't feel real, it doesn't feel real. So, honestly, I don't appreciate any problem with this when it isn't real." Even if somebody is conscious of their dissociative process, until you name it and normalize it as understandable and not a sign of insanity, your patient may hide it or simply have it tucked away just outside awareness or beyond the realm of having any meaning at all.

Clinicians need to be good listeners. It's also true that when it comes to things dissociative it's important to notice, out loud, the small inconsistencies, incongruencies, interruptions in a train of thought; intervening facial expressions that are out of context; and other minor disruptions of the flow of consciousness in your patient. The task is to be curious, with your patient, about their experience.

A sign is something you observe. A symptom is something subjective that is told to you. Exploring the actual detailed subjective experience of a sign or symptom is important. It's not enough to know somebody feels depressed. What is that? What is their personal experience? When there are elaborate behavioral scripts involved, it may require a kind of creative curiosity.

For a patient with bulimic symptoms, for example, there are several kinds of questions I would thoughtfully put on the clinical table with appropriate timing as we engaged an exploration of those symptoms. Repetitive behaviors often repeat in the same exacting manner, a script. I want to know what's behind the script (s).

"It sounds like you had the experience of doing something with a
    kind of intention when at the same time you really, emphati-

cally, had not wanted to do it, not at all. Is this an unusual experience for you, or are there other times when you've had something happen similar to this?"

"You talked about stuffing the pizza in your mouth. Do you remember this with clarity? What was it like in that moment? Did you feel in charge of the stuffing?"

"What was your mind doing while the stuffing was happening?"

"You said you weren't quite sure if you tasted it. Is this unusual for you? Are there other times when you don't taste food? Does taste have any importance in these scenes? Do you sometimes have tastes in your mouth that don't make sense, or that you don't want to have? Do you ever eat in a way that is somehow automatic? Are there other things that you do at times that seem to have a mind of their own?"

"I'm curious about the pain you had after you were well beyond full. It seems like the pain launched you into a dissolving experience, like your awareness disappeared, somehow. Can you tell me what goes into dissolving, you know, what that's really like, please? Are there other things that help you get to that dissolved place?"

"What do you think of that dense foggy calm you mentioned? Is it a problem? You said it actually felt good. Does that mean it helps in some way? How does it help you?"

These questions open discussion about subjective experience during a bulimic episode. This is a nonjudgmental and curious perspective that we can hope our patients will model if we consistently maintain it. Nothing "just happens" no matter how much your patient insists it does. Even if a person has little recollection of what happened or little consciousness for their subjective experience, these questions are likely to open up new ways of becoming aware of experience as it unfolds for them in future episodes. Once they have a reasonable intellectual frame and some new language, as well as your nonanxious and nonjudgmental curiosity, they will have more capacity to remember and more interest in noticing what's always been there but which has never really felt like it merited the focus of their attention. This increase in consciousness for these experiences primes the psychotherapy engine and adds clinical traction. It also helps for a clinician to be primed with an understanding of self-states and something about their organization so he or she can hear the music, the siren call of self-state activity, and make that background symphony fully audible.

Mind as a Conglomerate of Self-States

In general, a human mind is a conglomerate of self-states. An aggregate is like a rock composed of particles that are nearly the same size, whereas a conglomerate includes variably sized components of varying composition that are stuck together. Similarly, although all self-states tend to have core emotional content, behavioral coordinates, worldview, fund of knowledge, and varying degrees of embodiment, they are not all equal in stature because some are relatively dominant and may be broadly inclusive of personal experience as well as frequently occupying the role of the regularly presenting aspect of self.

Self-state formation is a normal developmental process (Bromberg 1996; Davies 1996; Davies and Frawley 1992; Flax 1996; Fonagy et al. 2003; Gergely and Watson 1996; Mitchell 1991; Putnam 1997; Schwartz 1994; Siegel1999; D. B. Stern 1997; Wolff 1987). Some self-states occupy more mental real estate than others and are more elaborate, more far-reaching in their capacities, and more easily able to creatively bridge to other self-states. There are always numerous guests in Rumi's house, my house, and your house, too. Some are more familiar than others. Each guest has active associative and dissociative processes at work, sorting experience for salience and creating coherence. Sometimes the equilibrium between these processes is off, way off. The bottom line is this: self-states each have at work a unique balance between associative and dissociative processes. Associative processes glue things together coherently, and dissociative processes support coherence by ordinarily discarding the chaff. This produces a cultivated degree of mental coherence with access to a base of knowledge, worldview, behavioral patterns, emotional capacity, physical coordination, embodied experience, and so on A frightened and overwhelmed mind sometimes hits the dissociative deceleration pedal so hard it gets stuck to the floor. Its persistence creates real problems as useful information is pruned from experience. This creates big gaps, or as Philip Bromberg so eloquently put it, spaces that eventually require therapist and patient being able to stand in them and look around together (Bromberg 1996). Big gaps provoke the need to make leaps. Thus, the often notable signature of a self-state looms into view when a change in the environment requires a person to jump from one relatively isolated state to another, rather than to slip seamlessly from one relatively integrated state to another.

It is not unusual for me to hear a thoughtful clinician, well studied in the psychoanalytic literature of our time, for example, become both curious and perplexed as to how they can bridge the gap between what they have studied and what I am talking about regarding the isolation of self-states, different ways of being, and so on (Chefetz 2004, 2008, 2013). It's even a bigger leap for them to tune in to the subjective experience of self-state switching and the delusion of separateness that identity alteration implies. In this next section, I spell out some of the latent allusions to dissociative process in a body of theory with which the reader is likely familiar. The goal is to appreciate the theory behind what it's like to have the subjectively alive experience of different ways of being (i.e., alternate self-states), not all of which feel under a person's control or even under the same umbrella, so to speak.

Self-States and Subjectively Alive Experience

Dissociative experience is all over the psychoanalytic literature if a reader is educated and prepared to notice it. Fairbairn first identified the patterns of internal object relations (W. R. D. Fairbairn 1941, 1944). David Scharff, a Fairbairn scholar, told me (personal communication, 1996) that Fairbairn knew he was working with "children with multiple personality disorder" when he developed his object relations theory. Skelton comments on this from a historical perspective:

The subject of dissociated or divided consciousness has been of interest in psychopathology from the time of Charcot and Janet. Dissociation of parts of experience is a normal process, but its excessive use figures in the pathology of dissociative disorders, including multiple personality, or "dissociative identity disorder," states which are often the result of trauma. Fairbairn was interested in the comparative study of dissociation and repression throughout his academic career. In his MD thesis he argued that repression was a special case of dissociation, being the dissociation of unpleasant mental content. Though he did not address the issue directly in his later writings, Fairbairn regretted the lack of analytic study of dissociation, aware that the concept was crucial to the study of the multiplicity of internalised ego-object interactions that characterize his endopsychic theory. (Skelton 2006)

Winnicott and Guntrip were close on the trail of the significance of dissociative process when they offered their descriptions of true and false self (D. W. Winnicott 1949) and schizoid phenomena (Guntrip 1969). Winnicott in particular seems to have been well aware of dissociative process—he expressly uses the word *dissociation* in the passage that follows—but it seems neither he nor Guntrip were aware of the full extent to which these processes influenced their patient's productions.

When a False Self becomes organized in an individual who has a high intellectual potential there is a very strong tendency for the mind to become the location of the False Self, and in this case there develops a dissociation between intellectual activity and psychosomatic existence. (In the healthy individual, it must be assumed, the mind is not something for the individual to exploit in escape from psycho-somatic being. I have developed this theme at some length in "Mind and its Relation to the Psyche-Soma" [1949].

> When there has taken place this double abnormality, (i) the False Self organized to hide the True Self, and (ii) an attempt on the part of the individual to solve the personal problem by the use of a fine intellect, a clinical picture results which is peculiar in that it very easily deceives. The world may observe academic success of a high degree, and may find it hard to believe in the very real distress of the individual concerned, who feels "phoney" the more he or she is successful. (D. W. Winnicott 1960a, p. 144)

The extent to which self-state compartmentalization is quite visible in the clinical data is striking in Winnicott's further description. Likewise, Guntrip's words have always put a smile on my face in appreciation of his painfully honest descriptions.

> One patient, a single woman in her early forties . . . would rave against girl children and in fantasy would describe how she would crush a girl child if she had one, and would then fall to punching herself (which perpetuated the beatings her mother gave her). One day I said to her, "You must feel terrified being hit like that." She stopped and stared and said, "I'm not being hit. I'm the one doing the hitting." (Guntrip 1969, p. 191)

It seems reasonable to surmise that his patient was very much in a "state" given that Guntrip used the word *stared* to describe her reaction when he spoke. His patient was almost certainly in a trance-like place and spoke through her stare about the perceived difference in her sense of agency. On the next page Guntrip described another patient who was even more easily recognizable as having had an active internal landscape and isolated self-states as he struggled with his "depressed childhood self" while getting ready to head off to his session with Guntrip.

"Just before I set out I felt apprehensive, as if I could burst into tears: a reaction I suppose to coming here." When I asked him why he should feel depressed in coming to see me, he replied: "I see a picture of a little boy shut up alone in a room, crying. If one were in a house where there was such a child, it would depend on how interesting one's work was whether or not you were aware of him. Sometimes I am aware of him and at other times when very busy I forget him." I said, "Your fantasy is really that you as a grown-up person are working in one room and wanting to forget a crying little boy shut up in another room. What about that?" He answered, "The obvious thing is to go to the child and find out why he is crying and comfort him. Why didn't I do that at first? That strikes me as very odd." (Guntrip 1969, p.192)

Guntrip's clarification of his patient wanting to forget the little boy joined the patient in reference to the boy with language that drifted toward the patient speaking of his having an *active* experience with the boy, as if *being with him*. This kind of metaphorical "being with" experience of the patient crosses a line from imagining the little boy in a kind of fantasy to the patient making it sound as if he had an actual interaction with the boy. However, Guntrip seems to hear this only as the patient's fantasy rather than as an experience that is *subjectively alive*.

Guntrip's later response in exploring what he considered fantasy was to ask the patient why he shut the boy up in another room in the first place. This is a wonderful and brilliantly put, breathtaking leap into the patient's inner world. The patient replied in that alive context, "He's a nuisance. You can't get on with your work with a child crying around." But here was lost a clinical opportunity as Guntrip slips back into thinking of this patient as having a fantasy rather than the patient describing a scene he sees and lives in his own mind, a transitionally alive space of a sort, filled with sensorially vivid experience. The patient interacts with the little boy in this space, and it is alive with "a kind of pretend" that ought not be questioned any more than one would disobey Winnicott's admonition to not analyze the transitional object (D. W. Winnicott 1953). The patient shifts back and forth in his language, as if the distinction between internal and external[1] is temporarily lost on him: "I see a picture . . . when very busy I forget him . . . obvious thing is to go to the child. . . . Why didn't I do that at first?" Guntrip could have said: "I know you didn't go to this child and comfort him, or find out why he was crying, earlier. What do you imagine it would be like to do that now? Can you see him now, if you look for him? Okay, good. Could you move over toward him so that he sees you gently approaching? What kind of thoughts and feelings do you see on his face? What concerns him?" In saying such things, the therapist would join the patient in his internal lived transitional space, in his sensorially alive fantasy, and respond to the patient's curiosity about the common sense thing to have done. An interaction with the child, the patient, and the therapist could follow. The therapist would "play" with this reality, not analyze or criticize it. It is not psychotic. It is an alive dissociative transitional space in which the patient is sometimes immersed and through which the patient may have had an alternate place for living when reality was too much to bear. Exploring the space—the thoughts, feelings, and sensations of it—could be transformative. When clinicians can work creatively with different self-states in transitional spaces and guide their patient's exploration a bridge is formed between self-states. Talking with and about self-states builds bridges and links states together. It does not reify the patient's experience and make things worse; it makes things better (as the first longitudinal outcome study on dissociative disorder treatment shows) (Brand et al. 2012).

It can be difficult to ferret out dissociative experience and the signs of self-state trajectories that behave more like the vapor trails of jetliners on a windy day than an enduring sense of self. Alice, whom you met earlier, had struggled with her angry snit by trying to banish it from mind. She told me, some time later, that it was her fantasy that

---

[1] See the discussion of the work of Fonagy, Target, and colleagues later in this chapter regarding psychic equivalence and pretend modes of thinking.

if we used hypnosis to help her explore her mind by reducing her anxiety, she expected her experience would be one of being in a state of mind where she was certain she was faking both having DID and being in a state of hypnosis. Without missing a beat in the rhythm of our conversation, she was quick to add she also knew that at the conclusion of the hypnotic work she would try to return to her normal waking state and discover that in fact she couldn't alert herself—she would actually be in trance!

"You know, Alice, what you are saying is almost the equivalent of the classic statement 'We are not multiple.'"

"Yes, I know," she said, authoritatively. Her acknowledgment that she finally understood there was a part of her who deflected our work by being in a complex state of denial and disavowal prefaced much deeper work as well as frightening her about the extent to which her mind was foreign territory (see chapters 10, 11, and 12). This particular kind of deflection from the exploration of inner experience Alice wrestled with is comparatively extreme, though it's also true that deflection in general is a relatively routine finding. The point is that a clinician listening to Alice must have an appreciation of complex phenomena to make sense of what she says. It's not impossible to understand Alice without that knowledge base. It's just a longer and more difficult process. The best way to track the comings and goings of self-states is to be alert to the discontinuities I mentioned before and watch your patient like a hawk. If you can't see their face, or you're looking elsewhere, you lose a whole lot of what could be useful. Studying hypnosis helped me learn to be a much better observer of the physiological state of my patients. Eye-lid flutter, swallowing, twitching movements, flush, change in posture—all have meaning.

All this attention to detail is in the service of making conscious the stigmata of self-states and the distinctions that describe their emotional and intellectual territory. The attention paid to making self-states distinct and conscious might seem counterintuitive given that the eventual movement needs to be toward an integration of self-state functions. Wouldn't making the states more distinct increase the sense of separateness between self-states? In fact, just the opposite happens—a paradox. Why? The compartmentalization of self-states erodes as familiarity with the content of the individual compartments increases. It's important to recall that dissociative process increases the sense of detachment from thoughts, feelings, sensations, behavior, and so on. Thus, the fruit of the therapist's noticing connections between self-states and component experience (especially feelings) out loud and engaging the patient in detailed discussion about their meaning and the relationship to the patient's experience is the creation of an obligatory associational experience in the patient. Clinicians are unable to foster associations to what they don't know about. The exploration of compartmental content is essential to the clinical process on the road to tolerable association.

In the example I briefly explored regarding Guntrip's patient, the supplemental questions I posed served the purpose of raising consciousness in the patient for the thoughts, feelings, and sensations in a different self-state while being conscious of a whole sense of self. This is a linking function (Putnam 1989). Creating a broad span of conversational attention that absorbs more than one plot of mental real estate in conversation is a linking activity that creates association where once there was just a dissociative gap. Our ability to automatically and naturalistically knit together or integrate the multiple self-states that exist in a human mind requires the assistance of a reliable other person who can reflect back and accurately confirm what is displayed in our behavioral, cognitive, somatic, and emotional expressions. This reflective feedback creates a reliable sense of me-ness. Good parenting regularly provides this.

Once a clinician identifies several self-states related to an area of dysfunction, then a kind of "linking group therapy" starts where the positions and attitudes of different states are openly recalled by the clinician when speaking with states that contain conflicting views. "I know you are telling me you don't want to eat and gain weight. It's also true that two days ago a younger way of being you told me the only pleasure they get in life is to eat. It doesn't sound like that discrepancy concerns you." The intent here is to create conflict in the service of eventually resolving it. But conflict is not noticeable when the dissociative process uses trance logic (Orne 1959), the juxtaposition of logically incompatible realities without anxiety. Dissociation is a smooth talker. He is a slick deflector of unpleasant or grossly painful reality, and he does his work while you're looking, although you don't see him. We must be prepared to engage him and not give in to subtle misrepresentations of experience if our patients are to feel real, eventually. A real pickpocket, as subtle as he is, is not as good as dissociative process is in emptying your mental wallet so that you can't find your license to live a life, when you need it.

If a clinician is to have some sense of coherence when standing in the dissociative therapeutic landscape, then the landmarks need to be made familiar; otherwise the clinician may find he or she is standing alone in those spaces without the patient, and that is certainly not what is intended or useful (Bromberg 1996). The finest compilation of dissociative experience in terms of its depth and breadth was written by Richard J. Loewenstein, and it is worth obtaining a copy of his article (R. J. Loewenstein 1991). Studying this work creates a situation that is much like what fishermen know about seeing fish in water. If you wear polarized sunglasses to sift out the scattering light rays, you can see below the surface of the water. Still, it doesn't mean you'll know what a fish looks like in water. It means you'll have a much better chance of looking right at a fish when it moves and then noticing the subtle camouflage that made it invisible a moment before. "See that long dark area in that place with white gravel? Yes, right there. Watch. It's going to move; and when it does, you'll know what a fish looks like in water because you'll see the fish above its shadow." Once you see it, you won't forget. The same is true in treatment: You become aware of a dimension of subtlety that may have previously escaped your attention, a dimension where dissociative process is visible beneath the surface of dissociative waters, hidden right in front of you in beautiful daylight.

Some Discontinuities of Experience in Other Psychiatric Disorders

The activity of self-states is a given in human beings. Sometimes that activity isn't noticed, nor is its salience appreciated. Thus, in the absence of a working knowledge of the way in which some psychiatric disorders mimic or overlap with dissociative processes and self-state formation, some symptom complexes may become confounded with each other. Two straightforward examples of the confounding of subjective experiences related to dissociation and the creation of diagnostic misadventure occurs in attention deficit hyperactivity disorder (ADHD) and the rapid cycling version of bipolar disorder. In the case of ADHD, PTSD rarely seems to be included in the differential diagnosis of children with this and other emotional disturbances. Neither the word *trauma* nor the word *dissociation* appears in the text or references of a recent authoritative review of the potential for an association between childhood ADHD and adult bipolar disorder (Duffy 2012). (Incidentally, no association is actually shown between ADHD and bipolar disorder in this thorough analysis.) Yet another recent paper showed significant overlap between PTSD and ADHD diagnoses in a highly traumatized patient population in the New York City metropolitan area (Szymanski, Sapanski, and Conway 2011). These authors make a plea for consideration of this finding of high levels of comorbidity. Here I would add that in considering the comorbidity with PTSD, one should automatically be primed to think about dissociative process as well.

It's been clinically clear for a long time, and more recently well documented, that there is a reexperiencing hyperarousal model of PTSD and an emotionally overmodulated version (Lanius, Vermetten, Loewenstein, Brand, Schmahl, Bremner, and Spiegel 2010). Some people with PTSD present with flooding, and others are so emotionally shut down that they present as emotionally flat, detached, with active dissociative process. It is now well established that PTSD and ADHD are highly comorbid in adults with burnout—people who have emotional exhaustion and end up on long-term sick leave (Brattberg 2006). Fifty-two percent of a cohort of 62 individuals had PTSD and 24 percent had ADHD in this study. Nineteen percent had both PTSD and ADHD. There is thus a distinct risk of undiagnosed PTSD in populations of ADHD patients. Because PTSD and dissociative processes go hand in hand, and it is well established that PTSD is highly comorbid with dissociative disorders, there is a problem in the literature with under-recognition of disorders related to dissociative process that are comorbid with ADHD. Would ADHD symptoms remit with treatment of comorbid PTSD and dissociative processes? I'm not aware that anybody has conducted that study. But if you see somebody with ADHD in your office, it would seem to be prudent practice to screen for PTSD and for dissociative processes.

Rapid cycling in bipolar disorder means more than four cycles in a given year (American Psychiatric Association 2000). Four per year— that's not four per month, four per day, or four per hour. The concept of rapid cycling has been expanded to include much more rapid changes in mood (Papolos, Veit, Faedda, Saito, and Lachman 1998): "In addition to regular circannual episodes, a spectrum of cycle frequencies has been observed, from the classical rapid cycling (RC) pattern of four or more episodes per year, to those with distinct shifts of mood and activity occurring within a 24-48 h period, described as ultra-ultra rapid cycling (UURC) or ultradian cycling. RC has a female preponderance, and occurs with greater frequency premenstrually, at the puerperium and at menopause." The nature of the similarity or differences between the actual switch process that produces four cycles in a year or a cycle within a 24–48-hour period is not addressed. This is a serious omission. It is well established that antidepressant induced shifts in neurotransmitter production take at least two and often three weeks when a pharmacologic dose of an antidepressant is taken regularly. A theory based on a neurobiological construct, bipolar disorder, seems to have been corrupted to the point that now it is implied that there are putative changes in brain chemistry that cause rapid cycling in a day or two or over hours. That may point to a conceptual problem. In a small clinical study of the clinical characteristics of bipolar disorder in very young children, based on a chart review of 26 cases, ages three to seven (Danielyan, Pathak, Kowatch, Arszman, and Johns 2007), very high rates of both remission and relapse were noted in a population often treated with antipsychotics and mood stabilizers for demonstrated irritability and aggression. These treatments do not seem to have been effective and call into question the diagnostic validity of the construct of bipolar disorder in this age group. In addition, other studies show that there is documentable comorbidity between adult bipolar disorder and PTSD (Freeman, Freeman, and McElroy 2002). Is this evidence for a misinterpretation of the constructs for bipolar disorder patients? The burden is on both ADHD and bipolar research clinicians to review the literature on the phenomenology of dissociative disorders and PTSD. The job is then to parse out what is consistent with the existing knowledge base across diagnostic entities.

Although there are other psychiatric disorders where self-states play a role, these two suffice to make the point that self-state psychology and dissociative experience are worth considering when making a psychiatric assessment. Self-states are ubiquitous and normal. When they are linked to each other and knowledge, behavior, emotion, and sensation flow freely from state to state, then we are in relative harmony with our sense of self and the world. We all benefit by being able to seamlessly trot out one or another authentic versions of ourselves to function in various situations. It can be the same person who is an authority on rocket safety, the coach of a Little League team, the parent who calms a distraught child with her first scraped knee, or the spouse who listens attentively to their mate after their own exhausting day, knowing that they will get their own turn soon enough (or maybe not). Yet the particular constellations of knowledge, range of emotion, possible behaviors, and consciousness for one's own needs can vary considerably. A healthy mind has the capacity to shift from state to state in a way that is unimpeded, and there is unrestricted and free flow of knowledge, emotion, behavior, and relational capacities. A person with persistent and excessive dissociative process, on the other hand, may get stuck in a self-state to maintain the isolation, exclusion, or deflection of psychological content that is unconsciously or consciously feared or has simply previously led to physiologic destabilization. There may be a mismatch of social context and self-state when that occurs. A self-state might be present that lacks social graces, or is unable to access a subset of knowledge and skill (driving a car or operating a computer), or may even lack knowledge of important people in their lives (R. J. Loewenstein 1991).

Self-states can even show up in competent and sophisticated clinicians when they feel shamed,[2] and when they do they can provoke stunning disorientation and confusion, as boldly described by Marg Sperry when she was shamed by a patient (Chefetz 2013; Sperry, 2013a, 2013b) Self-states are normal. Getting stuck in a contextually inappropriate self-state and losing emotional and intellectual flexibility or creativity speaks to compartmentalization of self-experience and the relative isolation of self-states via dissociative processes. Like the Japanese soldiers in World War II who were first planted on and then later abandoned on Pacific atolls, forming an early warning system for the imperial forces of Japan, isolated self-states may lack updated knowledge of the world and behave outside the current context. Then they "shoot" at the people who come to tell them the war is over. However, it is also typical for people without DID to have "not-me" self-states, which are also dissociatively held. It's just that there is not the same constellation of dissociative processes (depersonalization, derealization, amnesia, identity confusion, and identity alteration) maintaining a multiplicity of the not-me self-states in the non-DID population. Instead, it has been my observation that these self-states often form the core of enduring patterns of behavior, personality disorders, eating disorders, and addictive behaviors among others, whether or not there is DID.

Some Clinical Context about Self-State Presentation

I was once asked to interview a young man with a kind of "adult failure to thrive" syndrome and prescribe medication to have him improve his functioning in the world. Having survived a several-years-long period of illicit drug use, he finished college and entered graduate school. In treatment for about 18 months in individual and group therapy, he had failed to create a sense of stability in his life. His therapist recognized dissociative symptoms, but could not figure out the extent of his disorder. Here is a brief review of the consultation

---

[2] See this brief collection of papers based on Sperry's case, a discussion, and Sperry's confirmation of the speculations in the discussion.

interview. Of particular interest to me in discerning the potential for a complex dissociative disorder was to take note of possible changes in state; put another way, were discrete self-states visible and, if present, to what extent did they represent identity alteration? If identity alteration was present, or if he had a principal diagnosis of a dissociative disorder, what would be the rationale for prescribing?

An obviously bright 26-year-old man tried unsuccessfully to relax in the chair next to me, as he described how it was a miracle that he actually completed a year of graduate school. His inability to focus and finish a task was marked. He didn't know why he couldn't follow through. It was not that he didn't want to. It was that he often found himself doing one thing after he had intended and even started to do another. It was as if his mind had a mind of its own. Our discussion was pointing in the direction of the presence of self-states. I inquired about the salient aspects of dissociative experience to get a better picture of what might be generating behavior that confused him.

I asked him about depersonalization (see Chapter 6). "Do you have a sense of being in your body, being a physical person?" He didn't know what I meant and was clearly confused. I said, "You are sitting in that chair. Do you have a sense of speaking from the chair, from your body, your body that is in the chair?"

"Yes," he replied, still somewhat confused.

I took note of this by simply saying, "You look confused."

"Well, I am, kind of. I don't really understand what you are asking me."

"Okay, let me tell you why I am asking, and what I am trying to understand. Some people, when they are scared, experience a change in their relationship with their body; you've probably heard about people having out-of-body experiences. But there are other, much more subtle changes in people's experience of being in their body. So let me ask again. When you speak to me, or as you move through the world, do you do that in a body which feels like it's yours, one in which you live?"

"Oh, well, I know this is the body in which I live, but frankly, I don't really feel like being in this body is like what people call 'feeling alive.' It's like the way I see the world, everything is always kind of detached, not real. But I know it's real, it just doesn't somehow look like it's real. It's always that way. I don't know. I always get confused when I think about this stuff."

The interview continued as I noted out loud that it seemed there were a number of instances in his adult life where he showed evidence for being constantly frightened. He proceeded to tell me about his father's tendency to violence and his mother's extramarital affairs. Expressions of rage were routine at home. He then spoke more about his own abuse.

After telling me that when he was five years old he had been sexually abused by the family doctor, and then stating that he was becoming nauseous, the cadence of his speech changed. In an anxious, apologetic, and somewhat halting speech, he said: "I . . . I . . . don't know . . . I mean . . . you should know . . . I feel compelled to tell you . . . I don't know why . . . but I feel compelled to tell you that I may have just made all that up!" This kind of disrupted narrative is typical of adults with Type D patterns on the Adult Attachment Interview (IJzendoorn 1995). It hinted that his internal world had a lot of discontinuous experience. I needed to pursue that. It also seemed that he was saying to me that he wasn't at all sure why he was telling me he might have made this history up, but that he knew he had to say so. I wondered about the presence of a subjectively different state of mind. Did he have an alternate state of mind impinging on his efforts to tell of the abuse?

The difference in his emotional presence was striking. In a matter-of-fact tone I said, "I'd like to ask you a question. Would you be willing to tell me the first thing that comes to mind if I ask you a question?"

"Yes."

"Okay, here is the question: How old are you?"

With his eyes suddenly becoming wide open he spoke: "Seven."

I said: "Feeling seven when you have such big problems must be very hard. May I ask you another question and you tell me the first thing that comes into your mind?"

"Yes."

"What is your name?"

"William."

"You introduced yourself to me earlier as 'Will.' Is that your name?" I was interested in his subjective experience of himself, and attempted to create consciousness for having different ways of being Will or William.

"I am William. Nobody called me Will until after my uncle got killed when I was eight years old. I don't know why that started. I am William."

"Where is Will?"

"Oh, he is sticking his head in from behind and listening."

"Does Will know about you, William?"

"No, he doesn't want to know about me. He doesn't want to listen."

"How is he doing with you talking with me?"

"He's not too happy about it. He doesn't know what to think."

I spoke directly to Will: "Will, what is it like listening to William?"

He shook his head, as if rousing himself from a foggy place, and said, "This really makes me nervous. I have heard his voice before, like in my mind, but he has never spoken to anybody. I just feel so freaked out. Are you trying to make me think I have multiple personality disorder or something?"

"No, Will, I am not trying to make you think anything. I am just trying to understand how to figure out what it means that I have been talking with you and with another part of you who says his name is William. Seems like you experience different states of mind, and that is probably an important thing to know. Maybe it has something to do with why you have so much trouble finishing a project in school. You know, like who is working on this project anyhow?"

"Yeah, that makes sense. But it really makes me nauseous to be talking about this. My stomach is all tied up in knots."

Some Theoretical Background on the Formation of Self-States

It's important to understand some of the theory of how self-states and dissociative disorders are generated. Patients read about these theories and expect clinicians to know at least as much as they do about the origins of a dissociative disorder. Moreover, if you become articulate about the theoretical underpinnings of self-states, that working knowledge will help you be better prepared to hear a patient's reference to self-state experience and be openly curious about it.

The earliest theory about self-state formation was Richard P. Kluft's four-factor theory, predicated on (1) the capacity to dissociate, (2) the occurrence of a profound trauma, (3) alternate personality development based on naturally occurring phenomena like Hilgard's hidden observer (Hilgard 1986) or imaginary companions, and (4) the failure of caretakers to protect the child and help him or her resume normal development. Braun and Sachs went on to propose the 3-P model predicated on: (1) predisposition, (2) precipitation of dissociation as defense, and (3) perpetuation through repetition (Braun and Sachs 1985). For many years, these were the prevailing, state-of-the-art theories regarding the origin of the dissociative disorders. Both models pay credence to trauma, attribution of otherness to a self-state, chronic repetitive abuse, and failure to protect the child. These are multiple-blow models of dissociative outcome (Terr 1991) based on inherent capacities and environmental impingement. The models do not include an intrapsychic component per se except for the implicit appreciation of dissociative processes as being part of having a mind. Kluft is a psychoanalyst, and I have heard him present complex cases over a number of years, so I know he is masterfully aware of the intrapsychic dimensions of treatment. In his formulation of the genesis of DID, however, he does not emphasize intrapsychic factors.

Putnam proposed a third model based on the normative and naturalistic evolution of discrete behavioral states (DBS) (Putnam 1997) in all children. He looked carefully at normal developmental processes and the construction or absence of transitional capacities to help infants move from one state of being to another. He thoroughly took in the work of Peter Wolff, whose observational studies of the islands of relatively discrete kinds of infant behavior were revealing (Wolff 1987). There is an obvious need in infancy and very early childhood to move from island to island to keep up with physiological and environmental demands like hunger, contact with a caretaker, active alert states, and a need for sleep. Transitions represent the need to move or jump from one behavioral island to another. Especially abrupt movement from one discrete constellation of capacities or qualities has the feeling of a "switch" from one way of being to another. The formulation of meaning structures and links between behavioral states is associative in nature. The integration of these structures provides a sense of continuity and coherence as perspective changes with movement between islands and the construction of bridges. But what happens if there is no parent providing transitional, bridge-building guidance, no transformational object (Bollas 1987)? Putnam's model also makes use of the powerful cognitive-behavioral perspective of infant attachment research, other infant and self-state research, and trauma studies (Emde, 1983; Horowitz, Fridhandler, and Stinson 1991; Main and Hesse 1990; Main and Morgan 1996; Ogawa et al. 1997; D. N. Stern 1985; Terr 1979). Putnam argues that multiple personality disorder can be understood as "arising from a traumatic disruption in the early acquisition and control of basic behavioral states coupled with the creation of highly discrete dissociated states organized around differences in sense of self" (1997, p. 152).

The separation of and gaps between islands of subjectivity are reminiscent of what Mrs. Klein called splitting (Segal 1979), but I prefer to think of it as unintegrated experience. Clinicians see the behavioral results of this and have attributed to their patients that the good and bad are split from an object representation. Was something whole and then split? There is no evidence for that. An inability to keep both the good and the bad about the same person separate may be a necessity for the child who must remain in proximity to an abusive or emotionally toxic caretaker. Preserving the good parent is a paramount task if you are living with someone. The child may actually take up residence on unlinked specific islands of perspective as a parsimonious and automatic unconscious response to a changing mother (Lyons-Ruth, Bronfman, and Parsons 1999; Main and Hesse 1990), as seen in Type D attachment, and preserve the good mother lest their safe enough compromise on reality simply collapse. Who could tolerate

being close to someone who might change in a flicker of time? Dissociative process is sometimes very useful. A child really does seem to
experience the good and bad mother as separate, but they were never
together in the first place.

For a clinician, thinking about a child with unintegrated perceptions and isolated self-states *feels* different than considering a child
who splits the internal objects in their mind into good and bad. Anya,
who teaches us about dissociative process in Chapters 2 and 7, was
in the middle of the task of seeing both the good and the bad in her
parents, and wrote:

> I feel like it's because when I was young—and for a lot
> of my life really—it was good and then terrible. When I
> was around my dad—I'd have a good day at school or a
> fun experience out in the world—then I'd have to go back
> home—and my happiness usually was taken away from
> me. It wasn't just a feeling then—it was a reality. I also
> think it was impossible/too painful to know then that my
> mom and dad were hurting me and so I felt instead like I
> was bad and/or being punished by God because I'd been
> bad.

Anya anticipated states of feeling bad, especially when she was
around her father. When she initially presented for treatment she was
in a quandary when I asked her if she had any good memories about
her father. After several weeks of struggling, she finally found one
moment in her memory. She kept separate her knowledge of the hurt
coming at her from her parents, but the only way she could do that
was to see herself as bad. Otherwise, the things she recalled were too
painful and filled with intolerable feelings of betrayal (Freyd 1996).
Anya thought her mother might have self-states, too. When a mother
has unresolved islands of her own, she provides a template for her
child that a priori predicts the child will have her own archipelago
of self-states to add to the burden of trying to make living coherent,
efficient, and satisfying. Profound, unmodulated, and emotionally

intense parental state change maintains the value of having isolated islands of experience for the child (Lyons-Ruth et al. 2006), good ones and bad ones. Putnam's DBS model is less about the fragmentation of a mind that was once whole and more about the failure to develop transitional linking that would integrate the various normal or trauma related self-states into a working and coherent whole.

Infant attachment theory can be seen as a model of self-state formation and elaboration through understanding the relative discreteness of behavioral states, segregated subsystems, defensive exclusion (Bowlby 1980; Bretherton 1992), and the insecure patterns of attachment, the anxious-ambivalent (Type C), avoidant (Type A), and disorganized/disoriented (Type D) modes (Main and Morgan 1996). Beatrice Beebe and her team have used microanalysis of mother–infant interactions and been able to predict 12-month attachment patterns based on their findings: "Future disorganized infants represent states of *not being sensed and known* by their mothers, particularly in moments of distress; they represent confusion about both their own and their mothers' basic emotional organization, and about their mothers' response to their distress. This internal working model sets a trajectory in development which may disturb the fundamental integration of the person" (Beebe, Lachmann, Markese, and Bahrick 2012). Infant attachment theory is a strong evidentiary line of research that holds promise for expanding our understanding of what happens in the mind of a child when the relationship with their parents fails to meet their needs. Dissociative experience appears to be related to the emotional disrecognitions of insecure attachment.

Longitudinal studies have corroborated the maintenance of Type D patterns from childhood into adulthood as demonstrated by correlations in the Adult Attachment Interview (IJzendoorn 1995; Lyons-Ruth 2003; Ogawa et al. 1997). Attachment research shows unequivocally that childhood patterns of coping persist into adulthood. While Type A patterns may be associated with adult dissociation, Type D seems nearly always to be present. The best predictor of adult dissociation is emotionally unresponsive parenting (Lyons-Ruth et al. 2006).

Infant attachment paradigms are especially helpful because they predict transference patterns as well as providing some scaffolding for potential reconstruction of relational constellations in childhood. They are also guilt- and shame-free, in a manner of speaking, because the infant child is simply responding to the parental environment and trying to stay safe. There is nothing bad about the child. Bretherton was also clear that Bowlby understood there was active dissociative process when describing the defensive exclusions and other operations infants used to eliminate conscious threat to their maintaining connection with their caretakers (Bretherton 1992).

These two models (Putnam and Bowlby/Main) are less about trauma and more about normative developmental pathways gone awry owing to a lack of transitional and linking processes between one self-state and another—relational or developmental trauma if you will. (This parallels the work of Bucci in her use of the idea of referential processes and their relative paucity that is typical of dissociative process; Bucci and Maskit 2007.) These unlinked self-states are a by-product of inadequate relational activity that is somehow unresponsive to the particular needs of a child. Trauma need not be excluded from the generation of isolated self-states. However, a process more complex than trauma often seems involved in the creation of self-states and creates vulnerability to trauma and difficulty recovering from it.

Attachment theory pays attention to the emotional qualities in the caretaker as predictive of the emotional strategies the child develops to maintain proximity to the parent as a kind of emergency strategy (Bowlby 1980; Cortina 2003). When a parent is compromised, the child suffers. When rat mothers are provided with a crafted environment in which they feel quite safe, they respond to their pups differently and levels of pup PTSD are greatly reduced. Rat living conditions that do not ameliorate social defeat increase levels of PTSD (Pulliam, Dawaghreh, Alema-Mensah, and Plotsky 2010).

Peter Fonagy, Mary Target, and their colleagues have tracked the development of a child's capacity to be reflectively aware of their own mental states and those of others (Fonagy et al. 2003). Importantly, Type D infant attachment was interpreted by these researchers in reference to adult borderline personality disorder, not adult dissociation. The work of Main, Lyons-Ruth, and Ogawa (Ogawa et al. 1997) on adult dissociation as predicted by Type D infant attachment[3] has not had the impact on the theory related to mentalization that I might have hoped. In some respects, the work on mentalization parallels other work by Luyten, Blatt, and Fonagy on cognitive-affective interpersonal schemas and cognitive-behavioral approaches that focus on mindfulness and acceptance (Luyten, Blatt, and Fonagy 2013). The emphasis in all this work on mental processes and mental states parallels the approach I am spelling out, but omits the critically important role of dissociative processes in the distortion of meta-cognitions and the attribution of mental states as existing in others. If there was recognition of the major role dissociative process often plays in the presentation of borderline phenomena, then experiences like depersonalization and derealization might have influenced the resulting perspective. Significantly, in this regard, in a 10-year follow-up study of borderline personality disorder, while the severity of dissociation declined significantly with less absorption, depersonalization, and amnesia, dissociation remained a "recurring problem for over a third of those with Dissociative Experience Scale (DES) scores that were initially in the range associated with trauma-spectrum disorders" (Zanarini, Frankenburg, Jager-Hyman, Reich, and Fitzmaurice 2008; see also Zanarini 2009). The qualifying DES scores in this study were over 30, a number often reflective of DID. There is an apparent dissociation of things dissociative in the literature on borderline personality disorder, and the educated reader needs to keep this in mind.

A salient contribution of mentalization theory is its elaboration on how an awareness of mental states in others is achieved, in part through a resolution of psychic equivalence, pretend, and teleological modes of thinking (Fonagy and Target 1996). Psychic equivalence is the tendency to equate what is real in the world with what is imagined

---

[3] Adult dissociation, not necessarily dissociative disorder, is predicted by Type D infant attachment. U.S. researchers are wary of doing confirmatory studies and opening up the need to find treatment for adults with dissociative disorders who might destabilize if studied diagnostically.

in the mind—mental events have the same power or causality as events in the real world. "If I think I am shit, then I am shit and everybody knows it." Pretend modes of thinking are the tendency to assign qualities of realness to what is imagined or wished so that pretended personal qualities and fantasies become real and what is real in the world is of no consequence. In other words, in the pretend mode a child is not pretending to be a bird, he is a bird. What goes on outside him is of no consequence or influence on his behavior (Fonagy and Target 2000). Teleological thinking would state that a tree exists because people need shade on a hot day. In the teleological mode, an event or reality is explained by an attribution of purpose that is convenient or apparently parsimonious rather than veridical. These three modes of thinking are essential in the construction and maintenance of the transitional spaces characteristic of DID. They allow for an internal experience that is felt and alive and is not accompanied by a logical challenge of "that's just what you sense in your mind, it's not real, it's just a special kind of mental state."

Two other perspectives related to mentalization studies are especially important if we are to understand the impact of dissociative processes on the internal transitional space and real relationships: markedness and the concept of the alien self. Affective marking occurs when parents' response to a playing child is a reflection of what is emotionally real in the child; it includes behavioral cues in the parent, like minimal exaggeration, which lets the child know the parent recognizes the child is at play, for example, having super powers. The child does not frighten the parent and the parent goes along with (but not quite) the fantasy play (Fonagy et al. 2003). The child's capacity to discriminate between the rational and nonrational actions of parents, emotional accuracy, allows the child to recognize the parental response as almost a match with the child's fantasy. This capacity of the child has been demonstrated as early as nine months of age (Gergely, Nadasdy, Csibra, and Biro 1995). For example, a parent can playfully remonstrate with the child who says they have super powers: "Yes, I see what you are saying, and there is some truth in it, and it's also the case that you have to go to sleep now." The parent who beats a child for asserting their superpowers or who ridicules him for it in effect makes false attributions of a powerful and scary mental state in the child; in turn the child comes to believe there is within him a dangerousness that feels alien. This alien self (Fonagy 2000) is what Fonagy identifies as at the center of the fray in the borderline condition. "There is something frighteningly bad in me," is the simplified nontechnical version of this perspective.

A structural theory of dissociation was developed which conceived of an apparently normal personality (ANP) alongside a number of emotional personality (EP) states (van der Hart et al. 2006) and makes good use of attachment theory and self-state theory. The structural theory of dissociation is easily adopted by newcomers to the literature. However, in its efforts to parse out the observed tendency in self-state genesis to segregate intellectual and emotional ways of facing the world, the theory creates an additional level of jargon. It is absolutely the case that younger ways of being, younger self-states, tend to have more emotional activation, whereas older self-states tend to be more intellectual. However, there is quite a mix and variability. I prefer a more conversational language, different ways of being you, to the ANP and EP signifiers, which I believe go past the capacity of the metaphor to flexibly represent reality when the complexity of a self-state system becomes fully visible. What the structural theory does best is provide clinical wisdom from some of the finest minds in the field.

Crafting a Heuristic for Considering the Dissociative Disorders

Each of the theories described has value in helping us understand the clinical presentation of people who have a mind guided significantly by persistent dissociative process. If we combine these theoretical perspectives, we have a powerful collection of handles we can use in the clinical setting to hold and contain the work. We can be aware of the potential heritable contributions of capacities for hypnotic and dissociative experience, and the implications of trauma for the developing mind, including the particular vulnerabilities of children to physical and emotional abuse. We can stay tuned to the double binds that accrue during early development in terms of the activation of conflicting infant attachment patterns, such as the simultaneous contradictory internal working models of Type D patterns. These leave small children stuck in unresolvable behavioral dilemmas that parents can misinterpret, too, and lead to interpersonal misadventures replete with shaming or confusion for both parent and child. We can remain aware of the logical constraints that may be active, at times, for adults who did not fully advance in their patterns of thinking but have active remnants of psychic equivalence, pretend, and teleologic modes of thinking. All this may exist on a foundation of relatively isolated islands of experience associated with idiosyncratic behaviors because no bridges were constructed.

For the fortunate, only the vague memory of islands exist where now there are rivers of freely flowing thought and emotions in a fertile mainland of working self-states. For others, the persistence of dissociative process truncates psychological development, impairs the capacity for human relatedness, and leaves severely affected people guided through their lives by distorted forces they hardly notice, if at all. Multiple self-states exist in these circumstances, as they do in all of us, but the ability to make the use of the best these states have to offer is undermined by the self-state isolation that can produce the identity alteration seen in DID.

Counterfeit Coherence and Dissociation

In due time, our patients with persistent dissociative processes will ask our help in the task of resolving a dissociative inner space that no longer serves them well. However, in the initial period of their clinical presentation, the responsibility for increasing curiosity about things dissociative falls to the clinician. We must speak up because our patients are unlikely to do so. Increasing consciousness for the subjective experience of dissociative process is a central pillar of treatment. Attention to affect metabolism is part of that consciousness. The particulars and peculiarities of each self-state tend to sustain relatively distorted core beliefs and create a significant impediment to developing a coherent sense of self and the world. This lack of coherence was perhaps once of value as a cloud inside which could be hidden great fears and painful humiliations. However, as childhood fades into the background, adult requirements of living make the incoherence of childhood nearly intolerable. This creates massive vulnerability for an adult who wants to maintain his or her academic or professional standing or simply participate in an ongoing important relationship. The lack of coherence creates a situation in which it is more appropriate to feel that there is not a sense of multiple self-states but that it's overwhelming to approximate having even one clear sense of self. Lack of coherence is a central issue when dissociative process fills a mind's wallet with seemingly blank cards and runs a life long after the operating license has expired.

There is an orderly disorder to the manner in which dissociative processes organize. Counterfeit coherence generated by persistent dissociative process distorts the experience of experience and creates the illusion of a safe internal and external world at the price of falsifying reality. It's time to take a deeper look at dissociative processes and their clinical presentation, and then dive into understanding more of the role of emotion in the persistence of dissociative process.

Chapter 4

Opening a Treatment for Persistent Dissociative Processes

In his clinical work, D.W.W. made it his aim to enter into every situation undefended by his knowledge, so that he could be as exposed as possible to the impact of the situation itself.
—Clare Winnicott speaking of her husband, Donald W. Winnicott (C. Winnicott 1989)

THE FIRST REQUIREMENT IN THE ASSESSMENT OF A PERSON'S MIND FOR THE presence of dissociative process is that the clinician have a mind familiar with and curious about dissociation in its myriad manifestations. There are multiple dimensions of dissociative process, for example, psychodynamic, physiologic, and neurobiologic. In earlier chapters I spelled out some of the neurobiological processes that contribute to generating dissociative experiences and then provided some theory on the basis of self-state formation. In this chapter I elaborate on the clinical presentation of people who have lives directed from a sort of airport control tower where a portion of the window is blacked out, some of the keys to the supply cabinets have gone missing, the radar and two-way radio sometimes work and sometimes don't, and from time to time an employee from the maintenance department finds they are on duty in the tower, can't leave for fear of everything being out of control, isn't sure what to do, and doesn't know how they got there in the first place. Even in the face of this kind of chaos, some people with active dissociative processes have been able to maintain other compartments of function so that they do things like Babe Ruth, of baseball fame, and just seemed to be able to hit home run after home run and then some, with gracefulness and without any apparent effort. This apparently mystifying reality is normal for many people with elaborate and persistent dissociative processes.

In the first visit people make to my office, care is taken to methodically and intuitively provide a sense of safety and quiet but active listening. In that way, a person who is frightened might have the seeds of some hope planted that I might not be going to hurt them, and if they risk speaking, I might actually hear them. For many people who come to see me these two concerns are paramount, even if the person is not fully conscious of it at the time.

We each have our own hard-working dissociative little engine that could (Piper 1930/1976) who climbs up mountains of unintegrated experience in our lives. By the time he clears the top and looks back, he sees nothing behind and leaves us feeling like nothing's missing, everything is normal. As these overlooked spaces and places tend toward the excessive, discontinuity of experience enters mental life. Behavior becomes inconsistent. Memory fails for details even if the gist of them is preserved, though sometimes that is lost, too. Sense of self becomes confused or altered. As self-states become more isolated but still responsive to the environment, simple greetings like "How are you?" feel impossible to answer. It's not that there is no answer; it's that often enough the question provokes floods of internal responses that are too complex to sort or resembles the stark emptiness of a mind like a harvested corn field where all the birds foraging for loose kernels suddenly take flight and leave the field bare. The question of "What do you think?" may also generate multiple responses entangled in some minor or even contradictory disagreement. There is often a feeling of being a fraud. Tolerance for physical pain increases, and the sense of being embodied may feel like a foreign concept. Feeling unreal is often a regular experience. Food may have no taste or texture for the person who was sexually abused via fellatio. Willingly being sexual with a valued partner may be an exercise in frustration when being present in a body feels impossible and frankly not wanted. "Fake it until you make it" long ago failed to bear fruit.

The saddest part of it all is that dissociative experience often starts in childhood and thus enters awareness without adult intellectual capacity or knowledge to monitor it, in which case it may simply take over with devastating consequences that may be invisible to an outsider. In the words that follow, a middle-aged man who is quite far along in treatment writes to me about an internal conversation he has with a child-sized self-state, a repository for untold stories of anger, humiliation, and frustration. We enter this scene in the middle of the conversation, as both child and adult are reminiscing about feelings of loss in the past. You can see the world through grade-school eyes as the child is betrayed by a struggling dissociative mind.

ADULT: Yep. It was like a part of life that seemed almost from another life—like we knew about it, we felt we lived it, but that it no longer existed somehow.

CHILD: Right. It's like we lost it.

ADULT: What else do you feel like you've lost?

CHILD: Everything.

ADULT: Everything?

CHILD: Yes. Everything. I feel like everything has been erased. Like it happened, but it didn't happen. Everything seems like a blank to me. Like I'm looking at a blank sheet of paper at school and I have to write something down but I can't remember anything.

ADULT: Well, you remembered Mrs. E and Mr. R, right?

CHILD: Yes, but it's like I saw a movie about them, not that I was in the movie.

ADULT: How do you feel about that?

CHILD: Sad. Angry. Very, very angry. Like someone stole something from me. Like I had it, but it was then taken away. Like it happened, but then someone told me it didn't happen.

ADULT: What about your anger. What are you angry about?

CHILD: Everything. I am angry about everything. I guess the easiest way to explain it right now is that I can't think of shit to write on the blank sheet of paper. But I'm told I have to. But I can't think of anything. Everything is blank to me. I know I should wrote [sic] something, but I don't know what to write. It's too hard. Too hard.

What is it really like to have a dissociative disorder? Here we have a view from this child-sized part of the mind of a man who is boldly making contact with anger, sadness, and despair left behind in his childhood. You heard Alice's perspective in the first chapter. It's time to meet another person, a woman in her late twenties, Samantha, and see what she can teach us.

The clinician-reader may not be able to meet so many people with dissociative disorders in his or her practice at this point. My intent here is to help you become familiar enough with the recognition of dissociative experience that you can make an assessment for a dissociative disorder if a person presents with these subjective experiences. As always, a clinician must become attuned to the subjective experience of the patient to bring a treatment to life and create a sense for the patient of being heard. There is also a need for a clinician to become attuned to and aware of their own dissociative experiences.

While I discuss dissociation and countertransference in Chapters 8 and 9, it's important to at least briefly take a moment here to appreciate that if every mind is organized around basic building blocks of self-states, then it's reasonable to expect that a patient's self-state might resonate with a similar state in a therapist and activate that self-state. Such a response in the therapist is potentially diagnostic in its own way. I outlined such a case in a paper titled "Waking the Dead Therapist" (Chefetz, 2009) (see Chapter 8). The countertransference analysis there has continued for a number of years. At the time of that paper, my sleepiness in session could be appreciated in two ways. First, there were self-states in the patient and me that were relatively closed to knowing about the horrors of her abuse. Second, we both moved toward sleepiness when there was associated unbridled rage that was approached in her (and obviously resonated in me, too). What I want to stress here is that the sleepiness was specific in terms of being responsive to a dissociative field. Loewenstein wrote at some length about dissociative process and the dissociative field in regard to his own experience of being in trance after a session and having a minor automobile accident (R. J. Loewenstein 1993). A number of clinicians who have consulted me have reported nearly complete amnesias for sessions with their more dissociative patients. In addition to sleepiness and trance-like phenomena, it is not unusual for some clinicians to have psychophysiologic reactions to visits from patients that may include gastrointestinal disturbance, muscular aches, and pains. This degree of physiologic countertransference responsiveness, perhaps from emotion in the therapist that has never been desomatized, is unusual in my consultation work with clinicians without dissociative disorder patients. It is important to appreciate that clinicians with dissociative responses to dissociative patients may benefit from personal consultation regarding their responses if they continue to treat the patient.

Now, let's meet one of my patients at a point when they were new to my practice.

A Young Woman with Nightmares

Samantha demonstrated the tension between dissociative process and the problem of having coherent experience in her initial visit. She was plagued with posttraumatic nightmares, and the apparent onset of her distress was contingent on the untimely death of a loved boyfriend two years earlier. In the initial evaluation session, it became plain she also had massive amnesia for her life before graduating from high school. I felt cautious about proceeding with any specific trauma work regarding her recent painful loss before understanding more about why her amnesia predated the onset of her current symptoms. This approach is consistent with the general guidelines inherent in a phase oriented treatment (Courtois 1999; International Society for the Study of Trauma and Dissociation 2011; Loewenstein 2006; Steele, van der Hart, and Nijenhuis 2005). I am fond of saying that the three phase model is really five phases where the first three are all sta-bilization and are followed by working through of traumatic memory, and then by integration and rehabilitation. There is regular overlap of phasic work, but the bottom line is that trauma work waits until stabilization has been demonstrated.

Samantha and I spent a lot of time exploring her recent life and shoring up her capacities to function in the world. We noticed her strengths, helped her become more conscious of feelings as they emerged conversationally, supported coherent perceptions about fam-ily members' functions and dysfunctions, and connected the dots of seemingly stray experiences when they became visible to me, if not to her. She felt stronger, more coherent, better able to cope, and had fewer nightmares. There was more useful language to express what had been unintegrated. Less toxic dreaming occurred regularly, and she made good use of dream work in session. Eight months into the therapy, when she wrote me an email about some distress she had, I wrote back and invited her to just notice and describe any experiences she had where things didn't fit together like usual or as expected or wished. Essentially, I was asking her to notice discontinuities in her experience.

Things I notice

He [new boyfriend] has said I've been distant. I notice this too.

I mainly notice being foggy/not "being me" because I noticed the opposite. Yesterday morning when I drove to work to grab my computer I was totally functioning. I felt like a great driver, not missing a turn. I felt intelligent. I felt on, sharp.

This is different than how I've been, going about my days.

I have trouble with math. I have trouble paying atten-tion. I hear but don't listen. I get pissed off pretty easily. I'm holding grudges (like against my dad).

Math is my BEST subject, and something I truly understood.

I find it hard to be truly happy. Again, I know what this feels like because I remember being truly happy recently—when [my friend] was on TV, I was overcome with a wave of happiness. The rest of my happiness is logical happiness. Jokes are funny, I can be in a good mood, but being overcome with happiness, happiness that I can't control, that takes over, that's something that's rare.

This wave of happiness could probably be compared to the wave of sadness, when my girlfriend got fired. Most of the time I'm in a cloud in the middle.

I think that when I'm in this cloud I'm not really experiencing anything. I want to be present at my wedding. I want to enjoy it, remember it, and not just go through the motions. I AM happy about it, but I want to feel it, not just know it.

I worry all the time that [my old boyfriend] died. I'm worried about that right now. It scares me.

I wake up with my heart racing. My chest hurts. The other night I woke up at 12:30 and had to flip my pillow over it was so wet. I asked [my fiancé] to feel my heart in the morning and he said it was pounding hard, not fast. Strong.

I'm so tired it makes me not remember things—like I don't have the effort to even try to remember. Like my dreams. I'm glad I wrote them down.

I hear myself talk in my mind and analyze myself as I'm talking, which is distracting. I worry about how I'm coming across and comment on things I'm doing. This is mainly at work. Actually no, it happens with friends too.

My hands feel like they're not attached sometimes. Mainly when I notice them, am looking down at them. When I'm typing for work, when I wash my hands after going to the bathroom or cooking. When I wash them and rub them together with the soap they look distant.

I want to remember things when I see a picture of them.

[My girlfriend] said that the [old] picture [of me and my girlfriends] on Facebook from [the school play] was from junior year of high school. I want to remember that. I want to remember even doing a show like that. Did we do musical numbers, that weren't full musicals? I guess so. And did those girls actually participate? I thought they did sports.

Let's look at this communication through the lens of dissociative process. Feeling "distant" is a complex statement. In this case it seems to point in the direction of feelings of depersonalization and dereal-ization (see section on SCID-D later) as in foggy, not sharp, and not intelligent. She oddly has trouble with math, her best subject. There is temporary loss of skills. She's behaving unusually and keeping grudges, like with her dad. Her emotional life is blunted. She intel-lectually knows she's having a feeling, but it's not alive in her expe-rience. She has "logical happiness," a brilliant and sadly descriptive term. There is lots of isolation of affect, emotional numbing. She's having posttraumatic nightmares and panic attacks in her sleep. (This had increased after about a year to the point that intervention was required and her distress was ameliorated with prazosin (discontinued one year later), an antihypertensive medication found to be effective in treatment of posttraumatic nightmares related to combat (Raskind et al. 2003). Clonidine, a similar drug, may have similar efficacy in select patients.) Her hands felt detached, a depersonalization experience. She saw a picture of herself with her friends, knew what the activity was about, but couldn't recall being there or engaging with her friends or the activity. The central features of this communication are about iso-lation of affect, depersonalization, state changes with loss of skills, and amnesia. These things predated her traumatic experience. The wisdom of waiting to deal with her recent trauma became more apparent.

Using the Dissociative Experiences Scale

The Dissociative Experiences Scale (DES-II) is a nondiagnostic screening tool (Bernstein and Putnam 1986) for dissociative experience with 28 scaled items that take an average of 10 minutes for most people to complete. If someone fills it out in five minutes or less, it raises my index of suspicion as to whether they are actually thinking about the questions and responding, or just blowing the testing off. People who take 15 or more minutes tend to be highly obsessional.[1] Some are also dissociative.

The first question of the DES looks like this:

> 1. Some people have the experience of driving or riding in a car or bus or subway and suddenly realizing that they don't remember what has happened during all or part of the trip. Circle a number to show what percentage of the time this happens to you.
> 0%   10   20   30   40   50   60   70   80   90   100%

The DES is a screening tool that has been in use for many years.[2] Its format is simple, as are the questions. It's straightforward to administer and easily becomes part of a clinical discussion. However, the examiner cannot explain the meaning of a question. The intent is for the patient's own idiosyncratic interpretations to direct the response. If somebody objects to a question or can't figure it out, then you may instruct the person to write their concern in the margin of the paper for posttest review, and then make the best choice they can in responding to the question. All items must have a response for the test to be valid. Review of the controversial items is worth its weight in gold in many cases.

The best use of the DES may be to quickly explore a wide range of dissociative experience in a short period of time to get a sense of

---

[1] One person who was obsessional and took 20 minutes to finish wrote private notes all over the test paper and could not tolerate me not reinterpreting the meaning of the questions. They turned out to be psychotic, too, but not dissociative, on further formal testing, consistent with the clinical exam. They badly wanted to be dissociative because it would have served their social situation well by providing an excuse for their behavior.

[2] The DES is readily available online at http://traumaanddissociation.files.wordpress.com/2014/01/des-ii-copyright-free.pdf.

what's happening when there are conversational indicators of dissociative experience. The assessment should always be taken in front of the clinician. The reactions are too valuable to miss. The risk of somebody dissembling responses must be avoided. The posttest discussion of the reasons for robust endorsement of an item (or not) is often the entrance to a whole realm of experienced but never discussed subjective moments of distress and concern for the patient.

Samantha robustly endorsed a number of items on the DES: lack of recall for all or part of a trip—50 percent; not hearing what somebody said—50 percent; approached by people who seem to know you but you don't know them—30 percent; no memory for important life events—70 percent; often accused of lying while thinking there was no lie—70 percent; becoming absorbed and losing track of surroundings—90 percent; can ignore pain—70 percent; losing time—60 percent; talk out loud to themselves—100 percent; can't remember having done something or not—90 percent; and done things but don't remember doing them—40 percent. She did not endorse hearing voices commenting but, as described later in this chapter, 100 percent of the time she heard thoughts that commented and didn't feel quite like her own thoughts. I do not ask people to substitute "thoughts" for "voices" in question 27 until after they finish the test and hand it to me. Since the test instruction is to circle responses, I ask people to put a box around their response with "thoughts" substituted for "voices."

Samantha's endorsements point to high levels of absorption, an ability to ignore pain consistent with that, and potential self-state phenomena with amnesia for actions and experiences. Her raw score was 800, obtained by adding the endorsed numbers, and the adjusted score after dividing the raw score by 28 was 28.57, which rounds to 29. Scores of 30 and higher suggest the presence of a dissociative disorder; scores above 45 are highly suggestive of dissociative identity disorder being present.

Samantha had known about these experiences but never coherently put them together. She was deeply reassured that somebody understood something about her that had been missed and that she felt was quite important, as did I.

Collecting Clinical Information

Several months into her treatment, Samantha brought in a picture of herself at camp, sitting with her favorite counselor. In the picture, he is smiling, and she is stone-faced. Her hand is resting on his knee in the same way one might expect a boyfriend and girlfriend to sit. At the time, she was 12 years old. He had regularly commented on "how mature you are for your age." As she looked at the picture while sitting in my office, she became quite distressed. "It feels like something happened with him. I don't know what happened." We continue to explore associations to this picture.

As a child of eight, Samantha wrote a school composition that was replete with an apparent discontinuity of experience in her thought process. She wrote a book report kind of composition on a neutral subject about an adult male whose name she could not recall. The handwriting changes are typical of people with a dissociative disorder and may signify switches between self-states. Here is the text and an image of the composition as I first saw it with identifying information obscured. (I've used different fonts to illustrate the changes in handwriting. The original punctuation is preserved.) Notice the shift in the leaning of letters to the left and the right. That's more significant than the block letters. Notice the change in argument and the loss of meaning. What was the subjective experience of this child?

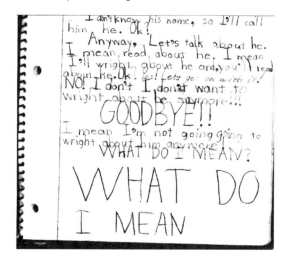

I don't know his name, so I'll call him he. Ok?

Anyway, Let's talk about he. I mean read about he. I mean I'll wright about he and.you'll read about he. Ok?

Yes! Lets get on with it! NO! I don't I don't want to wright about he anymore!!!

GOODBYE!!

I mean I'm not going going to wright about him anymore!

WHAT DO I MEAN?

WHAT DO I MEAN

In my office, Samantha was frankly distressed about this small piece of notebook paper and what it meant to her. Her family had saved this notebook as part of a collection from her childhood that they gave back to her some months after she began her therapy with me. She independently recognized the handwriting change and the experience of an internal dialogue in her mind that had her asking, as a child, what she meant by what she heard in her mind. It still left her feeling upset to read it, years later.

In Samantha's case, in addition to experiences of depersonalization and lost time, long after taking the DES she revealed that she had the experience of hearing a voice in her mind, several times. Around the time of her recovering the notebook, she had this experience when waking from a nightmare: "Then I heard that raspy voice I mentioned to you before. I didn't hear it outside my head, it was more of a thought, but a thought with a voice that doesn't sound like how I normally talk to myself. It said 'don't judge me.' And that was it." She had no clarity about what that meant. She was quite clear there was an active internal conversation in her mind, all in her voice, but not the raspy one.

She could not understand what she was doing/experiencing, and it bothered her. Lack of coherence can be an indicator of underlying dissociative process. People are obligatory meaning makers. Dissociative processes shut that meaning making off or skew it in interesting ways. Though I was not happy that she was distressed, I was very pleased that she noticed the discontinuities, sought an explanation, and remained aware. Too often moments of incoherence or discontinuity are momentarily noticed and then forgotten, as if they never happened. Dissociative processes spackle over the cracks in our experience, leaving an apparently smooth wall, nothing out of place, everything just fine—counterfeit coherence. All these strategies create the kind of coherence that is at the expense of knowing what is real or feeling real and reduces our fears about a mind that is not working like it ought to. "I've just not been myself, lately."

At the center of the clinical dialogue was a question I keep in my mind: What's it really like to be Samantha from one moment to the next? Sometimes I simply asked her, "What was that like for you?" Or I might ask, "What was your moment-to-moment experience when that happened?" I am cautious about and avoid language that favors glossing over discontinuities of experience rather than describing things in detail. When somebody says they feel hurt or uncomfortable, I may refer to that as a watered-down psychiatric term like *distressed* or *unpleasant*. There is no information of any specificity in those words. I especially want to know the specific feeling words that might accurately describe the experience. If somebody is relatively alexithymic (unable to describe emotions), I want to discover that fact early in our conversation. If their alexithymia is related to specific self-states, then I want to figure that out. When there is active and persistent dissociative process, there is almost always difficulty with processing emotion, knowing feeling, and mastering the call to action in a feeling like anger or shame.

Years ago I adopted and adapted much of the language and technique of dialectical behavior therapy (Linehan 1993) into my everyday psychotherapy practice. It has been a valuable piece of practical theory. Consciousness for all manner of experience, especially emotion, is a cornerstone in any approach to psychotherapy for persistent dissociative processes. Frankly, an emotion-focused psychotherapy is a highly flexible and enduring approach (Greenberg 2004; Johnson, Hunsley, Greenberg, and Schindler 1999; Paivio and Nieuwenhuis 2001) that regularly pays rich dividends in the treatment setting and goes on to benefit my patients outside the session because it gives them new perspective and flexible functionality. A focus on emotion has been important for Samantha in helping her work through and move beyond her logical feelings.

The central challenges Samantha and I seemed to face at this point were twofold. First, how would I help her feel safe enough to begin to tolerate knowing more about that for which she had amnesia, in high school and earlier in her life? Second, how could I help her become more conscious of the ongoing discontinuities in her experience as a naturalistic extension of her awareness without frightening her?

Alice, whom you met earlier, had been terrified of knowing her mind, and her deep fear was quite unlike Samantha's relative curiosity and drive to "get to the bottom of things." One consultant on Alice's case quipped that she was "too smart for herself." When I reported this to her in the context of appreciating how some parts of her mind seemed to be sabotaging her ability to know herself, she agreed that this was likely. Her choice of that word was legalistic and part of her refusal to confirm what I knew about her mind (as well as what she knew) in some places and spaces within her own mind. She had effectively used externalization of her conflicts over knowing her own mind by falling back onto strategies of challenging her diagnosis or dismissing the utility of psychotherapy. Alice's ongoing struggles occupy us at length in later chapters. Not every person will have as prolonged a diagnostic crisis. Most people come to appreciate the implications of having a lot of active dissociative process and actively pursue understanding it. That was too threatening for Alice. Nobody wants to think their mind is a repository for a large amount of emotional pain. When a mountain of pain confronts an already wounded mind, the tasks of psychotherapy can quickly overwhelm.

Samantha began to actively dream several months after the start of our sessions. Dissociative and associative processes are at work during waking and sleeping periods. While we sleep, our minds are still busy. Sleep has its own active processes manifest by slow wave sleep (SWS), rapid eye movement (REM) sleep, and dreaming. Although sleep disturbance is a hallmark of PTSD (Mellman, Bustamante, Fins, Pigeon, and Nolan 2002; Ross, Ball, Sullivan, and Carof 1989), not all dreaming is REM dreaming, and posttraumatic nightmares may occur in non-REM sleep (Hefez 1987). Non-REM nightmares leave beds looking like battlefields. Dreaming is also involved in the consolidation of long-term memory (Stickgold 2005), an associative process. The return of dreaming in a person in treatment is encouraging, for it is an indicator of a mind that is spending less time hiding from itself. I take this to mean there is more safety in the life of my patient. Samantha demonstrated this robustly. Remember the picture of her with her counselor and her sense that something happened? More than a year after she showed it to me, she had a disturbing dream about being out in the woods with him and another couple. The other couple were having sex. The dream was viewed as if from above, a depersonalized view. Though we didn't yet know what it meant, the form of the dream suggested we needed to be alert that this was not a "dreamy dream" in the sense of regular dreaming, but instead a communication with trauma narrative from an isolated self-state leaking through into a dream narrative. People with DID often have the experience of "witnessing" communication between self-states while asleep, and they naturalistically assign this communication the status of a dream, since of course it occurred while asleep.

Persistent Dissociative Process and the SCID-D

Dissociative process occurs in several dimensions of experience. I have been talking about isolation, exclusion, and deflection as psychodynamic processes. Consider, in contrast, the five main criteria of the Structured Clinical Interview for DSM-IV Dissociative Disorders[3] (SCID-D) (Steinberg 1993): depersonalization, derealization, amnesia,

---

[3] The SCID-D is a semi-structured guided interview with a manual containing numerous questions which the examiner asks of the test subject. It takes two and a half hours to administer and can be done in several sessions. Scoring is based on the robustness with which respondents endorse the five domains of dissociative experience the questions address. The SCID-D is a marvelous teaching tool for the clinician new to understanding dissociative experience. Its test results have been the gold standard for dissociative disorder diagnosis.

identity confusion, and identity alteration. Although we can neurologically see the differential brain map of alternate identity (Reinders et al. 2003, 2006), there are little data to convince us that the map we see is the result of a process of altered neurobiology predicting alterations of identity, rather than a neurobiology that is driven by psychodynamics. How is it that psychodynamics can have such an apparent influence on neural function? The translation of lived experience into an influence on biology is an extraordinary event and should provoke an abiding curiosity. One study makes clear that in comparing electroencephalograms (EEGs) for three people with DID, the graphs of alters are less different from each other than the graphs between different persons with DID (Lapointe, Crayton, DeVito, Fichtner, and Konopka 2006).

What we can say at this juncture is that taken together,the SCID-D criteria describe a mix of experience based on perceptual distortion, neurological disturbance, confusion (like that of the child-state talking about losses and a blank paper at school), and the complex multidetermined psychodynamically endowed experience of identity alteration. These SCID-D categories illustrate how the subjective experience of a person is distorted via dissociative processes.

In tandem with the criteria of the SCID-D, it's worth noting that basic lines of cleavage in dissociative experience were also explored some years ago in the BASK model, which defined dissociation in terms of behavior, affect, sensation, and knowledge (Braun 1988). In general, ordinarily expectable underlying perceptual and referential processes (Bucci 1997) are impaired in dissociation,and coherent consciousness cannot be achieved without inventing a contextual explanation, ignoring the incoherence, or allowing confusion to occur (American Psychiatric Association 2000; Armstrong and Loewenstein 1990; Frewen and Lanius 2006; Simeon 2004).

The actual SCID-D interview is a superb learning tool and worth the time it takes to go through all the questions. Once the drift of the questions is mastered, then the body of knowledge from the frame of the interview easily informs a more conversational approach to asking about the subjective experience in the SCID-D categories. This can neatly fit into a standard psychotherapy hour or less. It is worth taking a moment here to review the subjective experiences named in the SCID-D. Although these experiences may become woven into a psychodynamic structure, they may have quite variable psychodynamic meaning. In any event, they are essential in making an assessment of dissociation.

In depersonalization, the sense of a person being physically located in their body is distorted. The classic description is the out-of-body experience. However, depersonalization has also been simply conceptualized as thinking without feeling (Phillips et al. 2001) and feeling unreal (Simeon and Abugel 2006). Depersonalization appears to be associated with functional abnormalities in visual, auditory, and somatosensory pathways, as well as in those areas responsible for an integrated body schema. (Depersonalization is explored in additional depth in Chapter 6.) Importantly, while these abnormalities occur, it appears that the reduced response to external stimuli occurs so rapidly that people with depersonalization experience are in a heightened state of alertness that is isolated from emotional awareness (Sierra et al. 2002). It is my observation that people with depersonalization have grossly decreased attunement to their emotional life and may feel bereft of their feelings. In other words, depersonalization is a process in which there appears to be a dissociation of perception and emotion in addition to or leading to the subjective symptoms of depersonalization (Simeon, Guralnik, Hazlette, Spiegel-Cohen, Hollander, and Buchsbaum 2000) while reality testing remains fully intact. Derealization often occurs along with depersonalization experience and creates the sense that rather than the self being unreal, the world is somehow unreal. In derealization, it as if the world is seen through a veil; objects may not have sharply defined edges, colors can be muted, the intensity of light dimmed, or the world may simply take on the quality of feeling somehow phony (R. J. Loewenstein 1991). In my experience, depersonalization is much more common than derealization as a presenting symptom.

Amnesia in dissociative disorders is generally described as forgetting outside the normal range of experience. What is most typical of dissociative process is what is commonly called a "Swiss cheese" amnesia,[4] where only key pieces of information are missing—the pieces that would contextualize experience and allow a person to make sense of their personal narrative. This often happens in the midst of a therapy session where there's been a conversation about an important topic and several minutes later the patient seems to be responding to the continuing conversation as if we hadn't just discussed the issue at hand. Clinicians looking for global amnesias, like having no memory before senior year in high school (Samantha), will not find as many of those as they will these micro-amnesias. In a typical scene that evolves while simply talking with a patient, there is a subjective moment of discontinuity. These moments can become visible when, for example, you observe that your patient's eyes become fixed at a distance and their gaze somewhat trance-like. If this is interrupted by calling their name, they may appear startled. If this happens in a diagnostic interview, I often gently ask the following question: "Could you please tell me what we were just talking about?" The nondissociative person will easily respond and clarify. Some people will have amnesia and no recollection, a clearly abnormal situation. Others will hesitate, often avert their eyes at a sharp angle, as if they are looking somewhere for the information, and then tell you about what was said, but usually it is only an approximation of the conversation. The question then is: "Do you know this because it feels like it is your fully alive and recalled experience that you are reporting to me, or is this more like reporting something you read in the newspaper rather than what happened two minutes ago to *you*?" It always astonishes me how many people have the newspaper experience (R. J. Loewenstein 1991) even though they have the ability to mostly repeat the material. This is part of why I am fond of saying that in the clinical interview there is a part of me that has to listen like a lawyer and think like a clinician. The nuances of language that are abridged by minor discontinuities in discourse or fleeting facial expressions that signal confusion are wellsprings of valuable information. The concentration required of the therapist in an effort to catch these opportunities is significant.

---

[4] This term is not original to me, though I regretfully plead source amnesia for the reference.

In addition to what we usually think of as amnesia, there are several varieties of loss of memory worth mentioning: lost time and black-outs, disremembered behavior (not recalling eating, buying clothes, writing a note, or a sexual act), fugue/mistaken identity (the patient meets people who know them by another name), and unexplained ownership (how did those clothes get in my closet?). Memory distur-bance is also noticeable with a sudden change in relating, skills, habits, or fund of knowledge and can generate a fragmentary life history (R. J. Loewenstein 1991). (Loewenstein's article is a brilliant synthesis that is not only informative but rather humorous.)

In addition to the three SCID-D criteria already mentioned (dep-ersonalization, derealization, and amnesia), a fourth process is iden-tity confusion, an experience of not being able to know one's name when directly asked. It is as if somebody lost their mental road map and has no appreciation of who they are or what is going on in their life. They may know they know but become flustered or baffled as to why they don't. The information is inaccessible and likely would remind a person about things that have gone on in their life that are simply unacceptable and unknowable, in a given moment, because of the emotional gravity involved. What is sometimes remarkable about finding identity confusion in a person is their indifference to the lack of this knowledge. This is the classic "la belle indifference" (Janet 1901), and it speaks to the divestment of personal information that in the service of mercifully diluting the impact of experience under-mines the capacity to make identity coherent. Rather than a not-me divestment of selfhood, this is a global "who, me?" divestment of identity toward the same kind of deflection of knowledge, experience, or emotionality, that would be more typical of the not-me of actual identity alteration. Not all self-states in the not-me position are iso-lated via depersonalization nor by the other SCID-D criteria of DID. Nevertheless, the not-me self-state influences conscious behavior and the interpretation of events through implicit processes.

In my clinical experience, I have been much more likely to see identity confusion in a cohort of inpatients than in my regular psy-chotherapy practice unless there is the spontaneous emergence of a previously isolated self-state that is frankly disoriented on very basic levels—person, place, time, and situation. In one memorable event, a patient became visibly confused and upset, looked around the office, and then with real and compelling distress said, "Who the fuck are you and what the hell am I doing here?" I was glad this happened after many years of working with her and other people with DID. It was much easier to internally experience the jolt of her confusion and disorganization and then reply gently, "I can see you're upset. I'm Dr. Chefetz, your psychiatrist. This is my office and we are talking in a psychotherapy session. It seems like you may be dealing with some confusion."

The fifth criterion of the SCID-D, identity alteration, is the experience of an individual as having several different identities with subjectively different characteristics, for example, age, sex, face, body size, thoughts, feelings, personal history, and worldview (R. J. Loewenstein 1991). The not-me experience (Bromberg 1996) is a more subjective psychoanalytic approximation, but even closer to the subjective experience of alternate identity is the experience of having an additional sense of self, of not being alone in one's mind (Way 2006). The psychoanalytic not-me (Chefetz and Bromberg 2004) has a broader range of experience under its umbrella, and includes what some people would call ego-states (Watkins and Watkins 1997), psychodynamically disavowed and denied self-state characteristics, dissociative disorders without identity alteration, and DID. Typically, according to Putnam, on the basis of a review of 100 consecutive cases, 8 or 9 alternate identities are present (Putnam, Guroff, Silberman, Barban, and Post 1986). That earlier review of seems to be an underestimate of what I actually see in my practice, where 15 to 20 self-states are not unusual. The core number of self-states tend to increase with the severity and chronicity of abuse. If you are skeptical, put yourself in the shoes of a child who is prostituted by a betraying parent for 15 years (until they somehow escape to college), raped, sodomized, beaten, choked, tortured, and more, and then imagine how you would have coped. What's really amazing is that anybody can survive that kind of experience and still function at all. Skepticism about numbers of self-states is a potential intellectualization and deflection of the sad reality I report in these pages, an intolerance of the reality of severe abuse. The most extensive and erudite practical review of understanding the multiple self-state organization of DID, alters, is by Richard P. Kluft (2006) and I refer the reader there for a detailed discussion. The capacity of a mind to modify subjective experience and produce this kind of perceptual distortion that is stable over time is extraordinary.

Given all this distortion, discontinuity, disruption, isolation, exclusion, and deflection, it might make sense that a person with active dissociative process and identity alteration would have a life that was very messy. Instead, what is typical about my patients clinically is that they have extraordinary capacities to lead highly productive lives in very compartmentalized ways, such that different constellations of self-states tend to be active in different compartments of their experience, for example, work, home, school, parenting, play. Upon reflection, this makes sense given their broad general intelligence, long history of adapting to adversity, and resilience. However, it is certainly true that for some of my patients, unfortunate combinations of adverse psychological, physical, medical, and social situations have created a confluence of disadvantages that has made for very difficult and ongoing challenges.

The dissociative symptoms in the SCID-D are ubiquitous and profound, and they influence subjective experience. They can also be subtle and overlooked, seemingly by design. As one person put it recently,

> I was sitting at the conference table with all these people
> who had flown in from across the country when I real-
> ized that I could hardly speak and that somebody else
> was going to have to run the meeting I had called. I spent
> the next hour having the weird experience of feeling like
> my feet couldn't touch the floor and repeatedly pushing
> myself back in the chair so I would not fall off. I finally
> realized that the part of me who feels like being five
> years old was present and had left me feeling completely
> deskilled and like I had the body of a child. Once I real-

ized I had felt at risk and this part of me had come forward, then I could work with it.

Noticing Discontinuity of Experience

On a kind of psychological "molecular level" of what a person is most likely to notice as an epiphenomenon of active dissociative process is the experience of discontinuity. The flow of consciousness is interrupted. Of all the things a clinician new to thinking about dissociative process might do I recommend something simple: watch your patient carefully so as to notice discontinuity of experience in them. You really have to look. Yes, you are fishing in dissociative waters; once you see a fish finally move, you won't forget what it looks like. The capacity to observe discontinuity will provide many hours of clinical traction for you and your patients. Much of what you will see is a fleeting glance; smirk; shift of eyes up, down, or to the side; grimace; furrowing of forehead; glazing over; quiver of a chin muscle; and so on.

> Like the musical score of a movie, the memory of a thought or a feeling is encoded with contextual physiologic accompaniment. If we want to know about unconscious process, then we need to become keen observers of our patient's physiology and the associated bodily changes. Typical representative changes are: change in body position, shift in facial expression, shift in eye gaze, eye closure, swallowing, and skin flush. I include tears that flow onto cheeks and tears that well up but do not flow, finger, ankle, or other repetitive movement (both onset, and ending), rooms that suddenly get too hot or too cold, and so on. (Chefetz and Bromberg 2004)

The traditional psychoanalytic chair behind the couch may create literal impediments to the recognition of these moments. What is more typical is that some clinicians don't spend as much time as needed actually making and keeping eye contact with their patients, even when they sit in the chair opposite them. Truthfully, it's not easy to do that for many hours each day.

These discontinuities might be related to the presence versus absence in a patient of certain skills or abilities or the sudden inability to recall thoughts or information, or they might be due to experiences of emotional intensity that happen without an apparent context. The absence of continuity creates the experience of loss of mental coherence. If noticing discontinuity can be tolerated, then healthy curiosity can pursue the reasons for it. Much of what you can discern about state change will occur from a "close process" observation of your patient's body. For Freud, the first ego was a body ego (Freud 1923). Damasio has written a modern version of this old dictum in regard to the neurologic basis of conscious awareness and its reliance on somatic experience for development (Damasio 1999). Additional robust models deserve discussion later (P. Levine 1997; Ogden, Minton, and Pain 2006; Ogden, Pain, and Fisher 2006) with attention to bodily states (see Chapters 5 and 6). It ought to be a given that attention to somatic experience will pay deep dividends in the psychotherapy of persistent dissociative processes.

Identifying Dissociative Process in the Service of Providing Mental Coherence

Much like syphilis was known in internal medicine as the great imitator (White 2000), unidentified dissociative processes produce all manner of clinical presentations in psychiatry. For example, a 50-year-old woman came for a medication consultation because she suffered from depression, ostensibly related to the potential breakup of her marriage. Her husband was away for the summer and had taken their two children with him because he could no longer tolerate his wife's relentless harangues about his habits and her disappointment with life. She would move in and out of depressed periods; when she was depressed, these outbursts were more likely to occur. She missed her children and her husband terribly, had no idea why she berated him so, but also knew she did so with quite a bit of energy. She was very unhappy with herself, felt she was an inadequate person, understood why her husband had left her, and wanted relief for her depression with medication, as recommended by her therapist. She had come for a medication consultation to rid herself of these outbursts. She believed that if she could stay on track and be her usual self, her husband might forgive her and come back. He had said as much, but was at his wit's end as to how to deal with her vitriolic outbursts, which left the whole family upset. All in all, it would be an understatement to say that this woman had problems with remaining coherent in her understanding of herself. She could not hold her experience in mind and come up with an explanation. She had been taught to not have a mind that held experience for later consideration.

She was an intelligent and attractive woman working in a technical field and traveling frequently as a consultant to solve her clients' problems. She was articulate about the extent to which her behavior made no sense to her. She knew about it, but she couldn't stop herself from doing what she did. That did not make sense to her. Not only did she berate her husband, but as we talked she called herself stupid, and I noticed and inquired about this. She had an ongoing process in her mind that was brutally self-critical, but nobody had ever asked her about it. The self-critical voice she heard was her own, and the tones were heated and spewing forth with some viciousness, an experience she could barely tolerate when it was active. She could not turn it off, and she only knew that any small "defect" in her actions turned on a torrent of verbal abuse in her mind and interpersonally. She had a history of sexual abuse by an uncle in her childhood. This was well known to her and her family, but everybody had told her she simply needed to get over it and get on with her life. She felt like she had done that. She made no connection between her angry outbursts and anything in her past.

This visit was a medication consultation. My job was ostensibly to ascertain whether medication would help this person, who had been in treatment with a capable therapist for several months without any relief of her symptoms of depression. I was intrigued by the way she glossed over the issue of sexual abuse, her ongoing internal experience of verbal abuse, and her desperate cluelessness about her outbursts toward her husband, but I was aware that I had only 50 minutes to deal with both psychodynamic issues and psychopharmacological ones. To speed things up, I gave her two simple questionnaires to fill out, a Dissociative Experiences Scale, version II (Bernstein and Putnam 1986), and the Beck Depression Inventory, also version II (Beck, Steer, and Brown 1996). Her score on the Beck was a high 33, clearly indicative of an overwhelming depression. Anhedonia (inability to experience pleasure), fatigue, difficulty concentrating, irritability, mild sleep disturbance, and marked self-criticism were endorsed. The DES score was 27.86, indicating a relatively high level of dissociative experience. It was endorsed at the 50 percent level or higher for a number of items where her subjective experience was the following: she would lose track of travel in a car or subway, be in conversation and not know what had been said, could ignore pain, often would find herself staring into space, talked out loud to herself when alone, would have changed behavior to the point where in two different situations she felt she was two different people, and sometimes did things with amazing ease and at other times could not do those same things without difficulty. With regard to hearing voices inside her head that told her "to do things," she endorsed zero. When I modified the question and substituted the word *thoughts* for *voices*, it was endorsed at a level of 90 percent. We had a brief, animated discussion about how busy her mind was with thoughts that she knew intellectually were hers but that didn't always feel that way.

Aware of the lack of change after several months of psychotherapy, the extremity of her social and marital situation, her apparent affective lability, aimed at her husband and herself, and now her score on the Beck and DES, I offered her a selective serotonin reuptake inhibitor (SSRI) that had a neutral side effect profile, citalopram. My reasoning was that the medication would blunt her emotionality in general, have few side effects, not risk disinhibition of her cognitive abilities (as might happen with a benzodiazepine that might address her anxieties); in addition, SSRIs are generally safe medications. I also contacted her therapist to engage in discussion about my findings.

Two weeks later, there was no change as reported in a phone call and a desperate plea for more help. A week after that, at a follow-up visit, the Beck was scored at 9. She attributed the change in her mood to something good happening at work, after which her mood shifted "as if a switch had been flipped." Her mood had been stable for about five days. Several months later she had quit therapy and still had a stable mood. The switch from critical to good spirits is descriptive of a state change, rather than a shift in mood over time. She didn't notice that there was a gradual lifting of a depressed mood over several days and then a change in tolerance for her feelings or a gradual return of interest in things that had given her pleasure previously. It changed all at once. At the next follow-up for medication, we discussed the inadequacies of her previous psychotherapy and a referral was made to a clinician who was experienced and savvy with DID. She reported a month later that she was comfortable in therapy with this new clinician and it had been a good match.

This kind of consultation experience around medication is not unusual in my office. At another consultation for a change in medication due to recurrence of depression, I met a man previously followed by another psychiatrist. The patient described his central problem as depression. "What's it like for you to be depressed?" "Nobody has ever asked, really. I have trouble focusing." I asked him about the moment-to-moment experience of trouble focusing and feeling depressed. I wanted to know how they went together. It turned out that his depression turned on and off without rhyme or reason. His focusing was described as "I can be sitting at my desk, and it's like all of a sudden I recognize I really haven't been present and an hour has gone by. It makes me feel crazy and it's depressing for that to happen and know I'm not getting my work done." Lost time experience speaks to dissociative process (R. J. Loewenstein 1991). This person had a score higher than 30 on the DES.

The awareness I have for dissociative processes and my willingness to ask about them means I can cover a lot of ground quickly. The biggest problem I have after a consultation like this is trying to tune the referring psychotherapist in to these processes so they can be addressed in a long-term therapy. Many therapists are uncomfortable with these kinds of findings and prefer to either refer the patient or ignore the findings while proceeding along lines of inquiry they are more comfortable with or are a better match for their training. When that happens, I am very sad and honestly frustrated. The search for healing and coherence may be deflected. Clinicians are sometimes needlessly frightened of things they don't understand and that have been hyped in the lay press and movies. In this person's case, I was delighted with his therapist's curiosity and open interest in figuring out how to break through what he had experienced as a clinical logjam.

Coherence, Interior Decorating, and Tethered Memory

Samantha had no detailed narrative memory of her life before her teenage years. Yet like most people without such memory, she did recall the actual home in which she lived after her parents' divorce. She could see it with clarity in her mind. Amnesia for events or behavior is not the same thing as amnesia for everyday environment.

There is a temptation to approach a clinical scene of amnesia like this and imagine creating a kind of "surgical" intervention with the use of special techniques like hypnosis or eye movement desensitization and reprocessing to discover what was so terrible about the past to create amnesia. The idea is that without doing so, the patient cannot heal and will not get relief from his or her symptoms. I have never been comfortable proceeding in that manner, so I have cultivated other less intrusive means for stimulating memory of the past that is conversational rather than incisive.

I asked Samantha for a tour of the home in which she grew up. I requested that she use her powers of visualization, and we walked together down the front walk and through the front door. As we went I became a highly obsessive real estate agent, curious about every little detail of the house. What kind of walkway was it? Was it straight? Did the concrete have cracks? Was it crumbly anywhere? Was there a lot of stone in the concrete, or was it the smoother variety? What was the doorsill material—wood, metal, or aluminum? What kind of doorknob was there? Did the key fit into the knob, or was there a key cylinder next to the door handle? Did you turn the knob to open the door, or was there some kind of latch you pressed? We spent more than half an hour getting into the house, walking down the hall, and going into the kitchen. I regularly put lots of effort into getting descriptions of kitchens, basements, attics, closets, bedrooms, and bathrooms. I really don't leave out much, although I'm less inclined to spend time in a den or living room unless they turn up on a list of places in which people spent a lot of time. Care must be taken in requesting descriptions of areas that might be associated with a scene of abuse. There is a need to watch body language, stay aware of the cadence of speech, and to be aware of eye movement and facial expression because disruptions in the normal physiological flow of experience may signal a discontinuity of the patient's experience. In some cases, flashback phenomena may occur. Standard and simple stabilization techniques are useful at these moments (Boon, Steele, and van der Hart 2011; Brand 2001; Turkus and Kahler 2006; Vermilyea 2000).

It's my intention to activate memory for whatever is associated with the implicit memory for the facts about a home. During scenes of abuse, it is normal for people to focus on an inert object, like a doorknob or ceiling fixture, and they enter a spontaneous trance state. I want to tug gently on all the potential tags of latent memory that associational capacities can activate. After all, if dissociation is partly described by the isolation of knowledge, manifest in amnesia, then what better antidote for dissociative process could there be than an associative review of a relatively inert physical structure? I'm aware of how important homes are to children, as well as spaces in those homes. That's exactly the point. The person who has amnesia for early experience can benefit from an associative review of seemingly neutral memory, and then their natural associative processes pull up the detail over time. Although dissociation is indeed about disconnection and breaking associative links, it doesn't mean that the now unknown chunks of unremembered material concerning a previously fully memorable item is now on the other side of the universe. The associational link may have broken or not been established, but the plug and socket are still in proximity to each other, tethered and still aligned in the previous configuration.

Tethered memory is ubiquitous when there is active dissociative process. The memory is just outside our reach. The content of what could be remembered is implicitly known while continuing to guide behavior. Stern called this weak dissociation, the content of our mind that could be known if only a minimal effort to know could be made (D. B. Stern 1997).

Interior decorating is a lovely metaphor for a simple neurobiological reality: the conscious stimulation and recall of neutral items of some interest to a person will activate memory and cognition for those items (Strahan, Spencer, and Zanna 2002) and associated items including some that are simply "tethered" nearby. Memory researchers talk about this phenomenon in terms of "priming." "Priming refers to facilitative effects of an encounter with a stimulus on subsequent processing of the same stimulus (direct priming) or a related stimulus (indirect priming)" (Tulving, Schacter, and Stark 1982). If priming processes are used to activate emotional responses, then unconscious negative affective processing often guides the outcome and may play a role in the genesis of both sympathy and empathy (Yamada and Decety 2009) because threat associated with pain may inform the development of empathy. Painful emotion may also unconsciously distort time perception (Yamada and Kawabe 2011). Moreover, a simple experiment in the political arena makes clear that visualization influences decision making. In a close contest, a photograph of Bill Clinton was placed on the website of a Democratic California politician, and it positively influenced voters (Weinberger and Westen 2008).

In studies of memory and association, it's clear that if the subject is motivated, associative recall is more robust. In fact, experimental activation of psychodynamic unconscious conflict is well known (Weinberger and Westen 2008). In understanding memory function, it is useful to know that persons who are impaired on tests of recall and recognition memory nonetheless exhibit intact priming effects; their memory can be facilitated or biased by recently encountered information (Shimamura 2007). In short, amnesia and priming effects are dissociable. Thus, even though unconscious dynamic conflict may be activated, the priming effect of a tour through the childhood home (or a similar memory exercise) stays intact.

What effect did this motivated review of a childhood home have on Samantha? Her own words from an email subsequent to the home tour tell part of the story:

> Another thing I noticed that we didn't have time to talk about today was how I felt walking you through the house I grew up in. I wonder if you noticed actually. I felt pretty dizzy while telling you about it. I felt it come and go in strong waves, versus suddenly like normal. Normal. . . to me :)
>
> Then the entire next day at work I was insanely dizzy and felt incredibly sick, and was definitely in a bad mood. At one point I picked up the phone, was talking to my boss [while typing], and saw the words come out of my hands onto the computer screen, but they didn't hit my brain and I had no idea what was going on. It felt like something I never felt before, perhaps that "out of body experience" you've mentioned a few times. I read my notes later and luckily, as I had hoped, they were a transcript of what she said to me, so I coped yet again.

There are several things of note here. First, the experience of talking about a childhood home was physiologically and psychologically disturbing. She was dizzy. She had memory of a certain kind and beyond the descriptions of objects in the house and the house itself; there was an emotional stirring. Nausea often speaks to a sudden release of adrenalin; perhaps this was the mechanism for her feeling "incredibly sick." Second, the dizziness she felt was something she had been experiencing as relatively normal for her, and yet she knew there was something "off" about it. Many people describe mild depersonalization as the experience of being dizzy or lightheaded. Third, there's an interesting description of something like depersonalized action—the

125

observation of doing something, like typing, but not having a sense of being in control of it, not having it "hit my brain" (R. J. Loewenstein 1991). This is a dissociative experience.

Several weeks after the priming process, Samantha wrote to me about an experience she had when she was thinking about a dream. She was taken aback by what happened.

> The past few nights, as I'm doing this, thinking about my dream, a strange voice commented. I couldn't "hear" it, but rather it was inside my head. But normally when I "talk" to myself it's in my own voice. This was startling. It was as if I was trying to do a James Earl Jones imitation. A few nights ago I vaguely remembered dreaming about a supply closet, full of brooms and things, and the voice chirped in "Is there anything in the closet?" It comes out like a punch. Kind of angry. Deep. Scratchy. Enough to make me go "holy shit, what the hell was that." Then last night, I had a dream that you, Dr. C, had a new suit, pointing out to me that the label said Armani, and then I heard "Label whore." This is new and very strange to me. I'm not alarmed, but now it's a new weird pattern when I'm in that state of mind.

From another email that followed soon after, Samantha produced information about the extent to which memory could be isolated in her mind and had been since childhood, so she couldn't access it. Nevertheless she learned early on to cope with the problem. As an adult, she functioned at a high level and had seemingly adapted well to her memory problems. The compartmentalization of the problem jumps out of her words:

> There is something else I noticed which I think is worth mentioning. I remember having memory problems as a kid—that's ironic!
> I went to a book group at lunch in elementary school

and never seemed to have done the homework, which is very much unlike me. I remember feeling embarrassed that I had no idea work was assigned. I didn't admit it, and just faked my way through the hour.

The same thing happened in middle school, where I showed up [for] English class and the teacher had apparently assigned reading from *Huck Finn*, and I had no recollection of homework being assigned. She realized it, because I was usually the kid who sat in the front row and raised my hand a little too often. I must have started developing mechanisms to avoid this in the future—I had a planner, where I wrote my homework down.

I remember in second grade I couldn't find my bike anywhere, for a week or so. One day walking home from school I saw it on the bike rack. I refused to believe it was mine, because I didn't remember riding it to school and not home, and just leaving it there. I saw the registration number, and the bike lock—both that were specific to my bike. I still left it there for a couple days, in disbelief that it was in fact my bike.

I had to go back to school a lot after going home because I forgot books that I needed to do homework.

I left my lunchbox at school a lot, versus bringing it home. I could swear I brought it. So I started paying more attention to if I had it. Kind of like how I check my space heater and hair iron now. "I'm turning you off. You're off."

Once when I was walking home from school, probably third or fourth grade, I heard my mom calling my name. I went running home to see what was going on. I got there and she said she didn't call for me. I thought that was odd, because I heard it.

In their everyday way, these recollections and observations are not dramatic, but for Samantha they were quite new. Through general discussion and "interior decorating," through my making connections and labeling processes, she was becoming increasingly conscious and aware of the dissociative processes that had always been there. This consciousness is essential in changing the clinical course of her treatment and making it safe for her to be in the world. Otherwise, she remains confused about why things are happening and feels subject to the processes in her mind rather than that she has a mind with some understandable processes that previously scared her.

Samantha has continued to be curious about her subjective experience related to dissociative processes. Her continued curiosity bodes well for her. She was a bit undone about seeing her hands typing while having no idea what she was writing or why and hearing a "deep scratchy" voice speaking in her head. However, she has a basic sense of wanting to understand what isn't working well in her mind that trumps her anxiety. She walked into my office with a positive attitude and determination to find out what was going on with her life that was in the way of having more satisfying relationships. Although her initial presentation related to the upset around the death of a boyfriend, it became clear that her childhood was a very mixed and problematic time. She got it about this reality. She wasn't happy about it, but she knew what living a painful life is about, and she was on the path to making changes.

Ten months after the start of our work together, she continued to report and notice her dissociative experiences. One day she came to her session and announced that for the first time in several years, her memory was working. She was remembering details of interactions at work that other people couldn't pull up. She was delighted. We still didn't have autobiographical knowledge of her past, but she was not so afraid. It was okay to be living in the world and have a mind that could remember.

Samantha's presentation of adult PTSD-like symptoms was predicated on a foundation of dissociative process that went unnoticed by previous clinicians. The gradual unfolding of her consciousness for these processes will serve her well, and will help keep her functioning at her normal high level. There is no particular need to use technical maneuvers to "get at the trauma" while she is developing conscious-ness for things that are potentially frightening. What is most impor-tant is to strengthen her ability to be conscious for the events that occur in her mind and tolerate the emotional surges that accompany the unfolding of the story of her life.

Here I have made a concerted effort to highlight the everyday con-versational nature of asking about dissociative processes and their relationship to function in a person's life. Although isolation of affect can make it easier to do a perfectly unemotional and professional risk management task (people with abuse histories often make excellent corporate risk managers), it does little to create intimacy in relation-ships. When associated with depersonalization experience, the exis-tential sense of emptiness created can be profoundly painful. My intent has been to normalize dissociative processes and explain them in a way that almost anybody could understand, to demythologize them. Although it is not possible to omit a discussion of identity alteration, which often provokes incredulity in clinicians who have not observed it, it is most important to appreciate a focus on dissocia-tive *process* rather than on dissociative disorders. I believe clinicians will find many more people with dissociative disorders by staying aware of dissociative processes than they will ever notice if they are intent on looking for identity alteration.

Compartmentalization and Discerning Reality

The occurrence of compartmentalized function in human beings is normal. The central issue is not whether it occurs but the extent to which the compartments share information, emotion, worldview, and so on. In the midst of the fog of dissociation are the tethered ends of unlinked and not yet formulated (associated) elements of experience, the qualities of which lead a healthy mind to doubt and deny their very existence because those experiences feel far outside the normal realm of human experience. "That's just how I am. I don't know why I did that." The disowning of initiative for a particular behavior in this statement is subtle and rationalized. Perhaps this is the statement of someone playing out a trauma from the past as enacted knowing (Bardy and Mottet 2006) where knowledge is implicit in behavior but not explicit in thought. Perhaps this is an allusion to another aspect of self of the quality of an isolated self-state, an alter personality (Kluft 1984) of DID, if you will. If so, then let's be clear that this partakes of the quality of a pseudodelusion rather than there being present in the mind of the patient an intruder who has engaged in a land grab of neural real estate and taken up residence. There are not separate people in the mind of the person with DID—there is difficulty feeling like one whole person. A persistently dissociative mind holds disparate and contradictory reactions that resemble the simultaneous and/or sequential contradictory internal working models described years ago in the infant attachment literature vis-à-vis the disorganized-disoriented classification (Lyons-Ruth 2003; Main and Morgan 1996; Solomon and George 1999).

Pseudodelusions and pseudohallucinations (Howell 2011; Kluft 1983; R. J. Loewenstein 1991) are at the core of a mind's creative capacity to reorganize reality in just the right way to make it into what it needs to be to provide a context for living in the face of an unacceptable internal or external reality. Counterfeit coherence is the result. An example of a pseudodelusion is the belief that different self-states, alters, are separate people—the delusion of separateness. This naturalistically derived belief gives way with regularity to challenge regarding the lack of physical evidence for multiple bodies and the preponderance of evidence for one body. Although people don't give up this delusion immediately, they do give it up, and this is in contrast to a standard delusional belief that can persist for years and perhaps never change.

Pseudohallucinations, like seeing a child self-state when an adult looks in the mirror, gives way to the same processes as do pseudodelusions. In regard to metaphor and what is in the therapist's mind about the patient's mind, imagine what would happen if the therapist believed the patient had a mind with fully developed alternate individual selves, centers of initiative that could run the person's life? This would support the patient's pseudodelusion of separateness, as Kluft wisely described years ago, and would lead to clinical misadventure. The point is that the education and beliefs of the therapist about things dissociative, and about what it means to have a mind with massive persistent dissociative process, are critically important to any treatment.

More than one of my patients with DID have asked about the difference between my mind and theirs. Is that a moment to inquire with some curiosity about why that question is being asked? It depends. If there is an ongoing deflection of some content in the discussion, then perhaps such an inquiry might make sense. On the other hand, perhaps it is a moment of honest curiosity. If so, then deferring a response until after hearing a patient's fantasy might not make sense. This is a place where the art of psychodynamic therapy relies less on rules than on intuition. To always respond in a particular way undermines making use of feeling in the relationship. I don't have a set way of responding, and I tend to lean in the direction of responding and then asking about fantasy if it feels like that is unexplored. I believe it is important to remember that many of the people I see come from a family environment that would never have entertained the kind of question being asked about my mind and theirs. Steve Gold made that point eloquently some years ago by calling attention to the reality that our patients experience more than blunt trauma (Gold 2000), and it can be important to be responsive to and not just curious about what's in a patient's mind. Avoiding responding has potential serious negative consequences in a repetition of past neglect or dismissiveness. So I have often simply replied that part of what distinguishes my mind from that of my patients is that I have a generally free flow of information, skills, abilities, and emotions between my own self-states; the degree of isolation, exclusion, and deflection in my mind does not too often impair my ability to relate, work, play, love, or create. Once this is on the table, we talk about it, and in doing so we are negotiating the model of mind my patient has about their own mind. Multiple self-states? For me it is a much more parsimonious model of mind than Freudian structural theory, object relations, and so on.

I am not being dramatic; I am being honest. The degree of fear—terror if you dare empathize with it—and the corresponding sensing

131

of personal failure that includes a sense of being mortified, rendered worthless, dripping with shame and humiliation, is the kind of experience that activates dissociative process. There is nothing nice or casual here. Recall the scenes described in the first chapter of the prototypical emotional substrate for activation of unconscious dissociative process and the need to maintain coherence in the face of the discontinuities that result. Counterfeit coherence might begin to look somewhat more attractive than reality. As clinicians, however, we can't afford it or we fail our patient's trust.

In the previous chapters I provided a general introduction to the topic of dissociative process and the theoretical underpinnings of the elaboration of dissociatively organized self-states. Here I have tried to provide a window into the experience of opening a treatment and proceeding with care. I hope this levels the playing field for clinicians who might be relatively uninitiated into the world of dissociative process and chronic complex trauma and embellishes the knowledge base of more experienced clinicians. I could not imagine writing in detail about casework without constructing a logical basis for holding and containing the ways a person with a complex mind organized around dissociative process approaches psychotherapy or psychoanalysis.

There is one more puzzle piece to convey before I launch into casework and that is the relationship between dissociation and our emotional lives. If there is anything that creates context and meaning for me as I listen to my patients, it is tracking the emotional dimension of experience in the room, theirs and mine. In the next chapter we can explore the neurobiology of emotion and how it applies especially in the realm of persistent dissociative processes.

Chapter 5

Affect, Neurobiology, and Dissociative Processes

WHEN I FIRST BEGAN TO STUDY THE NEUROBIOLOGY OF MIND, I WORRIED THAT we could eventually lose sight of our humanity should we overemphasize and privilege the biological over the personally psychological. Having immersed myself in this area of study for a number of years, I find that just the opposite has happened for me. I am more convinced than ever about the wonder of the essential psychological complexity and magic that goes into giving birth to a mind and then growing it. I suppose that is in some part related to watching my first grandchild grow, up close, and being a witness to the leaps her delighted mind makes from week to week. Magic!

The study of emotion is central to the treatment of the dissociative disorders. No other dimension of experience is as powerful an organizer of mind as emotion is. To emote is to react to life—both the life inside and out. In this chapter I explore the power of an emotion-focused approach to the psychotherapy of persistent dissociative processes. Cognitive approaches are valuable and are part of my approach. Underlying it all is the neural fabric of mind that generates the experience of emotion and predicts the trajectory of a not-so-lived life, especially one where dissociative process gets out of hand.

How does the brain create the experience of having an emotionally capable mind, especially a mind of our own? That's a mystery, yet it's also true that we know associative and dissociative processes are involved. Notice how central emotion is to the story told by Kevin, writing about his wife, Denise:

> On the drives back and forth to the hospital, inspired by
> Denise, I found myself thinking quite a lot about the life

that I had been missing, not just since her surgery but for the 35 years of our marriage. I am a survivor of severe sexual abuse that went on intermittently throughout my childhood. It happened, I know that it happened, and I have to live with it every day. When you grow up like that you are wary all the time; you rarely get close to anyone and you don't go around having feelings where people can see them. My method of coping was my manner: low visibility, in and gone; distance. Denise saw through me and signed on anyway, when we were both young. I had never considered that I could be loved by anyone. When I met Denise I was, to my great benefit, open enough to understand that she was a person with whom I could share myself. I committed to her and to a life together. There have been only a few occasions in my life when I've looked and actually seen what was in front of me and fully felt the feelings I was feeling. One time was watching her walk down the aisle toward me, beaming, on our wedding day. I never looked away. (Kelly 2013)

Kevin Kelly has emerged as a writer after surviving severe childhood sexual abuse. He brings gifts for us all as he continues to write and tries to fully feel his way through life. He shows us what dissociative processes are like and teaches us about the centrality of emotion as the great contextualizer of experience. He reminded me of the essence of the tension inside me when I write about emotion and the psychotherapy of people struggling with the unrelenting gravitational pull of demanding dissociative processes that have run their lives for many years. These are feelings that need to be borne by both the patient and the therapist on the journey they make together—feelings that stop us in our tracks, leave us awestruck, call us to action with a vengeance, and more. There is also an emotional separation between patient and therapist, a distance of some necessity so we can stay on task. As the years go by, that distance feels like it has become less and less, much less. Yes, we need to understand the neurobiology and the theory, but let's not forget that we are all quite vulnerable to life's surprises. We are also capable of standing up in the midst of it all and engaging in creative acts of art, relatedness, and healing, among other paradoxical assaults we make on the entropy of life when we risk loving and being loved.

If It's All about the Relationship, Then It's All about Feelings

There is an intimate relationship between emotion and the body that is mediated by neural processes (Damasio 1999) that can be impaired when dissociative processes are active. Feelings are the physically sensed—in the body—alive experiences that provide moment-to-moment context and meaning for human experience (Ogden, Minton, and Pain 2006), especially human relating. Dissociative processes interrupt the flow of interaction between the mind, the body, and the neural structures that mediate and predict some of the size and shape of our emotional responses. Dissociative processes take the texture out of living and life, making it into a meal without tastes. We need to understand how this happens and then take advantage of what we learn so we can focus clinical attention on how to facilitate as full a healing experience as possible for our patients.

Why the emphasis on emotion and its neurobiology? The metabolism of emotion is what predicts a lot of what we see clinically when dissociation has gotten out of hand and just won't quit its isolating, excluding, and deflecting of mental content even thought it makes no sense to an observer for dissociation to persist. People who have depended on dissociative processes for their emotional survival have found a way to stay alive but hidden, to find a private alternate space for living when there is no more room in reality.

Emotion is at the core of self-organizing systems (Stechler and Kaplan 1980), an activity that is part of self-state formation. All self-states seem to have a central emotional valence (Bucci 2009), often holding sequestered toxic emotional content at a distance from consciousness as a way of avoiding hyperreactive and frightened states of being. Fear or shame are often at the core of especially aggressive self-states, some of which are laden with all the attitudinal issues of a rebellious teenager. The politics of these self-states predict that they are often repositories of visible rage, utter contempt, paradoxically hidden shame, profound humiliation, and fear of reexperiencing these toxic feelings. Contemptuous self-states can recoup marginal amounts of self-esteem and a brief assertion of competence by holding other self-states in disdain (Almond 1997). This is made possible by maintaining these disdained self-states in a not-me position (Chefetz and Bromberg 2004). If a fear of other people is prominent, and retaliatory urges are inhibited by that fear, then internal psychodynamics predict that some isolated self-states will become a target, a requisite whippingpost. This is not all that different than what Freud proposed as the theoretical backdrop of melancholia, that is, taking part of the ego as an object (Freud 1915). He just didn't think of things from the perspective of a multiple self-state model of mind.

Self-states are sometimes introduced by patients as "the one who is sad," "the one who is scared," and so on. Appreciation of the normal developmental tasks leading to adulthood and the trajectory of emotional development that occurs in tandem are useful perspectives in anticipating some of the emotional content of self-states in DID. As language replaces the facility of images in childhood (Bauer 1996; Grandin 1995), most of us leave behind a relatively autistic stage of thinking and feeling dominated by visual and other sensory imagery. However, child self-states of DID retain more of this kind of feeling and thinking, such as magical thinking and imaginary friends, which are normal in early childhood. The emergence of dominant emotions in particular self-states follows the trajectory of emotional injury at different times during a person's life, and the expression of the emotion takes on the shape of the typical developmental modes in which children process emotional experience. This requires us to be aware of potential shifts in modal processing of thoughts and feelings (psychic equivalence, pretend, and teleologic explanations) and make use of it in treatment (Fonagy et al. 2003).

Feelings, even after trauma and years of fearfulness, remain the mortar that cements together and shapes relationships with self and others over a lifetime. Again, it's all about intense feelings and the self-states that organize around them. For example, the intense emotion left behind by childhood is visible in the story of a professional woman who was an accomplished amateur musician but found herself unable to practice at home. Very cautious and protective about her inner world, she revealed carefully titrated amounts of her experience to me. She told me she could go to a studio and play, but those rooms were not frequently available. She became aware that the source of her inhibition about playing music at home came from a child self-state or two who wrapped themselves in a curtain and could not be seen. Of course, they couldn't see out either. As she talked about how she had been nicknamed "Mary Curtains" (Mary is not her real name) I began to have a sense that her child-sized self-states were still perceptually oriented to the past. From that perspective the mother they feared could assault them if they played music too loud or not in the right way. Mother could also be confused with the adult voice of the patient. Additionally, having once had a neighbor complain about "noise," there was a real-time fear of conflict if she played music at home. What to do?

"Have you ever heard about a window that was made so that it reflected from one side, like a mirror, but from the other side you could see right through?"

"Yeah, I know about that. I read about it in a book about therapy and hospitals."

"Okay, well, is there any reason you could not mend part of the curtains inside so that child parts could see out but nobody could see in?"

"Oh, this sounds like fun! Yeah, they've already got it going."

"Well, that's cool! It may not be as good as Harry Potter's invisibility cloak, but it will work just fine!"

"What's the Harry Potter thing?"

"Oh, it's just a special fabric you can put over yourself and then you can see through it but nobody can see you! It's kind of fun, too. Of course, you might already have one and I'd never know it!"

"Yes, I might have one already!"

"I've been thinking that when you've been hiding in the curtains there might be confusion about who is talking with you and who can keep you safe. Do you know what adult Mary's voice sounds like?"

"No, all we hear is our mother, and so we hide."

"Would it be okay to look through the new one-way window in the curtain while Mary looks at a mirror at home so you can see and hear adult Mary while she's talking?"

"Yeah, I can do that."

"Mary, can you use a mirror like that?"

"If it's to help me play music, then I can do it. I don't think it will be a problem."

"Good. I hope everyone inside the curtain can look out through the window now and see how capable Mary is at getting through the day. She's really doing a good job, and you haven't even known it! Once you know it, then you'll be able to relax and enjoy the music. Mary will keep you safe, won't she?"

"Maybe, but I need to check this out before I'll know."

In this vignette I made use of a kind of playful magical thinking with which the patient was already familiar (Bandler and Grinder 1975). Gregory and Musttata (2012) have written about how magical thinking represents a presymbolic mental state that processes and organizes distressing emotions through the body schema (in regard to their work with adolescent self-harm through cutting). I combined this kind of information with the knowledge that even in the face of intense emotion logically incompatible and contradictory information can be juxtaposed without anxiety thanks to the trance logic (Orne 1959) that is typically present in dissociative experience. The resulting perspective allows a clinician to be able to honestly play creatively with reality in a positive manner. There is an ease with which the internal transitional space of self-states can be modified with straightforward suggestion that allows a person to approach changing her reactivity with a sense of control. Imagining the conditions under which a child was terrified and hid inside curtains set the stage for this intervention. Emotional reactivity was the focal point of what I proposed to Mary to initiate change in a nonthreatening manner appropriate to the cognitive set of both child and adult self-states. The patient underwent a temporary switch in a conversational manner moving from adult to child and back to an adult state as we talked. The center of authority in regard to initiating change resided with the patient; I was a consultant and coach who was willing for the patient to try something on their own and tell me about the results. At the center of all this was a focus on the emotional risks the patient experienced in talking with me about something for which she was brutally punished as a child: playing music the "wrong" way. Consciousness for feelings and tracking the emotionality in the exchange were what I held in mind as we talked. Voice tone, facial expression, and body language were as significant as any of my words. I was genuinely delighted to be playful with her, and I sensed she knew it.

Some Notes on Emotional Development

Emotional development tends to be orderly and yet complexly tied to other domains. Cognitive and social growth involve the emergence of feelings and emotion regulation. The adequacy of such a developmental account is based on converging lines of evidence across domains that provides explanatory power for describing transformation and process throughout development (Sroufe 1996). For example, some children's understanding of facial expression may be poor and change qualitatively and slowly over the course of development. What children may often do is categorize emotional experience more simply into "feels good" and "feels bad" categories that are differentiated sometime later in development. A child's understanding of emotion may be less predicated on recognition of facial expression than it is on contingent social antecedents and behavioral consequences (Widen 2012). For example, children (ages four through nine) shown "disgust" faces were as likely to label that face as showing anger as were children who were shown an actual "angry" face likely to label that one as showing anger (Widen and Russell 2010). Without priming from a social script, the emotional meaning of the face was not entirely discernible. We know that infants engage in sophisticated communicative activities with caretakers even at age four months (Beebe et al. 2012). There is a developmental pathway to emotional understanding that seems to track the establishment of an appreciation of social contingencies and behavioral scripts (Ryle 1999). The cognitive-analytic therapy of Ryle and colleagues focuses attention on the expected behaviors of others in interactions. These behaviors tell the story of activated states of emotion, but they are often poorly understood.

Much the same kind of emotional-behavioral analysis takes place in a novel group therapy, the Circle of Security, designed to change attachment styles (Marvin et al. 2002). Parents whose own attachment status (as determined through the Adult Attachment Interview) has led to children with disorganized/disoriented patterns of infant attachment watched videotapes in a group therapy session of their children's behavior, and then engaged in therapist-guided speculation about what the behavior meant. What was that child thinking or feeling that produced that behavior? Mothers with impaired emotional capacities slowly learned the language of emotion and behavior, openly speculating about the mental state of their child, and eventually recalling their own mental states from childhood. Out of curiosity, I sent Marvin et al.'s paper on this intervention to the prominent psychoanalyst Philip Bromberg, and in his classically understated manner, he quipped to me, "Rich, don't let this get around or it's going to put us all out of business!" (personal communication, 2002). Of course, the circumstances of this intervention are unique, based as it is on a research protocol, yet it's also true that with a focus on the emotions and mental states generating behavior, and after 20 sessions over six months, these attachment-insecure mothers and children developed secure ratings. This result is consistent with our knowledge that emotions activate behavior and that the story of behavioral scripts tells the story of the action potential in emotion (Paivio and Nieuwenhuis 2001). Emotional development needs to be understood on a systems and organizational level that pays homage to the complexity of inherited neurobiological capacities and the wide variation in social and familial circumstances that predicts what an infant will learn about and come to understand as their own emotional responses to the world around them (Sroufe 1996).

It's really too bad that as we become adults there is no particular requirement that we review childhood experience for accuracy of perception and memory and then reformulate the meaning of our experience and the associated emotional responses. Imagine how much different adulthood would be! The kinds of errors of judgment or perception we might have made regarding disgust and anger remain embedded in our private child-sized interpretative library of experiences while we are oblivious to the idea that we conduct our adult lives using an emotional rule book from childhood. For example, one person spent a great deal of time attributing negativity to their own actions before they discerned that their mother's anxieties often translated into miserable and exaggerated facial grimaces. She can now recognize her mother's face-making as a display of her distress and feelings of vulnerability, whereas previously the mother was experienced as angry and shaming. It took a number of years to figure that out, and this person is still aware that her default reactivity to acute distress in her mother (or in some other people) can still evoke a fear of humiliation, especially if there are matching social contexts and the facial grimacing resembles the scenes earlier in their life. The social contingencies can inform the emotional attribution.

Early experience may require significant review and reformulation by an adult before childhood emotional content can actually become more clear (Bauer 1996; Terr 1979). Even with that review, the emotional qualities of early experience may only be sensed rather than known, and the likelihood of those experiences achieving felt coherence (Chefetz 2010) might be limited. Moreover, the content of what might be remembered may be limited to nonverbal pathways of experience. What does this clinical knowledge and appreciation of early emotion and nonverbal pathways look like when applied to a treatment?

Kelly had been in treatment for seven years before she came to me for consultation. She had chronic depersonalization as the most outstanding feature of her presentation. She told me, in tears, that on a high-pressure business trip she had fallen apart and had never been the same since. Previous therapy had helped her get back to work, but she could not . . .

recover the feeling of being connected to myself, and not be constantly depersonalized, which to me feels as though someone else is looking out from behind my eyes. None of the experiences I am having are my own; this detachment is confusing and frightening. It's not so much that I can't recover the feeling of being an efficient, organized, totally focused business person because if you asked my current boss he'd say that I'm exactly that. I can't recover MYSELF.[1]

The shame, the emotional instability I feel has kept me in this hiding place. I can't return to my old career not because I don't feel I can perform the tasks, but because I don't feel emotionally stable to deal with the pressures of life. So I hide in a job where I'm overqualified and the demands are not too high, I don't have to travel, be up for promotion, or sit in performance reviews. I hide in a place where the risk of unraveling again is lower than it would be if I returned to a career where I had competitive co-workers and demanding bosses.

I really just want to feel like I can feel connected to myself, participate in life, and not feel scared I'm going to unravel and become depersonalized again.

For Kelly there were profound periods of depersonalization and deep depression that seemed to come and go as if the depression had a mind of its own. At other times, there were "definite triggers, especially things that remind me of the life I have not been able to return to. It can be as simple as meeting someone at a party and finding out they work in my old career. That usually leads to a fast downward spiral into depression."

---

[1] Kelly reviewed the material in this vignette in some detail, and we discussed her comments in session, a useful reiterative process. I am partly quoting her written review. She said that she cried when she read the vignette because she was so relieved to appreciate that somebody "got it" about her and glad that she might contribute to other people getting relief.

On one particular morning, Kelly remarked to me that her night-time sleep disturbance had improved with minimal medication and she was feeling better. Her days were still plagued by the frequent appearance of what she called her "dark mood." Oddly, when her husband returned home from work, this mood would suddenly lift, and it never seemed to appear while he was around in the mornings. Her moods certainly did not depend only on her husband's presence or absence, but she said that talking with him "helps me with the feelings of shame that seem to accompany these dark moods more than any other emotion. . . . I think it is true that he serves as an anchor for me in my dark times."

Kelly was concerned about the metaphors I had introduced to understand her inner experience. In previous discussion when she had a felt and coherent experience of a sad child-oriented self-state, and then in a later session, a feisty teenage-oriented self-state, she balked at the experience because it didn't have the heft of a real, alive experience. She wondered if she had made it up. People who present with gross depersonalization as a regular part of their lived experience have a very profound emotional detachment and distrust of feelings that seem unfamiliar or foggy. In Kelly's experience, her mother's regular dismissal of emotion and coercive-doubting (Kramer 1983) created a situation in which Kelly learned to not trust her feelings, a situation made worse by depersonalization. She was also "really frightened of any bad feelings I have, like sadness, or fear, or rejection. Those feelings make me feel very unsafe." This was not a casual experience but a repeated one that continued to influence her sizing up what she experienced emotionally as frightening and not worthy of trust. Moreover, Kelly was familiar with the literature about dissociative disorders, and had certainly read enough to have been exposed to controversy about the validity of the dissociative disorder diagnosis and concerns about iatrogenesis.

"It just feels artificial, made up, but I know I've learned things from it. I just don't trust it." After reading this text she added: "Even though I know we're accessing something because of how quickly the flood-gate of emotion comes pouring out, when I'm asked to imagine 'six-year-old Kelly' or 'dark mood Kelly,' it's not totally clear to me that this is where the crying is coming from." (Editorially, she also wrote: "Even though I named the age, or gave it the name 'Head down–Knees up' from the image I saw in my mind, I'm having a hard time trusting the process of how this will help me recover my connection to myself and feel less depersonalized.") What Kelly is specifically referring to in this comment refers to a session that will be recounted shortly. The topic was her images and metaphors, but at the same time she and I were engaged in a very important conversation about doubting and trust.

I replied to her straightforwardly. "I think it's hard to trust things inside you that really tell part of the story about your feelings, but perhaps it would make some sense to you to consider that people often talk about their feelings in a mostly left-brained operation, logical, linguistic, and mathematical. In novels and in poetry, people talk about feelings in a much more emotionally expressive, right-brained operation that is hyperlinked, not bound by time, and makes use of images and sensations rather than words. The metaphors we're using make use of these right-brained processes, and they may not seem real familiar or comfortable."

"I understand what you're saying, and I like how you are distinguishing the left- and right-brain thing. It makes sense to me."

"Tell me more about what it's like to be in a dark mood; let's get into the details of your experience."

"It's not always the same, but often enough there is this sense of anxiety, a nearly helpless feeling. It's like I feel frantic. I just want the feelings to go away." She began to smile a very lovely smile, something I enjoyed, but something which didn't fit with the current conversation.

"Your smile is here, Kelly."

Through her nearly perfect smile, she spoke, while her eyes averted downward, "I don't know why. I'm just smiling." I had activated a shame sequence; it was apparent from the turning away of her gaze. I knew extra care need be taken to avoid humiliation. I proceeded gently and with permission.

"I have a speculation about your smile, given what we're talking about. May I speculate?"

"Sure." I was aware that her apparently well-practiced smile was an unconscious habit and some basic neurobiology informed what I said and did next. It turns out that facial expression has its own neural real estate that is responsive both to what we see on the faces of other people and what we do with the sensory experience of the mostly unconscious feeling of muscle movement on our own face. There's increasing information that an area of the brain related to the temporal cortex (on each side of the head near the ear and temple), the fusiform gyrus, responds preferentially to faces over other classes of visual objects and may be involved in early perceptual processing of faces and in facial recognition (Adolphs 2002). It also assists in forming an internal representation of faces (Pizzagalli, Lehmann, Hendrick, Regard, Pascual-Marqui, and Davidson 2002). Facial recognition can occur in a blink, between 80 and 170 thousandths of a second. It is speculative to assert this, but clinical observation suggests that when somebody smiles at a time when their mood is sad, for example, facial muscle tone and facial sensory images counter the feeling of sadness and may even make it impossible to notice the sadness. The smile misleads an observer, too. Some politicians may have mastered that one. We can also fool ourselves, somewhat, via contradictory signals.

"I have a feeling in me about your smile, Kelly. It's like it's present because it hurts so much inside you that the smile is like an antidote for you, and a signal to me that everything is fine, not to worry, not to probe." She began to cry in earnest. Later she added to her account: "Having thought about the smile more, I think there's also resignation, and a belief that no one can help me through my pain. I have memories of thinking as a very young child that mothers and fathers can't help you with your pain (probably because they felt so burdened or clueless about it, or maybe they believed the same thing), and I remember feeling as a very young child so alone, and so scared and devastated by this conclusion I made about life."

"I can see there are a lot of feelings," I said in the session. Tears were getting wiped away.

"Yes, and this is what it's like. I don't know why this is happening. These dark moods just happen." This kind of independent appearance and disappearance of an intense emotional state is a standard signature of isolated (dissociative) self-state-related activity. Since this often constitutes a concentration of intense emotion around which is collected a worldview, I chose to investigate my private speculation via nonverbal right-brain-bound sensory and imagistic approaches. At one point in what follows, I give names to self-states based on her visual imagining of them. The names I give are descriptive of the emotional constellation represented by her physical posture. It's simply a short-cut language, a signifier that quickly references an experience. I don't assign proper names. That's a patient's choice, if it happens at all. If it does, then I'm curious about the name and why it was assigned.

"Please focus on the dark mood, for a moment, okay?

"Okay."

"I'd like to invite you to look around in your mind and check to see if there are any images that go along with how you're feeling now, and the dark mood. Close your eyes if that's helpful to focus."

With her eyes closed, she spoke nearly immediately and said, "I see a little girl. She's frantic, she's desperate. It's like she's seeking something and she can't find it. I think she feels helpless. It's like she's going in circles."

"It sounds like the image holds a lot of the feelings you've been talking about with this dark mood stuff. Are there other images?"

"Yes, there's another little girl, but she's very different. She's sitting on the ground with her knees drawn up, and her head down. She's really in despair. She's given up."

"She's resigned to whatever it is?"

"Yes, she just feels helpless and nothing can help her."

"Does this resonate with something in your life?"

"Yes, it's all about my mother. She wasn't the stereotypical Tiger Mom talked about in Asian families. You know—standing over her child playing the piano for hours endlessly until she plays Beethoven to her standards. My mom wasn't this person. In some ways I wish her abuse was this obvious. I think my recovery would be easier! I think more of what was happening between my Mom and I was that she couldn't handle the emotional demands of being a mother. When

I had emotional demands and they couldn't be met, this put me in a very dark place, and naturally as a child I would rebel in some way, and then my mother handled me by shaming me, "You ruined the family vacation," or "Whenever we try to do something nice, Kelly has to ruin it."

"So, we can understand Frantic who is trying and trying to get your mother to see her and make contact with her."

"Yes, that fits and feels right."

"How do we understand Head down–Knees up?"

"She gave up. I sometimes feel like I am at the bottom of this abyss, just sitting, alone in the dark."

"Yes, that fits with the helpless despair and resignation we talked about earlier."

"How am I ever going to resolve these feelings? It just feels like an endless dark place. It really doesn't help to see these images. Nothing changes."

"Before this is going to move toward resolution, I believe we need to better understand what's going on. I'm sure you remember me talking with you earlier about using a right-brain metaphor rather than a left-brain language-bound experience."

"Yes, and that makes sense to me."

"Okay, then let's go with that and see what we can learn. Take a look around inside at Frantic and Head down–Knees up. Can you see them clearly?"

"Yes."

"Good. Now gently walk forward and step into the space near Frantic, and being careful of her space, sit down near her." This suggestion, and that's exactly what it was, comes from a hypnoanalytic tradition (Brown and Fromm, 1986; Watkins 1992; Wolberg 1945) that is extraordinary in its depth but is rarely discussed today, with some lovely exceptions (Bromberg 1998; Fine and Berkowitz 2001; Kluft 1983, 1989, 1990, 2013). The related idea of walking into a dream space is also not new, though it's also true that not everybody can do this. People with high hypnotizability often can, and people with dissociative disorders are often highly hypnotizable (Frischholz et al. 1992).

"Okay"

"Nod your head when you're seated." She nods. "Does she notice you are there? Is it okay with her to have you visit?"

"Yes, it's okay. She feels terrible. She's really anxious. Things are awful for her."

"Sounds like she's really been having trouble with the feelings left over from the early relationship with your mother and she's remained frantic for somebody to recognize her feelings and validate what she's feeling."

"Yes, she's never seemed to notice me, not really. I didn't know what to do to help her. I've been really angry with her for not being able to let go of her pain. I probably also hold her responsible for my emotional unravelings."

"Kelly, would you check with Frantic and see if she'd be willing to take your hand and go visit Head down–Knees up? Nod your head if she is willing." She nods. "Okay, now take Frantic's hand and walk over into the space where Head down–Knees up is sitting and if it's okay, then please sit down near her with Frantic so that the three of you are in a little circle. Look over at Head down–Knees up, look clearly at her face and tell me what feelings you see there, please?" Sitting in a circle is an inclusive approach, not the confrontational constellation of a face-to-face position. Looking at her face and speculating about feelings borrows from our knowledge of the Circle of Security exercises and is meant to initiate a reflective awareness and process of mentalization, the appreciation of mental states in ourselves and others (Bateman and Fonagy 2006).

"She's just given up. She's exhausted from trying to make my mother notice me. She's in a place of deep despair."

"Would it be okay with you if you reach out with your hands, and gently place one hand each on the shoulder of Frantic and Head down–Knees up and let them know you are there for them, that you see them, and that I know they're there now, too. Let them know they are no longer alone."

"Okay I did it."

"How does it feel, now?"

"I feel more relaxed, more calm, but I don't really understand what's happening."

"You're getting to know your feelings, Kelly, and the little girls inside are teaching you. By the way, could you check in with them please and see if they would like to be known by you and me as something other than Frantic and Head down–Knees up? That's a little unwieldy as far as language goes, and doesn't quite fit being a little girl with important feelings."

"Okay I'll do that."

"Good, thank you." Kelly began to open her eyes, taking my thank-you as a cue to resume conversation in the space we were in and leave the space in her mind. I dropped the task of finding new signifiers for the personified states she had visualized. Perhaps she had wanted to drop it, too.

"I'm dizzy." She had spontaneously entered a hypnotic state, perhaps when she entered the dream space at my suggestion or perhaps just with inward absorption.

"Thanks for letting me know. In a few moments, I'm going to count back from three to one, and then say that word that signifies the end of work in trance, at that time being the word *open*, at which time you'll be fully alert and present in your normal waking state, as I count, three, two, one, *Open!*" These are standard re-alerting instructions in posthypnotic work.

"Okay. That's much better. I'm fine now."

"So what was it like working this way?"

"It was very nice. You're the opposite of my mother. You seem so accepting of my feelings, and you're not afraid of what I feel. Some therapists I've talked to seem to get upset about things I tell them and then I'm just back in the place where I was with my mother. You're just so calm. It's very nice."

"Good. I'm glad it works for you. I think these little girls are going to teach us both a lot."

"Well, I don't know what's going to happen, but I'm willing to try and work on it. It feels okay to do that."

"I'm glad, Kelly."

What happened here? Kelly got in touch with several of her feelings as represented by the images in her mind. What could be better to represent an emotional constellation of experience than embodied emotional images of little girls, Frantic and Head down–Knees up? There was no formal hypnotic induction, but she nevertheless entered a clinical state of hypnosis spontaneously, likely via intense absorption in the imagery. She needed help to emerge from that absorption. With just the exercise, but without knowledge of hypnosis, there might have been a very difficult time for her to get oriented again and that might have created an aversive experience from the disorientation.

Kelly also identified several cognitive perspectives related to her experience with her mother. Her dark moods became symbolized in a naturalistic manner and lost a great deal of their mystery. These emotions and the context in which they were viewed had the opposite impact from the smile that was incongruent with her spoken words. Noticing that inconsistency, knowing about the fusiform gyrus and its function in facial recognition and in potentially coopting facial expression to detach a feeling state opened a window into Kelly's emotional world, and we went through it together. My assigning the names of Frantic and Head down–Knees up combined the language of the body with the mood, the prevailing emotional climate. The images in her mind had embodied the feelings. This is a kind of synesthetic language, a language where a bodily image has a feeling, just like in classic synesthesia where colors are heard and sounds are seen.

I followed right-brain rules in asking Kelly to enter the space in which the images resided. I was not bound by left-brain logical, mathematical, sequential, time, and space parameters. The logic of emotion is right-brained. Interestingly, it turns out that the right fusiform gyrus is more reactive to positive emotions and the left is more reactive to negative ones (Pizzagalli et al. 2002). It's not that the left brain is not involved in our emotional lives; it's that there is specialization of the hemispheres in knowing some things and not others (Bermond et al. 2006). Specialization of brain regions and the modular nature of brain organs means that our brain is prone to lose only part of a complex function if one area goes offline. The punch line here is that we're prone to dissociative experience when, for example, we lose body sensing in an emotional moment and feel unreal, not just like there's part of a process missing.

What Are Emotions?

It's not just that I think it's intellectually useful to have a working model of emotion. I think it's essential to have a thoughtful appreciation of the role of emotion in human life and one that guides clinical activity. My views about emotion are informed by the wisdom of my patients, my own experience as a patient and clinician, and by a number of theoretical models that have informed my understanding of the apparent therapeutic action of an emotion-focused intensive psychotherapy (Damasio 1999; Davidson, Abercrombie, Nitschke, and Putnam 1999; Demos 1995; Emde 1991; Horowitz et al. 1991; Hurvich 2003; Jones 1995; Lane and Nadel 2000; Lansky 1992; LeDoux 1996; Lewis 1987a; Lewis and Haviland 1993; Morrison 1989; Panksepp 1998; Panksepp and Biven 2012; Scheff and Retzinger 2001; Siegel 1999; Sroufe 1996; Wolff 1987; Wurmser 1994). Notably, the authors I have just cited certainly do not always agree with each other. The controversy is most useful, though. Although my interest has been heavily weighted in the direction of affective neuroscience, I have benefited from the emphasis cognitive neuroscientists place on the role of cognition in emotional life, and find their arguments persuasive as to how emotional appraisals influence perception of complex emotional experience. I am especially indebted to clinicians who have struggled with the exploration of shame, one of the most toxic emotions. In the treatment of complex trauma and dissociative processes, a clinician needs all the help available. There can be little purity in the theoretical views of a clinician; applicability and utility are the gold standards by which I have measured the value of theoretical persuasions. In what follows immediately I owe a large debt to the work of Silvan Tomkins, especially as interpreted by Virginia Demos (1995).

There is a clinical need to distinguish between emotion considered as a cognitive appraisal process versus as a visceral affective experience modulated by subcortical (limbic system) neural real estate (Panksepp, 2004). One interesting line of evidence about the cognitive versus visceral origins of emotion is that removing the cerebral hemispheres of a dog or severing its spinal cord did not alter apparent emotional displays by that dog (Sherrington, 1900, p. 397, cited in Cannon 1914). Today we know that emotional circuitry, especially fear circuits, are mostly not in the cerebral hemispheres but are in the diencephalon, the midbrain, as part of the limbic system (Ledoux 1996). Removing the cerebral hemispheres might have no effect on the observation of a basic emotional response, as can readily be observed in a laboratory animal. However, a reflexively displayed feeling, such as Sherrington's dog showed after the cortex was removed, is different than a felt feeling with associated contextual meaning and higher-level consciousness (Damasio 1999) in a human subject. Damasio's somatic marker hypothesis (Damasio 1996) postulates that there are bodily signals, markers, that arise in bioregulatory processes, including those that express themselves in emotions and feelings, that influence behavior, such as decision making. This influence can occur both consciously and nonconsciously (Bechara and Damasio 2005).

Panksepp and Biven (2012) argue that Damasio's view in the somatic marker hypothesis (bodily information, unconscious visceral experience, is transformed into feelings that guide action), has not been adequately tested in the laboratory and prefer their perspective that the stuff of raw emotion arises from subcortical structure (2012, p. 79). Damasio's heuristic, however, is a hand-in-glove fit with my clinical observations. People get a bodily stirring of some kind, often referred to as something like a gut feeling, and they eventually may be lucky enough to get clarity on whether they are sad, angry, and so on. The subcortical areas, those below the cerebral cortex (most of what we see when we look at an image of the brain is cerebral cortex), in which Panksepp takes appropriate interest, mediate emotional experience and have several really important brain organs like the amygdala and hippocampus. These two organs figure in fear responses and short-term memory, respectively. The working knowledge about living that accrues to these brain organs predicts much emotional responding, and that's part of why I like the subcortical hypothesis combined with a cognitive neuroscience view of appraisal processes alongside Damasio's emphasis on embodied experience. Bodily sensory outputs interact with cerebral libraries of past experience and subcortical patterns of activation to produce consciousness for a sensation we eventually call a feeling (more on this later). All these components constantly communicate back and forth, honing our experience. Although there is strong evidence for the growth of emotionality as predicated on human relatedness, there is also good evidence that self-perception relies on appraisal of bodily states, as in Damasio's work. The neurobiology of emotional experience is more like the weaving and reweaving, each moment, of a tapestry strung between disparate subcortical, visceral, and cortical poles than it is like activating a switchboard where an emotion lights up.

Emotional appraisal reflects a constantly changing person-environment relationship (Lazarus 1984). Perhaps no better example of the value of this perspective occurs than in the cognitive psychoeducational treatment model of panic attacks where people learn that the fear they have of being frightened (second fear) is causing them more trouble than the fact that they had a first episode (first fear) where they were afraid (and possibly nothing really happened beyond their fear) (Weekes 1969/1990). In the treatment, they learn that with each second-fear worry they "squirt" a bit of adrenalin into their bloodstream, and that in 20 minutes it will all be gone, metabolized by their body unless they provoke another release. The skewed appraisal process for their emotional distress is undermined by new knowledge of the meaning of their embodied experience. They suddenly appreciate how much control of their situation actually exists. Effective cognitive therapy for panic pivots on this physiological-emotional reality. Do emotions take origin in the body? Yes, and it's also true that once the frontal lobes and other brain organs develop an interactive library of emotionally associated experience, there is little reason to be a purist and separate out either felt emotion or appraisal processes as not being of relative importance (Lane and Nadel 2000).

Given the last hundred years or so of the body being relatively ignored in the psychological treatment of trauma,[2] what's important is that we now know the body is involved as a major player in emotional experience (P. Levine 1997; Ogden, Minton, and Pain 2006; Rothschild 2000; Scaer 2001; van der Kolk et al. 1994). This provides a needed clinical window of perspective for us to use in understanding dissociative processes if we just notice the opportunity. If we are going to help our patients, we need to understand emotion. We need to know what it's about, and how to intervene on basic levels, sometimes as a bottom-up rather than a cortex-focused top-down thinking model (Schore 2003).

Definitions of Affect, Feeling, and Emotion

No discourse on the subject area of emotion can tolerate a tangle of terminology. I am referring to the problem that arises in the use of words like *affect*, *feeling*, and *emotion*. Some authors use these words interchangeably, excusing the confusion and loss of clear definition that results. If there were no consequences to this tangled linguistic spaghetti, I would follow suit. But the consequences are symptomatic of the fix we've found ourselves in regarding the loss of an appreciation of the somatic origins of our emotional lives and the functional reality that the body is part of the mind (Panksepp and Biven 2012). My patients seem to benefit from the definitions I present here by gaining increased clarity about their own experience; the usage we adopt gives them a simple outline they can apply to things emotional. My intent in spelling out these definitions is to add clinical utility to the traditional distinction, which the reader will certainly be familiar with, between affect as something we surmise and emotion and feelings as something we feel or experience. I realize that in proposing a somewhat revised scheme I am potentially perpetuating the terminological problem. But that won't happen if the reader joins with me in this usage!

---

[2] As a former family physician in rural Virginia, I appropriately note a long-standing tradition of psychosomatic studies that sometimes were related to trauma. However, the use of this perspective in psychological trauma did not seem salient.

Where there is a degree of controversy in a field, as there is in the study of emotion, it is not possible to formulate strict operational definitions that will satisfy everyone. So one turns to heuristics. A *heuristic* is a learning tool that can hone or sort knowledge toward having a working understanding of something that outstrips our current knowledge base or lacks certainty. Working with a heuristic, we can see that an *affect* arises from the kind of bodily tensions that accumulate from the interaction between brain, mind, and bodily processes (the functioning of body organs, e.g., the gastrointestinal tract) on an unconscious level. If intense enough, an affect is associated with the release of stress-related hormones, cortisol and adrenaline, even if we're not aware of being stressed, and we end up with a pounding and racing heart beat, perhaps even a panic attack, but we don't know why. Affect is part of what is associated with the muscle tensions in chronic pain syndromes, for example, fibromyalgia and chronic fatigue syndrome, that are stress-related (Hauser, Kosseva, Uceyler, Klose, and Sommer 2011; van Houdenhove et al. 2001). Accumulated affect is what some clinicians are talking about when speaking of a failure to desomatize emotional experience in somatization disorders (Krystal 1988). In more technical language, *affects are nonconscious, protosensations arising from visceral and neuromuscular tensions that reflect an overarching summation vector of the moment-to-moment equilibrium of the physiological state of a human being.*

A classic example of somatic-affective dysfunction is irritable bowel syndrome, where antidepressant therapy and psychological therapy may have equal efficacy (Ford, Talley, Schoenfeld, Quigley, and Moayyedi 2008). In one study two-thirds of patients were responsive to psychotherapy alone, among a group of medical patients unresponsive to medical therapy (Guthrie, Creed, Dawson, and Tomenson, 1991). In another study in patients with symptoms of heartburn (dyspepsia) who had no medical reason for their symptoms, a 16-session psychodynamic psychotherapy improved gastrointestinal symptoms and decreased alexithymia scores as well (Faramarzi, Azadfallah, Book, Tabatabaei, Taheri, and Shokri-shirvani 2013). Somatized affect can influence our physical sense of well-being enormously.

A *feeling* is a sensed accumulation of nonconscious somatically generated affects that crosses over an imagined threshold of intensity to reach a level of consciousness. A feeling is a felt sensation, a conscious embodied sensing. We feel feelings in our bodies, we don't think feelings. Before my perception of feeling(s) becomes more organized and subject to reflection, an associative process, I might just privately notice to myself, "I'm really feeling 'on' today." I might also be inclined to respond to an inquiry by a friend regarding a requested decision on a difficult issue by saying, "I don't really know what to think about how to respond. All I know is that I have a lot of feeling stirring inside me about it and it's making me feel pretty uncomfortable." We sense feeling, the stir in our bodies. Something is happening, but we have yet to name what it specifically means. The right brain helps us associate to and organize the felt sensation of what we might call a feeling, and then later construe as an emotion, but it is the left brain that must name the emotion (Bermond et al. 2006). If left- and right-brain communication is already impaired, as has been shown in the case of patients with a history of being verbally abused, then naming feelings might be neurologically less possible for verbally abused people (Teicher et al. 2010), as noted earlier in Chapter 2. Less interhemispheric information transfer (corpus callosum), less executive control (precuneus), and impaired working memory (hippocampus) can all lead to impaired learning of feeling states and associated named emotions. Given that psychotherapy with a focus on emotion has increased efficacy for people abused in childhood (Johnson et al. 1999; Paivio and Nieuwenhuis, 2001), this kind of impairment predicts a less positive outcome if not remedied by a psychotherapy that spends at least some of its time focused on developing emotional competence (Monsen, Eilertsen, Melgard and Odegard 1996).

Emotions are the names we assign to the familiar and well-worn paths of felt sensations we associate to the cortical libraries of personal and interpersonal experience, the social contingencies (Widen 2012). This is consistent with naming recurring states of feeling. We are either taught to assign the name of a specific emotion to the felt experience by somebody who observes a change in us (part of good parenting) such as facial expression or body language, or else we see emotions in others (especially on their faces) to which we resonate, and we learn what emotion they identify when they have that kind of feeling. Mirror neurons may play a role here (Gallese, 2001; Gallese, Eagle, and Migone 2007; Iacobani 2009). Social and relational contexts and contingencies may guide our naming of feeling states with emotion names. When Mary has a frown, pouty lips, tears, and sunken shoulders, her mother might teach her she's feeling sad by saying, "Oh my, Mary, you look so sad! What are you so sad about? What happened?" If Mary's mother is verbally abusive or emotionally dismissive (avoidant attachment, Type A), then her reaction might stifle Mary's emotional development by responding to her tears with a backhanded slap across her face followed by an admonition: "Stop your crying! You've got nothing to cry about. Keep that up and I'll really give you something to cry about!" Emotion words are shortcuts to personal and interpersonal experience. Extreme experiences may lie outside our emotional ken. Associative processes fail when we don't have emotional definitions that include an experience of rape, for example.

Neurobiology may be against us in efforts to remain coherent under stress. For example, the hypoperfusion of blood in Broca's area (responsible for verbal expression) in the left brain, which occurs with trauma, may deprive us of word-finding ability and a capacity to verbally express our experience (Rauch et al. 1996). This represents a neurological dissociation of the capacity to create autobiographical narrative from the capacity to know behavior or feeling. This is not a failure of will, an important distinction for our patients.

Silvan S. Tomkins, on whose work my definitions are mostly based, first proposed his theory of affects in 1954 (Demos 1995, p. 86) and talked about the relation of affect, feeling, and emotion in this manner:

> 1) by the terms "affect" or "innate affect," we reference a group of nine highly specific unmodulated physiologic reactions present from birth. 2) We use the term "feel-

ing" to describe our awareness that an affect has been triggered. 3) The formal term "emotion" describes the combination of whatever affect has just been triggered as it is coassembled with our memory of previous experiences of that affect. Tomkins eventually dropped the term "emotion" in favor of the much larger category of these coassemblies that he called "scripts." (Tomkins 2008)

Others have called similar organizations of experience emotion schemas (Greenberg and Pavio 1997). Tomkins's innate affects were startle, fear, interest, distress, anger, joy, contempt, disgust, and shame (Demos 1995). It seems less useful to argue about which emotions are primary and more important to hold on to the idea that some emotions tend to be primary, bred in the bone, so to speak; perhaps these are subcortically scripted. These are the relatively simple emotional concepts with large associational personal and interpersonal contexts as well as physiological effects. It is clinically wise to try to find the most primary named emotions in a situation and not allow primary emotional intensities to become hidden behind watered-down psychiatric terms such as *disappointed* and *unpleasant*. Specificity in naming the emotion of sadness is much more powerful and engaging than talking with someone who says they are upset or depressed. Those words are sopping wet with dissociative deflection, have little utility, and could mean many things. A sequence of primary, secondary, and tertiary emotions based on the degree of processing involved, for example, joy (primary), cheerfulness (more complex), optimism (even more complex and especially imbued with cognitive components), adds complexity to interpersonal responses and social contingences while providing for more precise empathic resonance.

Emotional awareness correlates with health. My interest in emotion is not simply a matter of personal preference. It's a matter of clinical efficacy (Gratz 2007; Linehan 1993) when working with people who have unbearable emotional pain warehoused beyond normal capacity. A scale was constructed to measure levels of emotional awareness as a means of assessing a cognitive-developmental understanding of emotion (Lane, Quinlan, Schwartz, and Walker 1990; Lane and Schwartz 1987). Individuals with PTSD showed lower levels of both emotional awareness, as per the scale, and emotional adaptability (Frewen, Lane, Neufeld, Densmore, Stevens, and Lanius 2008), as evidenced by shifts in activity in the anterior cingulate cortex (ACC), an area of brain that is correlated with consciousness and emotional awareness and performs evaluative functions and initiates problem solving activity with intention. The ACC is part of the anatomic limbic system, the subcortical system that Panksepp investigated diligently as he constructed his theory of emotion while making extensive use of the groundbreaking work of Joseph LeDoux, a cognitive neuroscientist (Ledoux 1996).

Research on emotional processing in an experiential therapy was revealing in terms of the value of consciousness for emotion. *Global distress* was defined as unprocessed emotion with high levels of arousal and low meaningfulness. Distress, fear, shame, and aggressive anger showed evidence for undifferentiated and insufficiently processed emotion. Assertive anger, self-soothing, hurt, and grief were signs of advanced emotion processing (Pascual-Leone and Greenberg 2007). Movement toward grief is impaired when dissociative processes hold sway, and there are many ways we can deflect the process of grieving (Kavaler-Adler 1992). The point is that with increasing differentiation an individual adds complexity to their emotional life, with a consequent relief of distress and increase in the sense of well-being. Dissociation creates less complexity and less emotional meaning, and leaves us more vulnerable to disturbance with stress.

A Note about and Definition of Anxiety

Psychoanalytic theories of affect have been predominantly derived from considerations about anxiety. Novey (1959, p. 95) comments:

> Anxiety is not a typical affect, and a theory of anxiety
> is not a theory of affect. It is more than likely that it is a
> connecting link between all the other affects, and there
> is reason to suspect that the energies of many, if not all,

the other affects may be translated into anxiety or may emerge from what had been an affect state of anxiety. In view of the special problems related to the operational aspects of anxiety, therefore, a general theory of affect cannot be based upon the particular unique characteristics of this affect alone.

Anxiety is the physiologic leading edge of not-yet-felt feelings and not-yet-thought thoughts that threaten to unacceptably alter implicit or explicit reality. As such, when implicitly held knowledge or unconscious emotion is stirring, we can experience physiologic distress, complete with a circulating chorus of adrenalin, telling us to pay attention and notice there's a disturbance in our mind. A panic attack occurs when the adrenalin becomes excessive, and this may be precipitated by a particularly intense need to both feel the feeling and not feel the feeling when there is a failure of traditional mechanisms to resolve internal conflict (Moore and Fine 1990). If healthy, we work things out and feel unfettered. If neurotic, we work some things out but may metaphorically shoot ourselves in the foot as part of the effort. Anxiety is thus an amplifier of a feeling. There is shame-anxiety, anger-anxiety, and so on. From a cognitive neuroscience perspective, anxiety is a lesser version of fear, and represents an appraisal for the anticipation of danger; anxiety disorders occur when there is no real danger (Shin and Liberzon 2010). Since cognitive neuroscience doesn't include work with a dynamic unconscious, this burdens cognitive neuroscience theory with the need for a workaround for unconscious process.

Samantha, whom you met in Chapter 4, eventually began to develop consciousness for the somatic states that were precursors for feeling her feelings, not just having logical feelings, as she put it. One weekend she developed chest pain and nausea. She became frightened. Her husband advised her that given what she had been doing, she was probably not medically ill but simply anxious. She was startled by the realization. She considered the context of her experience and realized he was correct. In session with her the day after, we talked about adrenalin, chest anatomy, muscle physiology, and muscle cramping from breath holding. She now had consciousness for the functioning of her body as related to feeling states. She needed a cognitive education about the basis for feeling a feeling. The decrease in overall worry was palpable.

Emotion and Pain

Many patients with trauma histories have problems with physical pain, numbness, or hypersensitivity to pain. Pain affect is different than pain sensation (Rhudy, 2000). A frightened patient in physical pain called me back after a phone intervention to tell me that he had finally calmed down and that when that happened his pain felt much more manageable. Pain affect is encoded in the anterior cingulate cortex (Rainville, Duncan, Price, and Bushnell 1997), the same anterior brain organ in Paul Frewen's study showing decreased emotional awareness and decreased emotional adaptability in PTSD. Pain affect and pain sensation are potentially dissociable because they are mediated by the anterior cingulate and somatosensory cortex, respectively. It's also true that short-term working memory, which is hippocampally facilitated, can play a role in ameliorating pain affect when the patient is adequately prepared beforehand (Ploghaus, Narain, Beckmann, Clare, Bantick, Wise, Matthews, Nicholas, Rawlins, and Tracey 2001; Ploghaus, Tracey, Gati, Clare, Menon, Matthews, Nicholas, and Rawlins 1999). Hippocampal-associated knowledge can mediate activation of stress responses (Preuessner et al. 2008) and deactivate limbic system emotional responses through inhibition of the hypothalamic-pituitary axis. We can willfully suppress a stress response to some degree.

When I worked as a family physician, I unknowingly made use of this reality in working to overcome needle phobias by resting the sharp end of the needle on somebody's forearm and having them talk with me about what they actually felt, right in that moment. (There was a safe enough trusting relationship with me that my patients could allow this. Psychotherapy is little different in this regard.) By focusing on the sensation of the pain, rather than the emotional hijacking by pain affect, they learned that if they anticipated having the needle pierce their skin on the count of three, they could control their behavior and reactions. The fact was, as they discovered, I inserted the needle on the count of two, and they could not discern the sensation of the insertion from the sensation of the needle just resting on their skin! "Doc, you said three but you didn't put the needle in?!" This created a teachable moment about fear of pain versus pain sensation. I have come to appreciate that what's important is the clinical assessment of an emotional state in an adult and how it involves physiological, hard-wired emotional patterns, modified over time by experience, interacting with activated associated patterns of thinking and appraising a scene (Greenberg and Pavio 1997; Oatley, Keltner, and Jenkins 2006; Sroufe 1996). We cannot follow paths of emotional healing without a healthy look at appraisals of emotional experience and the associated deeply felt and lived meanings.

Affects, Feelings, and Emotions as Probes for Dissociative Experience

From a psychodynamic psychotherapy perspective, sorting emotional experience into a tripartite model of linked concepts (affect, feelings, emotions) provides a heuristic perspective from which dissociative processes can be probed. Dissociation's influence on emotional experience can be explored through understanding its tendency to unlink normally associated elements of experience or to prevent linking from taking place, and then maintain the nonintegrative constellation. In some circumstances, dissociative processes can be accessed by focusing on processes related to somatized affect (e.g., pelvic pain, vestibulitis, pudendal burning, low back pain), nondescript but felt sensations (feelings) that have not been associated with an emotion (chest pressure, throat pressure, and difficulty swallowing), and named emotions without associated content ("I feel sad and have been crying but I don't know why. It makes me feel crazy."). Attention to somatic states as a focus of interest often leads to emotional expression (Ogden, Minton, and Pain 2006). The bodily state acts as a kind of physiological screen, much like a psychoanalytic screen memory, from behind which raw emotional content can emerge, if it is only noticed and focused on. This is illustrated in the case work in a later chapter on the negative therapeutic reaction and in the following vignette.

Marla was a consultant now, rather than an employee of a large agency, and the clothing she wore to her therapy sessions had changed from business suits to casual—shorts and a series of T-shirts from one of the scenic locations she visited as asides from her business trips. She hardly ever called attention to what she wore, but on one particular day I thought she would, until she pulled down the collar of her crew neck shirt, rather than pointing to it, and said: "I thought I might ask you to put on your medical hat. I've got this rash, and it really itches badly." She let go of the collar, but the image of thickened, dry, nearly scaly, angry, red skin, washboard layers of flesh, stayed in my mind. An eczematous reaction. High-potency steroids. Yes, my medical mind was still intact. But why did she have a rash, now?

"How long have you had it?" I asked.

"Since last session. It started the next day really, but the itch started not too long after I left the office."

"Sounds like an allergy to the session," I said with seriousness. She looked down, hiding her eyes, shame-laden. She caught herself quickly, and yet her face had changed. "I've started to remember some things, some things about the gang rape. I know we've talked about it before, but this stuff is new. I don't know how to talk about it with you." I replied gently and said, "I know how much you hate to discover new layers of your experience. Tell me what you've learned so far." She rubbed her chest.

It was another half an hour before she was able to tolerate knowing the feeling and thinking that went along with the memory. Her older brother had invited her to go fishing with his friends. They all piled into the van. She was excited. She didn't get to go many places, and in the summer her home was too dangerous to hang out. Her brothers were bored enough that they often abused her as a distraction. They had been especially abusive since her father had stopped abusing her (because he had died). As they barreled down the road, her excitement about going fishing was truncated by a wide movement from her brother's arm as he slapped her across the left side of her face. She was suddenly startled and terrified. They never did go fishing.

She had remembered the gang rape some five years into this nine-year therapy. Now something else had come to consciousness. She was afraid to tell me. We talked about her fear. Would I hurt her, too? Would I be disgusted by her? How could I listen to her and not react more? Why didn't I show more expression on my face? What was I hiding? Did it excite me, too? Her sexual excitement disgusted her. Would I change suddenly like her brother, like her father, and be somebody else? Would I surprise her with a slap? If I tried to hurt her, would she try to hurt me? Could she hurt me?

She sobbed in the way she had many times before. She did not simply cry. Large, full tears ran off her face as fast as they could flow. Sometimes I heard them hit the leather chair as she leaned forward to take another tissue from the box she habitually moved right in front of her on the ottoman. I could feel the rage inside me, the rage I understood must still have been inside her, as I thought how good it was that her brother lived in another city. I didn't want to test my fantasy of killing him. Was my murderousness truly just "in the countertransference"?

A week later, she told me the rash stopped itching just after the session. And yesterday, there was no sign of it. She never did call her internist. It had helped to remember she had been sodomized, face down, chest in the grass. It had helped to talk. For the first time there was a felt and coherent narrative of this story, terribly and miserably alive with feeling and sensations in a body that first told the story without words.[3]

As a result of this work, she had begun to sense the rage inside herself. She was frightened. It felt "too big, suicidal, and homicidal," she said in affectively bland emotionless speech.

"Where was your brother, when the sodomy started?"

"He was first. He showed them what to do. He showed them what my father had taught him."

---

[3] The fibromyalgia that had been diagnosed by her internist and rheumatologist also eventually resolved with psychotherapy.

These scenes sadly illustrate the link between mind and body, the symbolization of conflict between knowing and not knowing, shame, rage, sadness, more. She told her story, and here I tell hers and a little of mine. We all tell our stories, one way or the other, however we can, with words and bodies.

The word *somatization* is a sterile shadow of the angry, red, swollen folds of skin on her chest. The therapeutic modes of action desomatized the embodied affect, the prefeelings, until they were felt. The shame and rage in her body, the emotions, were named and the healing work continued with a comprehensive new narrative filled with all the elements of the BASK model (Braun, 1988) (behavior, affect, sensation, and knowledge), which roughly describe the dimensions of experience in a narrative when there is full integration.

In this vignette, no special technique like hypnosis was applied. My clinical preference is to reserve special techniques for impasses or situations that require rapid resolution of some tension as a matter of safety. I'm of the opinion that my patients gain strength and confidence in their ability to self-right after discovery of something painful when it occurs as they think and feel through their experience in conversation with me rather than in a moment where I "do" something to or for them. I have no proof, but my intuition is that this message to my patients about their own strength is a factor in keeping people out of the hospital.

The entry into Marla's story lay in the recognition of her somatic shame reaction and a focus on emotional experience. She didn't know how to tell me about what happened. I heard that not as inability but as painful reluctance based on her fear that my feelings toward her would change if I knew what she knew or felt what she felt. We learned that she believed I would see her as disgusting because of the involuntary sexual arousal that occurred with her rape, a reactivity we had worked on for a while. She survived these scenes by changing self-states, becoming hypersexual, and taking charge of the situation when that was possible. Shame, self-hatred, disgust, contempt, anger, rage, terror, sadness, helplessness, hopelessness, and more were endemic to the constellation of stories she told regarding the multigenerational intrafamilial scene of abuse from which she had emerged. Her somatic reaction was the physiologic re-creation of the skin irritation she experienced when she was abused. If I had sent her to a dermatologist rather than explored the meaning of it with her, then we would have been ignoring the story her body was trying to tell us while her verbal mind was unknowing. This kind of knowing is coincident with the anoetic (without external knowledge) (Tulving 1985) primary process core affects that are thought to represent intrinsic unreflective brain knowledge (Panksepp and Biven 2012) and seem roughly equivalent to the level of mentation to which Freud assigned what he called primary process[4] modes of thinking (Laplanche and Pontalis 1967).

Gut Feelings and the Body in Psychotherapy

Marla, with a rash on her chest, implicitly knew all about "gut feelings." This colloquial expression is a way of saying that in each of our very human bodies there are disturbances we recognize as somewhat intuitive and have informational value about the condition of our condition (Newbury 1967). Any physical disturbance we sense has a physiological basis that is directly linked to the centers of emotion in the limbic system of the brain. When it comes to our actual gut, there are in fact both physiological connections that are direct through the wiring of the nervous system and connections that are indirect through the influence of more local and circulating (e.g., adrenalin) hormonal activity.

It's the tenth cranial nerve, X, the vagus nerve, that provides the

---

[4] "The bewildering array of seemingly irrational or meaningless phenomena . . . the concept of primary process embraces such characteristics of unconscious mentation as the disregard of logical connections, the coexistence of contradictions, the absence of a temporal dimension and of negatives, and the use of indirect representation and concretization (imagery)" (Moore and Fine 1990). This description fits nicely with that of trance logic as the juxtaposition of logically incompatible elements of experience without anxiety (Ornel 1959). Primary process as described by Freud holds much of what we describe more specifically in the language of dissociative experience that holds explanatory power that is neither bewildering nor meaningless.

connection to visceral (internal) structures in the neck, chest, and abdomen, and importantly carries some fibers from the autonomic nervous system (ANS). The ANS contributes to the regulation of brain stem–initiated automatic, involuntary control of bodily processes, for example, heart rate and respiratory rate. Autonomics integrate many self-regulating and interacting neural, neuroendocrine, and regulatory behavioral responses that are of interest to us (Porges 1995, 2011). The vagus influences and is influenced by the hypothalamus, the home of the pituitary gland (Sawchenko 1983), a central structure in the hormonal stress response.

Things that happen in the physical brain and things that happen in the physical viscera are linked in a complicated feedback and feedforward manner (Menon and Uddin 2010) that again make it clear the brain has wide and profound connections throughout the body, in particular with the viscera. For example, cholecystokinin (CCK) (cholecyst = gallbladder) and vasoactive intestinal polypeptide (VIP) have receptors near the emotional centers of the brain and in the bowel. Stress creates watery diarrhea, which is the province of VIP, and stress also changes CCK levels and may decrease small bowel rates of peristalsis (Cao, Wu, Han, and Wang, 2005).[5] Centrally, CCK-4 is panicogenic (Kellner, Wiedemann, Yassouridis, Levengood, Guo, Holsboer, and Yehuda 2000) and induces states of fear and anxiety, as well as neural activation of fear circuitry in the amygdala,[6] insular cortex, cerebellum, brain stem, and anterior cingulate cortex (Shin and Liberzon 2010). In addition, gastrin, a hormone released in the stomach that induces acid secretion and has other local effects (Giles, Mason, Humphries, and Clark 1969), also has an active neuropeptide, gastrin-releasing peptide (GRP) that has major roles in the gastrointestinal tract, including the release of insulin and other gut hormones, as well

---

[5] Medical lore speaks to the experience of physicians in noting that gallbladder attacks are often associated with emotional distress.

[6] The amygdala is a bilateral brain organ in the limbic system and behaves like a sentry that sounds an alarm when danger is perceived. We considered the amygdala in Chapter 2 and we'll look at it in more detail in Chapter 6 on fear and depersonalization.

as in thermoregulation, anxiety, and peristalsis (Gonzalez, Moody, Igarashi, Ito, and Jensen 2008). Additionally, GRP plays a role in the stress response, amygdalar activity, memory formation (Chaperon et al. 2012), consolidation of hippocampal memory (GRP-receptor) (Dantas, Luft, Henriques, Schwartsmann, and Roesler 2006), and in the interruption of neural processes that allow forgetting of emotionally traumatic experience (Dudai 2003). Disordered eating, gastrointestinal hormone analogs in the central nervous system, and stress eating all help us make sense out of the finding that there is a high incidence of abuse in people who present for treatment of obesity (Kubzansky, Bordelois, Jun, Roberts, Cerda, Bluestone, and Koenen 2014). This is a neurobiological reality that weight control clinics must confront. To be sure, regardless of the psychodynamics of abuse, obesity presents its own biologically driven homeostasis that requires a multipronged approach to this complex set of issues.

The Body Is Part of the Mind

Mind is a more inclusive concept than the physical limitations of a central nervous system, a brain. The body has been the missing link in many failed treatments where going beyond words seemed impossible. Just adding a somatic perspective to thinking about things dissociative, or even just things human, changes the landscape of a treatment for the better.

Freud said that the ego was "first and foremost a body-ego" (Freud 1923, p. 27); more recently Damasio has presented a coherent argument that extended and expanded consciousness takes the body as an orienting roadmap in developing a core sense of self (Damasio 1999). Panksepp also ties his affective neuroscience perspective to bodily states (Panksepp 1998). Cozolino has argued persuasively regarding the neurobiological mechanisms underlying the therapeutic action of psychotherapy (Cozolino 2002), as has A. N. Schore (Schore 1994, 2003), and these clinicians recognize the importance of the body in what they have conjured as a "top-down and bottom-up" perspective regarding cerebral insights in tension with somatic experiencing as important in healing. I have found these kinds of perspectives useful in psychotherapy, but there are limits to the utility of any theoretical persuasion. To the extent that neuroscientific information is used to shore up positions of already established psychotherapy principles, for example, transference, neuroscience is incredibly interesting but not indispensable. What I want to know is how does neuroscience change what happens in a psychotherapy session? How is neuroscience indispensable to the practice of psychotherapy?

Somatotopic maps, those funny-looking bodily artistic renderings that tell us how much neural real estate is dedicated to function of the lips versus the kneecap (big lips, tiny knees), are found all over the brain and are fundamental to sensory processing (Kass 1997). Multiple areas of brain have their own somatotopic organizations and can thus more easily communicate with each other. Research into perception of what actually is real vs. the construction of a cognitively meaningful internal representation of that reality (Longo, Azanon, and Haggard 2009) showed that there is variation in somato-representation with changes in posture. I have learned that asking my patients to stand (experiencing the gravitational weight of their body) while speaking about a particularly meaningful subject, when they have had an apparently emotionally flat connection to it, can change their experience of the subject and increase their emotional connection. Knowledge of somatotopic mapping and shifts in somato-representation with change in posture provides a neat and simple aid to psychotherapy. This is a simple example of relevance. More profound is that the presence of somatotopic maps in diverse regions of the brain teaches us to maintain inclusion of embodied consciousness as a path through which we can probe a mind for psychologically relevant associations by speaking to the language of the body. Somatotopic maps are not just found all over the cortex, there are maps in the cerebellum and its midline vermis (Manni and Petrosini 2004) (linking emotion and movement), the insula (Menon and Uddin 2010) (linking emotion and the viscera, in particular disgust), and the periaqueductal grey area (Denton, McKinley, Farell, and Egan 2009) (related to nonconscious emotional reactions), among other locations. The bottom line in relation to psychotherapeutic utility is that attending to and pursuing the sensations of movement, gut feelings, and even fleeting, barely worth mentioning somatic experiences that somehow get mentioned can be pursued through focusing on the sensation (Gendlin 1978).

Stomach Feelings Open a Clinical Avenue of Exploration

One of the powerful benefits of working with somatic experience as a gateway to additional emotional content in a person's mind is what I think of as psychotherapeutic ratification. In the practice of hypnosis, there is the experience of trance ratification that occurs when a person becomes aware of a nonconscious occurrence of movement in their body like an experience of involuntariness of action with arm levitation. This is an experiential validation of the power of their nonconscious mind and a kind of proof of both their hypnotizability and their capacity to work hypnotically (Hammond, 1990). Likewise, when making emotional and intellectual connections on a visceral level in psychotherapy, the value of the process can be ratified and a clinical alliance more quickly established. Knowing that the body is part of the mind is the essence in this approach.

For example, in her very first session, Jackie, a middle-aged woman, complained of increasingly intense stomach upset as she talked about her childhood. She'd had this stomach feeling before, and she didn't like it. She usually tried to ignore it or distract herself as a way to make it go away. As we talked, it got worse. She was visibly uncomfortable. Her face began to redden—not a blush, but a hue. I asked her if she would be interested in learning something more about the stomach feeling. She agreed. I suggested that she focus on the feeling and let it intensify. She described an intense nauseous, empty feeling in the pit of her stomach and began to cry. Increased focus on the feeling led to a "floaty" experience, and while she was still able to communicate, I helped her break off the focus, aware that her mild depersonalization experience indicated overwhelming anxiety. As she decompressed from the anxiety, we talked about how the floaty feeling had been a regular part of her life for years. In social gatherings she nearly always felt floaty, and she had the experience of not really being present while she watched herself interact and be social. She had made the connection between anxiety and floaty feelings for the first time. Her depersonalization had been persistent and its significance was not known to her.

Twenty weekly visits later, she reported that since the previous session she had "hit the wall." Though she had wondered why former therapy attempts had been so superficial, she now thought that in having remembered that she had been sexually molested by a member of her extended family, she was clear that she had to either shut down and talk about everyday issues or quit therapy. Then she said with the nervous laughter that was a personal signature, "that isn't something that is really an option if I am going to change."

Jackie spoke of a kind of sensing of something in her mind, something without words, and wondered how we would ever talk about it. I asked her to describe the sensing. She drew a blank. I suggested that she just sit and focus on the blank feeling, try and get comfortable with it, and see what she noticed. She became tearful after about two minutes of silence, during which she had closed her eyes. She said that she couldn't talk about what had come into her mind because it made no sense and she didn't know if it was true. She said there weren't any words, but there were images. How could she talk about something that might be a lie? I responded, "Whether you know it's true or not, it's still something in your mind, and the more controversial it is, the more your mind will spend time and energy trying to figure it out." I asked what might be in the way of her prefacing what she might say with the words: "This might or might not be true, but it is in my mind."

"Do you know those cartoons with classical music where the cat chases the mice?" she asked. I did, and said so. She continued, "I got sexually aroused when I saw one a few years ago. I don't know why I am telling you this, but it seems like part of what I am thinking about." There was silence. She became red-faced. She went on, "I once bought a Betty Boop calendar for a girlfriend. I opened it to look at it before I gave it to her. Same thing. I couldn't look at it again. I put it away somewhere and never gave it to her."

171

I didn't know where she was going with her associations, and she seemed in pain, not wanting to continue, and clearly not able to stop. After another silence she said, "You know, little children are good targets for someone who is going to abuse a child because they haven't really learned how to speak about what happens to them."

"Yes, small children are vulnerable to being hurt, especially if the people who are supposed to take care of them don't do their job well."

"I just remembered that when I was little, and my parents were fighting, my father would be sleeping on the couch in the living room. I would get up early and watch TV. I would get on the couch with him and snuggle." There was silence. Her eyes were still closed. She became agitated and upset, tears streaming down her cheeks. "How can I say things that might not be true; things that might turn out to be lies?"

"It's important to look at what is in your mind, even if you don't understand it, or can't figure out whether it is a lie, or the truth, or some combination that you will revise later when you understand more about your life."

"I remember my sister telling me, a few years back, something I had forgotten she'd said. It was about my father confiding in her, sometime before he died. She said he had suddenly remarked to her: 'You know, your sister has a goldmine between her legs!'" She burst into tears. A blank feeling had turned out to be something covered with a blankness related to stomach feelings that for a small child might have been in the vicinity of other feelings, sensations that were too young to have words.

Affect Phobia as a Trigger for Dissociation

At this point we've covered a lot of territory about emotion, feelings, and affect as neurobiological givens. We still need more clinical material to flesh out the flexibility inherent in this approach. Jackie was fearful of her feelings. She didn't tolerate having them and ended up depersonalized as a response to her approaching intolerable emotion. Also known as *affect phobia* (McCullough, Kuhn, Andrews, Kaplan, Wolf, Hurley, and Hurley 2003), this is a ubiquitous condition, lasting sometimes for nearly the full duration of DID treatment, though it changes in tenor as affect tolerance increases. When dissociative processes are in full sway, the circuit breaker–like activity of isolation of affect creates an experience of the sudden loss of feeling, like going over a dissociative cliff, and the very memory of having had a feeling often gets lost. Children learn to anticipate the cliff, and then later make use of this knowledge to instigate dissociation, a kind of paradoxical affect regulation. This generically sounds like: "If I scare myself silly, then I'll be so frightened I'll get calm, just like I always do." Provoking a dissociative reaction through misadventure, mishap, conflict, or other catastrophe can become an embedded regulatory behavior. These chaos-creating strategies, leading to a "familiar chaos," are the things that frustrate clinicians, but alas, there is order to this disorderliness, and figuring out the script is useful. To do so a clinician must be tolerant of the chaos, observing it but not participating in it. That sounds like: "You know, this certainly is a bit chaotic for you, something we both noticed last month when you were so upset. The outcome then was for you to end up rather blank, numbed out, and then we pieced together a script of self-regulation. Perhaps we would be wise to speculate about the possibility of a regulating script rather than have you play it out all the way to numbness, if that's what this is. You might be a whole lot better off if we pause the script, and take a look at it. What do you say?"

From this perspective, the self-regulatory nature of something like cutting often becomes visible. An extremely self-destructive patient with a long history of serious overdoses and deep cutting was baffled by my telling her that I had begun to appreciate how she had learned self-hypnosis, "the hard way," by cutting herself. She had just told me how calm she had gotten after she had cut herself in her car immediately prior to her session. She also had just said that she felt like going out and "chopping" herself up. My reply was that I didn't think I could stop her from doing that now, or eventually, if she really wanted to. "No you can't, that's right!" was her emphatic, triumphant reply. This patient expected a battle for power and control over cutting. Instead, I offered to teach her how to enter a hypnotic state without needing to cut herself.

My suggestion did not deprive her of soothing; it provided a substitute method to enter a sought-after state through a less humiliating and dangerous pathway. My attunement to her desperation left me in touch with helplessness, sadness, and loneliness, a noncombative set of affects. My countertransference urge in response to her walking into my office bleeding was to have her locked up (a sadistic thought). The wish to be controlled, as enactment, was in the transference. She tried to provoke my response according to her script. As a child she had come home from being sexually assaulted, bloodied, and her mother's response had been to be sadistic, calling her a whore and beating her. Sadly, this happened when my patient was a preschool child. Her father and his friends abused her at a neighbor's home. Being aware of the pull to become role responsive (Sandler 1976) as a sadistic transference object meant my holding those urges to become controlling and letting other miserable feelings emerge in my consciousness. She hoped to elicit expected behavioral patterns (Ryle 2001). I was stuck with the loneliness, fear, and the sadness of having to make a hard decision to hospitalize or not, while realizing I could lose my patient, who could lose her life. I could be sued, I would feel ashamed.

I told her that I thought cutting was much less efficient and neat than hypnosis. Wouldn't she prefer hypnosis to calm herself down? She replied, "It really bugs me that you are not trying to control what I am doing but trying to teach me a way to help myself. I don't understand you at all!" It was later in that session when she surprised me by volunteering what I had been thinking peripherally. She said sadly that she thought she used hospitals to escape from the world. I would have used sending her to the hospital to escape, too, from my own intolerable feelings, rather than sitting with them and doing what I asked her to do, develop tolerance for feeling. This woman was escaping from what I only found out years later was ongoing and continuing sexual abuse by her now elderly father for which she had complete amnesia (Middleton et al. 2013), a 50-year history of incest.

Affect phobia is gradually modulated by combinations of the psychotherapeutic discourse, naming feelings and consciousness for associated bodily responses (Monsen, & Monsen 1999; Monsen et al. 1996), self-hypnotic tools to "slow leak" emotions (Kluft 1983, 1989), related hypnotic techniques for controlled and fractionated abreaction (Kluft 2013), EMDR with concomitant self-soothing techniques applied, and variations on somatic experiencing (Ogden, Pain, and Fisher 2006), as noted by my focus on the body as part of the mind. The strategy is to provide a safe enough clinical environment in which a person can feel, but not so safe as to disallow any upset, any safe distress. As Kelly noted, earlier, a clinician who is intolerant of intense emotion is not going to teach a lot of affect tolerance to their patients. Likewise, a clinician who is completely unmoved by their patient's emotional expressions will demonstrate a lack of receptivity that may prompt more and more violent emotional displays from their patient to evoke a response that indicates the clinician can feel the real presence of their real patient with real feelings.

Guided imagery and other strategies may be useful to counter emotional arousal with top-down cortical inhibition of reactivity via absorption to pleasant imagery; grounding with novel, soothing tactile objects; counting exercises to tolerate the feelings, and so on (Boon et al. 2011; Napier 1994; Vermilyea 2000). Fear of feeling also succumbs to uncovering meaningful contexts in which the original sources of dysphoria are identified and placed in the context of a person's autobiographical narrative (Foa and Kozak 1986).[7] Above all else, a feeling of safety in the relationship with the therapist must be established for any of these techniques to be of use. The trajectory of a treatment always needs to be toward safety (Brand 2001).

---

[7] Though I heartily endorse emotion processing as useful in the treatment of complex PTSD and the dissociative disorders, I feel much more cautious about applying exposure therapy techniques to this population because of the risk os overstimulation and flooding that can create safety issues and retraumatization, especially in an outpatient setting. Anecdotally, this may be one reason that exposure therapy is less used in treatment of PTSD in Veterans Administration hospitals, even though it is an approved therapy.

Emotional Fluency

I have a somewhat yellowed and tattered copy of Roget's Thesaurus sitting on a book stand of reference volumes within my reach as I work with my patients. This particular thesaurus has accumulated little colored tabs in places where primary emotions and their synonyms are listed. When the timing is right, out comes my trusty thesaurus, and depending on the clinical moment either I or my patient will read out the synonyms for an emotion word like anger. The contrasts in synonyms for anger versus rage shows the difference between anger as energetic protest and rage that destroys first (clears a safety perimeter) and then looks around afterward at what's happened. For people who are especially tending toward the alexithymic end of the spectrum, I pull out some paper and we construct a hierarchy of the relevant synonyms in rank order, sorting by intensity, and see where they fit on the feeling spectrum. This ranking and extension of nuance to the experience of anger is essential to modulating an individual's responses to stress. With more words, and the admonition to find the word that matches the scene before taking any action, there is both a requirement to stop the impulse to act and a new categorization of reactivity that can make sense. That is not to say somebody will change their life the first time they use this strategy, but change does eventually happen. If not the first or second try, then the third or fourth works just as well to put a smile of self-efficacy on somebody's face if you have predicted from the start that each person finds their own trajectory for this kind of learning, as they are ready. This cognitive-psychodynamic strategy works well for anger, sadness, guilt, shame, and more. The clinician can enjoy being creative in applying this in his or her own office.

A Language for Emotion

Words are symbols—shortcuts that convey the meaning of personal experience when formulated and spoken with care, and sometimes with more than a little passion. The language of emotion is often conveyed by the poets who teach us imagery to tell the story of that for which the simple use of words may feel inadequate. For

Rachel, whom you will read about in Chapters 8 and 9, words were not trusted. At one particularly difficult time of her treatment, she proposed we find a nonword means of conveying what was in her mind, but only in pictures. She had done loads of artwork, but that hadn't reached the level of intensity she needed. She proposed music, and when we played some, she wanted to do modern dance. We video-taped her dance and her discussion with me after she watched the video. Though unusual, it created a rapid and profound sense of embodiment that broke through her chronic depersonalization. This mode of reiterative communication was very helpful and made all kinds of neurobiological sense, given what we know about the cerebellum and emotion (Lemche et al. 2008). As she put it, "You can't dance if you're not in your body."

The material covered in this chapter puts psychotherapeutic flesh on the bones of the neurobiology of emotion and makes plain the central role of the body in the intensive psychotherapy of the treatment of persistent dissociative processes. We looked at a balance of research and vignettes, moving back and forth, to show how immediately applicable is a knowledge of the neurobiological mediation of experience in psychotherapy. This is the story of the neurobiology of a mind, not simply a brain, alone. The body is part of the mind, and the psychotherapeutic work here is part of a relationship between two people. We have to hold this reality close or the work of an intensive psychotherapy is not tolerable. No amount of knowledge or technique can substitute for the earned trust that flows in both directions in a clinical dyad. This is a cognitive-psychodynamic approach, and it relies on the growth of relatedness between two people who both have to tolerate their feelings to make a go of it. If it's all about the relationship (John and Lambert 2011), then it's all about feelings. In the next chapter, the focus is on fear, an experience that is of a degree of intensity beyond what we commonly call anxiety.

Chapter 6

Fear and Depersonalization

THE TREATMENT OF DEPERSONALIZATION HAS BEEN DAUNTING, WITH A number of serious researchers coming to the conclusion that psychodynamic therapy seems to work (Sierra, Baker, Medford, and David 2005; Simeon and Abugel 2006), but without any certainty about why that might be the case or the specific salient issues in the psychodynamic realm. In this chapter I build a case for understanding depersonalization as arising from catastrophic levels of fear. I show how fear is neurobiologically different from anxiety and intimately involved in the capacity to perceive bodily sensation, and I discuss how this viewpoint can guide the kind of interventions made in treatment.

Sustained and repetitive fear create a profound insult to a person's ability to go on being (Winnicott 1960b). Profound neglect also seems to provoke a crisis of being, with efforts to self-stimulate through rocking or self-mutilation, the last alternative to emotional deadness (van der Kolk, Perry, and Herman 1991). That deadness, in turn, can be the last alternative to profound fear. Kelly, whom you met in Chapter 5, is clear that when she realized as a child that her mother didn't "get" her and her sensibilities, had an "avalanche of fear" that her mother would emotionally abandon her; that fear, in turn, "triggered my depersonalization." This is a good example of how disrupted attachment can unleash fear (Lyons-Ruth, Yellin, Melnick, and Atwood 2005). When depersonalization enters the scene, it functions as an unconscious affect regulator. Given our the discussion in the last chapter about distinctions between affect, feelings, and emotion, it's not a big leap to appreciate that if a body feels unreal or detached, feelings can't really register or be felt. No feelings, no pain, no fear . . . no problem.

What is a catastrophic level of fear like? We could ask child-soldier Ishmael Beah, who was unable to turn off his mind.

> I had passed through burnt villages where dead bodies of men, women, and children of all ages were scattered like leaves on the ground after a storm. Their eyes still showed fear, as if death hadn't freed them from the madness that continued to unfold. I had seen heads cut off by machetes, smashed by cement bricks, and rivers filled with so much blood that the water had ceased flowing. Each time my mind replayed these scenes I increased my pace. Sometimes I closed my eyes so hard to avoid thinking, but the eye of my mind refused to be closed and continued to plague me with images. My body twitched with fear, and I became dizzy. I could see the leaves swaying, but I couldn't feel the wind. (Beah 2007, p. 50)

I have little doubt that this kind of knowledge was in part what moved Seneca to write:"Show me a man who is not a slave; one is a slave to lust, another to greed, another to ambition, and all men are slaves to fear" (Seneca, Epistle XLVII).[1]

Anxiety, Fear, and Dissociative Processes

How are fear and anxiety related to one another? It has taken more than a century to sort out the issues. Darwin's volume on emotion, first published in 1872 (Darwin 1998), was an important first step, a truly extraordinary scientific treatise oriented to the cognitive aspect of emotion in its approach, highly detailed, and tied to his theory of evolution as he proposed that emotions also evolved over time and had become more nuanced and sophisticated while retaining primitive characteristics. Darwin followed this contribution up with his pioneering observations regarding infants and fear almost two decades before Freud originated the psychoanalytic method (Darwin, 1877). Although Darwin influ-

---

[1] See http://www.stoics.com/seneca_epistles_book_1.html'XLVII1

enced Freud in many ways, his notions about affective development in childhood did not find their way into Freud's thinking. Walter Cannon, who studied fear (fight or flight) a few years later, was hot on the trail of the relationship between fear and adrenalin (Cannon 1914). Freud did not take time out to meld that work with his own, which is curious, given his wish for a scientific psychology and his continuing interest in the study of hormones (Freud 1895, 1905). What he did do was try to make sense of anxiety as a distinct clinical phenomenon.

For Freud, anxiety was finally thought of in two main respects: the kindling of a sense of danger, using the moment of birth as a model of danger to life, or a small signal anxiety that unconsciously told us to get ready for some bigger anxiety that was just around the corner (Freud 1926). Prior to this perspective, anxiety was considered within psychoanalysis from a variety of perspectives. To begin with, it was part and parcel of what had been thought of as the "strangulated affect" at the core of hysteria, which required abreaction to relieve it (Breuer and Freud 1895). There was also the anxiety neurosis (Freud 1900), a diagnosis Freud was initially enamored with that linked coitus interruptus with a transformation of libido into anxiety. But Freud's notions continued to evolve. In 1917 he spelled out his view of hysterical anxiety as having no discernible relation to danger (Freud 1917). In 1920, he proposed that trauma was the result of piercing the stimulus barrier, allowing a surfeit of stimulation into the psychic interior (Freud, 1920). One commentator has noted this constant shifting about in terms of models: "Freud's theory of anxiety is an illustration of how very far it is possible to go by making assumptions which cover without contradiction what cannot, at the given time, be understood—a successful exercise in ambiguity" (Compton 1972). This is a place where Freud's habit of abandoning one theory in favor of another, without reconciliation, did not serve well. He worked heuristically and without apology when he changed his mind.

Yet we need to get clear on the difference between anxiety and fear to make headway with the affective phenomena found in dissociative disorders. In Chapter 5 I proposed a definition of *anxiety* as the physiological leading edge of a not-yet-felt feeling, or a not-yet-thought

thought, that threatens to unacceptably alter implicit or explicit reality. The physiology of anxiety is dominated by the biochemistry of adrenalin, which activates physiological systems. This creates a primarily embodied experience to which we attach the name *anxiety*. Affective-cognitive appraisals of the meaning of anxiety and other perceptions rely on recognition and matching processes that are ubiquitous in the hippocampus and amygdala (Fried, MacDonald, and Wilson 1997). Neurons essentially vote via activation if what is presented to them is familiar. It is reasonable to hypothesize that cognitive processes of assimilation and accommodation ensue in this manner and that affective processes are at work in the background simultaneously, given the anatomy involved. Felt anxiety is related to the result of activation of central adrenocorticotrophic hormone at the level of the pituitary (the hypothalamic-pituitary axis) and peripheral adrenalin that causes an accelerated heart and respiratory rate, sweating, muscle tension, and other peripheral effects—the stress response (Horowitz 1986; Yehuda 1998; Yehuda and LeDoux 2007).

When it comes to considering how fear is different from anxiety, all roads of investigation eventually lead to the little inverted dome of cerebral cortex called the insula. We have seen how little curls can make a big difference, and it turns out that little brain organs are the same. Located at the juncture of the temporal, parietal, and frontal lobes, the insula plays a role in consciousness, emotion processing, and interoception, which is the ongoing sense of our "gut" responses (Critchley, Wiens, Rotshtein, Ohman, and Dolan 2004). With such an important set of integrative functions, what better place for the insula to be located than next to three major cortical areas? Location is important for this piece of neural real estate not just for the local geography but because of the robust connections it affords with wide-open access to the amygdala, that sentry standing guard against threat, and the thalamus, the major switching station for neural connections related to sensory and motor processing between body and brain, and pain perception, among other functions (Yin et al. 2011). The insula is in the perfect place to mediate awareness for somatic experience. Big things come in small packages.

An emphasis on attention to somatic states pays dividends in thinking about the difference between the experiences of anxiety and fear. One way they differ has to do with the processing of the cues that trigger them. To be frightened, filled with fear, is about perceivable danger and invariably involves the activation of the adrenalin-related neuroendocrine pathways as well as neural cascades of emergency circuitry systems (LeDoux 2012). It is hard to think clearly when frightened. Explicit fear cues activate the amygdala. Nonspecific cues activate a related structure, the bed nucleus of the striaterminalis, "which in turn activates hypothalamic and brain stem target areas involved in specific signs of fear or anxiety. Because the nature of this information may be less specific than that produced by an explicit cue, and of much longer duration, activation of the bed nucleus of the striaterminalis may be more akin to anxiety than to fear" (Davis 1998). The bed nucleus helps us be alert to danger. Anxiety is useful to prepare us for dangerous settings. To understand more of the difference between anxiety and fear, we have to dig a little deeper into functional neuroanatomy.

Phelps and colleagues (Phelps, O'Connor, Gatenby, Gore, Grillon, and Davis 2001) add an important piece to the puzzle by describing how the left amygdala can be activated by a cognitive-linguistic representation of fear in a nonexperiential fear-evoking situation, for instance, when people are told about a potential adverse outcome. Visual stimuli, however, are more likely to activate the right amygdala (Phelps et al. 2001). It is well known that symptom provocation activates the right amygdala and deactivates Broca's area, creating a fear-laden speechlessness (Rauch et al. 1996). Fear makes it harder to express thoughts with words. Some trauma memories may have visual coordinates but no verbal script. Fear makes it harder to think, whereas during anxiety worried thoughts are the norm.

Thus, neurobiological evidence points in the direction of there being a specific right amygdala–mediated fear response that interrupts the process of narrative formation, and a less intense left amygdala–mediated linguistic and intellectual response (LeDoux 1996; Phelps et al. 2001) that I'm inclined to also think of as anxiety or worry. Anxiety and fear seem to be neurobiologically different. Fear has powerful subcortical cascades of reactivity that can change our capacity to perceive and process emotional states and personal narrative, whereas anxiety is much more about a worried, language-bound left brain and a more emotional embodied right brain no longer working together in the presence of peripheral release of adrenalin and a racing heart. It's not that anxiety has no somatic markings or never leads to fear, but it is distinguishable in the manner described.

Is this distinction between fear and anxiety clinically useful, or is this just one of those interesting neuroscience things? Consider that states of anxiety have more verbal content and are more approachable via linguistic modes of interaction, either cognitive or psychodynamic. Fear, in contrast, is less likely to have verbal signifiers associated with it, is more likely to have both visual and somatic representations, and might be more effectively approached via nonverbal means, for example, somatic focus of attention, hypnosis, or EMDR. If you are not getting anywhere with a problem filled with anxiety, consider that you might be working with fear, not worry, and change the approach as neuroscience would guide you.

Attending to nonverbal somatic modes of experience can also be helpful in fostering efforts at soothing. Ongoing anxiety may respond to cognitive interventions more readily. Approaching modulation of fear experience by teaching hypnosis can be highly effective. Just the experience of entering trance and feeling relaxation in a body is reassuring and self-reinforcing each time it's done. That's a powerful way to imbue self-confidence and a sense of efficacy. Teaching a standard self-hypnotic technique with an open-eyed method can allow somebody to be stressed out at work and relax. This is empowering. In general, I wouldn't want to do this work with traumatized, dissociated patients without skills in hypnosis. EMDR can be too activating, but the supplementation of EMDR with hypnosis and guided imagery often makes it quite tolerable.

Neurobiology has even more to offer a clinician interested in fear and anxiety. Consider that the amygdala potentially teaches us an important lesson about our emotional life in that it is known to activate in regard to intense negative and positive emotional experiences (Hamann and Mo 2002; Metcalfe and Jacobs 1996; Phan, Wager, Taylor, and Liberzon 2004; as cited in Shin and Liberzon 2010). The clinical significance of this is that if we open our patients to intense emotion, good or bad, the intensity may leave them flooded with negative experience, even if they started out with a positive emotional set. People become affect phobic (McCullough et al. 2003) when intensity is unmanageable. It's like once the valve is opened on the pipeline to emotional intensity, both pleasurable and painful intensity flows. This is part of why our patients often avoid all emotional intensity when they are dissociative or posttraumatic. Emotional intensity in and of itself is feared. When emotional capacity increases, it is an achievement and a burden. More capacity means more impact when new traumatic experience is explored. Less dissociation may mean much more emotional pain to manage. The effect of this on treatment is profound when healing produces increased vulnerability. It is worth warning people about this, casually, and then bringing it up again if it seems to be happening. That approach is stabilizing of their new experience.

Fear extinction is what we all hope for after we've been scared. After a while, we're hoping to feel safe again because the danger is over; from a neural processing point of view, this means we hope our fear reaction will go the way of the dinosaurs: extinction. Failure of fear extinction (Milad et al. 2009; Milad, Rauch, Pitman, and Quirk 2006), in my experience, is often secondary to lack of access to persistent dissociative process related to compartmentalized experience. This makes the treatment of complex PTSD and dissociative disorders more complicated than the cognitive intervention for panic I described (Weekes 1969/1990) in the chapter on affect and dissociative processes. The persistence of PTSD is hypothesized to be related to higher responsivity, heightened conditionability, and reduced extinction of aversive responses (Peri, Ben-Shakhar, Orr, and Shalev 2000).

Part of the picture of failed fear extinction, as well as the source of some confusion in clinical presentations of PTSD is that there is both a hyperaroused, undermodulated, and sometimes flooded profile in PTSD, and a hypoaroused, overmodulated, and often numb profile in the dissociative subtype (Lanius et al. 2010). This means that some people with massive PTSD present with apparent placid exteriors; in fact, their PTSD may be missed in a clinical exam. Testing for dissociation in the face of even routine PTSD ought to be considered essential (Brand, Armstrong, and Loewenstein 2006).

Given the way emotional intensity is avoided in PTSD, it's useful to have a model of what the brain is doing when affect phobia rules the day. A useful approach to considering the neural management of intense emotion is rendered intelligible by a two systems approach— the"cool" and "hot" system model of memory advanced by Metcalfe and Jacobs.

> We proposed that the "cool" hippocampal memory system records, in an unemotional manner, well-elaborated autobiographical events, complete with their spatial-temporal context. In contrast, the "hot" amygdala system responds to unintegrated fragmentary fear-provoking features of events, which become hooked directly to fear responses. The hot system is direct, quick, highly emotional, inflexible, and fragmentary. The cool system is cognitive and complex, informationally neutral, subject to control processes, and integrated. Hot-system memories are stimulus-driven and entail a sense of reliving—more like simple responses (often fearful) than like recollections. Cool-system memories are narrative, recollective, and episodic. (1996, p. 1)

Metcalfe and Jacob are clear that the "cool" system does not always function properly. We now know that hippocampal and amygdalar coordination breaks down under stress (Rauch et al. 1996; Shin, Rauch, and Pitman 2006). The functional expressive aphasia of stress is potentially reflected in the impaired capacity for narrative creation and loss of hippocampal short-term memory capacities with decreased hippocampal volumes related to stress (Vermetten et al. 2006). Hippocampal time-keeping is also impaired, and suggests a role in the generation of "trauma time" misattributions that lead to reacting to the present as if one were living in the past, a phenomenon that is regularly seen during flashbacks or normal waking periods for people with dissociative disorders. Trauma time issues can contribute to failure of fear extinction.

Metcalfe and Jacob's incisive logic and accessible language help us appreciate the underpinnings of the trauma response and reactions to increasing stress or fear:

> It follows that at low levels of stress, both the fear evoking features (hot) and the contextual and narrative features (cool) of a situation show enhanced encoding with increasing stress (or arousal). However, at traumatic levels of stress, the cool system becomes dysfunctional, while the hot system becomes hyper-responsive. This means that the encoding under such conditions should be fragmentary rather than spatio-temporally bound, replete, and coherent. At high levels of stress the individual will focus selectively and, at traumatic levels, exclusively, on the fear evoking features that are peculiar to the hot system. These hot features or triggers provoke fear reactions, and condition such reactions to them. Memories and reactions that are attributable to the isolated hot-system encoding may seem irrational both to the individual, and to the therapist, since such fragments are ungrounded by the kind of narrative and spatio-temporal contextual anchors that tie our ordinary experience to reality. Such memories are disturbing, not only because of the direct fear they evoke but also because of their strangeness. (1996, p. 2)

In the recovery from trauma this hot-cool system distinction predicts that emotional memory may have little or no verbal content. However, the hot-system memories do consistently have visual associational content that is linked to function of the amygdala (Vuilleumier, Richardson, Armony, Driver, and Dolan 2004). This is consistent with the well-established qualities of emotional memory and state-dependence (Eich 1987). The bottom line in this discussion is that states of fear are much more likely to involve somatic and sensory encoding of trauma and are less likely to be responsive to cognitive interventions than are states related to anxiety.

The failure to appreciate the differences between fear and anxiety, and the outward placid presentation of people with dissociative regulation of intense emotion, can leave an examiner perplexed as to the origins of behavior. Flatness can be misinterpreted as being associated with psychotic process, especially when a clinician has little experience with self-state activity and a patient is confused by their own behavior, feels disoriented, and has only hidden fear, which has been estranged by dissociative process. It's worth considering what this can look like clinically.

Robert, a man with a sexual addiction, was seen in consultation to assess his failure to progress in treatment. His own work required the maintenance of scrupulous interpersonal boundaries. He was failing at that and deeply frightened by his behavior. He had the experience of "waking up" as "Jack" in the midst of giving anal sex, and the consciousness that was Robert was horrified by what he was doing. Robert had given his sexually addicted self the name of Jack after a former colleague who had died some years before. His therapist felt Robert to be delusional in regard to his state of mind when in the thrall of his addiction. Although Robert did not describe depersonalization or derealization, he did have a dramatic change of state when behaving as Jack and partial amnesia for events. Though confused by what happened, he described how with some mental effort Jack banished Robert from awareness after a brief moment of interference. Robert was frightened and ashamed because Jack behaved in ways that were anathema to Robert's upbringing.

Dissociative processes allowed the compartmentalization of Jack's behavior in a self-state that was mostly isolated from awareness. His therapist viewed talk of Jack as representing psychotic process. This foreclosed the possibility of talking with Robert about Jack's perspectives and motivations, something the patient readily did in the consultation when he easily shifted to Jack's perspective with the simple invitation of my open, nonjudgmental curiosity. "Robert, would you mind if I addressed my next question to Jack? I'm quite interested in his perspective and doubt anybody has ever asked. [He agreed.] Thank you. Jack, it seems that people have not understood what you're about. May I ask you about your views?"

It turned out that Jack was much more emotionally alive than was Robert in general. Robert used obsessional activity to isolate affect (Freud 1909). Obsessional strategies are a poor man's dissociative process. They do their magic by focusing attention on thoughts and actions at the expense of consciousness for emotion. Excessive thinking blocks feeling (Bermond et al. 2006). Exclusion and deflection helped maintain the isolation. Jack could banish Robert's consciousness, with effort. Jack was another way of being Robert, which Robert personified with a name. Robert did not believe he was inhabited by another person. He just found a signifier name to explain his behavior and keep track of it. He had a self-state that was sexually active and emotionally alive. He also had amnesia for his sexual acting out. In DSM-5 the patient would meet criteria for dissociative disorder not elsewhere classified (American Psychiatric Association 2013).

Robert was stuck, in large part because there was no appreciation that his addiction was a zone in which he, as Jack, was actually emotionally alive. Robert's emotional life was held secondary to a diagnostic category. There was a kind of deadness in him that gave him the feeling of being made of cardboard. However, when I met him and shook his hand, his palm was moist, a result of circulating adrenalin. He was quite anxious, probably frightened, though there was neither a facial nor nonverbal hint of it. His addiction seemed to be both a potential effort to heal and a respite from the emotional desert in which Robert lived as a reaction to a family life (and its internalization) that was likewise emotionally desolate. In his case, anxiety and fear about his behavior led to the dissociation of a more alive self-state, which in turn became dismissed as psychotic, with the net result that an experienced clinician was unable to help this patient. An appreciation of the relationship between fear, self-states, and dissociative process opened up the treatment.

The dissociation and compartmentalization of fear and the chronicity of PTSD create an important punch line: PTSD criteria have a dissociative engine under the hood. Intrusions are of nonintegrated experience, dissociative in nature. Avoidance is provoked by intrusions of trauma-related thoughts. Negative alterations in cognition and mood, including constricted affect, partial amnesia, out-of-context persistent trauma-related emotion (e.g., fear, horror) are all dissociative in nature. Problems with arousal and reactivity inconsistent with current levels of safety, that is, failed extinction, are related to a nonintegrated, implicitly understood need to be hyperalert for a danger that no longer exists, dissociated knowledge. PTSD is essentially a kind of dissociative disorder with a trauma criterion tacked on. But trauma is more than just a frightening experience. As we approach the clinical issues posed by depersonalization through considering fear and anxiety, we should pause and think about how we define trauma and appreciate its relation to fear, emotion, and the mind that mediates those experiences.

A Definition of Trauma

What makes a trauma traumatic? What is a trauma, really?

An early and considered definition of *trauma* was "an emotional state of discomfort and stress resulting from memories of an extraordinary, catastrophic experience which shattered the survivor's sense of invulnerability to harm. . . . A catastrophe, the situational prerequisite for the emergence of a trauma, is defined here as an extraordinary event or series of events which is sudden, overwhelming, and often dangerous, either to one's self or significant other(s)" (Figley 1985). The DSM-5) essentially talks of trauma as a stressor:

> The person was exposed to: death, threatened death,
> actual or threatened serious injury, or actual or threatened
> sexual violence, as follows: (1 required) 1. Direct expo-
> sure. 2. Witnessing, in person. 3. Indirectly, by learning

that a close relative or close friend was exposed to trauma. If the event involved actual or threatened death, it must have been violent or accidental. 4. Repeated or extreme indirect exposure to aversive details of the event(s), usually in the course of professional duties (e.g., first responders, collecting body parts; professionals repeatedly exposed to details of child abuse). This does not include indirect non-professional exposure through electronic media, television, movies, or pictures.(American Psychiatric Association, 2013)

In the DSM definition of trauma in PTSD, the notion of trauma is defined around the size of the bang, or the fact of an external event. The architects of this definition had the miserable job of protecting the science behind the PTSD concept while also dealing with the politics of PTSD and criticism that the diagnostic criteria were too loose, resulting in too many claims of PTSD disability. In a study of drive-by school-yard shootings, there was ample evidence that a model of PTSD applies to children as well as adults (Pynoos, Frederick, Nader, Arroyo, Steinberg, Eth, Nunez, and Fairbanks 1987). It is a mystery, though, exactly why some children not at school on the day of a shooting also developed PTSD. Likewise, other research has shown that predisaster factors had more predictive value than an actual traumatic event in the development of PTSD (McFarlane 1988; Karlehagen et al. 1993; Nolen-Hoeksema and Morrow, 1989; as cited in Peleg and Shalev 2006). Clearly, there is something about PTSD that has less to do with an actual event and more to do with who is at the event and what has happened in their lifetime that has accumulated. Yes, normal people break down in combat, but the ones who don't seem to recover from that are those who have antecedent histories of trauma. This is based on my anecdotal observation and questions to Veterans Administration clinicians who have attended my lecture presentations through the years. I have made it a habit to routinely ask about the histories of unresolved cases of PTSD. The straws that accumulate on a camel's back come in all sizes and shapes, so to speak.

We know that specific events are traumatic for some people but not for others. But how can we define *trauma* in a way that takes an individual's characteristics into account? Even a more nuanced definition of trauma leaves us in the same bind: "Psychic trauma occurs when an individual is exposed to an overwhelming event resulting in helplessness in the face of intolerable danger, anxiety, and instinctual arousal" (Eth and Pynoos 1985, p. 38). Intolerable for whom? Tolerance can vary from person to person. If something horrible happens that is tolerated, will it not be traumatic?

In the spirit of providing something psychotherapeutically useful, I propose a working definition of trauma that is consistent with the discourse of this volume and pays attention to what it means to be an individual with a mind and body:

> Traumatic experience has occurred when there has been sudden or cumulative experience that alters the developmental trajectory of an individual through changes in the organization or constitution of their self-states, the ability to have emotional experience, the capacity to think and balance associative and dissociative processes, the capacity to live in relationship with self and others, and the maintenance of an enduring sense of self, all of which is reflected in altered neurobiological function.

I like this definition for several reasons. First, trauma is mostly about the challenge of being a person, not about what happened in the world. Second, the mind of a person is at the center of what it means to have been hurt. Thinking and feeling processes are altered by trauma. Our neurobiology is changed by it. Third, it is the creation of new state-dependent processes (Eich 1987, 1995), perhaps including isolated self-states, maintained by dissociative process, that is part of what generates the PTSD symptom complex as well as the orderly disorder of dissociative adaptations. Self-states are at odds with each other. "I want to know" versus "I don't want to know"; "I want to feel" versus "I don't want to feel." PTSD and DID both describe the scene of a mind at war with itself. These states are a core feature of traumatic experience, even at the level of "simple" PTSD (Berridge and Waterhouse 2003). (Read the spectacularly painful clinical descriptions of soldiers struggling to emerge from trauma under narcosynthesis for a description of their state-dependent experience; Grinker and Spiegel 1945.) Fourth, living in relationship with self and others is inclusive of living in a body and coming into both physical and emotional contact with others. Healing is not complete if these relationships are not truly alive. Fifth, the balance between associative and dissociative processes has been upset. That's what people talk about: "I'm too nervous and frightened to put my thoughts or feelings together." As much as this book is about dissociative processes becoming persistent in the wake of trauma, it is also meant as an implicit treatise on the importance of reestablishing a capacity for association as a central goal of an intensive psychotherapy for persistent dissociative processes. Last, a sense of self is only marginally possible when the activity of isolated semi-autonomous self-states, dissociative or not, cause a person to feel that they can't rely on themselves to be present and accounted for at home or at work. The urgency with which people with PTSD may feel the need to isolate themselves socially or the power with which emotional numbness leaves them feeling like an alien presence in the midst of family can be devastating. All too often this is the result of PTSD for soldiers. Sense of self can be deeply altered as a result of trauma. It's a *person* who has experienced trauma, and it's a *person* who deserves the focus of a definition of trauma. And that person is still afraid. Let's take a look at the clinical presentation of somebody with such fear and depersonalization in the context of DID.

Depersonalization and the Psychodynamics of Mary's "John"

It's hard to absorb the realities of neurobiology and the division of labor in "brain organs" without something to hang your hat on. Toward that end, I'd like to introduce you to John, an alternate self-state of Mary. Mary had several self-states, but John was the only male one. The creation of a male self-state may have unconsciously taken advantage of robust fear-driven depersonalization in Mary, leading to a loss of body sensing. This probably made it easier for her to develop a sense of John having a different body than her, as if being a separate person—the delusion of separateness. For Mary and John, though, this is not as "as if" experience, it is "as is." With depersonalization there would be no somatic perception opposing this sleight-of-mind magical thinking. This is a pseudodelusion, as will be seen shortly, since real delusions don't give way to the incremental pressures of a conversation. In DID, the pseudodelusion of separateness is a regular occurrence and often remains hidden until the therapist is curious about physicality in their patient or hears about a blunt disowning of the person of which a self-state like John is part. The disowning is often mutual: Mary disowns the self-state of John, and John sees himself as separate from Mary. That keeps the emotional and narrative content of John isolated from Mary.

John, who confronted me about my views in the vignette that follows, was probably a creation of psychodynamic realities, neurobiological givens, and especially the advantages that depersonalization created for him to live inside a delusion of separateness. If you can't feel your body because of depersonalization and don't have a sense of being detached from physical reality, and if you have a wish (as an abused woman might) to be a man who can use bluster and aggression to keep people away from you, the delusion of separateness is a parsimonious solution. This perspective is illustrated by a sample from the collection of statements made under the aegis of this delusion that I've heard through the years. "It happened to her, not me! I don't have *those* feelings, she does, the slut." "I don't have feelings at all. Who needs them?" "I don't have those thoughts. I don't have flashbacks, she does." "She just cries in the corner. She's such a cry-baby. I am a separate person and nothing happened to my mind. It means nothing. I don't feel those yucky sensations; it's not my body!" "Nothing bad happened to me, and there is no proof that anything did!" "He used to change at the drop of a hat, and I'm not like that." "I like getting lost in the confusion; it's a lot better than the pain of living in this stupid world of yours!"

When I am confronted by the delusion of separateness, an emotional wall built of sturdy bricks of denial and disavowal and the creative use of the perceptual distortions of depersonalization, my own gut feelings tell me a lot about what is going on. I sometimes need to buy time to figure things out and not take action to challenge my patient's reality too soon. I have found it useful to take an attitude of "Yes, this is a problem, and we're going to have to study it a bit before we come up with something workable to approach it." Often, an exploration of what led to the creation of the problem contains the keys to relieving the pain hidden within the delusion.

John's opening gambit was sexual acting out that nobody could control. Mary, who had the experience that John was separate from her, a not-me self-state, tried to turf the problem of John's acting out to me: "Well, you're the expert here, and you need to do something to fix this."

"It's true, I'm the therapist. It's true I may know more theory about things dissociative than you do. It's also true that you have a lot of internal resources that are not being utilized in problem solving on this issue of what to do about John's threats of sexually acting out again. We need to figure out what is going on that John has been able to pull this off for so long, right under the nose of everybody else inside. I'm uncomfortable suggesting any change before we've really talked with all the ways of being you who have an interest in this scene, directly or indirectly, known or unknown. So, sure, I can suggest to you, John, that you increase the respect others inside might have for you by putting aside your actions until we complete a discussion about what's going on. How would you feel about that?" This approach is called talking through, since John was "in the background" and Mary was presenting as herself. My intentionally logical and likely unacceptable suggestion did the trick of evoking John's presence.

"I don't give a shit what anybody else thinks. I'm going to do what I want to do and tough crap on the rest of them."

"Thanks for coming to talk with me John."

"Fuck you."

"Gee, it sounds like you don't really value the others inside, or me." My language was intentionally understated to be less inflammatory.

"Who cares about you or them?! They're just a bunch of wimps!"

"Actually, John, it's unclear to me about whether you really understand that you and the others are all part of the same person, Mary, but you and the others each have your own territory, of sorts, and are somewhat compartmentalized, one from the other."

"That's what you think. So what?!" I had a sense that John was actually listening and taking in what I was saying. He was being dismissive, but not invalidating.

"You're all in the same boat, John. Isn't it true that Mary, Jill, and Jane, spend a lot of time organizing and ferrying the rest of you around, guiding Mary through the day?"

"That's got nothing to do with me. I'm separate. I'm different. I am not them. I rule the night."

"Well, you can say that you are separate and different until the cows come home, but it isn't going to make it true. In your heart of hearts, I'm sure you know better, but it just might not be that easy to own up to it. After all, what's a guy like you living in the mind and body of a person like Mary? Do you look in the mirror, John?"

"When I look in the mirror I see me, John, and my muscles. Nobody is going to get the best of me."

"Okay, what happens when you look down at your legs, right now, and your feet; have you looked yet today?" Mary was wearing a smartly tailored gray pinstripe business skirt and jacket over a silk blouse, nylons, and high heels.

"Jesus! What the hell is going on?"

"I know it's a bit of a jolt, John, but I think things are a little more complicated than you've realized. You are not alone in your mind, have you noticed that?"

"Uh, well, yeah, but I just kind of blew it off like I had a headache or something that went away when I focused my attention and got busy on what I wanted to do."

"Focusing your attention is a nifty trick and helped you to switch into the full extent of being you, but it isn't going to help you figure out how to deal with those nice-looking high heels you're wearing. I think we need to talk. Do you know what I mean? You need a consultation."

"Yeah, doc, I hate to say it, but I think I do."

The somewhat comic aspect of this interaction is not unusual in this work. It's important to have a sense of humor. The shared attuned space created in each psychotherapy contains all manner of idiosyncratic meanings of experience, unique to each clinical couple. "If somebody listens in to this conversation between us, Dr. Chefetz, they're going to think you are as loony as I am. At least we understand each other," one patient volunteered.

In this interaction with John as a self-state of Mary, I talked through to John on an emotionally important level, evoked his presence, tracked the emotional tone of the conversation, and responded accordingly. A useful perspective in working with contemptuous self-states like John is twofold. First, contempt is an efficient means of disposing with challenge if the challenger backs down (Jones 1995). I neither backed down nor intensified my challenge. My voice tones remained conversational. Second, contempt that is offered immediately is a signal of deep vulnerability. You might say that's nearly always true with DID. The issue, though, is that John, an abuser-protector state (Blizard 1997), has concentrated amounts of vulnerability—a reservoir, not vulnerability in general. So while challenging him is important, it has to be especially respectful. The self-states that have the most vinegar are the ones who have the most potential to spend that energy for living. Once converted to an ally in the treatment, they tend to be unflagging supporters of the psychotherapy. John was a very important figure because of both his negative emotionality and his storehouse of energy that could be used for living. His demeanor is rough-tough dismissive, and this keeps us away from the pool of pain deep inside. The Kohutian bipolar self describes the use of grandiosity and dismissiveness as a way to protect from isolated fears of annihilation. This is the "vertical split" (Kohut 1979) that in my view walks and talks like it's dissociative, and in a manner of speaking has webbed feet, too—ones that few people seem to notice. The rule of thumb is valuable: Contempt and grandiosity are often used to create distance from fear and humiliation. In all likelihood there is also intense shame in John, and that's part of why he rules the night, believing he can undo the sexual abuse Mary suffered and be dominant rather than the one who submitted.

John was focused on Mary's other self-states as being wimps, and that suggested to me that at some point in his (or some other way of being Mary) experience there was a gross humiliation, a sadly normal event for people who were abused. He was going to be tough in relation to the other self-states and also in relation to me, which meant that he was frightened of me and might feel like he was at an additional risk of humiliation or gross attack. If I responded to John by being fearful or humiliated in the face of his contempt, then I would have reified his pumped-up efforts to shore up his vulnerability by implicitly telling him he was scary; this is akin to the process of affective marking (markedness) we looked at earlier (Fonagy et al. 2003) in Chapter 3. But my matter-of-fact voice tones and even-handed treatment of John versus other self-states left me in the useful position of a consultant to Mary and John rather than an enemy of John. In this way, avoiding the antagonism he spread out in front of me spared the two of us a confrontation with risk of shaming, humiliation, or raging. It is interesting that John is a male self-state, and culturally fits a pattern of men who hide their shame by setting up chaotic and angry confrontations rather than be exposed as feeling vulnerable or as having failed (Lansky 1992). It is likely that John is modeled after a figure from Mary's past who did the same thing. That is worth a direct inquiry to John, at some point: "You know, I was thinking again about what it used to be like to be you, all the sense of risk of being wounded and that kind of thing. I was wondering, is there some person who used to behave in your family like you were behaving with the other ways of being Mary? What do you think?"

For our purposes here, it's useful to think of the delusion of separateness as highly dependent on depersonalization experience, which allows the creation of a feeling of bodily separateness or difference. When the body feels unreal, and there are few physical coordinates of being, dissociative transitional fantasy reigns. In this respect, as in other ways, depersonalization serves as a global regulator of the elements of the BASK model (behavior, affect, sensation, and knowledge) (Braun

197

1988) by creating a not-me self-state, an isolated self-state of the kind that Richard Kluft memorably dubbed an alternate self, or alter, many years ago (Kluft 1984). The conversational language I prefer challenges the delusion of separateness implicitly by talking about "different ways of being you" instead of making reference to alters. That doesn't mean my patients don't read the literature on the dissociative disorders and talk with me about the meaning of alters (some of them have read quite extensively), or that the term isn't used in their treatment. It does mean that by offering an alternate language, we get to negotiate the meaning of the language used to describe their own compartmentalized self-states. That's the key, here—negotiation—and the goal is consciousness for nuance and emotional meaning. When something is subject to negotiation, then the rigidity of beliefs surrounding it erode, bit by bit. The delusion of separateness, like depersonalization, is fear-driven and regulates emotion through gross disowning, denial, disavowal, isolation of affect, and so on. Talking with John about the clothing Mary put on that morning challenged the delusion of separateness and brought into focus his wearing high heels, something that under the umbrella of trance logic (Orne 1959) he had been able to ignore or not notice. At the core of John's ability to maintain the delusion of separateness was depersonalization experience. We now turn to that, with an emphasis on the neurobiology involved.

Depersonalization Experience: Gateway to the Clinical Neurobiology of Dissociation

Detailed study of the subjective experience of depersonalization has revealed four (Sierra et al. 2005) or five (Simeon, Kozin, Segal, Lerch, Dujour, and Giesbrecht 2008) underlying general dimensions in depersonalization: anomalous bodily experience, emotional numbing, anomalous subjective recall, alienation from surroundings, and temporal disintegration (time disturbance). John had a male orientation, had different memory than Mary, was detached from knowledge of what he was wearing, and saw the world differently than Mary did. All these things made the delusion of separateness workable for John and useful for Mary, who had been sexually abused and now had her own bully to protect her. Under John's hard outer shell could be predicted the soft vulnerable burden of intense shame and humiliation, a constellation easily conveyed to people by talking about a chocolate candy, the M&M. Depersonalization is a profound experience that is generally unresponsive to psychopharmacologic intervention. Psychodynamic psychotherapy may be the most effective treatment (Simeon and Abugel 2006). Recent reports of the use of transcranial magnetic stimulation (TMS) to remediate depersonalization (Mantovani, Simeon, Urban, Bulow, and Lisanby 2011) are reminiscent of the shotgun-like treatment of depression with electroconvulsive therapy, which nevertheless may be lifesaving in properly selected cases. Since TMS is generally safe, it makes a nice addition to the clinical toolbox. Caution should be taken to not generalize the striking 70 percent initial efficacy noted for the use of TMS with depersonalization disorder to the dissociative disorders. Regardless, if we're going to understand the neurobiology of dissociative process there is no better thing to study than depersonalization.

One of the curiosities of my clinical experience is the preponderance of people with significant depersonalization experience and the rarity of classic out-of-body experience. The Dissociative Experiences Scale's (Carlson and Putnam 1986) question number 13 is for depersonalization, and it wisely does not ask specifically about out-of-body experience: "Some people have the experience of feeling that their body does not seem to belong to them." I find I am much more successful in discovering the extent of depersonalization experience if I am less specific about what I am asking and leave room for an idiosyncratic meaningful response: "Do you ever have the experience of somehow not being connected to, fitting into, or being present in your body?" "Some people have the experience of their body as a kind of suitcase rather than a place where they feel alive. Do you ever have an experience like that, or something else that is similar and might even be hard to describe?" "Are you fully in your body and present when you are sexual?" (Asking about sexual things requires getting permission first: "May I ask you a question along these lines but related to your sexuality?") It is wise for a clinician to look for disturbances that may appear not as agitation but as emotional flattening. "I have the feeling that after asking you about this stuff, there is a way you could be feeling somehow detached."

The bottom line with depersonalization is that if you screen for it with one question you are not likely to discover it. I ask about depersonalization in several different ways and then follow it similarly with questions about derealization (a feeling that the world is unreal or phony). If I get a negative response at one point of a diagnostic interview and the feeling of the interview moves into a less coherent space, I may ask about depersonalization again at that later time. If a person does not recognize the repeat questions, then there has been a state change. They often are able to confirm depersonalization at that time. The Cambridge Depersonalization Scale (Sierra and Berrios 2000) is an additional useful source of items one can use for inquiry with patients about their depersonalization experience. It contains items such as things looking flat, like in a picture, or one's voice sounding remote and unreal.[2]

What is depersonalization experience? It would be foolish to say it is an out-of-body experience. That would simply be circular. Depersonalization is the subjective experience of somehow feeling unreal (Simeon and Abugel 2006), but that's not exactly informative either, however accurate it is. It is more apt to say that depersonalization is an inaccurately perceived somatic experience that involves feeling partially or completely disembodied in ways that often defies verbal description and may have both a neurobiologic and a psychodynamic basis. This experience is illustrated in patient artwork when my request to "draw a picture of yourself" is met with a simple stick or balloon figure drawing where arms, hands, legs, feet, and head are detached from the trunk of the body. Samantha, whom you met earlier, had the subjective experience of watching while her hands seemed to type on their own. The language that usually describes depersonalization is familiar when you hear it: "detached," "disconnected from my body,"

---

[2] The scale is freely available at:
http://www.iop.kel.ac.uk/iopweb/blob/downloads/locator/1_911_Scale3.pdf

TABLE 6.1 Items in the Cambridge Depersonalization Scale
(Abstracted from Sierra, M., & Berrios, G. E. (2000). The Cambridge depersonalization scale: A new instrument for the measurement of depersonalization. Psychiatry Research, 93, 153–164.)
Scale available at: http://www.iop.kel.ac.uk/iopweb/blob/downloads/locator/1_911_Scale3.pdf

1. Feeling unreal or cutoff from the world,
2. Things look flat, as if looking at a picture,
3. Body feels as if it didn't belong to oneself,
4. Not feeling frightened in normally frightening situations,
5. Favorite activities no longer enjoyable,
6. Feeling of being a detached observer of oneself,
7. Flavour of meals no longer gives a feeling of pleasure or distaste,
8. Body feels very light, as if it were floating on air,
9. No emotions felt when weeping or laughing,
10. Feeling of not having any thoughts at all,
11. Own voice sounds remote and unreal,
12. Feel like hands or feet becoming bigger or smaller,
13. Surroundings feel detached or unreal,
14. Recently done things feel as if they took place a long time ago,
15. See oneself outside, as if looking in a mirror,
16. Personal memories feel as if one had not been involved in them,
17. When in a new situation, feeling as if it had happened before,
18. Unable to feel affection towards family and friends,
19. Objects look smaller or further away
20. Unable to feel properly things touched with hands.
21. Unable to picture things in mind,
22. Feeling detached from bodily pain,
23. Feeling of being outside the body,
24. Feeling mechanical and robotic when moving,
25. Smell of things no longer gives feeling of pleasure or dislike,
26. Detached from own thoughts like they have life of their own,
27. Urge to touch oneself to be reassured of body existence,
28. Unable to feel hunger or thirst,
29. Previously familiar places look unfamiliar.

"coming apart," "falling apart," "disappearing," "falling down a black hole," and so on, but these expressions can have many meanings that need to be explored when these words and phrases come up in the patient's conversation.

Perhaps the simplest and most directly descriptive way to put it is that depersonalization is a dissolution of the subjective unity of coherent embodied experience. Being able to feel alive and present in your body is a prerequisite for feeling feelings. Clinically, depersonalization seems often to be a product of sustained overwhelming emotional experience on the level of terror that has become persistent (fear extinction fails). But the knowledge of a sense of ongoing terror disappears, dissociatively, perhaps via functional unlinking of cortical contextual libraries from subcortical stimulus-bound reactivity; in particular the prefrontal cortex may be unlinked from amygdalar alarm functions and insular interoceptivity. These decouplings happen outside of our self-monitoring capacities. In other words, we're not conscious of the shifts in physiology signaling distress, aren't aware we've been triggered, and instead have a stealth experience of lack of reactivity. This really is no different than having amnesia for having amnesia. We lose track that we're numb until a recognizable personal or social situation is not accompanied by emotion we know ought to be there. For a child, there may not even be this kind of cued experience of absent emotion if there's no memory for really feeling feelings. For an adult, the lack of feeling can create distress and sometimes painful concern about not being able to feel.

The underlying science describes how people with depersonalization unconsciously, implicitly, respond to an emotion-laden stimulus faster than it can consciously register; yet their emotional numbness, tracked by decreased skin conductance (emotional arousal causes increases in sweat secretion due to adrenalin release and salty sweat is a good conductor), is maintained even in the face of what control subjects experience as startle (Sierra et al. 2002). From a neurobiological perspective, one group of authors has proposed that out-of-body experiences are related to a failure of "proprioceptive, tactile, and visual information with respect to one's own body (disintegration of personal space) and by a vestibular dysfunction leading to an additional disintegration between personal (vestibular) space and extrapersonal (visual) space. We argue that both disintegrations are necessary for the occurrence of OBE [out of body experience] and that they are due to a paroxysmal cerebral dysfunction of the [temporo-parietal junction] TPJ" (Blanke and Arzy 2005). The TPJ includes the insula, the cortical structure which as we have seen is associated with visceroception and interoception (Paulus and Stein, 2010). The TPJ also includes areas responsible for vestibular processing (balance, orientation in space), multisensory integration, and perception of human body parts. The TPJ is where the Montovani group applied TMS. The TPJ is also the neural real estate involved in a study that showed stress creates alterations in neural function that are consistent with the neurobiology underlying conversion disorder (Aybek, Nicnolson, Zelaya, O'Daly, Craig, David, and Kanaan 2014). In Turkish populations, dissociative disorders often present with conversion (Sar, Tutkun, Alyanak, Bakim, and Baral 2000).

Although it is difficult to assess what exactly is happening for a specific person with clinical depersonalization, it is clear that the neurobiological underpinnings of it go far and wide in the brain and influence a number of different self-referential experiences including agency. What I find provocative is that it seems that most of the areas of the brain related to affect, feeling, and emotion relate to depersonalization.

Depersonalization involves dissociation of perceptions as well alterations of the experience of subjectivity (Simeon et al. 2000). The ability to feel a feeling is markedly diminished when somatosensory modes of experiencing are reduced or go almost entirely offline. Indeed, autonomic arousal is blunted in depersonalization, as is sensory processing of body schema (Stein and Simeon 2009). The cognitive evaluation of emotion-related sounds in depersonalization disorder patients is disconnected from their autonomic responses to those emotional stimuli (Michal et al., 2013). The nervous system reacts but there is a lack of attention to this. In response to images of increased intensity for happy and sad faces, people with depersonalization showed less fMRI signal intensity than a control group (blunting), but reacted faster than controls in terms of changing cerebral blood flow to affected brain areas (hypersensitivity) (Lemche et al., 2008). In a parallel study on visual images and the subjective experience of emotion, depersonalization patients had reduced responses in emotion sensitive regions of the brain and increased responses in emotion regulating regions of the brain (Phillips et al., 2001). People with depersonalization are less likely to consciously respond to emotional intensity and more likely to unconsciously over-respond to stop emotion from emerging into awareness. Depersonalization may be the opposite in some ways of mindfulness and reflective awareness, given that mindfulness training may decrease depersonalization (Michal, Beutel, Jordan, Zimmerman, Wolters, and Heindenreich 2007). An approach to depersonalization experience ought to focus on the emotional qualities of experience, on what's present and what's missing.

For example, much emotional expression is conveyed through facial expression (Adolphs 2002) and if visual cortices are disturbed, then the ability to discern feeling in others may be grossly impaired (Lemche et al. 2007). When working with specific self-states in relation to other self-states, I often ask my patient to describe to me the feeling they can see on the face of the self-state they are watching with their mind's eyes. (Recall Kelly's internal experience of Frantic, and Head down–Knees up.) This has both informational value and is a matter of therapeutic neurobiological "weight-lifting," exercising the visual associational cortex, to grow a stronger emotional associational capacity through modeling repetitive reflective awareness (Fonagy et al. 2003) for a mental state, as viewed via the imaged face of an internal self-state.

Early in treatment it is useful to be alert to a person's implicit sensitivity to feeling and to be cognizant of what is likely too much for them to take in without destabilizing. Neutrality in this instance means taking the side of the patient and speaking up to alert them to potential unconscious distress is useful as long as it is neither alarmist nor a matter of telling them they are weak. The issue is that their adaptive dissociative capacities are turned up a tad too high. An outwardly quiet and even placid patient is not a guarantee of physiological quiet, as the science shows.

In my practice I often invite my patients to indirectly track their level of fear by noticing the extent of depersonalization experience in a given moment to help understand what is happening as we work together in difficult territory. After a while, depersonalization begins to function as a barometer for emotional tension, and as it becomes a tool it is much less feared on a cognitive-behavioral and psychodynamic level. The healing is in a safe-enough-feeling relationship.

The bottom line in considering depersonalization is that it is a stealth finding in many patients; you have to ask about it to learn it is present, and you need to be skillful in the asking. Moreover, once you know it's there, making sure you keep it in mind and protect your patient from overstimulation is important. Demystifying the experience of depersonalization and normalizing it in context goes a long way to reducing anxiety in general, and reduced levels of anxiety contribute to less depersonalization response in the nervous system and a more clinically capable and resilient patient. This is much easier said than done.

Working with anxiety and fear in a patient with profound depersonalization can be a rather chaotic experience if the tolerance for emotion is limited and the ability to sense feeling alternates between limited and flooded. This may occur as their dissociative adaptations respond to treatment by eroding. This sometimes leaves people feeling naked and defenseless. It's as if they are confronted by their emotions, which want to run up and hug them after years of not hugging anybody and being frightened of registering any intensity at all. Rachel, whom you will meet in Chapters 8 and 9, had a major breakthrough in treatment when she reported that for the first time in her 40-something years of life she felt like people could see her. She said it was weird, and it frightened her. "It's like wearing a raincoat for 40 years, and going out into the world with it every day. Then, one day, you go out, and it's not on, and it's like you're exposed." On this particular day she was also telling me about soothing a child she was visiting who had knocked a stack of dishes onto the floor. She intuitively and wisely hugged that child gently, asked them if they were okay, and really didn't care about the dishes. We took that experience and made it into an internal one for self-soothing. An internal hug has made it easier to be in the world without her raincoat.

Emotion is feared for many reasons, and many of these have to do with experiences from earlier in life where displays of emotion met with dismissal and being told they were of no value, or by being physically silenced by a sadistic other. Speculatively, one way in which a person might develop depersonalization is through practicing the admonitions of a Type A emotionally dismissive parent who forces their child to stop displaying emotions. These children display no particular distress but are actually in physiological disarray and quite stressed (Main 2000). In these kinds of scenarios, there is little affect tolerance, and the feeling of an impending feeling is frightening. Recall Kelly, earlier in this chapter, whose mother didn't "get" her; Kelly's mother who had characteristics of both a preoccupied (Type C) and disorganized-disoriented (Type D) adult. Emotional dismissiveness and disorganization can be profoundly disturbing. The fear stemming from the disrupted attachment was profound.

Such was also the case with Alice, whom we met in Chapter 1. Alice's disrupted attachments with both parents left her at the mercy of intense fear and anxiety when new separations threatened. Her dissociative devices were her chief resource in dealing with the potential chaos of feeling. At the time of the vignette that follows, Alice was in a very unstable place in her treatment, felt like she was threatened with the loss of her beloved job, and had been recently actively suicidal. She still has lots to teach us, so let's return to her treatment.

Fear, Attachment, and the Relationship

The crisis that is the subject of this vignette began when Alice's absence from work surrounding a hospitalization had worried her boss. (This was about five years prior to the work depicted in Chapters 10, 11, and 12.) He depended on her to do the work of three people, and in their small business she could not be replaced, nor could anyone else really do her technically sophisticated work. He asked to speak to me about the possibility that she would be absent from work again. Alice very much wanted me to do that, and after talking about it for a session, I agreed to the conversation, which we did by speakerphone in her presence. What Alice took away from the conversation was that he was trying to get rid of her. What I understood was that her boss was frightened of the implications of her being unavailable, didn't want to lose her, and was trying to understand how to protect his business. Alice was distressed during the remainder of the session after the phone call, but seemed to settle down as the session drew to a conclusion. The calm did not last.

I choose to explore this evolving scene because it illustrates a number of different issues in working with a patient with DID from an emotion-focused psychodynamic perspective that makes conversational use of somatic states and employs a self-state perspective typical of DID treatments. The attachment I had with Alice, and she with me, was disrupted by a fear of abandonment, and this fear was matched by her focus on a fear of not being normal and the potential loss of a job she loved; all this was destabilizing enough that it impaired her ability to think. As we will see, when the emotional connection with Alice was restored, her cognitive abilities immediately returned. Prior to that happening, self-states with toxic shame and fear experience were prominent and painful emotion precluded cognition.

The reported clinical sequence includes in-session, phone, and email communication. Much of the work was done by talking through to self-states in the background, rather than exclusive direct conversation with a fully embodied self-state. Alice was regularly seen on Tuesday and Thursday, and it was a Thursday session where the discussion with her boss took place. The evening after, I received an email from her:

> I slept an hour in front of your house in my car. I know
> I wasted my session today but I don't know why. I really
> wanted to talk about my fiancé and how much he hurt me.
> I hadn't really thought about him in years until last week.

She had mentally erased much of the content of the session while she slept in the car; in particular, she lost the discussion surrounding her safety.

> My problem is that I just can't work. I have not been at
> the top of my game all week, although last Sunday was a
> very productive day. I came home at 3 p.m. today, think-
> ing I was going to work on this web project that my client
> is screaming for, and I did nothing at all but watch TV and
> read the newspaper. I don't know what is wrong with me.
> Am I somehow rebelling against my boss? Am I doing this
> on purpose? I almost feel that this is intentional. In fact, I
> am sure that it is. Wow, that was a revelation. What do I

do to get back on track? Now I'm really pissed at that part of me. Who is it . . . I don't know.

There is some work going on here, but at the same time there is a block to knowledge about her feeling of rebellion and the source of it.

My emailed response to Alice was very simple: "You're angry with your boss." My intention in writing that to her was twofold. First, it was a message that she needed to pay attention to that part of her she feared, a part who had lots of anger. Second, in writing a simple note, it set a tone that said: This is a problem that you need to work on and it's okay for you to do that without a lot of input from me. However, as she put it in her replay, she felt like I was "either busy or blowing me off." I responded to that with a thoughtful denial (clearly in a negative countertransference mode, retrospectively), and a more detailed description of the scene I imagined in her mind:

> I'm not blowing you off, Alice. I am perfectly serious. I don't think it's super-complicated. The part of you who does anger is sitting in the driver's seat on this, I believe, and if not her, then it seems likely there is another way of being Alice who doesn't give a hoot what your boss thinks. You need your Feeling parts to help you on this. Spend some time thinking about this and considering how to find out more about your anger, and I think you'll find that very fruitful.

Of course, from Alice's perspective, my telling her to work on this alone is blowing her off. My telling her it's not "super-complicated" is indeed potentially dismissive of her experience. I had recently been through a very tense time with her being suicidal, and I didn't want another such scene. I was trying to not get entangled in a scene about anger and also to encourage her to work on her own with self-states, though in fact that was something she had not be able to do with any ease.

Alice did, in fact, hear my message and responded appropriately, containing her experience and acknowledging it:

Well, I'm sitting here in my bathrobe. Can't work. Can't get in touch with my anger. Just a fucking waste of me. I can't pull myself out of this and I know you are telling me to get in touch with my anger but it's just not happening. I am so frustrated.

For me, the presence of clearly stated frustration devoid of threats of self-harm was refreshing. It suggested that after the recent suicide crisis there was a new capacity for affect tolerance. However, nothing is ever as it seems, and I was left wondering what would happen next. I didn't have to wait too long. By the end of the next day she had written a long email detailing how she felt like her boss and another employee were ganging up on her, how she hated herself, how she didn't go to work, and that she needed either my help or someone else's. She finished her note by saying: "I have to snap out of this." What she didn't write about was my suggestion that she deal with her anger. A second brief note from her stated she had the thought that she would quit her job. I took this as an antishaming script of action, reminiscent of what Tomkins (1995) would have called an "anti-contamination" script, that is, viewing shame and disgust in terms of a feeling that one has been contaminated.

Later that evening, when I saw her notes, I wrote back and suggested she would rather quit than risk being humiliated, but that she was in a doublebind because she was actually angry at her boss for mistreatment that was ongoing but felt unable to express her anger at the same time that she felt like her job was on the line. From that perspective, quitting solved the emotional doublebind by opting out. I suggested to her that she could simply provide her bosswith a thoughtful plan to deal with a possible brief hospital stay and that what he probably wanted most was for her to be collaborative with him on this issue. I then wrote on late Friday eve:

Don't quit. Just tolerate the feelings and try to understand where they come from. You will pull through this if you just tolerate the feeling without taking action. What are the links to the past? What ages does this fit? We can work on this, Alice.

I didn't hear from her at all on Saturday. Sunday morning, as I sat down early to do some desk work, I saw a message from her from just past midnight on Saturday:

> I didn't bother you all day, but now it's Sunday. I still haven't done any work, although I did clean my house. What am I going to do? This "state" has apparently not abated and I am scared to death. Do you understand I have to show the client my work on Monday and it's not done? Why can't I get my head together? Why is this happening to me? I am a broken woman and I desperately need help. I am flipping out.

This is part of where email may fail as a means of communication; it is very unwieldy when dealing with intense emotion, especially in the wake of suicidality. I wrote and suggested that she pull up the emails I had written to her, consider them, and write to me with whatever came into her mind. I was foolishly hoping she'd connect with her anger on her own. By late in the day, I had heard nothing. I began to anticipate a late evening crisis on Sunday, something I did not want. I wrote a brief note rather than wait for her, and did so while wondering about my motives and whether I was inviting trouble or giving her the wrong message if I interrupted her quiet. Here's what I wrote:

> Perhaps there is a part of you, Alice, who isn't really sure what your boss will do, or why, and so this part of you has tried to figure out a way to make him mad, or to make you feel badly, by not doing your work, so at least there will be something "concrete" to point to about why he/ you might take action.

An hour later, she wrote that I was correct, and asked if I could call her if I was in my office. I did, and this is the conversation that took place, as best as I can recollect.

"Hi Alice."

"Hi," she replied, and then with verbal pressure of an almost manic quality she went on: "I'm losing it. I'm not getting anything done. My client expects me to produce this project by 2 P.M. tomorrow, and I have nothing to show them. I don't even think I can do it. I just don't really have the skill. I've wasted all this time and now there is nothing to show."

"So, you think there is an attempt underway to find a way to leave your job for failing to do a project as opposed to feeling you're not able to live up to some personal standard?"

"Absolutely. I just can't stand the way I feel. I don't want to be doing this, but I can't seem to stop myself. I have no access to anything going on inside me. It's all quiet."

"If it's all quiet inside, then I suspect there is a way in which a thinking part of you is furious about having to deal with feelings and just wants to get rid of everything so that the feelings just go away."

"That sounds right, and when you say that my whole body suddenly aches."

"What does your body have to say about what I said?"

"You were right when you said I felt like I was in a double bind. I don't feel like I've been working well enough over the past several weeks to protest anything my boss is thinking of doing, and I can't stand the tension inside me."

"Sounds like this is something that the 'one who gets the job done' [another self-state] might try to deal with. You said you were thinking you were attempting career suicide since body suicide was 'off the table' for now. She was very much part of the suicide thinking before. It makes sense she would be involved in this, now. What do you think?"

"Yes, I know she is. She'll do anything to stop the feelings. It's driving her crazy. She just can't stand it."

"You know, I don't think you appreciate that the reason your boss is so worried is that he is so dependent on you that he gets scared when he thinks about losing you. It's not that he doesn't want you at work—just the opposite. Have you thought about that?"

"No, but it makes sense."

"You've been thinking you need to solve the tension by quitting before he humiliates you, but in fact, he values you and is afraid of you not being there. Right? This must resonate from something in your past;what's the connection? Can you sense it?"

"The only thing that happened when you asked that was that my stomach was suddenly upset, nauseous."

"What does your stomach have to say about this?"

"It's Twelve, she thought everything was fine, but then everything suddenly fell apart. She thinks it's going to happen again."

"So, speaking to the one who gets the job done: Seems to me that Twelve has her default set to expect bad things to happen and for the world to fall apart so that she ends up feeling ashamed. When she gets upset in that way, and there is anger heating up, no wonder you get upset and just want to resolve the tension." (We learn more about her anger in Chapter 10 as this treatment evolves.)

"She understands what you said about my boss needing me. I don't know why I didn't see that."

"Twelve really is set to a hair trigger after being humiliated at school. What does she need to hear from you now about this situation?"

"She needs to know I can handle it and that everything is going to be okay. She's already feeling better. But now I'm feeling nauseous, but not like with Twelve. I see myself on the floor in the bathroom, sick like I'm really going to throw up."

"What is this scene about and which way of being Alice is there? How old is she?"

"It's Emily. She's six. She's really worried that she's done something wrong and is going to be punished. She's frightened."

"What does she need to hear from you?"

"She needs to hear the same thing, but I don't think that is going to be enough for her."

"She wants you to keep an eye on her, pay attention to what she feels?"

"Yes."

"So . . . what does she need to hear from you?"

"She needs to know I will look after her and not let her get hurt."

"Will you?"

"Yes, I can do that."

"And how does she feel about what's happening as we talk?"

"She doesn't know if you'll be there for her."

"Did you notice how when I wrote to you and made specific suggestions about how you could work on this stuff on Thursday, your initial response was that I was blowing you off?"

"Well, you made a one-word response."

"No, it was not one word."

"Then it was just two."

"I made a specific suggestion in a couple of sentences and then when you replied later, I made a one-sentence reply to help you focus on the task, but I'm not sure you ever did. I didn't make a one-word reply, and I've responded to your emails. So if you are saying you can't count on me to respond, then there are some wires crossed here somewhere. What was it like for you this afternoon when you got my email that started with 'perhaps'?"

"I knew you were thinking of me and that you cared."

"And so I have a mind where I think of you, even if you don't prompt me to do that. Did you know that?"

"Wow, that's really big. I know that's true, but I never thought about it, really. It's having a big reaction inside."

"I've been sticking with you and responding to you for nine years, Alice. There must be a way that you anticipate being blown off and not cared about that's so painful that it's been hard to learn something else exists in our relationship."

"I can feel myself relaxing."

"I'm glad. So what's happening for the one who gets the job done?"

"She's feeling better. Actually, I just got an idea about how I can do some of this project."

"How many hours do you need to really finish this if you were able to work on it?"

"Just eight or so."

"So you could work on it tonight and finish it after a good night's sleep before the 2 P.M. deadline tomorrow."

"Yes, actually, I could do that."

"How are Twelve and Emily doing?"

"They're both feeling better."

"Have you noticed how context-sensitive Twelve and Six [a younger self-state related to Twelve] are? It's like you find a situation that matches their experience and it's almost as if you've double-clicked their icons on your computer desktop, isn't it?"

"That's really true. That amazing! It is just like that."

"So, if Six or Twelve become active, then you have a head start now on what kind of issues are cooking, right? And how is the one who gets the job done doing?"

"She's better. My whole body feels better, and she's relaxed now, too."

"So, speaking to the one who gets to job done, was it of value to work with your feelings?"

"Yes, it really makes some sense" (said in a child-like voice).

"Well, I appreciate you saying that, but I really want to hear from the one who gets the job done, please? What did you learn about working with feelings rather than trying to get rid of them?"

"It really did help. I never would have guessed it could, but I do feel much better."

"Good, is there anything else we need to talk about today before we stop?"

"No, I don't think so. I think I know what to do."

"Good. By the way, we've been on the telephone for quite a while, how do you feel . . . "

"Go ahead and bill me for the session. That's fine with me."

"Okay, see you Wednesday this week since you're away on Tuesday."

"Okay, goodbye."

"Goodbye, Alice."

For Alice, her own feelings were dismissed by her boss and to some extent by me, an instant replay of parental emotional dismissiveness, especially associated with her father. The negative transference was also father-based, as in "You won't be there for me." The negative countertransference was: "I'm worn out from being there for you. Work it out on your own, it will be good for you." The internal psychodynamics and politics of her self-states were: "I hate my feelings. I don't want to be dependent. I want someone I can trust. People want to get rid of me. I am shameful. I don't know what I did wrong but I'm going to be punished for it. I'm scared and lonely. I need to be rid of these feelings, even if that means I'm dead." I reframed her perceptions regarding her boss from punishment to respect: "Your boss is dependent on you rather than wanting you to leave." I decreased some of the emotional weight of the current situation with a transference clarification. My message to her, in effect, was that it was no wonder she was upset if her old feelings were matching the new situation and she thought the intensity was from the current situation.

My agenda going forward was somewhat more complex. I had to stay alert to the way Alice's experience was parceled out among different self-states: Twelve and Emily had old worries they needed to talk about. Dealing with feelings was actually useful rather than always a problem; different ways of being Alice emerge in a context, not randomly, and Alice could figure out these contexts and deal with the issues. I went on to link self-states while behaving opposite of her emotionally dismissive parenting: "What does Twelve need? What does Emily need from you?" This encourages a kind of theory of mind by challenging her to figure out what is in the part of her mind she usually doesn't consider. This is much better than me telling her what to do, or what is needed. If she doesn't know, then we play Twenty Questions until she figures it out. If she never does, then I rescue her and we discuss that.

I also connected bodily sensations with psychological states, part of an effort to desomatize affect. I made clear that bodily sensations were associated with psychological states. She was able to respond immediately after several years of work like this. Many sensations represent conflict between self-states, and at times abject terror emerged as she climbed back up the dissociative cliff she long ago fell off. The transference was active and challenged by my activity in writing an unsolicited email, something I rarely do. When Emily says she's not sure if Alice will look after her, my warning lights go off about dependency themes, including the potential for abandonment feelings, and avoidant attachment themes where absence doubles for lack of interest or dismissiveness. I have wanted her to work alone on some things, and she feels dismissed. I could have been less confrontational in my tone, and that might have been helpful, but in fact, she responded well to me laying out the reality of my thinking about her without her having to prompt me to attend to her. I modeled reflective awareness and theory of mind for her in presenting the idea that I had a mind that had thoughts about her, even if she didn't prompt me. That was big for her because she never had the experience of someone anticipating her needs. It's also true, at this point, that she is mostly unwilling to believe someone will actually meet her needs if she doesn't ask. That was part of her birthday dilemma, when people planned things for her but didn't tell her ahead of time, then she felt hurt because nothing visible was going to happen for her. Twelve, who felt abandoned and discounted by peers, and Emily, who didn't know what she did wrong, were both despondent in resonance with Alice's 50th birthday. Context isn't everything, but it's a lot. Fear of abandonment, a repetition of childhood issues, got tangled up at her job and in her therapy. The delusion of separateness was prevalent, as if self-states were independent agents and could or would not be reasonable. An integrative model of interaction challenged that delusion in the creation of a safe-enough caring relationship with me. She modeled that with herself, and feelings of fear of abandonment dissolved with a return of creativity.

The fear spectrum of emotion is complex and grounded in a neurobiology that predicts anxiety may resolve with cognitive interventions and that the origins of fear may become accessible with affective-somatic linking through attention to bodily states. Depersonalization fuels the delusion of separateness and represents a paradoxical unconscious hypersensitivity to intense emotion while simultaneously unlinking capacities for consciousness about emotional states. People can be internally hypersensitive and externally placid. Depersonalization may be unknown to the patient, and careful inquiry must be made about a number of dimensions to rule it out. Distress is often invisible and not conscious. This creates major pitfalls in any psychotherapy, and the therapist must constantly be alert about the potential for even seemingly small missteps to create major reactions, give the underlying neurobiology and complex psychodynamics of the scene.

Chapter 7

Incest, Sexual Addiction, and Dissociative Processes

CLINICIANS WORKING WITH SURVIVORS OF TRAUMA REGULARLY CONFRONT the problem of addictions to food, alcohol, drugs of abuse, gambling, and sex, among other domains of behavior. My argument here is that the behavioral focal point of the addiction is not nearly as important as the factors that generate the emotional and behavioral scripts that produce the addictive behavior (Goodman 1998). The intersection of traumatic experience and dissociative process has a lot to teach us about addiction. In recent efforts to medicalize and depathologize addictive behaviors, there is risk of throwing out the wounded baby with the bathwater and saying it's all in their genes, for example. What about the wounds?

Consider the legacy of an incestuous relationship, such as what my patient Anya endured for years. It's impossible to know or catalog all the variations on how such a relationship begins, and yet before we hear Anya's story it's worth taking a moment to provide some general context and ask a simple question: How might the sexual abuse of a child start? Often enough, an apparently understanding and caring adult becomes a special friend to a lonely and vulnerable child by first playing with them, reading to them, buying them ice cream and snacks, doing special favors, and then teaching them things like the "tickle game" that leads to sexual activity. In a rare moment for our society, the public was recently shown a sad and vivid picture of these kinds of activities, called "grooming" by law enforcement personnel, in testimony before a Pennsylvania grand jury investigating allegations of sexual abuse committed by Jerry Sandusky.[1] In a context of incestuous abuse within a family, the grooming of children through fondling, masturbation, and penetration sadly occurs with some frequency in the first several years of life, as part of a grotesquely "normal" part of introducing sexual activity to a small child. In some children, dissociative processes regularly create multiple layers of self-states, depersonalization, derealization, and amnesia that insulate knowledge of painful experience from awareness. The day child is often not aware of the events occurring for the night child, as one Miss America taught us some years ago (Van Derbur 2003).

The subtlety to be observed here is about how carefully crafted coercion is followed by entrapment. This can evolve into slavery played out over decades into adulthood (Middleton 2013). Middleton collected from the popular press 44 cases of enduring incestuous relationships from 24 countries over a five-year period, his sample beginning one year prior to the famous case of Josef Fritzl in Austria. Fritzl, an outwardly friendly man, imprisoned his daughter, Elisabeth, in a locked cellar beneath his family home for 24 years, during which he fathered seven children with her, three of whom he raised with his wife while Elisabeth and three of the children (one had died) remained in the cellar. A neighbor reported the Fritzls appeared to have a "perfect family unit."

Incestuous abuse and pedophilic abusers do not have a personal social signature that is distinguishable from normal. Thus, the repetitive sexual abuse of a person from early childhood into adulthood creates an extraordinary burden for a surviving adult to manage when much of their daily and nightly life was organized around various sexual acts and other acts solidifying the power and control of an outwardly simple and hard-working "family man." With pedophilia of the Sandusky variety and incestuous abuse, there is no visible marker of ongoing abuse, no sign of it, not even a hint of it unless someone escapes or the abuse is observed by someone outside the perpetrator's realm of sovereignty and is willing to speak up. In the Sandusky case,

---

[1] See http://www.attorneygeneral.gov/uploadedfiles/press/sandusky-grand-jury-presentment.pdf

that proved difficult enough and nearly didn't happen. In the incestuous family, the pressures arrayed against consciousness are even more extraordinary (Freyd 1996), and the risks to family members' safety are often high in the face of potential disclosure.

Disclosure of incest in the Middleton study occurred at an average age of 25.9 years (Roesler and Wind 1994), a chilling indicator of how hard it can be to speak out. Some of the factors arrayed against disclosure are accommodation with distortion of reality, guilt and self-blame, helplessness, attachment to the perpetrator, illusory self-idealization of control, mistrust of others, dissociative amnesia, concern for others in the family, family loyalty, norms of obedience, and fear of blame (Somer and Szwarcberg 2001). I would add to this list what I commonly hear in my practice: threat of harm to self or other. The power of these threats, often delivered in moments of sadistic triumph during episodes of abuse, constitutes a highly imperative behavioral injunction woven with threads of physical and emotional pain, terror, hopelessness, and humiliation.

Incest Set the Stage for Sexual Addiction

Anya was struggling to understand her sexual behavior.[2] There was a history of incest that she believed went on for many years, apparently until the end of high school, ending when she went away to college. This had been followed by an enduring sexual addiction. After seven years of intensive, twice-weekly psychotherapy, Anya still experienced herself as unable to fundamentally alter a pattern of having sex with men who were clearly not interested in her for any other reason than to be sexual. Four years after she began to use the concept of performance art as an avenue for self-exploration, her psychotherapy was going well, but her relationships with men

---

[2] Graphic descriptions of sexual experience and traumatic events are used in this chapter. These are contextual rather than gratuitous and create an appropriate sense of the gravity and depth of the subject. Some readers may find it helpful to be aware of and anticipate the need for additional efforts at self or affect regulation while reading this material.

were still chaotic, on-and-off, emotionally painful experiences. Performance art, as we learned in Chapter 2, was her way of saying how she sometimes ended up enacting the past rather than being able to speak about it. In our meetings the context of this relational chaos was speculatively tied to her father, but it was hard to figure out how he, as a feared and loathed person, could figure in the attraction phase of these new relationships.

Anya had gone back to smoking cigarettes. She knew this was somehow related to her teenage years, when she had a habit of smoking and putting out the cigarettes on her legs and belly. She was aware that restarting smoking, which she had not had done for years, suggested the reemergence of a way of being related to these earlier times.

She was 30 years old and working several unskilled jobs to make ends meet. She never missed an appointment, though occasionally she negotiated a miss when she felt exceptionally overwhelmed. She was never a no-show. For several years she had also attended a twice-weekly group therapy and met once a week individually with that group therapist.

Anya had two sisters and a brother. She grew up deep in the back woods of a Southern state. Her father worked in a mine. Mother was a homemaker. This was small-town America at its best, but this scene could have been anywhere. In therapy, she described being anally, vaginally, and orally raped by her father. The peak of incestuous activity occurred during her teenage years, though it had begun, by her description, when she was two years old. She once tried to run away from home, and the only thing she packed was underpants. She said that because her underwear was for some reason always getting bloody, she knew she had to have all the underwear she could find if she ran away. She regularly wore several pairs of underpants and underclothing that were as tight as possible, until very recently. Lately, she had realized that not only was she trying to delay someone getting to her genitals but that she needed the tightness of her underwear to create enough discomfort for her to feel her body.

Anya was quite aware that there were different ways of being her, but that awareness came at the price of "getting it" and appreciating its significance. If it was true that there were so many self-states, then something must have happened to create such a constellation. The whole idea of a multiplicity of self-states frightened her for this very reason: She couldn't bring herself to confront the "something" behind them.

She did not always have an awareness of her self-states—far from it. Prior to her starting psychotherapy with me, her boyfriend understood that something was quite wrong and asked his therapist for a referral for her. Two months after Anya started treatment, her boyfriend hung himself. It was a challenging beginning for any treatment. Over the years since that time, and with the exception of just a few three-day hospitalizations to deal with destabilization and self-harming behaviors (including superficial cutting), Anya had been stable in treatment. Her brilliance was obvious, and she was multitalented in music, the arts, literature, and poetry. She was alienated from her family of origin, but she had several long-term friends around the country in addition to her local friends. She stayed in touch through standard modern technologies.

She began one particular session by continuing the weeping that had started in the waiting room. She said there was so much going on she wasn't sure where to start. She had gone to see Chuck (a man she was seeing), and he disclosed that he was dating an unemployed stripper. Chuck made clear that Anya could still visit him, but he was going out bowling that evening with his date. Of course, the intent of Anya going to visit Chuck was, as she put it, to make sure they "fucked." She found herself oddly not in the least bit upset that he was going out with another woman. She was quite clear that he didn't care about Anya at all and was just interested in using her as best he could. His attitude toward her was summed up by Chuck using a metaphor that she had previously only known her father to use: "Hold out both hands in life and put shit in one hand and wishes in the other and see which hand fills up first." "No man has ever said that to me except for my father. I thought Chuck was a pretty good matching substitute for my father, but this was really too perfect," she said to me in session. "I've been telling Chuck what a mess I am, how upset I am that I keep coming to his place and fucking him, and that I don't want to be doing that." His response was to invite her to return.

As we talked, Anya and I arrived at the same conclusion: Chuck seemed to like feeling irresistible, liked thinking that Anya could not avoid having sex with him no matter what she declared. We also realized that there was a part of Anya who was totally delighted that Chuck was who he was. When she wanted to have sex, it was no longer covertly an effort to cover over the memory of having sex with her father by having a new intense sexual experience. The motive was the same, but it was conscious. In realizing this, she anxiously said, "Maybe I need to go in the hospital. Maybe this is just too much for me. I can't seem to control what I'm doing. Maybe we should plan a hospitalization for me because if I keep on doing these things, I'm going to destroy myself." We both knew that Chuck had a history of violence.

"That certainly does seem like the direction in which you are heading, Anya, though I'm not sure we need the hospital at this moment. You've always had difficulty dealing with the rage that's inside you and it's been very hard for you to become openly angry with your mother or father or anybody. The only person you've been able to really consistently be angry with is you." I was focused here on the self-destructive nature of what she said about her sexual activity, though I was certainly partly attending to her comment about self-destruction. But it was not a particularly useful thing for me to say, because it missed the point she was trying to convey, and she let me know it with the dripping sarcasm that came next.

"Okay. So, that's terrific. Tell me then that we're making progress. Tell me that what we're doing helps; because I'm hurting."

"Yes, we are making progress." I knew I was on the wrong foot with her, and this seemed the safest thing to say. In retrospect, it was ridiculous. I should have said, "I see your point." Along the lines of Sandler's idea of role responsiveness (Sandler 1976), saying "I see your point" would have acknowledged her perceiving something in me rather than my being defensive or illogical, like "we're making progress." Wearing the attribution (Lichtenberg, Lachman, and Fosshage 1996) instead would have been wise. By wearing the attribution of her hurting and me not helping her, I would have been responsive to the transference role, perhaps of her father, and then we would have gotten into more about visiting Chuck but with less tension between us. We weren't making the progress Anya needed, and she didn't pull her punches in letting me know it after I evaded my responsibility.

"Okay, then tell me why do I keep on visiting Chuck?! Tell me how that is going to stop. Because, you know, we've talked about how at some point I might somehow arrange for him to really hurt me in a way that I can't recover from, and then what? So, tell me we're making progress, please." She was now clearly identifying the issue, not self-destruction per se but her inability to control her sexual actions. The issue was less about sex than about seeing that she was not in control of what she was doing. Another, more sexual way of being Anya was calling the shots.

"We really need to talk in detail about what has been happening," I said.

"Okay, so what is going to happen is that maybe I'll have to cut my face up into little pieces and go further than I did before.[3] You know, two weeks ago he wanted to tie me up to the bed." I was privately horrified as she spoke.

"Well, what happened?" I spoke calmly with curiosity in my voice.

"I let him. And, you know, I didn't get into a panic at all. I was completely relaxed about it. That's what caught my attention. I was just waiting."

As Anya spoke these words, I thought to myself about how we were sitting on a powder keg of emotional energy inside her. Performance art was leading us into danger. Some part of her was trying to tell a story and was not using words. It felt to me that another part of her was observing the scene and moving toward panic about what she was seeing. An additional part of her might be using Chuck as a facilitator of suicide. Was she looking for a way to tell the story of

---

[3] This cutting had happened several weeks earlier. She and I discovered later that her facial cutting was related to her father's insertion of sharp objects into her rectum during particularly sadistic episodes as well as threats during her abuse that he would cut off her face.

a script by enlisting an outside actor, somebody to play the role she needed? Had she found that character in Chuck and his focus on his own needs and willingness to use Anya as a sexual object? The match to the incest scene was clear. But what was the specific story line? She was still on the verge of provoking a situation where she could be irrevocably hurt. She was clearly displaying anger and contempt toward me; her expressions about what I said continued to be dripping with sarcasm and belittling. This wasn't fun, yet I also felt reassured that she could express such intensity toward me—at least it wasn't aimed at herself. At least she trusted me with an expression of her anger and did not seem to fear retaliation.

"I told Chuck before I went to see him—since he seemed to hesitate about fucking me and reminded me that I told him I didn't want to do it anymore with him—I told him that he could fuck me now, or I could go on Craigslist and find somebody more than willing to fuck me later. I told him that I really wanted to go to graduate school, and I needed to earn some money, and why not do it by prostitution? Don't I give the best blow jobs you've ever had in your life? Don't you think somebody would pay for me to do that? His response was, to say 'come on up here.' And so I went. The thing I do with men, the thing I seem to be most satisfied about is when I'm face down, with my butt up in the air," she said, as hot tears streamed down her cheeks and she angrily hurled her words across the consultation room. "I don't seem to be satisfied until someone takes me from the rear. When I think about my father raping me, what I see in my mind, I see myself and him behind me, fucking me. It must be an out-of-body experience. I suppose that's what it is. That's what's always there. When I dated the first guy I dated in high school who I had sex with—and when I got him to fuck me from behind, it was absolutely completely satisfying. It was wonderful. It fits in with what's going on with Chuck. I just don't know how to understand it."

I thought of Ally. "Ally" was a way Anya had of being Anya during her teenage years, especially around issues of sexuality. On one hand, I had a sense that the absence of rage or intense anger at the people who hurt her in the past was important. On the other hand, this teenage aspect of Anya ought to have been present in the treatment with sexual issues on the table, but in fact she seemed to be nowhere in the picture. So, I said, "You know, I think it's time that Ally came to therapy to talk about this and see what's on her mind."

"What's in my mind . . . Do you want to know what's in my mind? I wouldn't do that, even if you paid me."

"Prostitution."

"That's right."

I was silent for a bit, and so was she. But she broke the silence with a torrent of vitriol tinged with a belittling sarcasm.

"You know, Richard, I'm really disappointed in you. You wrote this shitty little response to my email. How could you even have thought to send something that stupid and meaningless to me?"

"Yes, it's not a response of which I'm proud, not at all." (I honestly couldn't recall what might have been so awful, though I did know that one of my replies to her recently was superficial rather than my more typical thoughtful response.) Now she turned her head to the side and spoke in a wholly different voice of compassion and sadness.

"You know, I'm really grasping at straws. I'm willing to use even the smallest and littlest thing to tell you how inadequate you are and that you haven't been helping me." Then turning back toward me, she changed states again and went on to continue to criticize me about other email responses and how I was not really meeting any kind of standard of responsiveness that had any meaning for her. As I continued to listen to her harangue me, it dawned on me that this state change might mean that Ally was present and was giving me the kind of hell that in theory was reserved for her father. I took a leap of faith in my intuition.

"Welcome to therapy, Ally. I hope you appreciate that you can be angry with me and that I'll listen to you and hear you out."

"I'm really frustrated. There doesn't seem to me to be any way that I'm going to stop doing this stuff with Chuck. There doesn't seem to be a way out." It was Ally, after all.

"Well, what about the cigarettes? Did you smoke after having sex with your father? Did your father smoke?"

"You've asked me that before."

"Well, many people smoke after having sex."

"You asked me that before and I said no, and I don't know why you are belaboring this. Why do you keep asking the same question?"

I had begun to think that several other parts of her mind were involved in the activity with Chuck since I knew that cigarette smoking and putting out the cigarettes on her skin were part of the constellation of her abuse and her reaction to it in high school. I thought I might be on to something. Her irritation about my asking a reasonable question might indeed be a reaction to my having asked it before, but it was in excess and was being given more emotional energy than it deserved. She wanted me to stay away from the issue. Why? I wasn't sure what was driving her. I thought about the other cases in my practice and what typically is going on when there is this much energy and no visible script.

"There's more to this than what's been visible, and I'm trying my best to openly sort through the possibilities for why you are having this kind of relationship with Chuck. I'm actually beginning to think that you're having flashbacks of a sensory variety." In a determined voice, I went on. "I think you are having flashbacks nearly all the time."

Bursting into tears she spoke. "Yes, I am having flashbacks all the time. My ass is burning, all the time. And last night when Chuck fucked me in my ass thank God he did that."

"Anya, there's a way in which Chuck thinks that he is irresistible. But there's also a way in which he doesn't understand how you manipulate him up one side and down the other to get what you need. For you, he's just a piece of meat and he just doesn't get it that it doesn't matter that it's him and that he's a dime a dozen."

"That's right!" she said with emphatic relief.

It was important to say to her that I imagined there were other ways of being Anya who were active in this situation, and I did so. She agreed and then indicated that she was really upset that, when she was fucked in the ass last night, she had clearly switched self-states. I knew that noticing a switch tended to disturb her deeply and she confirmed it in the next breath.

"It wasn't like there was just this little change in how I thought, or what I was saying. I could feel the jolt of recognizing that I had become totally different. I've watched that *United States of Tara* show, and I've always said to myself that I'm not like that. But last night I knew better. I really do have multiple personality disorder, just like she does. I don't want to have it, but I know I have it. It's just horrifying to think that's the way my mind is. I don't want it."

Anya had confirmed my ongoing sense that not only were several ways of being her really involved in this scene of anal sex, but also that she was really coming to understand on an emotional level that she had a dissociative disorder, which was shocking to her, even after all these years. This kind of lag was not unusual in my clinical experience; here it spoke to the difficulties in the present and the kind of shock waves that might occur if more consciousness for her mind emerged from this discussion. Nevertheless, there was no premium in avoiding making contact with different ways of being Anya who were involved in scenes of abuse. That was a prescription for failure.

"Who else inside is involved in the discussion we're having about Chuck and what goes on but hasn't been participating?"

After some hesitation, she replied, "It's Jennifer. She was the one who was active at this time in high school. It was Jennifer. But you need to remember what her full name is, like I told you before. It's Jennifer Burns."

"Yes," I said sadly, "Jennifer Burns as in a burning sensation in your anus." Anya began to cry in earnest. She was clearly miserable. In a soft and caring voice I spoke, "You know, Anya, I can help you with these flashbacks; it doesn't have to be like this. Even before we start doing specific work to deal with the flashbacks, you can look around inside and find out who has been involved in these scenes with sensations in your anus, your mouth, wherever your body has been sensing abuse from the past. It will help a lot just to identify who inside has been involved and to get to know their story so they don't have to use sensory flashbacks to say what happened and get your attention and mine."

"I know, I know, it's just so hard."

"Yes, it is, and it's also true that pushing through the difficult stuff gets you a lot of relief, something you've known about for a while. But I wonder if you're going to have a hard time with me speaking to different ways of being you. You've always been anxious and upset about my doing that, and you've reminded me that your father did that. He manipulated you."

"No, it's not you, Dr. Chefetz. It's me. I haven't wanted to know what's going on in my mind."

"Yes, it really does make the past real in a way that you know you've been hurt."

She burst into tears again and sobbed.

"I'm really, really sorry, Anya. I wish there was a way in which I could erase what happened and make it all go away. And you have a life that is much more than what happened to you in the past. You have friends. You are gifted. You have a lot of living that you can do."

"Yes, all that is true enough, but I don't know how I'm going to stop doing what I'm doing."

I didn't know either, and I also understood that the gravity of her sexual actions dictated that something needed to change sooner rather than later or she would indeed end up physically hurt or dead.

Addiction

Sexual addiction is not about sex. It's not that sex is irrelevant, it's that sex is just the stage on which underlying concerns are being played out. These concerns usually involve intense emotions. Feelings like shame, terror, and helplessness often figure in affect scripts related to power and control, or the loss thereof. States of rage and powerlessness are often present in the scripts as are efforts to reestablish control. Dodes (1990) comments:

> The addictive behavior reasserts a sense of power by seizing control over the individual's own affective state. . . . Indeed, what is important in addiction, in my view, is to respond to the largely unconscious sense of helplessness

and to demonstrate to oneself that one has the capacity to control one's internal affective experience. For example, alcoholics regularly describe feeling better as a result of simply ordering a drink. I have regarded this as a signal satisfaction (analogous to signal anxiety) of the effort to reestablish a sense of internal mastery. (Dodes 1996)

Some psychoanalytically oriented authors like Dodes have further understood addictive behaviors along Freud's lines as compromise formations operating between a wish, a defense, and a desire for self-punishment (Freud 1894). In my view, the psychoanalytic emphasis on the analysis of fantasy as the source of the wish is somewhat at risk of repeating Freud's errors in his abandonment of the seduction theory. However, there has been significant movement toward an appreciation of what Ferenczi understood about the realities of child sexual abuse (Ferenczi 1955) and of the necessity to be able to formulate a person's mental life as a reaction to real and not just imagined events: "The real objects of a person's world influence the content of the fantasies that constitute that person's drive derivatives, affects, defenses, and self-punitive tendencies" (Rothstein 1991).

The presence of dissociative processes, however, makes the task of understanding historical experience that much more difficult. For example, Anya had little interest in sex, nor did she have any apparent interest in orgasm. Indeed, she had little sense of connection to her body except as a problem reminding her of her abuse, though occasionally she could experience her body as powerful while riding a bicycle or running. Sensuality was not an openly sought dimension in her experiential repertoire. What she had most of all were states filled with exquisite tension and a compelling sense of a need to take action in a sexual manner. Sexual action hid painful feelings of shame, rage, helplessness, and terror, among other things. This is visible in the self-state Jennifer Burns. How such a self-state can both hide and be present involves a variety of mechanisms we discuss later.

Given these kinds of multiple coordinates of experience and the complex interwoven psychodynamic and neurobiologic factors involved, it is reasonable, in at least some cases, to suppose that highly charged but isolated implicit memories of abuse can be responsible for feelings of sexual compulsions. A compulsion can be understood as a consciously unwanted action, including speech, both performed knowingly and experienced as irrational or irresistible. The potential implicit emotional origins of compulsion are often visible.

Addiction may not be conscious despite the fact that it may be performed in an impulsive and compulsory manner. Classically, psychological and physical addiction both show three main factors: dependence on a substance or repeated activity that is depleting of health, tolerance of that substance or activity such that increasing doses are needed to produce the same physical or psychological effect, and the fact that abrupt withdrawal of the substance or activity causes major psychological or physiological dysfunction. Additional characteristics of addiction are that efforts to stop or reduce the behavior fail, a great deal of time is spent in the behavior, important activities are given up or reduced, and the activity continues even after conscious knowledge of detrimental effects (American Psychiatric Association 2013). Even after Anya's eventual success in freeing herself from her sexual addiction, lingering attachments to the relationships with her erstwhile abusers caused major emotional distress at the level of suicidality. The presence of compartmentalized relational strata in her mind meant that even though the addictive sexual behavior had ended, the longing to be with an abuser and have the fantasy experience of safety in the predictability of his attentions, or other hidden experiences, had been maintained for several years.

Does it matter if we talk about sexual addiction versus compulsion? If the medical model of addiction is used, then the tendency is to consider the problem insoluble and a matter of tolerating, limiting, and managing the addiction that will continue for a lifetime. If we talk about compulsion at the level of obsessive-compulsive disorder (OCD), then the potential exists to reframe a sexual addiction as OCD, with all the attendant implications for behavioral and psychopharmacological treatments. These issues are effectively reviewed in detail elsewhere (Gold and Heffner 1998; Goodman 1998). As noted, there are advantages to considering that sexual addiction in the context of dissociative processes represents a complex weaving together of psychodynamic, neurobiologic, behavioral, and other processes that may be advantageously thought of clinically as a habit. Since people often talk about their addictions as their "habit," this is actually a naturalistic use of language. Habits can change.

A major concern in approaching Anya's difficulties was how to maintain a theoretical model that did not undermine the potential for change. A model for generating human factors toward healing was proposed by Antonovsky (1996), and at the core of it is a sense of coherence that emerges from the mobilization of factors he called generalized resistance resources. A person with a strong sense of coherence will "wish to, be motivated to cope (meaningfulness); believe that the challenge is understood (comprehensibility); believe that the resources to cope are available (manageability)." For Anya, after years of suffering sexual abuse in a family where she had no personal power and no decision-making potential, it was understandable that her sense of coherence and agency was in tatters. It's nice that Antonovsky's model has been validated across cultures and languages, but in Anya's psychotherapy, if anybody was going to have a sense of coherence about how to mobilize resources for her healing, then for the time being that responsibility to make things more clear was significantly mine.

The model I had in my mind about addiction was not just of theoretical importance but needed to translate more or less easily into Anya's personal narrative and language. There were two key parts to the model. First, it's been my observation that at the core of addictive behavior is isolated affect—emotional states that are dissociatively inaccessible. Second, while appreciating the biological givens related to addiction (Esch and Stefano 2004; Eysenck 1997), I am also fascinated by the theories of genetic expression and the extent to which genes are influenced by environment in the regulation of anxiety in general (Gross and Hen 2004) and PTSD in particular (Yehuda and Bierer 2009; Yehuda, R., Daskalakis, N. P., Lehrner, A., Desarnaud, F., Bader, H. N., Makotkine, I., . . . Meaney, M. J. 2014). This may be part of why addictive behavior seems to be so recalcitrant: The environmental-genetic fit has made it central to anxiety management. It is also true that in longitudinal studies of a colony of Rhesus monkeys at a long-standing laboratory, results of complex research have shown that good parenting can trump the kind of genetic loading that is usually predictive of misbehavior in young monkeys (Suomi 2006). What this means to me is that with enough time and energy, a positive change in my patient's emotional environment might tip the scales of their behavior, even at the level of genetic expression, in the direction of health, a salutary effect. Combining these perspectives with my appreciation of psychodynamics and dissociative processes means that addiction is more like a habit generated by core experiences, a habit with unknown motivation but with an effect on emotional regulation. A medical model of addiction as generated by biological givens and vulnerabilities may be written in genetic stone and implicitly predict that addiction is an ongoing and consuming lifetime management problem, at best. A psychodynamic model of addiction that incorporates an understanding of dissociation, when it is present, entails recognizing a habitual behavior with a hidden core affective script and unknown motivation with both writ large in the action like Japanese shadow theater, though the attendant dissociative processes mean that the written stage directions have been thrown away. Addiction is compulsive performance art.

Any psychodynamic approach to sexual addiction must appreciate that what is sexual needs to be made distinct from what is sensual. Lichtenberg's motivational systems theory (Lichtenberg 1989a, 1989b; Lichtenberg, Lachman, and Fosshage 1992) provides a framework for appreciating how sexual motivations are distinct from the sensual and how we are also motivated to maintain physiological equilibrium. The sensual-sexual axis includes bodily needs and hormonal tensions related to soothing and pleasurable sexual excitement. (Pain represents a change in the slope toward a rate of increase of sensation that exceeds pleasure; [Tomkins and McCarter 1995], though the pain may become entangled in a pain-pleasure enactment as a scripted precursor to orgasm). The embodied nature of all motivations was not emphasized by Lichtenberg, but is clearly and intuitively visible in his work.

From a dissociative process perspective, thinking about the normative but separate domains of sensuality and sexuality creates a need to discover the subjective nature of a person's sexuality and the extent to which real sensuality might exist during sexual activity. Sexuality without sensuality needs investigating. The absence of a clear and coherent sense of being present in a body and experiencing the sensations associated with sexual activity, including the simply sensual ones, is an indicator of the dissociative isolation of somatic experience from awareness. The human need to hold and be held is missing in action when this isolation of somatic experiencing occurs.

What is sexual must also be distinguished from notions of romantic love. Certainly the two may coexist, but it can happen that certain fantasies of romantic love can wrap around and occlude the visibility of aversive sexual behavior. The romantic fascinations of one self-state may lead to suffering sadistic abuse with some ease if the thrall of romance dissolves with a change of self-state, giving way to an alternate self-state inured to the pain of sadomasochistic relating. Amnesia for these state changes is often profound. However, even casual clinical inquiries can be powerfully undermining of the isolation of those states if they generate curiosity on a practical level: "Do you have a clear and complete memory for the time you were with him before sexual things began through the time after they ended?" "During intercourse are you aware of feeling fully present in your body?" The absence of consciousness for painful or humiliating sexuality enacted during a sexual relationship teaches us the extent to which an absorbing or obsessional focus can function as an exclusionary or deflective dissociative process. Then, too, orgasm may be a sought goal but have many meanings. Scripts with sexual behavior may tell a story. Sexual scripts replete with emotional or physical pain and ripe with humiliation and sadomasochistic activity can be so painful as to be fully or partially organized outside awareness. When the story is fully known, felt, coherent, and alive—when the patient finally "gets it"—addictive behaviors are more difficult to maintain.

In any treatment where there is sexual addiction, the behavior will become more open to exploration as the extent of dissociative process becomes visible. Clinicians must inquire about depersonalization, derealization, and amnesia. A detailed sexual history and a detailed history of a typical episode of sexual activity are critical. Discontinuities in the story may be a sign of dissociative experience, much like narrative incoherence in the adult attachment interview is characteristic of the parents of children with Type D (disorganized/disoriented) pattern of attachment (itself associated with subsequent dissociation as an adult;Lyons-Ruth et al. 2006). Listening for signs of the compartmentalization of experience is very important. Some typical signs are: "Oh, that. Well, my memory for those kinds of things is just terrible. It's always been like that. I don't think of myself as very sexual at all. But he says that when I get my engine started, there's no stopping me. Sometimes he complains that I seem more into what I'm doing than I am in being with him, but I honestly don't know what he's talking about because I have no memory for it." "I don't know how it actually happens, but there's this kind of energy I feel in my body, and then it's as if I'm watching the scene rather than in charge of what I'm doing." "I'm really frightened because I can see what I'm doing, and know that I shouldn't, but it doesn't seem to matter, I still do it. All I need for this to happen is a stray thought or a suggestion and it's like everything changes." "I'd rather be knitting than having sex, and while I'm doing it with him I'm a million miles away, but he never seems to notice." "I get in front of the screen of my computer, go to my favorite pornographic websites, and the rest of the world disappears. Hours go by. It's incredibly exciting, and I'm also terrified the whole time, on and off, because I keep on thinking of what will happen if I ever get caught. I just can't stop myself from doing it. I don't understand. I don't want to, but I must want to because I do it. When I'm not doing it, I live in fear of being discovered." A clinician benefits from having a cultivated knowledge of basic dissociative processes. This can be combined with a nearly obsessional detailed inquiry into the moment-by-moment sexual story, in as much personal detail as possible, while looking for discontinuities, compartmentalization, and the potential for a state change.

Stockholm Syndrome

My introduction to Anya of the Stockholm syndrome—hostages developing sympathy for their captors, and then adopting their captors' perspectives—was an intentional effort to normalize some aspects of her reaction to years of incestuous abuse. I made an effort to temporize the self-hatred and suicidality generated by the disdain, disgust, and contempt she felt for a particular self-state, Sue, who had refashioned her father as being in a romantic relationship with her. If abuse was going to happen, then at least some part of it might have some kind of redeeming value, sad as that was. In essence, this was Sue's perspective.

The grossly conflicting set of motivations—hatred and romantic love—was nearly impossible to tolerate as it became more conscious. Thus, in the context of our ongoing work toward ending Anya's sexual addiction, she increasingly displayed a roller coaster–like oscillation of emotion. Such was the case when at the start of Anya's next session she didn't so much greet me in the waiting room as she scanned my face to gauge my mood and then worriedly ushered me in to my office. There was a nervous energy in her body that told me to follow quietly, as if there was a secret to be told. When she sat down, her body folded, her elbows went to her knees, and her hands covered her face. After a short while, her hands parted and she spoke with her face framed between hands that compressed her face as they held up her tired head. She looked up into my eyes and started to speak.

"I need you to know that if you are going to have a reaction to what I'm going to tell you, then you need to keep it to yourself because I don't think I can manage it if you react to the terrible things I'm going to tell you about what I did." There was a history in our relationship of her having accused me of laughing at her when she was telling me something serious. We had come to understand that the extent to which her father ridiculed and dismissed any serious or important expression of hers had left her anticipating the same in our relationship. I sat, knowing that I had better steel myself against showing a reaction or we would be off into a transference enactment of sorts, and she manifestly seemed to know it, too. I was also aware that if I focused too much on her admonition, I would stop being able to listen to what she was saying in an unencumbered manner. This was her warning. It was a sign of her health that she understood that regardless of the mental space she was in at that particular moment, wanting to tell me something "terrible," she knew another line of thought in her mind was ready to pounce and take over if anything I did might lead to more humiliation and shame than she already anticipated.

Several weeks before this, she had carefully cut a dozen or so parallel rows of superficial wounds on her left cheek and right wrist with a box cutter she impulsively stole from a store. She was so miserably distressed that she had entered my waiting room bleeding and then interrupted someone's session by knocking on the door of my closed consultation room to ask for help. In her subsequent session, she and I had been unable to talk things through as to how she could cope with the erosion of the denial and disavowal of her incestuous relationship with her father. I arranged for a hospitalization. (As I had said to her, at the time of her cutting her face, it seemed to me something must be wrong or not working in our relationship for her to have done this to herself. She didn't know what that might be. She was telling a story. I didn't know the script, though we both knew it was at least partly about her father raping her for many years.)

Had she now cut herself again? Was that what she had done? I couldn't see any bleeding. Had she mutilated herself in some place I couldn't see? I dismissed the idea that she had hurt somebody else. She had been struggling to know her anger toward both her father and her mother, but she could not sustain it for long, even when she could spend a whole session feeling it. Her habit was still to treat some aspect of herself as the target, or to choose her body as the whipping post through the use of over eating, restricted eating, cutting, over exercising, and so on. I didn't think she had taken an overdose of medication and then driven to my office. She might not have been able to create this particular constellation of a scene with me if the drugs had worked too fast. That wasn't her style, in general. I finally settled on her having tried to continue the sadomasochistic affair she had been having with Chuck, but which she'd told me she would stop. Although Chuck was the latest in a long series of men with whom she had done this, this relationship was a victory of sorts for her because she was so utterly conscious of how inadequate a potential partner he was that the incongruity of the relationship had become obvious. Once, in an email, as she was ending a relationship where she had played out a similar script she had put it this way:

> I think the part or parts of me that wish I could hide
> behind him (or anyone or anything right now) kind of felt
> and feel pretty sad after having spoken with him. It feels
> like some important part of the thinking that pretended
> things in my head is no longer pretending and other parts
> of my mind are wondering and yelling, "WHY ARE
> YOU NOT PRETENDING ANYMORE?"

She understood that she was enacting her incestuous relationship with Chuck. She understood she was pretending and hiding something. She wanted to stop, and she hadn't been able to stop. In the last week she was determined to not call or text him. She had deleted her phone logs; she wiped her phone memory. She couldn't speed dial him, and then she had called him from her own memory. She was miserably caught between an apparent determination to enact the past and seemingly simultaneous wish to be free from absent-minded autopilot abuse. What was the motivation to enact? What might it have had to do with her previously cutting herself and presenting herself to me in an emergency situation? How did I get in that scene? Who was I?

But, now, in the moment, if in fact she had gone back and had sex with him, I knew it would provoke a crisis in her. She would have felt deep shame at having had sex with him and also for not having been able to resist the performance art she knew she was enacting. She was now aware that she was emotionally and physically absent in a way that had become painful. Worse, she still wasn't sure why she was acting out sexually. Chuck was not going to be of much help in figuring this out. While having a side to him that was generous to Anya—he gave her gifts from time to time—and having apparent sensitivity to his young daughter, whom he cared for as a single parent, Chuck was indifferent to the fact that the relationship with Anya had degenerated into a use-and-be-used mechanistic sadomasochism.

I was quietly delighted when she told me what the outcome was with Chuck. She had indeed gone to see him, approached him, and without further ado done the shameless thing of asking for sex. The only words from her were emphatic: "Do you want to have sex?" His reply was: "I have VD. I'm contagious, I think." With that, she turned on her heels, got back in her car, and went home.

The banality of the scene now shocked her. At the time, she privately mulled over replying to his "I'm contagious," with a flip "So what?" But thankfully she had enough self-esteem that she didn't do that to herself. I was grateful for the clarity of her action. What I didn't know was whether she would have gone through with having sex with Chuck if he hadn't been infected, and if so, then why? She was shocked and ashamed about simply asking if he wanted to have sex in such a casual manner. I had a sense that this was a repetition of the relationship with her father. Seduction of the aggressor (R. M. Loewenstein 1957) is a powerful childhood coping mechanism. The abused child learns to "turn her trick" with an abusive adult, much like an adult prostitute who gets her john to orgasm quickly and gets rid of the tension about what will happen next. Seduction of the aggressor is an affect regulation script. In the scene Anya described, her behavior with Chuck pointed in the direction of a repetition of action in the incestuous relationship. I kept that thought to myself as I preferred Anya discover this, if it was there.

I considered what had been happening recently in the work of the psychotherapy. There were several threads, two of which seemed crucial. First, there was another relationship she had with another man, interestingly enough called Charles. He preferred his proper name, and while he had his own sources of distress from his life, like Anya, he was clearly smitten with her, loved her deeply, was distressed about her distress, politely, and had been especially distraught with her suicidality just before she had cut her face. She had sought the safety of his relatedness the night before she cut, but neglected to tell him where she was going when she left the next morning, and did not call him when she was briefly hospitalized. He had called me to express his concern for her safety. His deep sadness, fear for her safety, and caring were painful to hear. But Anya couldn't tolerate the intensity of his loving feelings, even though she would temporarily enjoy Charles tremendously. She ran from him, and she routinely did things that hurt him deeply in her back-and-forth, on-and-off relatedness. She seemed to both enjoy and fear the connection with Charles.

A second thread of action was that Anya had been working pretty hard on spelling out what she knew and understood about the different ways of being Anya. In an email she said: "I sort of (SOME PART ANYWAY) wish I knew about the parts of being me—but I feel scared—mostly because I know it is attached to so much bad stuff. And so many bad feelings. So many feelings of being hurt. So it is hard to face that." This was the ongoing struggle, and we believed it was related not just to her fear of knowing she had different ways of being Anya, but that her father had known it, too, and took advantage of it. In that light, and in particular, we had been working on Anya's relationship with Sue. We had stumbled on Sue some years ago. This part of Anya owned a sheer green nightgown that she wore as a teenager when having a fantasy romantic relationship with her father.

Anya's rediscovery of the image of that nightgown, tucked away in the back of her dresser drawer under the rest of her clothes, had occurred some years back, and was the source of a major and enduring upset. She began to appreciate how she found a way to tolerate being raped by making use of a fantasy of being in love with her father. But this love was quite complicated. In fact, her feelings were congruent with Stockholm syndrome. Still trying to sort this all out, she had just read a chapter on anger from a self-help book (Boon et al. 2011). Here is more of the story in her words, via email:

> I was reading the chapter on ANGER. Hmph. Good timing. It was good. It was helpful. After I read it I laid in bed and thought about how I would like to tie up my father and

slowly torture him to death. But that was not a totally satisfying thought—I was thinking first that I would shoot him
(one way of being me), but then that seemed too quick,
then I was thinking I might like to torture him slowly to
death (another way of being me)—cut up pieces of him
and make a lot of cuts on him and pour acid into the cuts
. . . etc. Then I suddenly thought that was not satisfying
either because (you are sitting, right Richard?) BECAUSE
I LOVE HIM AND I DO NOT REALLY WANT HIM
TO DIE. (Okay . . . I am coping with this thought today
by remembering the term STOCKHOLM SYNDROME)
But also, really—I did (I just wrote the word "do" where I
meant to write "did". Um hm.) Anyway, I started thinking
that I would like to go to my parents' house and hold them
both at gunpoint and let my father choose (once and for
all) between me and my mother.

There were a number of things on the clinical table at the point
where Anya told me about her abrupt visit with Chuck. Most important, there was still the problem of what was being played out sexually
that had become dangerous and how to finally bring it to rest. In a session the week before, I had suggested to Anya that her own relationship with Sue was likely in the way of her resolving this performance
art. This had startled her and left her nauseated in the session. The
degree of hatred and blaming toward Sue was profound, as if it were
Sue's fault for what happened. Indeed, her father had contributed to
that myth by invoking words that I have heard again and again from
my patients as they talk about the father who hurt them saying, "Why
do you make me do this to you?"

Nevertheless, Anya rose to the challenge to get to know Sue. In a
painful memoir written over several pages of her journal, Sue packed
in not only a description of her romantic fantasy but the details of
how she had been raped and sodomized, often injured to the point
where she was unable to walk for several days afterward. She described
in particular detail the feeling of being jilted by her father when he

left her bed, the jealousy she had of her mother, and her belief that father would eventually leave his wife and live with Anya alone. She reasoned that she probably had to wait for her mother to die, given her father's tendency to go back her. In this elaborate disclosure there was clarity about the depths of rationalization to which Anya as Sue needed to engage to make sense out of why her father was not gentle with her when he had sex with her. She had to pretend it was love making when it felt more like rape and not attend to the twists and turns required of her in terms of pretending so as to hide the pain. (As an aside, my thoughts went to old psychoanalytic mythology about incest as both rare and also often consensual and so not always traumatic. In this disclosure by Anya we can see how invested Sue was in the fantasy pleasure of the experience. However, a clinician not aware of a change of self-states might have taken this pleasure as representing the whole truth.) Sue's dramatic account made it clear that Anya's capacity to absorb herself in fantasy and then pretend was part of what was mind-saving in her situation. Unfortunately, the fantasy and its enactment were a screen for so much pain that it was very difficult to end the action of the addiction all at once. It was ending incrementally. It seemed to both Anya and me that it was taking forever, and there was some risk in prolonging things.

As Anya and I talked about Chuck and her shame at having approached him so wantonly and brazenly, I was impressed by how disgusted she was with the idea and also how tightly she held on to the action. What was plain was that part of her mind disappeared when she took action. It was as if she didn't know better. It also might have been the case that an essential part of her relationship with her father was in the disappearing act itself, a painfully familiar parameter of their relatedness. We had had a conversation about this.

"One of the things we both know about this particular piece of performance art, Anya, is that it gives you an opportunity to speak in the language of action about the feelings that are emerging in your mind. The script seems to be about a man who hurts you sexually and doesn't really seem to care about you. The scene seems to be about the man you are with right now, Chuck, not your father. We both know

you can potentially hide the feelings and knowledge about your relationship with your father when you are preoccupied with a man in the
present. What's also been clear is that you've been frightened by the
extent to which you are aware now of how powerful and alive you are.
You shy away from the power, sometimes doing things to stop yourself in your tracks, yet still there seems to be a momentum building
for you growing and healing."

"Yes, I know that's true, and it's been showing up in my writing
and art. I just don't know why I can't stop this thing with Chuck. It
doesn't make sense."

"Perhaps one way it might make sense that we haven't considered
is that the intensity of your preoccupation with Chuck is a match for
the intensity with your father. In some ways you disappear into the
relationship when it is heated up. I think the disappearing has been
important to you, and that it feels scary to not have it so much."

"I think that's right, but I don't know how much it fits."

A day later, she wrote to tell about what she'd learned:

> The thing (the "relationship") with this guy Chuck has
> been going on for over two months now and I have felt so
> many times like I am trying to see the performance, the
> script I am acting out so that I can stop seeing him, stop
> acting it out, stop injuring myself, etc. And so many times
> in the past two months I have thought: This is about my
> dad, this is about me re-creating the relationship with my
> dad, Chuck is like my dad in this way and that way and
> this way and like this, etc.—so I think all of that and still
> I go there. But on Thursday night—when we talked about
> the relationship with him being a place to hide myself—
> that the one with my dad was a place in which I disap-
> peared—oh—so much felt like it clicked into place. There
> have been so many things that I have wished you and I
> could figure out in one session, in one sentence, so that I
> could stop the script/performance—even though I know it
> does not really stop until I am ready/able to know and tol-

erate what it is about and that even this is as much or more about being able to tolerate knowing this fact as it is about "figuring it out." But you are right—the relationships have been places for me to disappear into—which is what happened with my mom and my dad—I was not allowed or able to be "me" and then I have been unable and/or scared to be myself and so I have been hiding behind these different relationships and throwing myself and all of my time and energy and everything into them instead of into my own life and what I want to do as me. This feels so big, Dr. Chefetz. To finally see this. And it is painful to know that I was not able to be me when I was a child or teenager, or ever, really, not very much at all until very recently—but I feel like I have been working up to knowing it for a long time now and I feel like I am able to tolerate it.

The Role of Perceptual Distortion

The particulars of the distortions inherent in dissociative living make enactive repetition of past experience especially resilient to change. The multiple realities encompassed by the different ways of being Anya could include changes in the orientation to the present and the orientation to the childhood past and to the teenage past, and so on, all happening simultaneously. As Anya once put it, "How does someone hurt this much and be okay but the hurt is old but it does not feel that way?" The hypnotic phenomenon of trance logic, the juxtaposition of logically incompatible realities without anxiety, without noticing something is very wrong (Orne 1959), is part and parcel of dissociative experience.

While one way of being Anya might be in the midst of grieving, as she clearly was in the communication just quoted, another way of being Anya might still be isolated, unaware of the therapeutic gains being made, so to speak. It creates a situation where someone like Anya may become conscious of repeating the same learning, in differently nuanced ways, multiple times, and feeling like they are getting nowhere in therapy.

The bottom line is that in the context of DID, sexual behavior is subject to multiple disruptions of perceptivity (R. J. Loewenstein 1991). Some of these are attendant on the factor of time distortion so that memory of events from the past are experienced as if in the present or just a moment ago or ongoing. This can foreclose the possibility of a sense of safety. (A woman visiting my office in my home could not contain her anxiety over her implicit understanding that there were beds in the house. She could not tolerate continuing the consultation and had to be referred.) There may also be somatic distortion where memory of events may be experienced in the context of a child-sized body. ("I wasn't abused; it was that pathetic child I can see in my mind.") Other perceptual distortions seem more directly to reflect dissociative processes in all their variety. Facial recognition may be impaired, memory for faces may be absent, or there may be substitute faces that hide the identity of a perpetrator or victim. Hallucinations of both a positive and negative variety may add or subtract perceptual information from a given scene. Depersonalization may complicate memory and cause misattribution of who was being hurt, and so on. It may also create a sense of "I dreamed this" rather than "something happened to me." Spontaneous age regression into a child self-state may occur. This state change may contribute to maintaining amnesia for an event, or create chaos as a way of either telling part of the story or ending an inquiry into a story. There may be anesthesia or analgesia for bodily areas. The presence of these kinds of perceptual signposts may have self-regulatory function or contribute to deflection or exclusion of an ongoing somatic memory via physiological flashback.

Again, in the person with DID, the complexity of the behavior behooves a clinician to become nearly obsessional about discerning specific details of components of these behavior in addition to their dynamic meaning in the relations between self-states. Some self-states may engage in sexual activity while the general fund of knowledge available to other states remains restricted except for things like green nightgown surprises. This contributes to disremembered experience. Some self-states may start a sexual activity and not finish it. Some may find themselves engaged in an activity and not want to finish it. Some may use sexual activity to raise anxiety and fear to silence other states who may wish to convey a trauma story. Some may use passive influence experience[4] to interfere with or control other self-states via an internal script. Some self-states may end up at the end of a sequence of switched states and have to "clean up" the mess. Some may have the role of self-punishment or shaming, after or during sexual activity. Some may have the role of preventing a person from becoming conscious of the sexual activity. Suicidality, and much less frequently homicidality, may be expressed in a contingent manner around sexual activity in the service of preventing access to knowledge of abuse by provoking fear of death as a focal point. This may also be part of the script of an event replete with threats of murder. Some self-states may engage in current activity to obfuscate and confuse a person regarding the emotions, sensations, or behaviors in which they feel compelled to engage in a not-conscious effort to create misattribution of past experience as happening in the present. Somatic flashbacks may be obscured via new sexual activity that hides the origin of the somatosensory flashback disturbance: "Nothing happened to me before. I feel this way because this has just happened a moment ago." Here the self-state Anya called Jennifer Burns comes to mind.

We must also consider that perceptual activity may change during the addictive behavior for a reason that is potentially universal: Sexual activity can regulate emotion. This is both obvious and subtle. Emotional regulation may occur through efforts at self-soothing via relief of mental and bodily tension through *le petit mort*, that is, masturbating to orgasm. This also can include a nearly unnoticed "letting go" of

---

[4] Passive influence is the self-state version of implicit memory that influences choice. Self-states "in the back seat" actively change the action of another state that is "in the driver's seat" and seamlessly influence things like eating and sexuality without the primary self-state have a clue of the manipulation going on. The self-state center of initiative changes for just a moment, and the behavioral or perceptual trajectory changes, passively.

mental and physiological supervision as part of an orgasmic swoon that provokes or heralds self-state change. Emotion can be transformed via a flow of anger into sexual activity. Helplessness can be transformed into activities of pseudocontrol via provoking sexual abuse.

Orgasm thus has multiple potential uses. Orgasm can disrupt core affective flow and provoke a self-state change. Orgasm may signal the end of a scripted scene of abuse in a moment of loss of orientation. Sexual activity that results in disruption or loss of consciousness may both follow a previous script and create specific physical pain that disrupts consciousness. Sexual activity can be used to modify or occlude the hyperarousal symptoms of PTSD.

Orgasm also has involuntary aspects. Perpetrators of abuse note their victim's orgasm and use it to cement their sadistic triumph by exclaiming, as reported to me, "You are the slut I said you were. Look at you. You like this!" It is important to appreciate the decrement of self-esteem that can occur in a moment like this. More puzzling still, pleasure and pain have neurobiological similarities—the amygdala is deactivated during orgasm (Georgiadis, Kortekaas, Kringelbach, and Berridge 2009) and opioids are released into limbic and related areas with both pleasure and pain (Leknes and Tracey, 2008) and can become woven together experientially on several conflicting levels of experience. The presence of a sexual response during abuse is confusing for the person being abused. The association of relief from pain as an experience of reward may have similarities to orgasm. The excitement of sexual arousal can block experiencing negatively charged emotions or the ability to cognitively process experience or reflect on past experience. Sadomasochistic sexual behavior, excitement, pleasure, and pain can be complexly woven in an affect script so that emotional tension may persuade a person to undergo painful experience as they seek an ultimate state of relief and freedom from pain.

The Road to Compulsion

Gold and Seifer incisively identify an important overarching feature of sexual addiction and compulsion (SAC)—loss or absence of control—when they note that the syndrome "consists of sexual behavior over which the individual does not experience a sense of control, and which consequently repeatedly creates social, occupational, or legal problems for her or him" (Goldand Seifer 2002, p. 65). This raises the clear possibility of dissociative scripting. To be sure, Gold and Seifer qualify their position when they note that dissociative states may be less common for people with SAC who do not have complex histories of childhood sexual abuse.

Still, there is much in common between their approach and mine. A key provision of the Gold-Seifer procedure is explicit in how they introduce the therapeutic process: No attempt will be made to change behavior. The patient is asked to make a commitment to report every facet of a specific incident of sexual behavior to their therapist for discussion. As they then note, feelings of being coerced by a therapist are greatly reduced. Although this therapeutic approach seems cognitive-behavioral, the noncoercive approach is in fact quite psychodynamic.

SCAN-R, Gold and Seifer's interview protocol, stands for select, cue, analyze, note, and revise. This is essentially what I did with Anya as we carefully reviewed sexually charged scenes in her relationship with Chuck. A specific incident is selected, the triggers and cues to which the patient responds are discovered, the sequencing of actions and reactions are analyzed (in the context of the cues with a detailed moment-to-moment microanalysis of events), salient issues are noted out loud by the therapist (especially those that are newly added to the action script), and then the script is revised in the sense that there is new, more detailed understanding of what happens. This highly detailed process is reminiscent of the processing of a trauma scene, from before the beginning through and past the end, so that all contexts that both provoke and result from the script become known (Kluft 2013). The detailed analysis of the different elements of the action script create links between different areas of compartmentalization of behavior, affect, sensation, and knowledge (Braun 1988), essentially breaking down the compartmentalization that is typical of dissociative organizations of mind.

I believe there are three additional areas worthy of emphasis: the need to look for emotional scripts from SAC that match with SAC scenes other than the one selected; integration of the SAC script into the personal autobiographical narrative; and, most important, assessing the extent to which a person who works through a SAC script achieves a sense of personalization and embodiment in the process. Remnants of depersonalization, especially unchanged levels of depersonalization or derealization after exploration of a script, predict a lack of integration of the knowledge and a failure to achieve enough consciousness for the script to keep it in awareness when sexual impulses and compulsions arise.

From this perspective I understood how Anya's ability to tolerate knowing herself as having multiple self-states was compromised. It's not that she wasn't interested; she was terrified of what it would mean to her if she intimately knew the shifts, changes, and differences between states and consciously tracked the changes. It would mean that the story of her life, the one she had cultivated and held on to, was very incomplete. During one brief hospitalization, she spelled out her thoughts in a powerful and instructive way as she struggled to know what was in her mind and deal with sexual behavior that she struggled to control.

> Before I left the hospital on Monday I wrote on one of the first pages of a beautiful new little sketchbook the following: Two roads diverged in a yellow wood, AND I TOOK BOTH.
>
> And I meant this: For all of my life it is like I have been running down two roads—one road on which I knew about the abuse and another on which I did not and I was always imagining that the two roads would never meet. But the roads met. It makes me want to cry just to type that. Anyway—the roads met and the wish that my parents had never been horribly abusive was killed at their convergence. And I was thinking today how I had written yesterday that I went into the hospital because

I came to the understanding that I have to let go of the wish that my parents did not abuse me—which is sort of what happened. But it was also really that when I started to understand what was happening—that I had to fully stop pretending and wishing—I felt like I might hurt myself because I was so scared. I was so scared and lost and completely terrified about it all—I thought I might hurt myself—I wasn't sure what was going to happen. I was unsure what was going to happen next because I had never even imagined my life without the wish. And when I did—imagine my life without the wish—I felt like I might just not make it. So that is why I really went into the hospital.

I was feeling better through the metaphor about the two roads and how I had taken them both—I had come to understand something that had been really difficult to understand. But I felt like something was still not quite right—that some piece was still missing and then I came to understand that there was a third road. There was the knowing, the not knowing, and then the final road—the last piece and the most painful road of all: the road of Stockholm syndrome . . .

I spent the first several years of my therapy work literally running back and forth between the two roads of knowing and not knowing about the abuse. I would go to therapy and tell a detailed memory of my father raping me—feel a sense of freedom and relief—then run home filled with terror and anxiety over all I had said. I would call friends and write in my sketchbooks over and over asking the same questions: "Why am I saying these things? Why can I not stop saying them? Why would I be saying them if they were not true?" I would literally sit on the phone with one of my closest friends telling her the stories about my father that I had been spewing in my therapy and then go on to say: How could this be true?

One of the things I hate the most about the incest, rape, and trauma that I survived at the hands of my own parents—one of the worst parts is that they acted like it did not happen and that made me feel worse and crazier than all of the abuse ever had. They would hurt me and pretend they had not. My father would rape me and act like he didn't. And when—by the time I was in high school—I was a drinking, class-skipping teenager who was starting to have sex and put out cigarettes on my flesh—they said I was a failure—a fuck-up. But really—the real reason I was "acting crazy" was not because I was crazy at all—I was doing those things because I was in terrible, terrible pain and I was in that pain because they were hurting me.

The naturalistic scaffolding that Anya had created to compartmentalize knowledge of her abuse from the knowledge of being part of an apparently normal family seemed to have been a function of the ability of her parents to seamlessly collaborate in Anya's abuse. Since her mother was also a victim of the father's sexual sadism, and by Anya's reports had been complicit with him in Anya's abuse, it was mind-fracturing for Anya to emerge from physically punishing events into the family kitchen where dinner was on the table. No discussion was ever entertained of what had just happened to her when her father came home from work.

The usual emphasis in thinking about the creation of self-state compartmentalization is on the high impact of trauma. It's not unusual to hear clinicians talk about a "part of Mary that was created to deal with this episode of abuse that was different than others." However, it's worth considering discontinuities in the behavior of perpetrators, which grossly ignores reality as an inciting generator for compartmentalization of experience (Kramer 1983). The tension inside Anya as she struggled to deal with the contradictory nature of at least two versions of knowing the "story" of her life was also present in the context of the frame I had introduced to her as the Stockholm syndrome (Auerbach, Kiesler, Strentz, Schmidt, and Serio 1994).

The End of an Addiction

It was extraordinarily confusing for Anya to reconcile the strong feelings of love and hate for her father that contributed to discussions like the one she talked about with her girlfriend where she doubted what was in her mind. Healthy doubt is part and parcel of that for which every patient and clinician must strive. An ability to tolerate not knowing with clarity and to leave room for revision or discarding of recollections of abuse is important. The struggle over what to do with recalled memory belongs with the patient. There are no known characteristics of recall that predict veridical memory. The clinician is a witness to the recollection, not to the event. When Anya first nonchalantly mentioned in therapy a green nightgown she once found in her dresser drawer, hidden behind and under other clothes, she was horrified by what she heard coming from her mouth. She came to know both the supercharged hypersexual activities of her early adulthood that extended the picture of the incestuous relationship with her father into her mid-twenties and the Electra complex-like wishes and guilt she harbored in the hope of displacing her mother from her father's life. She was later baffled by recalling how her father could leave Anya's bed and go back to her mother, leaving her to clean up after anal sex. She was also horrified by the implications of only having cleaned up these messes in her teenage years, knowing her mother must have cleaned up earlier. The whole fabric of the life she thought she had lived was completely upended. Repeating sexual acts in her adulthood as a way to obfuscate the past and attribute her behavior to an addiction of sorts was a much more acceptable set of thoughts than the hornet's nest of her family scene.

Anya realized that the romantic love she had felt for her father was not something that was at all realized in fact; it was only a fantasy. Her version of the Stockholm syndrome was a useful pivot that helped her survive a number of years of particularly sadistic abuse. But again, it worked only in fantasy. She became clear that her father was never a gentle lover—quite the contrary. As she put it, tongue in check, she confessed to me that she really did have false memories: The story she had once believed described her childhood was mostly made up—so she could have something to believe in that would not frighten her.

We all tend to reenact, in whole or in part, the salient emotionally unresolved scenes of the past. Whether we think of these as model scenes (Lichtenberg 1989a) or reciprocal role responses (Ryle 1999) (the behavior that comes back at you when you behave in a way that is expected to generate a particular response) is less significant than keeping in mind that our behavior is often guided by unintegrated and unresolved past experience. We may contrast this point of view with medical models of addiction that interpret behavior as generated by biological givens that create compelling behavior through physiological imperatives such as abnormalities of dopamine metabolism (Eysenck 1997) and the complexities of reward and pleasure circuitry in projections of midbrain dopaminergic and limbic circuitry (Esch and Stefano 2004). In the medical model, "addiction represents a pathological usurpation of the neural mechanisms of learning and memory that under normal circumstances serve to shape survival behaviours related to the pursuit of rewards and the cues that predict them" (Fratta 2006). Of course there is physiology and biology. But people are not machines, and while it is exceedingly difficult and painful to do the work just described, it is a tribute to Anya's humanity that she did it. At the center of some addictive behavior is intense, painful embodied emotion. An emotion-focused treatment that pays attention to self-states, dissociative processes, and psychodynamics can be an effective treatment for these forms of addiction.

An Upgrade for the Repetition Compulsion

Why do we repeat? What good is it? Freud spoke of a therapeutic process in which we remember, repeat, and work through. In all these things the underlying agenda "is to fill in gaps in memory; dynamically speaking, it is to overcome resistances due to repression" (Freud 1914, p. 148). Yet a page later he notes: "It particularly often happens that something is 'remembered' which could never have been 'forgotten' because it was never at any time noticed—was never conscious"

(Freud 1914, p. 149). Repression of something previously conscious is thus not a factor here. Freud is clearly talking about unformulated experience (D. B. Stern 1997), dissociative process, and a lack of referential linking (Bucci and Maskit 2007).

At this time in the history of psychology we may not be able to figure out how to parse the difference between what is dynamically unconscious, and what is part of implicit, procedural memory. We can say with certainty that it is a reasonable heuristic to appreciate that for a patient like Anya there exists a relentless search for coherence and putting together in a common sense personal narrative the isolated, excluded, and deflected content of her feelings and thoughts that were incoherently jumbled together. For Anya and others, repetition is not about wanting to repeat. Ask anybody who repeats and they will tell you it's not what they want to do. What is it, then? Paul Russell comments:

> For the most part, the repetition is of something actually, or potentially, painful. We do not complain, presumably, about pleasant repetitions. . . . In fact, the suspicion begins to dawn upon us that the more painful the experience, the more we were injured by it, the more likely it is to be woven into something we find ourselves compulsively repeating. This is more than a little unsettling. It feels spooky; Freud used the word "daemonic." There is some powerful resistance that appears to operate against all efforts at learning to anticipate, to avoid, or to alter painful repetition. The repetition compulsion is education-resistant. (Russell 1998)

I wouldn't even call it "resistant." I think of it as reflecting a paradoxical self-protection without a knowable context. The repetition compulsion is a compromise formation: it is an unconscious process trying to relieve us of tremendous pain while it tries to protect us from knowing or feeling it. That's the one paradox in Russell's elegant work that he didn't specifically name. Until we are strong enough to tolerate what we need to feel to provide the associative links of which dissociative process robs us, we are destined to repeat the action that tells the story of what is too painful to coherently know. Anya had this experience and overcame the fear.

We take action—performance art—because that's all that's left to us when emotion is isolated alongside thought, behavior, and even bodily sensation (Braun 1988) as a result of dissociative process. The action tendency (Greenberg and Paivio S.C., 1997) of emotion energizes movement, often along the lines demarcated by old behavioral (Ryle 1999) or affective scripts (Tomkins 1995) that are implicitly held. We know that the right brain can dance to the music of a feeling while not being able to name it (Bermond et al. 2006), and it's not a leap of faith to appreciate that we take action without always being able to name what we're doing or why. Anya stopped her sexual addiction when she figured out what she was feeling and thinking underneath her action.

The apparent compulsion to repeat tragic scripts is about a desperate unconscious effort to create coherence when exquisitely painful and meaningful unintegrated experience lacks personal narrative and consciousness for intense emotion. The repetition compulsion reflects a tension between dissociative processes activated by fear versus associative processes undermined by irresolvable confusion (pieces of the puzzle are dissociatively inaccessible) that seek coherence and relief of emotional pain. We repeat because the dissociative process maintains the isolation of elements of experience often riddled with shame, terror, hatred, helplessness, and all the other miseries of human tragedy. This leaves only a narrow corridor of apparently addictive behavior down which action compulsively moves us as it tries to tell our story. We repeat by virtue of the magic of that thief who steals the links between the elements of experience and leaves us ashamed, once again, of how we failed to protect or heal ourselves.

Put another way, we repeat because the conditions under which the original experience occurred have not changed. It is still too painful to know. Thus, we repeat in shame what we experienced originally as ridden with shame. We tell out loud with obvious action the story of our silent, unspeakable shame when we repeat. We are disgusted with ourselves when we repeat, and thus, without a compassionate witness, we repeat, we feel shame, rage, disgust, despair, helplessness, and we don't resolve. So we repeat again.

Underneath all of it, there is a countervailing associative effort toward coherence. The repetition compulsion is a paradoxical compromise formation where we protect ourselves from knowing what we desperately wish to know with felt coherence.

Postscript

It feels appropriate to honor the courage in Anya by closing this chapter with her own words.

> I have so much grief inside of me about—all of the things I have been working to know about the past 6, 7 months and the past 9.5 years.
>
> I'm not fighting inside my head—between different ways of being me. I wanted to tell you that—since I (we) now have been reminded that you are not a mind reader. As my dad and family often felt like to me anyway. Starting to talk to you about different ways of being me—even just a little bit so far—it has taken a TON of pressure off inside of me. So I feel really happy about that.
>
> And also there is the stuff I am doing/thinking when I am not there, in sessions with you. I'm trying to be more aware—ask more questions—why do I feel this way? What is this about? What is this connected to? And it is helping me a lot. To feel more freedom in my head and in my life.
>
> But oh there is so much sadness inside of me. So much.

Chapter 8

Waking the Dead Therapist

THE PATIENT WHO IS THE CASE EXAMPLE OF THIS CHAPTER KNOWS THAT I write and give talks.[1] She once admonished me to be sure that I tell people the most important thing in our relationship was that I was *real* with her. Metaphors about feelings, emotions, and affects are helpful, but it is the emotional presence of the therapist that is required. For me, the times in treatment requiring emotional presence are often the "messy" ones; they are not times to which I look forward, but they often become the memorable times, the ones that patients and I may look back on as moments of real emotional growth, for both of us.

Rachel, 40 years old and widowed, had dissociative identity disorder.[2] For her, and for other patients like her at the start of treatment, there was a constellation of ongoing chronic depersonalization, derealization, amnesias, identity confusion, and identity alteration (Stein-

---

[1] This chapter was originally published as R. A Chefetz, "Waking the dead therapist," *Psychoanalytic Dialogues*, 19(4) (2009), 393–403, and is reprinted by permission of the publishers, Taylor & Francis Ltd., http://www.tandf.co.uk/journals/. A much earlier version of this paper was presented at the Massachusetts Institute for Psychoanalysis in May 2006, and a much shorter version at the meeting of Division 39 of the American Psychological Association in April 2008. At that latter meeting, a formal discussion of the paper by Wilma Bucci opened an important avenue of inquiry. I have specifically and gratefully incorporated what I learned from Dr. Bucci's insight into this chapter.

[2] You are going to read case material where I speak to the patient's shifting subjective experience as if I am talking to another person. That is not what I am doing. But that is what you may discern if you have no experience with these particular radical shifts in the subjectivity of your patients.

berg 1993). These criteria are based on shifts in the patient's subjective experience. In their most robust manifestation, dissociative alterations in subjectivity produce the experience or feeling of being "taken over" by a center of agency outside one's own will or by the presence of an additional sense of self (Way 2006). "I was appalled at how I was eating, just shoveling food into my mouth, but I couldn't do anything to stop it!" a patient may say. This part of the patient may insist she is a different person, with a different name, sometimes a different life history, and may use pseudodelusional beliefs to not experience any curiosity about how she somehow knows all about the life of the person to whom she believes she has no relationship! "That's *not me!*" Some people have these shifts in subjectivity in a seamless way and don't particularly notice the lack of connection to the rest of their being. Sometimes the shifts are noticed, and the clinical challenge is to make the shifts in subjectivity part of the psychoanalytic inquiry (Chefetz 2004). Here are the words of another patient struggling with the emergence of a new aspect of herself, who finds herself in therapy and doesn't want to be there (from an email in the voice of this alternate self-state):

> i don't know what i feel, stop bothering me and leave
> me alone. i didn't ask for your help and i don't want it.
> shame, what's shame? feeling like vomiting every time you
> see a child at risk or hurt or going to be hurt? who am i to
> feel anything? i am a nobody, now go and bother someone
> who wants to be involved with you because it's not me!
> You're not going to gain my trust and i am not going to
> give you my word! so we are at a stalemate!

Clinicians also have shifts in subjectivity, and some of them are too painful to fully emerge into consciousness, if they even emerge at all. Regardless, their magnetic influence on the treatment may become visible, if we're lucky. Dissociative process is characterized by disruptions in referential processing of experience (Bucci 1997). The unlinked referential tags of dissociated elements of experience stay in close psychic proximity (Chefetz and Bromberg 2004), and even if they are like small, very weak magnets, when they are close enough together the pull they exert on each other can be compelling. This is visible in the comments we routinely make: "I don't know why I do it this way; it's just the way it feels. I don't understand it, but it feels like the right thing." The implicit nature of the felt sense is clear, and the reference cues that influence this particular behavior are not visible but nevertheless exert their influence.

Rachel has a typical way of beginning the session that she initiated some three years before the scene at the center of this chapter occurred. She came into the room, paused by one of the armchairs near the door, picked up an overstuffed pillow, then placed it in the center of the couch across from my chair, sat on it, and said, "How are you doing?"

"Okay," I replied, "Just hangin' out in my office, the usual."

"Good," was her reply.

Some background: For several years Rachel had wished to know about my emotional state, how I was, before she would venture into open communication with me. "How are you?" thus came to be understood as neither a casual inquiry nor a social grace. During the previous year in her ongoing four-hours-a-week treatment (one double followed by two single sessions), she had become increasingly able to honestly voice her occasional upset with me. This was a major gain for her. It was also becoming increasingly important that she might be able to feel angry with me, considering my behavior. Recently, we had been tracking my sleepiness in her sessions, especially the two afternoon sessions, the first hours after lunch on Monday and Friday.

At the start of my noticing how hard it was to stay focused and not lapse into a sleepy state, I considered the extent to which I was physically exhausted. I pondered the size of my lunch and knew that after-lunch shifts in blood flow were going to be more provocative of sleep as I got older. I had even compared notes with another senior clinician who reminded me that he had battled this for some time. I wasn't reassured. It was a problem. I also knew that it didn't occur with only this patient. I had been working too hard. I knew it, and yet I had made a number of commitments that were important to me. I must just be tired, I thought.

During one previous sleepy moment of mine, she had nearly had enough of it, but then somehow made an accommodation that I felt was a remarkable sign of her growth. I had gotten sleepy in the session, and when she returned for our next meeting, she led off immediately with a cogent, accurate, and nonaccusatory statement of the history of how painful my sleepiness had been for her, how she had been made to feel invisible, and how she had come to appreciate that it was my problem, not hers. She told me that she had considered quitting treatment, but that I had been the only therapist she'd ever had who consistently helped her. She had decided not to give up on me, but instead she accepted that this was a problem I had to work out. I agreed with her, and I promised to keep track, as best I could, of what was happening and try and resolve it. I openly appreciated her willingness to work with me on it.

Now to the session at hand. After Rachel had checked in and discerned my state of mind, she got down to business rapidly. "I had a new memory last night," she then said, resentfully. She looked down at her lap as if she had been struck. She spoke in the emphatic, pleading, tearful voice of a child who was tired and despairing of working at a task with no apparent end. "I'm really tired of this, and I don't think it's worth trying to do this anymore because it is never going to end, never going to leave me alone, and I just quit. I can't stand it anymore! I get through something, and then there is no rest, there is just something else."

"Seems like this has just about blown your fuses. What's going on?"

"I was talking to my sister, Robin, and she's going on and on about how her boys are like wild Indians, driving her crazy and getting her frustrated. I called her because she was in this image that came to me. She was tied in a chair." Rachel became silent.

"Does this have anything to do with Mr. X?"

"Yes, Robin was watching."

"She was tied in a chair and watching!?" I spoke with a tone of incredulity. "How awful!"

With no pause in the conversation, and no hint of the impact on her, she said, "Yeah, and so I'm talking to her about her boys, waiting to tell her about my image of her tied in a chair, and not being able to figure out how to do it, and then she goes and says: 'I get so frustrated with those boys I feel like I have to tie myself in a chair!' And so I nearly yelled at her when I said, 'Robin, that's not normal, to say something like that. I mean, nobody says that they are so frustrated that they need to tie themselves in a chair?! That's got to mean something!' So, she said it didn't mean anything to her. It was just an expression, she said."

Having sounded incredulous in talking about her sister up to now, here Rachel began to speak in flat tones. It was as if she, and the animation that was present in her just a moment before, had been suddenly transformed into a deeply depressed prisoner on death row, hopeless, helpless, and only somehow able to speak. She continued.

"So I told her about my remembering that she was in the room when Mr. X hurt me, and she was made to watch. He taped her mouth shut, and tied her to the chair. Then he hurt me while she was watching. Sometimes he made her help hold me down while he hurt me. I don't know that I can talk about it with you. I just can't do it. I need hypnosis; I just can't get into it."

I had a sense that she was indeed on the brink of something so unbearable that she could not imagine talking about it without the insulation afforded by a hypnotic state. "Why do you think you need hypnosis?"

"It's just too much!"

"Does the story feel like your story, or does it feel like it belongs to a different way of being Rachel?"

"It's Joey's story."

"Joey, do you need hypnosis to talk about your story?"

Rachel shifted in her chair, her body becoming somewhat stiff, hands in her pockets, and as she spoke, her voice remained flat, no feeling at all. Joey spoke slowly, as if the words emerged with difficulty. "I want to be dead. I don't want to do this anymore. It doesn't get me anywhere. I've been talking about the same things, over and over, and nothing good comes of it."

"Joey, Rachel said she needed hypnosis to work on this. Why do you think she said that?"

"I hurt too much. My body hurts, my head hurts, I just hurt. Everything hurts."

"I hear you talking about how you feel right now, and I also hear you talking about how you felt when Mr. X hurt you years ago. It sounds like the feelings of the past are in your body right at this moment. When you look at your body, inside your mind, what is happening?"

"He's gone. I've fallen on the floor. I don't have any clothes on. I see my body, the legs are just stretched in front of me. There's blood on them. They're just there. I just hurt. I want to die." Rachel, as Joey, was speaking in a depersonalized, dissociative manner about "the legs."

It's very difficult in retrospect to remember the exact sequence of what I was experiencing during this time, and of course that is part of what the problem was for me, and in other ways for Rachel. What is clear is that during this session I was struggling to stay focused and attentive. I was, in fact, fighting to not drop into a kind of sleep. It wasn't just that every minute or two I felt a little drowsy. It was more that I was finding myself nearly falling asleep, much as happens when driving for many hours and being tired; no matter what kind of effort I made, lapses of attentional focus left me drifting into sleep for a fraction of a moment, head almost (I imagined) not quite falling forward, then lurching back to consciousness with an effortful force of will.

As I have mentioned, I had experienced some sleepiness in past sessions, but at some point in this session, I believe, not too long after this exchange with Joey, not only did my eyes close, but I must have fallen into sleep because I have a clear memory of my head actually falling forward, catching myself, and then jerking myself alert, only to find Rachel looking straight into my eyes with a mix of concern and fury.

She spoke first, in a forceful voice, completely uncharacteristic of her, as soon as my eyes focused. "Look, I know this is your problem, and you know what this does to me when you get tired, but whatever it is, you need to do something about this right now because this just isn't going to work if you keep doing this. So, what is it that's bothering you, what is in your mind that you are falling asleep? We're going to get to the bottom of this right now!"

I am aware of my own vulnerability to overreact to anger coming at me from my patients if there is a feeling in me of my patient being mean or having a wish to hurt me. I have been working on this kind of experience for a number of years. It is partly a fear of humiliation. In this case, I did not have such a fear. I actually thought about this odd absence of the threat of shame or humiliation and was privately grateful to Rachel for her ability to respect my intentions to be of use to her, even when I was in trouble with myself. It was very useful to feel this respect from her because it freed me to look for issues that were hidden from my awareness without having to spend inordinate time initially dealing with the shame spectrum of emotion as related to my sleepiness. In fact, I was so grateful to her, I had no fear of humiliation. I didn't think about additional possibilities for my sleepiness beyond my own avoidance of my patient's potential for sadistic expression. After a pause where I imagine I was visibly trying to get oriented, I finally spoke to her.

"Rachel, I appreciate very much what you are saying, and I couldn't agree with you more that I need to figure this out. I also don't think I can suddenly work on my stuff without having some private time to go with the material in the session, and see what kinds of things come into my mind from our work. I do that all the time, routinely, but I've obviously been missing something here that's important. And yes, something has to be done about this, now. Can we continue?"

"Yeah, but you've really got to get this under control, it just doesn't work for me."

"It doesn't work for me either."

I asked Rachel to focus again on what it was like to be Joey in the scene from her childhood, since that focus was where we had left off. At least I had some memory for what was going on! She moved immediately into being Joey, and she shifted the conversation to talk about how her protests only led to Mr. X being more violent prior to the sexual abuse he inflicted on her. Joey then described the miserable process of having to clean up the blood that was on the floor in a puddle underneath him, how Rachel and Robin had snuck downstairs in the middle of the night to wash sheets, pillow cases, and what was left of her clothes that she could wear. Joey made no mention of the feeling of sitting in blood or any feeling in the body. For the first time, I became openly aware of what must have been the depersonalized deadness in Joey. He had not spoken of this deadness at all.[3]

"Joey, I have such a sense of the deadness that was your body then, and how much you are feeling that deadness now as we sit and talk. What's it like to finally be able to tell somebody what was going on?"

"I've already told you. I just want to die."

"Yes, and I don't think anybody has ever understood why that feeling makes sense for you, or even listened to you say it, or even notice that you've been able to say it, perhaps for the first time."

"Everything is spoiled. There is nothing I can do. I have no skills. I have no interests. I have nothing. I am nothing. I just want to die."

The helplessness and hopelessness being expressed were very powerful, filling the room. I understood that there was a need to voice these feelings. I knew there would be no acknowledgement of Rachel's interpersonal skills, artistic talents, and organizational abilities. All that knowledge was isolated from the consciousness that was Joey.

I continued to struggle with my sleepiness, though I was much more alert than previously. I could feel the pull back into the place from which I had jerked myself alert. I don't know when it was exactly, but I remember that at some point in this continued discussion of pain and hopelessness, an image came into my mind. It only lasted a brief moment. I nearly dismissed it as annoying. This was an image that I had known and can still see, though now with a different feeling. I could see an image from my twentieth year, an image of my own father's shrunken, wasted legs sticking out from his pajamas as he lay in his hospital bed, about two weeks before he died of cancer. His skin was white, and the scales on his legs were thick, but somehow oddly

---

[3] I am aware of the movement back and forth between gender assignments in the way I refer to Rachel as "her" and Joey as "he." I go with the patient's regard for their identity, and use male and female pronouns as is contextual for the name of different self-states. There are times where gender seems to hold particular meaning and becomes the subject of inquiry.

translucent, the white edges curling up from the skin on the flat of his shinbone while the centers stayed tacked down to the skin beneath with a kind of brownish freckle; this was the skin of a wasting body that I had seen many times since then in working with patients in my medical practice.

I kept listening to Joey speak, and then it finally dawned on me, as I kept this image in mind, that the legs of death in my own image were what Joey had seen, his own dead legs attached to his own dead body. It was Joey's image of horror, but there was a profound resonance with my own horror, a feeling that I had not ever named to myself. It wasn't that I hadn't "sort of" thought "My father's legs look horrible." But I don't believe I had ever thought: "Rich, you are feeling the feeling of horror!" There's a real difference between saying "That's horrible" and being speechless with horror. So I thought, privately, "I am *feeling* horror!" I had been asking Rachel to speak about her pain, but I couldn't tolerate my own any better than she could hers. I had been asleep to my horror, and apparently, I had wanted to keep it that way.

I don't have a sense of how long it took for me to formulate what I was considering saying, but I had clarity that I needed to speak in a meaningful way about what was in me that was likely also in Rachel but didn't have a name. I waited a little while, letting my thoughts cook, perhaps 15 minutes or so, and when there was a pause in her story, I spoke.

"Rachel, I've been working on the falling asleep problem as we've talked, and I think I may have found something important about me, and also about you. I think it's about a feeling, and just like happens sometimes with you, the feeling made its way into my awareness as an image, not a thought. I'd like to tell you about the image, and I'm hoping it will help us figure out what's been going on in your treatment, as well as with my sleepiness."

Rachel looked at me with rapt attention. She moved quickly from being Joey into a more adult state. Her body was alive, and she leaned forward, open, receptive. "Sure, I'd like it if you would."

"The image is from many years ago, just before my father died of cancer. It was an image just of his legs, legs that had gotten very thin from the wasting away of his muscles. I'm sure you remember what your husband's legs looked like as the cancer attacked his body."

"Yes, it was horrible, they were so thin, and he was so weak. I can still see them."

"Well, Rachel, I am thinking that it's my own image telling me about my own feelings of horror that are vibrating in tune with feelings of horror in you, feelings related to you being abused by Mr. X, brutally, but feelings that you've been unable to know about or to speak. I think that I haven't wanted to know about my own feelings of horror either. I think that I haven't been able to know, so much so, that I unconsciously tried to avoid knowing by sleeping. I've also had a visual in my mind about what it was like to be you, as Joey, and to be on the floor of the bedroom, bleeding, and not in your body, the body feeling dead, detached, from the horror, the impossible horror of it all."

In a very thoughtful, considerate adult voice she replied, "I know it was horrible, but I can't feel it, it doesn't feel like it's mine, it's just like it's Joey's, but I know he is part of me. I appreciate you telling me about your father. It makes sense that you didn't want to know the feeling. I guess I don't either. How are you feeling?"

"I'm wide awake, now. It's a very curious experience. I think you've had it yourself, at times. Joey, what are you understanding about this?"

"I don't feel anything about it. I don't feel anything. I hear what you are saying, and I thank you for working on it, but it doesn't do anything for me."

"Joey, I am thinking that there is a way in which if you know about the horror, you'll get angry with Mr. X for what he did. I'm guessing that you're afraid to make the horror real because you're afraid of being angry. When you got angry with Mr. X for trying to hurt you, he beat you to within an inch of your life, throwing you against the wall. Remember when he threw you through the window? He had you lie to the doctor in the emergency room about the shards of glass in your skin. So getting angry with Mr. X might be terrifying. If you have a body that you don't live in, Joey, and you don't feel the horror of it, then you would never have a reason to feel anger in your body, and want to take action to protect yourself."

She began to have a couple of tears in one eye, and her face looked sad as Joey said, "He didn't have any right to hurt me. *Stupid*! You're so *stupid*. . ." and we continued on with the work of the treatment as the anger bubbled out. I thought I now had the full picture, but I didn't.

This experience of thinking I had found *the* source of my counter-transference sleepiness was repeated several times over the next few years. The examples are not without value. I learned that there were times Rachel spoke with a monotonic hypnotic speech that provoked a trancelike sleepiness in her highly hypnotizable therapist. I became aware of the murderous rage I felt toward her abuser, a rage that was alive in me, and enlivening, as I felt my response to her stories of abuse. Rachel discovered that as angry and despairing as she was about her abuse by Mr. X, it was her mother's controlling and emotionally dismissive behaviors that were most harmful to her. I discovered a painful countertransference identification with Rachel in discovering some latent anger toward my own mother. I heard from Rachel, in a painful session, that for some parts of her my sleepiness meant that she had lost her therapist, lost someone who could listen to her and be a witness. She was able to become somewhat openly angry with me as we worked on this feeling of loss, an anger that was healing and a match for the experience of losing a mother or father who couldn't or wouldn't listen to her.

I also discovered my own rage at having to listen to the stories of my patient's abuse that had the resonance of truth. The context was related to feelings in me of being overwhelmed, exhausted, and immobilized. On one day, I had just seen Rachel and then another patient in an equally painful place. I was unconsciously enraged, but at the time, consciously only annoyed and irritated about having to listen and struggle with the negativity that threatened their lives. I resonated with their despair, and I lost my energy. It must have drained into the affectively isolated pool of my own rage. The words in my mind were "I don't want any more of your truth!"

Then on one particular day, after the usual inquiry of "How are you doing?" Rachel pointedly spoke to me in a manner that made clear she needed a very real and up-front response from me: "Dr. Chefetz, what's it like for you to be doing this work with me?" Without hesitation I told her, "It's rather a horrible thing, Rachel, to work with this kind of pain. I know you feel the same way about it. I think you are aware of how I also have struggled with what resonates in me, and how it leaves me sleepy, at times. I still don't understand it completely, but I know there is no backing away from it. I know I'm going to honor my commitment to you. There are many times when I think of myself as awful and abusive for helping you discover what hurts so much in you, and leaving you at least temporarily miserable. At the same time I know that the only way for you to heal from what happened to you is to help you through the pain, not to go around it or to hide it. That doesn't work. I'm sorry it hurts you so much."

She replied very simply, in a clear, fully coherent adult voice: "Thank you for telling me. I needed to know." Since this session I have come to understand that her statement was only part of the story, and that Rachel intuitively knew the rest.

There is a way that Rachel's family was so "normal" that it defies my ability to secretly see them as abusers, which might otherwise be a way to distance them from my own family experience. I have become aware that I have implicitly wanted to do this to draw a line between my life and the lives of my patients. Of course, as I grow older, my awareness that the line is fantasy slaps me in the face with some regularity.

There is the growing knowledge that in my aging, in my doing this work for so many years with so many people, there is a way I become angry with Rachel for requiring my absolute presence with her as she goes through yet another graphic scene of abuse. The pain in her experience is extraordinarily visible in the writhing of her body, the contortions of her face, the alterations in her voice, and the violence of her displays of anger that are facilitated by using the props available to her in my office to safely be angry. The sound of her hitting a pillow with a foam bat splits the air so loudly it's like the retort of a gun.

I was being seduced by my dedication and commitment to my patient. It was a sadomasochistic relationship. I now knew the murderous rage in me, the terror of acting on it, the fantasized humiliation of having acted, the sadness of not being able to undo anything I'd have perpetrated in my rage. There was also sadness beyond words over what had been lost, what will never be, and what could have been.

The treatment of persons with dissociative adaptations to living is often filled with the stirring and emergence of intense affective states. Often bereft of words, these affective states remain to be articulated by either patient or therapist, as best they can tolerate, or perhaps to become part of an enactment (Bromberg 2006). As Bromberg points out, when there is something isolated from the consciousness of both patient and therapist, the scene is ripe for enactment. I would only add that what makes enactment become part of the treatment scene is the resonance of the intolerable emotional burden in the therapist with what is in the patient. Without this resonance there is not an enactment. Instead, there is enactive repetition. This is a simple extension of enactive knowing based on the influence of implicit process that I discussed in the chapter on performance art. When Joey and I resonated over dead legs, an enactment was activated. This was a co-created part of the scene evolving and describes the mutuality of dissociative process active in the clinical dyad.

Countertransference Analysis Interminable

It was with a smile of irony as I reread the words in the last two paragraphs above at the end of February 2008, that I realized that I had forgotten all about my sleepiness with Rachel, forgotten about it for over a month. It hadn't been a problem. I truly had forgotten about it completely—until I pulled up the file of this former paper in progress.

In the intervening period, Rachel had been furious with me for another reason. In early January I'd told her I was reconsidering my participation in Medicare. I had to decide by the end of February, and there would be no change in our arrangement until July. I told her I was committed to treating her, that my commitment was to her and not to a specific fee. She was very upset. It turned out that she'd had major financial problems when she was first in treatment and had been repeatedly hospitalized. Insurance companies dropped her. Hospitals discharged her. Doctors refused her. Therapists worked pro bono for several years and then quit.

When I brought up the subject in January, she accused me of controlling her life. She shut her eyes and refused to look at me in a subsequent session when I confirmed I would opt out in July. She yelled at me that she hated me. I told her I could understand why. She was sputtering her words in her fury, and she left that session without our usual handshake. Neither did she open her eyes more than a crack to track her way out of my office.

In the several weeks of her anger that followed, I had tolerated my own fantasies regarding how this was hurting her, how I shouldn't do this, and so on. I was fearful that she would turn her anger on herself and commit suicide. I felt ashamed that I was not being a good physician by opting out of Medicare. Of course, then I remembered the people I treat for nearly no fee, who had no insurance whatsoever, and those feelings of my being abusive became the focus of my curiosity.

Rachel remained openly angry with me, and I continued to feel guilty about what I had done. The strange lack of my fear of humiliation when I had fallen asleep in session now came to mind. My anger (really rage) was isolated, the subject of dissociative process. Perhaps that was the constellation. The old Karpman drama triangle—abuser, protector, rescuer—was active (Karpman 1968). I had been the dedicated and good therapist again, refusing the abuser role, and just like Harold Searles had written, my patient complied with my need to be good and was staying ill (Searles 1967). Old habits die hard. Of course, some old habits are destined to repeat. What was happening with my opting out of Medicare? What was that about?

In the analysis of my countertransference sleepiness, there had been a rich array of useful experience—near, alive, clinical material. The patient's willingness to tolerate and engage in the work had led to her own continued growth and mine in the service of becoming more human. However, the sleepiness had not truly resolved, and the treatment was now threatened by my decision to opt out of Medicare.[4]

---

[4] Medicare law changed in late spring 2008 and this discussion was mercifully truncated. The treatment continued.

Rachel reasoned that it was time to quit therapy in consideration of her belief that she could not afford to continue. She dismissed an out-of-pocket solution, which would have entailed a reduced fee, as something humiliating. It would have been a kind of charity, one that she believed I would resent on some level, regardless of whatever I might say to the contrary.

There were several phases and trajectories that were activated as a result of listening to the formal discussion of this case by Wilma Bucci at a conference in 2008. To understand them it is important to appreciate the deep respect and interpersonal warmth and affection that were part of the panel discussion experience. All the panelists shared in this experience. So it was in that emotional context that Dr. Bucci rather casually, and literally with a wink to me, remarked that the statement I had made about the Karpman drama triangle needed to be corrected. She knew I knew it, so she was just going to mention that the triangle was not "abuser, protector, rescuer" but "abuser, victim, rescuer." I had left out "victim." Why?

Given that I have taught this work for many years, I was quite clear I had unconsciously managed some mental sleight-of-hand to make sure I would not see, think, or feel the word *victim*. If I didn't want to know I was a victim, then the loss that I was avoiding was, at that moment, clear to me: I was avoiding knowing the loss of my father. And, I thought, what seemed most salient in the scenario of loss is that like my patient, I was furious with my mother. After all, I had been aware for a very long time of the difficulties in my family of origin surrounding the resolution of intense emotional experiences. The experience of my father dying was filled with emotion, as was the time prior to his death, and I knew that my mother still had great difficulty talking about it.

As it happened, I was staying at my mother's home during the conference, and there was ample opportunity to notice the effect of my new understanding on my relationship with her. There was a noticeable shift. I was no longer carrying an angry chip on my shoulder. I saw her limitations, but my usual frustration was absent and in its place was a pleasantly alive peacefulness.

I thought I had found the Holy Grail of the impasse with my patient. We had actually been talking about her difficulty with loss, even though I was not conscious of my own. I reasoned that there must be some way I was colluding with her in not knowing the real feeling of it. Now I had found a not-me aspect of my self, a self-state intent on not feeling the deep sadness of loss.

In my excitement about all this, I didn't notice I was relieved very directly from noticing my anger and shame. In retrospect, as I write this chapter several years later, I note that I had included not one but two rescuers. I suppose this was for unconscious emphasis, lest I did not pick up the first time what else was going on. I now see two inter-twined reasons at work: I unconsciously preferred to avoid knowing my rage, by overidentifying with the good rescuer, and my shame, by banishing the helplessness of victimhood.

At the time, I returned to work anticipating only that at some point what I had learned so far (the side-stepping of loss) would come up. After lunch and before Rachel arrived, I noted my usual after-lunch fatigue and was privately dismayed at the possibility I might again be sleepy in session. When Rachel arrived, I was not sleepy at all, but quite alert. She knew I was going to the conference to present our work together, and she asked about what had happened. I simply told her that I had bumped into the theme of feelings of loss as a result of the discussion that followed the presentation and wondered if we could review the losses from her life that seemed to stand out the most. Somehow, what we eventually focused on was not loss per se but a repeating scene from Rachel's life where she would be furious with her mother for changing states. Her mother would repeatedly change her mind about instructions she had just given to Rachel, not once but several times over several hours. She used to send Rachel to the market to buy a can of vegetables. Rachel would dutifully follow her instructions. But on her return, mother had changed her mind. It needed to be taken back, or it was the wrong thing. It felt crazy-making for Rachel. She would protest and be sent to her room to await her father's return from work and "adjudication" of the scene with mother. Father would listen patiently and quietly to Rachel, and then he would gently, almost in a pleading whisper of desperation, say to her: "I know how you're feeling, but just do it her way this one time, for me, please?" For Rachel, this was tantamount to having been made invisible. Father listened, but it made no difference at all. She wanted him to validate reality, to say that he knew mother was "off the wall." He remained always loyal to his wife, no matter how that invalidated Rachel's perception of what had happened, of what was real. Rachel believed that if she became angry with him, she would lose the affection she received from him at other times.

As Rachel was describing her experience with her father, I realized I had been wrong in my self-analysis of the omission of the word *victim*. To be sure, it was clear that Rachel was refusing to know how injured she felt by her father's repeated devaluing of her feelings, and his repeated pleas to "just this one time" give up her own reality and substitute her mother's skewed sense of the world. I, too, was refusing to be angry with my father—for his dying—but I was also refusing to acknowledge my anger at my mother. I had intellectually understood that I would naturally, humanly, be angry about losing him, but I had somehow managed to not connect the dots between my anger with my mother for never taking charge, never preparing the family for what must have been obvious for months, and my anger with my father. Never once had he stopped the action and told me he knew he was dying and created a moment where we could openly talk about the loss. (Of course, all this externalization of affect tacitly helped me avoid knowing feelings of helplessness associated with my father's death, a realization I came to months after I began rewriting this as a chapter.)

Neither of our fathers or mothers could tolerate what was real, and Rachel and I had been let down in that respect. (Here appears another cogent motive for why two rescuers had become part of the drama triangle. *Neither* of my parents could rescue me during my father's dying. Not my mother, certainly, and not my father, either.) While I have thought this was a story about isolated rage, which in part it is, I realize from the feeling in my body as I write these words that there is the heaviness of profound sadness as I now know my parents simply weren't up to the task. The same was true with Rachel. Neither of our fathers, let alone our mothers, could tolerate what lay before them. It's not like they tried to ignore things. They themselves didn't have parents who could have helped them be more present.

So it was, with all this complexity in me just coming to my awareness, that as I listened to my patient I was quite flooded with waves of anger and a wish to yell out and scream about my furious disappointment with the father I deeply loved. Several minutes passed, and my anger was gradually humbled by the sense of loss I now knew about, the sense of what was never to be and existed only in my own recognition of a missed opportunity for deep intimacy. In fact, as a family physician I used to take pride in my willingness to make housecalls when my patients were dying, and to help them die at home, surrounded by family, in familiar and comforting surroundings, and helping them literally say good-bye to all the people in their family. What an extraordinary and useful enactive repetition and undoing of my earlier traumatic experience! I have many times told friends it was about as intimate an experience as I had ever had with another person. As I type these words, the dots feel sadly fully connected between self-states as if "me," my deeply sad "not-me," and my angry "not-me" can truly know about this together.

I tried to help Rachel see her anger with her father. Over several minutes we danced around the usual territory: "How can I be angry with him when all he was trying to do was keep mother's chaos to a minimum? How can I be angry with him when he was just doing what he needed to do when he came home from work after such a hard day, and he was working so hard?" "How can I be angry with him and risk that he would hate me for it and I'd lose the connection with him that I value so much? I can't bear to even think about losing that connection with my father. If I lost him I wouldn't want to be alive." "What's the point of being angry with him now when he recently has started separating himself emotionally from my mother and will talk with me alone, privately, on my cell phone if I call him?" "He's managed to somehow tolerate my mother's tantrums, and that always meant I couldn't talk with him." "Being angry with my father doesn't really make sense to me anyhow. It's like it's not possible for that to happen. It's not a concept that makes sense to me. I get that it would make sense for a person in a situation like mine to feel anger with my father, but I just don't."

In listening to Rachel, I had a sense of having heard it all before, and indeed I had, in bits and pieces, but never before had it all seemed held together with such firm logical mortar. There appeared to be a massive edifice of dissociative not-knowing, an isolation of angry emotion where the link to the narrative was missing; the receptive tag ends of the thoughts and feelings were all tethered in sight, but the dissociative process still held sway. It occurred to me that I had been in no different a situation, for some 40 or so years. I had not been able to connect with the anger or sadness I felt in relation to my father after his failure to talk with me about dying. Of course, I couldn't name it, either. I was a too frightened and confused helpless victim of his death. I was intolerant of feeling it, knowing it. My father would have needed to show me the way, and even then, perhaps it would have been too much to bear.

In the session I thought about taking action and disclosing my own dissociation, my own not-me experience. How else would Rachel get to know about this if not in the tension of our relationship, in the context of my demonstrated lapses into incoherence? This would be the second disclosure of this type in nearly as many months. Was this for me and not for her? Was the pressure in my mind to speak out loud about my own pain, and not about hers? What if it was about both? Would that be a bad thing? Could it really be any other way? Was I crossing a boundary without enough thought? Would I lose this moment, pregnant with feeling, if I didn't act now? It would prob-ably come up again, but when? It's her 12th year of treatment; she's exhausted; should I wait months or years? What would happen? I wouldn't really know until afterward. I wouldn't know until the tra-jectory of the treatment changed or stayed the same.

With some trepidation, and wondering if the excitement of the case presentation and discussion was somehow influencing me to take action again, I did what I felt in my gut was the right thing to do.

I spoke: "Rachel, I think I know what that feeling of knowing about something but not making the connection is about for me. You can't figure out how it might happen that you could actually feel angry with your father. Well, as a result of the work I presented on my sleepiness reaction in our work together, I've come to understand that it's not simply that I could not tolerate the horror in my life, just like you couldn't, but that in my father dying, something you know happened, I became aware from the case discussion that I had been unconsciously avoiding feeling like a victim." I explained the Karpman drama triangle scene and then went on. "I didn't want to feel like a victim, I believe, because I didn't want to feel angry. And it wasn't until we were just reviewing your relationship with your father and mother that I discovered I was angry with my father! He never could muster the ability to tell me he was dying! [My voice was firm, determined, slightly raised in volume, and with clear additional energy above and beyond my usual tones.] He robbed me of being able to say good-bye to him. He robbed me of the intimacy we could have had. And I think that in your father repeatedly ignoring reality, and repeatedly telling you that he had to take your mother's side, and that you should swallow what you knew to be real and pretend, he robbed you of being able to know what was real and what wasn't. And in my mind, I can hear myself yelling and screaming at my father, and also feeling sad for what was lost, something I can never have with him. I can feel the tears in my eyes as I'm speaking. The opportunity is lost, forever. I can't get it back."

Rachel's reaction was swift. "I'm getting nauseous thinking about this. I'm not sure I can tolerate it. I just wanted to throw up when you said you were angry with your father for not talking with you. I can understand that. But I don't really want to think about it. It just makes me want to die. It's too much."

The session finished with a discussion of her feelings about the death of her husband, her statement that she thought that after five years she was still deeply grieving, and her observation that she knew she needed to consider what I told her about being angry with her father, but she just couldn't go there. While her autonomic activation made clear that there was a deeply emotional response, it wasn't clear what the details of that response were about. In favor of the response being useful was her ability to remain coherent, not switch into a child state of incoherence, and to elaborate and make associations to our discussion about the feeling of stuck grief related to her husband.

In the next session she started in a clear adult voice and said that the last session had been hard. I asked her what it was like for me to disclose my feelings to her. She said that it was actually very good because it gave her a sense that if I could be angry with my father then perhaps there was a way she could be angry with her father. She said that my disclosures had always been right on target for her, and she appreciated them. Wondering if she was just being kind and otherwise hiding a potential negative response, I asked if she had ever had a therapist who disclosed to her and the outcome was negative. She said, "A lot of my therapists have said things to me about what they were feeling, and it's mostly been okay. There was one woman I saw very soon after my first hospitalization. I told her that I had been in church and staring at a statue of the Virgin Mary, and that after a while the Virgin Mary appeared and talked to me."

"How did the therapist react?"

"Well, that was the problem," said Rachel. "What she told me was that she was glad I had visions because she did, too, and it was nice to be able to have someone to talk with her about these things! I thought to myself: 'Oh, my God, my therapist is a whacko! I don't need this!'"

I responded, "Yes, I can see where that became a problem."

Laughing, Rachel added, "You can sure say that again! That treatment ended not too long after that with me going back in the hospital."

Afterword

As I mentioned, Rachel insists that when I write about her I have to mention that from her point of view my most valuable trait is that I am "real" with her. Yet what I have written about is that in fact sometimes I get very sleepy with her. Not forgetting her vociferous protests about this, I find myself pondering the question: Is "sleepy" sometimes "real?" Or at least a potential stepping stone to "real"? Where does this sleepiness connect with her story?

I have come to understand that there is something in this clinical situation with Rachel that resonates so deeply inside me that from time to time I find myself slipping into inattention, and then trance-like sleepiness, even after years of ongoing countertransference analysis. The case continues to unfold and the patient continues to make real progress. The exploration of feelings of helplessness, profound sadness and loss, humiliation, shame, rage, and other intense affects continues in this treatment. It feels like a kind of mutual analysis, yet as the work continues there is more room in me to respond to the patient's direct questions about what is happening in my mind by saying: "That's private territory, and I'm not going to report on that unless it seems to me that it will benefit you. Let's work without my disclosing that and see how it goes." She is quite positively responsive to this. Of course, this does not mean there is no future role for self-disclosure, but I wonder about additional meanings of the disclosures, their significance, and their importance. From the patient's perspective, they have been essential. I am not as certain, but it does not seem that the treatment has suffered because of it. Quite the contrary.

The treatment of persons with chronic, complex trauma is invariably a treatment filled with overwhelming, intense, intolerable affect states that arise in patient and therapist with regularity. The ways these emotions show up in the clinical inquiry necessarily require a willingness to notice disturbances and disruptions in the flow of a session. Although falling asleep is an obvious disturbance, tolerating a lengthy countertransference analysis is still a daunting prospect. It seems quite worth the effort, however, and in my consultation room, I would be clear that to not make that effort is to close my heart and mind to my own growth and preclude the growth of my patients. To be sure, negotiating the boundaries and limits of that kind of treatment is a challenge that I don't so much look forward to as I have come to embrace as a necessary and useful part of any treatment. In my willingness to talk with Rachel about my experience in the countertransference, I helped level the clinical playing field and model exploration of what has felt uncomfortable and previously intolerable for both of us. This is at the core of the utility of understanding enactment. If this is mutual analysis, then so be it. It is useful in this particular treatment. I remain grateful to Rachel, my other patients, and my colleagues for their respectful assistance in joining in exploring the tasks of complex treatments.

Chapter 9

The Unconscious Fear of Feeling Real:
Negativity and the Negative Therapeutic Reaction

Wake up you idiot! There is no place left to hide. Open wounds must be filled with the stench of adulthood. There is no honor left in you! You filthy, threadbare, used-to-be imitation of a person. Own who you are. You're a raped bitch who has a problem with her mother and thinks it was tough growing up. No news flash . . . there's millions more wounded people getting along just fine.
                                             —Rachel (writing to herself in her journal)

TWO OF THE MOST DIFFICULT AND CHALLENGING CLINICAL PROBLEMS IN THE treatment of the dissociative disorders are the sustained presence of a biting and self-excoriating negativity and a repetitive negative therapeutic reaction. If you have not been exposed to these, it won't be long before you bump into this double constellation if you begin working regularly with people who have dissociative disorders.

Negativity often brings a treatment to its knees, wearing down both patient and therapist with relentless hours spent dealing with suicidal crises, hopelessness, and the pain of hearing yet another wish to die or statements like the one above from Rachel, whose treatment is further explored in this chapter. Her vitriol was as caustic as any I had encountered, but it was only part of who she was. I liked her tremendously. Her human depth and compassion were extraordinary. The contrast between her compassion and her negativity was the source of the clinical whiplash that is inherent in the treatment of the dissociative disorders. There were self-states pouring their pain into the treatment like a burst water main, only they seemed intent on drowning all progress (actually these self-states were desperately calling for help because they felt as if they were drowning), and then there were self-states so complexly sensitive and tender about the world that it was hard not to be captured and deeply engaged by the side-by-side juxtaposition of emotionally intense opposites.

Negative therapeutic reactions are thought to represent a minority of cases in treatment, but in the treatment of the dissociative disorders they are common, even normal. Not only is there the typical movement of a complex treatment from impasse to impasse, but as one layer of traumatic experience gets peeled off and resolved, the next layer rises to the surface with a vengeance and tends to have more impact than the last. Each increment of gain in being able to feel emotion is met by the reality that with increased tolerance for feelings, and less dissociation, the next worst thing that ever happened is now the trauma du jour. Who wants to keep coming to the table if that's what's going to be served? "You just can't win for losing" is the phrase that echoes in my mind from my days as a country doctor.

Negativity and the negative therapeutic reaction are responsible for a significant portion of the treatment of dissociative disorders that fail or come to me desperate for consultation. If a clinical pairing is to avoid that fate, then perhaps what I am going to lay out now about the functions of negativity and the negative therapeutic reaction will be useful. Rachel and I had to untangle the various kinds of negative therapeutic reaction as we worked together in a space that often felt only like the skinny edge between life and her suicide.

Paradox is at the core of the life-saving nature of both negativity and the negative therapeutic reaction. Just like for the young child who emphatically says "No!" as they enter the infamous terrible twos, the capacity to oppose is a sign of growing agency. This is especially true for a mind that is struggling to exit from the captivity inherent in chronic abuse (Herman 1992). The problem is that the deeply entrenched negativity in an adult not only asserts agency but also makes existing wounds deeper. I have come to believe that negativity and the negative therapeutic reaction are best seen as being used in a self-protective manner. What kinds of fear might exist that make healing and change threatening? Why is there such a relentless attack on meaningful existence? The self-state system of DID is complex, but unlike non-DID cases there is also the advantage that it provides a road map of sorts that somewhat predicts where negativity and negative reactions take origin.

A negative therapeutic reaction is defined by the specific circumstance where both patient and therapist may agree there has been a significant therapeutic gain and yet things get worse. Freud began to talk about negative therapeutic reaction several years before he wrote this clarifying definition:

> Every partial solution that ought to result, and in other
> people does result, in an improvement or a temporary
> suspension of symptoms produces in them for the time
> being an exacerbation of their illness; they get worse dur-
> ing the treatment instead of getting better. They exhibit
> what is known as a "negative therapeutic reaction."
> There is no doubt that there is something in these people
> that sets itself against their recovery, and its approach is
> dreaded as though it were a danger. We are accustomed
> to say that the need for illness has got the upper hand in
> them over the desire for recovery. (Freud 1923, p. 49)

In dissociative disorder treatment, the negative therapeutic reaction often reflects the dangers of feeling real in a real world and of making real the realities of past and present. A central dynamic in the inner world of dissociative experience is that the temporal coordinates of past traumas are copied and pasted into the present, seamlessly and unconsciously. It's the work of that little engine that could (dissociation), which leaves no telltale traces as it looks back over its shoulder and keeps chugging along. A person living in the present has the cognitive and emotional overlay of the past guiding them as if they are wearing tinted glasses that imbue the world with a threatening character. They live in the present as if they are the frightened child who will be hurt again at any misstep, and they see that fear as fully justified and realistic. Understanding this enables us to extend the insights of an extensive literature.

This perspective is implicit in Olinick's summary of much of the original psychoanalytic literature on the negative therapeutic reaction, but he does not specify dissociation per se as a factor. He views the negative therapeutic reaction as a derivative of sadomasochism and a special case of negativism in patients who have or have had excess aggression, special stresses in the early mother–child relationship leading to an ambivalent alliance, fear of object loss, fear of gratifications, rages, depression, and obsessional defenses (Olinick 1964). These things light up in Rachel's history.

The reader can recall Rachel's struggle as Joey when he emerged from the depersonalized deadness of bloody legs into calling Mr. X "stupid." This action is hidden in the more archaic language of Lampl-De Groot, but the unresponsiveness of Rachel's mother and the battering and abuse by Mr. X created the specific trajectory of what is described in this text afterward. Jeanne Lampl-De Groot emphasized four factors that she culled from Freud's writings: a strong need for punishment, an incapacity to "tame" the instinctual drives and a particularly unfortunate relationship between sexual (libidinal) and aggressive drives, an ego alteration or impairment which makes the patient incapable of coping with the instinctual demands in a favorable way or (put in another way) an irregular development of ego functions, and a clash between passive and active tendencies, including a repudiation of femininity in the sexual sphere (Lampl-De Groot 1967). Lampl-De Groot's psychology was influenced by Bowlby, Mahler, and Spitz, and she understood the great significance of impaired relating between mother and child. In particular, she identified scenes where the mother failed to respond to the newborn's original embodied aliveness with "the consequence that it is rigidly repressed and buried" (1967, p.27). She correctly perceived that a therapist's capacity to respond at this nonverbal level is essential if a patient is to heal, and the patient must be able to take this in. I have no doubt that Rachel would agree.

In *Nothing Good Is Allowed to Stand* (Wurmser and Jarass 2013a) the authors offer their own summary of much of the world's professional literature on negative therapeutic reactions and then add to it considerably. As noted by Lichtenberg (2013), the authors show evidence of moving toward and embracing a two-person psychology, and I submit that anything less would obscure the scene of a complex treatment. We can see how responsive Rachel was to my disclosures in Chapter 8, even after I had offended her sensibilities. Anything less than an acknowledgment on my part of something so egregious would have been deeply wounding to her, and a display of the misuse of my being in a position of some authority, a traumatic repetition in the sadistic transference to me as a potential abuser.

Karen Horney (1936) built on Freud's opening gambit by noting the presence of intense affects in the negative therapeutic reaction: resentment, envy, unconscious guilt, jealousy, and shame-anxiety masked by narcissism; these have also been summarized by Wurmser and Jarass (2013b, p.4). Grunert (1979) reminds us that defiance may protect from a fear of surrender to or fusion with another. Kernberg (1975) places an emphasis on masochistic triumph in the transference as part of a need to defeat those with life-affirming tendencies (Wurmser and Jarass 2013b, p. 8), a view that illustrates part of the problem of a one-person psychology. The therapist is indeed life-affirming, and the patient knows it, but the therapist doesn't appreciate how the patient's acceptance of a life-affirming stance would historically have put him or her at more than simply a risk of attack; it would have made him or her subject to truly merciless attack by others. Apparent masochism might be better than the real risk of annihilation. Enabled by the time-distortion of dissociative process (R. J. Loewenstein 1991), these attacks feel ever-present in the mind of the patient perceptually. The patient must oppose the therapist and defeat the therapist's efforts because it feels as if they will be literally destroyed if they don't. This gives great intensity to the affect in DID, and goes well beyond Horney's notion of narcissism and shame-anxiety.

Jack and Kerry Novick describe a dual track developmental model to explain the defensive omnipotent beliefs that anchor sadomasochism to negativity. In their view, there is an open system of self-regulation, which is "attuned to inner and outer reality, has access to the full range of affects, and is characterized by competence, love, and creativity." But there is also a closed system of self-regulation, "which avoids reality and is characterized by sadomasochism, omnipotence, and stasis" (Novick and Novick 2003). In their view, negative therapeutic reactions arise out of the closed system: "A sadomasochistic superego not only allows but demands the flouting of authority to demonstrate power; at the same time, however, the harshest punishment follows on ordinary acceptable actions, like having pleasure, being a separate person, exercising one's skill and competence" (Novick and Noick 2004, p. 236). Yet take away negative self-assertion and what is left? It may be the only tool that can provide a momentary boost to energy in a depleted self. This is a sad and brief sadomasochistic triumph that provides a kind of toxic but potent temporary refueling of narcissistic goodness. Still, negative self-assertion stabilizes. It preserves agency through shaming the self. Discovering that the harsh self-state is both born of modeling the harshness of a perpetrator and acts as a repository for unbearable shame-pain is often helpful in reframing this self-state's role as protecting the self from that pain. Sustainable increases in self-esteem only begin to occur when there is a willingness to begin to consider the possibility of a self that is honestly liked and enjoyed by an outsider. The person who is outside the closed system is often the patient's therapist.

Negativity in a Dissociative Context

Later in this chapter, I attempt to spell out some of the varieties of negativity and the negative therapeutic reaction as they appeared in a later phase of Rachel's treatment. First I want to highlight specific aspects of the phenomena in question so that the reader can better parse the case material. As we'll see, once a dissociative context is added, it lights up critically important details that can guide a clinician to respond more productively to negativity.

Shame-Rage, Self-States, and Paradoxical Agency in Negativity

What is it that fuels the destructive acidity (see epigraph to this chapter) in Rachel's language? Rage and shame become linked when the full force of a perpetrator's control so overwhelms the ability of the victim to protest that the victim's experience of their rage feels puny and wholly ineffectual. In other words, rage fails to protect the victim who is instead shamed and humiliated (Lewis 1987a). The humiliation of rage is an extraordinary event and signals the beginning of emotional captivity (Herman 1992) and the failure of a self to protect its territory. The global nature of this failure is appalling in its implications for loss of agency. The extraordinary pain of this combination, which Lewis called shame-rage, is often hidden by outward professions of contempt and inward hostility toward self alongside ruthless judging and negativity. The shame-rage is typically isolated from awareness and bereft of contextualizing narrative. To link to the narrative of a global failure of self-protection associated with captivity is too painful. The shame-rage seeks a contextual target, but the perpetrator of abuse as target is procedurally (implicitly) forbidden. Furthermore, the victim is unconsciously aware of a history of retaliatory rage in response to their protests. The isolation of self-states in a not-me fashion provides other self-states as safe targets for the burdensome shame-rage and hatred of the perpetrator. "I can attack Joan, she's not of me anyhow." Family dynamics may be enacted among internal self-states. This was legion in the case of Rachel.

Anzieu (1986) quotes Fairbairn (1952) in describing what happens when a child "feels that the reason for her (the mother) apparent refusal to accept his love is that his own love is destructive and bad." In such instances, withdrawal from loving becomes a lifelong pattern: "When an individual with a schizoid tendency (gives up) social contact it is namely because he feels that he must neither love nor be loved." But there is also an inward transformation that merits our closest attention: "Since the joy of loving seems to be barred to him, he may as well deliver himself over to the joy of hating. He thus makes a pact with the Devil and says, 'Evil be thou my good.'" Becoming an agent of destruction is better than having no agency at all.

"Attackment" Relationships

Negativity in a victim is acceptable to a perpetrator. It doesn't challenge their worldview, nor does it challenge their contempt for the victim. Just as in the infant attachment paradigms, negativity can be seen as like an attachment behavior that guarantees proximity to the power of the parent but doesn't threaten them, for example, Type A, avoidant infant attachment. It therefore safely joins the victim's mind with that of the perpetrator to maintain the perpetrator's stability, who otherwise would become enraged if there were disagreement with the perpetrator's view of the world. The rigidity of the perpetrator in this respect is necessary to maintain their omnipotent distortions, or else they run the risk of discovering their own fears. The victim thus creates a safe and paradoxical destructive assertion of agency right under the nose of the perpetrator by adopting negativity, a stealthy recouping of lost power. This is at the core of an "attackment" relationship, as I call it. There is enmeshment in mutual attack. Enacted reciprocal role responses (Sandler 1976) in the therapy become complex and unwieldy once the attackment relationship takes hold, as both patient and therapist behaviors are subject to potentially wide interpretation and begin eliciting nonmatching responses (Ryle 2001). A pattern can evolve featuring reciprocal attacks interrupted by isolated moments of intimacy. This was visible in Anya's story when she openly tried to humiliate me about my emails to her. Often, the only way I've found to exit these action-packed transferential scenes is to take a meta-position on the action and notice it out loud. Aggression must be noticed and not simply tolerated as if noticing would injure the patient. It may take several sessions or more for the noticing to calm things down. Nice therapists who are willing to suffer repeated attacks do poorly in these scenes. The patient must know the therapist is strong enough to oppose them or the lack of emotional marking (Fonagy et al. 2003) fails to reassure them they won't really hurt the therapist. There is nothing kind or nice about tolerating being abused. The signal to the patient is that they can enact the attackment with you if you don't name it with respectful firmness and gentle curiosity about what vulnerabilities in the patient are hidden behind the attack.

Alice, whom you met in the first chapter as we dealt with her angry snit, accommodated to the difficulties of the attackment relationship by telling me, "I want to keep you and get rid of the psychiatrist." My job with Alice (as with other patients) was to announce my recognition of the attack and be curious about what was going on. Aggression needs acknowledgment or it may remain unnoticed, even if it is rather obvious to the recipient. Alice was very aggressive for many years when it came to her efforts to dismiss the treatment as doing no good at all. She would start the session attacking the treatment, switch to another state and engage, and then just before the session ended switch to a dismissive state who had amnesia for the content of the session and declare that nothing had happened. When by chance an adult state noticed the momentary presence of a child-sized state, there might be a violent emotional reaction like, "There will be none of that here again!" Each increment of progress in helping her be conscious of her feelings, especially her anger, ended up threatening to end the treatment. For years, such progress precipitated crises where she would angrily bolt from the session, sometimes after only a couple of minutes.

In Alice's case, it eventually became clear that her anger had been pushed into the background by her parent's intolerance of her initiatives. Emergence of her anger was feared by her and was often volcanic in its quality. She would watch herself explode and feel helpless to stop speaking. With an aging mother to whom she was deeply attached but also deeply angry with due to the mother's inability to deal with reality, consciousness for anger frightened Alice because she believed she would get relief from the tension of jailed feelings only at the expense of angrily attacking her mother and losing that relationship. Thus, for a very long time, in the period before this was clarified, clinical progress was two steps forward and at least one step back. Every advance in the treatment was met with fear and the need to undo the gain rather than risk the treasured relationship with her mother via another of the angry outbursts that had characterized her childhood, teenage years, and much of her career. This was the context behind the fear of healing that prompted a negative therapeutic reaction each time we made progress.

A Healthy Superego?

A consistently thoughtful, kind, and openly firm noticing of attachments and negativity provide the basis for a good superego representation derived from observing and interacting with the therapist, which can be a novel and important addition to a patient's experience after being subject to a lifetime of sadistic abuse (Wurmser 2000). I would go further. In a multiple self-state model, healthy self-criticism (the function of a mature superego) conforms to the shape of a positive and growth-promoting internal dialogue between self-states in the therapist. It is a model for the patient. At appropriate times, the clinician in this scene must model a mature capacity to be self-critical without needing to destroy an aspect of their own self that erred in judgment. Being openly reflective and acknowledging errors and regrets is part of this process, but this does not mean working to artificially produce these situations; rest assured, they will occur naturalistically. This may be part of why countertransference disclosure is so powerful when appropriate (Bromberg 2006; Ginot 1997; Levenkron 2006). The mature inner critic eventually functions as a benevolent and growth-promoting source of authentic and accurate perception, a benevolent superego (self-state), if you will, who hopefully has as a model the benevolent relationship of a therapist between his own self-states.

Negativity, Contempt, and the Relationship

We all understand that physical and sexual abuse is brutal, but it's also true we usually only wince at verbal abuse. The neuroanatomic developmental delays in the hippocampus, precuneus, and corpus callosum associated with verbal abuse—associated, that is, with nothing more than "hurtful words" (Teicher et al. 2010)—are astonishing when visually represented with enhanced neural imaging techniques. Words are hurled like bricks through delicate webs of growing axonal and dendritic neuronal synaptic links, destroying the ability of a mind to communicate with itself as well as with others. Like the tenacity of shame spectrum emotions that defies clinical efforts, negativity, even of the seemingly puny verbal variety, is a relentless hulking twin. One version looks toward tremendous vulnerability and holds the self in contempt. The other version looks in the direction of the miserable experience of compressed rage still boiling under the felt threat of continued abuse and holds the world and others in contempt. This contempt is a kind of confident shadow of the emotional dismissiveness of the perpetrator, in some ways akin to a Type A infant attachment pattern. Contempt is an efficient means of dismissing a challenge to dominance without having to fight (Jones 1995). The fierceness of this assault on the self is painful to witness. Small wonder. Both shame and humiliated rage draw energy from a common source, a dissociatively tethered, crushed, and barely alive self-esteem for which it is implicitly forbidden to acknowledge what has happened lest it be attacked and finally killed.

Paradoxical Energy for Living in Abuser Self-States

Although it often feels easiest to form a compassionate clinical alliance with the nascent and wounded self of the patient, paradoxically it is only through an alliance with the self-states that promulgate negativity that we stand a chance of eventually bringing negativity to a healing conclusion. At its core, this means being able to honestly reframe negativity as currently self-protective, not just as a useful tactic in the past. To avoid clinical misadventure, care needs to be taken to form this alliance with abusive and negative self-states rather than seek to punish, confine, or disable them (Frankel and O'hearn 1996; Kluft 2006; R. J. Loewenstein 2006). Anger holds energy for action and living. Abuser self-states often display that anger as contempt. Harnessing this angry energy in the service of living is the challenge. For the patient without a dissociative disorder, this piece of self-state psychology still applies.

The healthy sense of self is visible in the reality that my patients with deeply entrenched self-excoriating negativity regularly have a highly developed sense of affirmation, truthfulness, and justice for *others*. Noticing this double standard is critical. But if the therapist belabors the point, he or she should be prepared for a strong push back from self-protective states who become terrified of feeling good, being real, or having an actual life. Talk of suicide often follows too strong an emphasis on the good in a person steeped in the bad.

Paradoxically Engaged in Treatment

The doggedness with which people living in a cloud of negativity tend to nevertheless slog through a treatment is confounding, given how often they are on the verge of giving up, quitting, talking about suicide, but somehow making it through the day and continuing to engage, albeit negatively. This juxtaposition of negativity and tenacious engagement has deep and important meaning. It supports the viewpoint of the tethered and isolated self-states who cannot be acknowledged but who want relief from pain, seek relatedness, and yearn to have a life. Negativity is not a game. It is desperation in action. It is neither bluster nor bluff, and should never be treated that way. If it is, then a person may feel the only way to validate their claim to negative self-assertiveness is via the ultimate negative: suicide.

Negativity and Omnipotence

People steeped in negativity are often simply baffled when others compliment them. They are always of two minds. They don't want to be alone, and yet they don't believe anybody would want to really know them and their core disgusting self. Paradoxically, they don't want to be invisible, and yet they aren't comfortable with the idea of being seen (Steiner 2011). They want to know what hurts and why, and they don't want to know.

The belief in one's overwhelming omnipotent badness is often the global explanation for events in the abused person's life. The default setting is fixed by typical beliefs: "I was born bad." "People hurt me because I am bad and I deserve to be hurt." "I am completely incompetent and deserve ridicule." "I am so bad that, if there is anyone to be hurt, then it should be me, or others will suffer in the place I should be." "If I were not so incompetent, then I would not have so much trouble in life." Knowing about one's badness predicts abuse because it holds the unconscious premise that the abuse occurs because "I am bad" rather than because "He is dangerous and scary." It protects from knowing about the badness in the other, a far more anxiety-provoking situation. Shame is more tolerable than fear (Chefetz 2000, p. 322).There thus arises a core belief in the patient's own essential badness, a sadomasochistic default.

Omnipotence is often visibly reflected in the internal relationships between self-states that play out scripts from the past; abuser/protector self-states terrorize child-sized states with threats of punishment or annihilation to silence emotional upheavals that are typical of these child states. The need to take things to an omnipotent extreme reflects the desperate wish to wipe out any trace of real vulnerability, helplessness, hopelessness, and loss (Almond 1997), all positive signifiers of having been wounded beyond tolerance. In this context a new capacity to feel feelings is too often like awakening to find your skin has been removed and everything emotional that touches you makes your soul shriek with pain. Who would want to heal?

Relating versus Accommodating

Conscious owning of a desire to understand or move toward the kind of vulnerability underlying negativity is not easily approachable and may be openly opposed, at times with incredulity. It would be as if one of my patients made yet another forced adjustment to someone else (Summit 1983) akin to what Brandchaft has called "pathological accommodation," which he depicts as a "response to the trauma of archaic object loss and designed to protect against intolerable pain and existential anxiety" (Brandchaft 2007). Importantly, these accommodations are seen as structures that exist in both patient and therapist, perniciously undermining the clinical dialogue and operating unrecognized, at least initially.

> By repetitive process, the child's first reality becomes patterned into a set of immutable belief systems. These subsequently find their place in retrograde social systems in which authoritative first truths remain absolute. Transgenerational transmission results here in the natural selection and preservation of entrenched characteristics impervious

to changing need and evolving circumstance. The ensuing pathological accommodation continues to operate as an entrenched system beyond awareness, to preserve life by imprisoning it in archaic bonds. (Brandchaft 2007, p. 668)

Stabilizing the Wish to Be Dead

The wish to be dead echoes with promises of relief of pain, a stabilizing fantasy; to voice this during abuse would have been unacceptable to a sadistic perpetrator who would have lost their recurrently surrendering victim. But the wish must eventually be voiced. It must also be respected and valued for its utility while not encouraging action. Death may have felt like the only escape from abuse, and that real feeling must be acknowledged. In fact, the feeling of and the potential for acting on the wish to die may be part of an ongoing psychotherapy for nearly its entire duration. The first time the wish is voiced may be in a moment of finally lurching into the reality of the feeling of abuse. Care must be taken to distinguish between a current wish and an old wish finally being articulated. That may not be so easy, but it is often of value in posing the dilemma to the patient. For an adult abused in childhood, the wish to be dead may speak literally of the body while figuratively pointing to the dissociative deadness of mind that may feel like a respite, a paradoxical goal, a place in which a person can hide from pain. Being numb to a perpetrator's abuse undoes the effects of the perpetrator's sadism, although it can often ratchet up the perpetrator's violence to produce a response confirming his or her prowess.

One middle-aged woman in treatment for DID, Scylla, had a long history of self-harm which resolved only after five years of treatment led to enough decrease in her general use of dissociation to numb herself that she became frightened when she cut herself badly and made a gory scene of her bath and bedroom. It was not until nearly 10 years later in treatment that she felt safe enough for child self-states to verbalize a wish to die that had started at age two as a result of sexual assaults by her father and beatings with an attempt to drown her by her mother. Having been sexually abused by a previous psychiatrist, the sense of safety in her therapy with me was hard earned. In several other psychotherapy settings, expressions of a wish to die led almost immediately to hospitalization and the loss of the relationship with her treating therapist. To have her plea to die heard in the context in which it originated, there needed to be enough basis for our relationship and her wish to be connected to me to sustain her life during these times. I am not being dramatic; I am being realistic. It was only after her fears of depending on me were voiced and her violently tendered plea to "Stop treating me like a person, I am shit!" was understood in context by both of us was there a chance that her archaic suicidality could emerge and be named. Hospitalization was something that nearly happened, many times. On one occasion she was positively livid with me for telling her at the conclusion of a difficult session, "I hope you'll keep yourself safe. Losing you now, after all the hard work we've done together, and all the ways in which you've grown, would be a miserable loss for me."

Language, Verbal Abuse, and Negativity

Negativity is often fueled by the verbal shaming and doubting strategies that are a sad experience for children in abusive families. Object coercive doubting is one version of the strategy of taking over the mind of a child (Kramer 1983). "How can you even think such things about me! That's not what I said and it's not what I meant. You are so incredibly sensitive! It's always about you! You are so full of yourself and your own puny excuses for having hurt feelings." Authoritative and contradictory admonishments about reality make the already confused child doubt his or her own perceptions (see Chapters 10 and 11). These kinds of systematic inauthentic relational strategies, which Feiner (1970) has discussed in terms of reification, mystification, doublebinding, boundary invasion, privacy intrusion, and attribution, undermine the capacity to have a mind, know thoughts, know feelings, and assert what is real. Reification might just as well be called by the more modern term *objectification*: The child is no longer treated as a subjectively alive person, but as a puppet, an object of an authoritative admonishment. Being mystified is often a result of contradictory admonishments. Boundary invasions and privacy intrusions override assertions of personal space, as in having no bathroom privacy. False attributions undermine reality testing.

It can be very challenging to keep separate in one mind the kind of content that would create robust conflict between the open and closed systems described by Novick and Novick (2003) if the content entered awareness. For example, Kelly, whom we met in Chapter 5, and Rachel, who we learned about in the previous chapter, had mothers who were at odds with them, but who my patients felt were in earnest in wanting the best for their daughters. This creates a potential conflict that must be approached indirectly via an examination of the actual relationships involved.

In Kelly's case, she longed for the feeling of being absolutely "on" regarding her professional skills. She recalled the days of being able to put her personal needs aside and without showing any signs of stress simply plow through her work, traveling the world, doing what needed to be done regardless of the personal cost. It had been years since that was a description she could claim. Instead, what she had been experiencing for years was chronic depersonalization.

As work with Kelly progressed, she became less concerned with the metaphors we were using to describe her background self-state activity, and more focused on what she was feeling and why. We learned about the intensity of the attachment she had to her mother and the ways in which her own self-esteem was a function of whether her mother was okay; this mattered far more than who and how Kelly was in the workplace. Mother was a harsh judge who expressed displeasure through action in decreasing her already minimal emotionally alive engagement with Kelly. "My mom has to be okay with who I am and then I'm okay. My mom is not okay if she's not okay with me." In this closed context, Kelly lost track of her own thoughts and feelings. In operational language, she could not tolerate being anybody other than whom her mother wished her to be since she would lose mother's support and have her wrath instead. "[The phrase] 'I'm worried about you,'" said Kelly, "seemed to lead to a verbal attack from mother." Mother would detail her worry in the context of Kelly having failed mother's view of how Kelly ought have behaved; what was involved was not contempt per se but a laundry list of failings that left Kelly devastated. If mother was not okay, then Kelly was anxious about what would happen next. This closed system of logic was slowly being eroded as Kelly began to appreciate how she regulated her mother's anxieties at her own cost, a classic example of pathological accommodation. Of course, as an adult she did this full-time with the other adults in her orbit, not just in the relationship with her mother.

Similarly, Rachel was clear that she could not have a mind of her own or her mother would think she was too "big" and that she was trying to upset the balance of power and authority in the relationship. This meant that mother's judgment ruled all. You can hear mother in Rachel's attacks on herself at the start of this chapter. If her mother was upset, then father would be upset. If father was upset, then Rachel would lose the only ally she had at home who might deflect some of mother's arbitrariness about Rachel's behavior and expressed attitudes. If mother was upset, then her father would betray Rachel's need for having her own perceptions of mother's unreasonableness by refusing to side with his daughter, ever. Father seemed intolerant of mother's anxieties. Rachel learned to misplace her sense of self because to have such a self would threaten mother directly or threaten Rachel via a disturbance with father. Her closed system of thinking was locked in place by fear of mother's relentless attacks on Rachel's agency. She was building an open system where anger with mother was considered, but she would quickly become suicidal if she thought about being angry with her mother.

Leon Wurmser spelled out the six factors he found repeating in his patients with an unremittingly harsh inner judge. They were a phobic core with affective storms and taboo objects, a mythical protective system and mythical belief, radical and irreconcilable value conflicts and split identity, impulsive actions of a nearly ritualistic kind, denial (blinding) and reversal (especially from passive to active), and multilayered core conflicts (Wurmser 2000, pp. 176–77). As I see it, the phobic core is an assignation of anxiety to a specific target, a facsimile of something to be feared as a deflection from an actual feared experience or person. The shape of the phobia is often congruent with the original scene. Mythical protective systems and beliefs summarize in two phrases nearly the entirety of the internal worlds of DID, and although Wurmser does not apparently appreciate that hidden richness, he does not ignore it but analyzes it, though at a distance from the subjective experience of dissociative process. The conflicted values and split identities are his sideways description of a multiple self-state model of a dissociative mind. Ritualistic impulsive action represents the replaying of affect scripts that rest beneath behavior and speak to addiction-like efforts to regulate affect that are isolated from consciousness. Blinding denial and reversal speaks to the insistence of the self-states in DID on maintaining their distorted views. This insistence erodes in the face of empathic exploration of why they hold the views they do, and it is essentially the same in Wurmser's cases though he calls it, appropriately, defense analysis. These are the multilayered core conflicts, which I think of as constituting a disorder of subjectivity and which create the politics of self-states.

A Mind Constructed of Painful Experience

Arthur Valenstein (1973) offered the thought that some patients may be attached to their painful affects because the "quality of the affects, may very well reflect the nature of the early object tie." As to the quality of these painful affects, Valenstein is clear: "A good deal impinges upon the infant from within, viscerally and autonomically in terms of his own physiological functioning; and from without in direct or indirect consequence of the (mother) caretaking surround" (1973, p. 373). For some patients, then, painful affects are where the heart lies. For this select group of patients, negativity makes sense since "such affects are emphatically held to because they represent the early self and self-object" (Valenstein 1973, p.376).

Early loss may precipitate what has been called a "fading" of early attachment to mother or father. Andre Green comments: "As this takes effect, the transitional phenomena become gradually meaningless and the infant is unable to experience them. . . . This fading of the internal representations is what I relate to the inner representation of the negative, 'a representation of the absence of representation', as I say, which expresses itself in terms of negative hallucination or in the field of affect, of void, emptiness or, to a lesser degree, futility" (Green 1997). I agree with Green about the quality of the representation, but I would speak of world transformation rather than fading because the transformed attachment maintains its intensity, albeit in its empty shadow form. The representation of emptiness is profoundly present and the source of great pain. It can be explored via focusing (Gendlin 1978), hypnosis, or modifications of EMDR much more effectively than in a psychodynamically informed conversation, in my experience. At the center of the transformation is incredibly painful nonverbal isolated affect and felt knowledge. Too painful to directly recall and not linguistically experienced, it often makes itself known through work similar to somatic experiencing, relying on associations to bodily states that emerge as the somatosensory work progresses. There is new access to language in the safety of the therapeutic relationship. The psychodynamic work then follows. The latter is illustrated in the clinical scenes with Rachel that follow.

Profound isolation of affect in the mother is experienced by the child as emotional deadness, or emptiness, or what has been called an evacuation of mind. When the child asserts his or her presence to the mother, the mother fails to provide an appropriate emotionally marked response (Fonagy et al. 2003) and instead mirrors back emptiness to the child. So the child has reflected back from the parent a great emptiness that is representative of the vacantly lived and unformulated interior of the mother. Emptiness in a child grown to adulthood may appear as an attachment to the presence of absence, or as Valenstein would have said, an attachment to painful affect. Negativity, in the face of this kind of emptiness, is preservative and self-protective of a presence, albeit painfully in negation.

Countertransference and the Negative Therapeutic Reaction

As patient and therapist travel along the clinical Via Dolorosa that I have just described, insights that initially feel like they ought to help and that a patient may actually value often result in the patient getting symptomatically worse as the work of the treatment progresses. *Negative therapeutic reaction* is in some ways too mild a term for this sudden change for the worse at the moment of expected improvement (Horney 1936). In my review of the literature, few authors take up countertransference issues in this situation beyond noting the difficulty of coping with the intense emotions involved, and with the projections and projective identificatory processes that ensue. One noteworthy exception is Jeffrey Seinfeld's object relations approach, where he reasons that a kind therapist is a lure to become dependent and that the patient must reject this or repeat their relationship with rejecting attachment objects of the past (Seinfeld 2002). He feels that in the negative therapeutic reaction the therapist always has a role in its appearance. I agree.

Orgel (2013) noted the tendency of his patients to block the passage of time. When dissociative process is especially active, then the stopping of time, maintaining trauma-time, or what I describe as the seamless copy-paste contextual displacement of the past on to the present, prevents the truth from being known and loss from being experienced. Countertransference deadness that was part of my trance sleep in my work with Rachel (Chefetz 2009) can be seen as my unconscious avoidance of intense emotion. Time stops for me, too, when I am in trance. I speculated openly about some of the sources of my sleepiness in Chapter 8. As for Rachel, trauma-time[1] adhesiveness protected her from knowing the reality of profound losses. After additional years of work from the time I first became sleepy, and when we focused on feelings of murderous rage in her, she became sleepy, too. It was an odd and unexpected confirmation of my suspicions of the resonance between us. It was still challenging to know if there was some equivalence in our emotional states, but I eventually came to believe that I became sleepy partly in response to her wish that she not

---

[1] The experience of living in the past, while living in the present, means that old fears and the assessment of risk are applied to the present context without noticing the misattributions and distortions of risk.

have a mind and that I not have one either. I believe this resonated with a wish in both of us for psychic deadness, but for different reasons. Although most sessions were not affected by my sleepiness, it was an ongoing challenge for me to stay focused at times, and get time flowing in pursuit of what was real in her and in me (R. J. Loewenstein 1993). Being a container for the patient's emotions is one kind of thing, but holding onto and becoming conscious of my own dissociative process and the isolation of intolerable feeling was daunting.

Schmithhüsen (2013) focused an exploration of the negative therapeutic reaction in patients who distort time by filling it up with verbalizations that control time. He referenced the work of Von Susani (Susani 2010), who talked about catastrophic fear occurring in an infant with too young a mind to manage the experience. When reading this material, it suddenly occurred to me that there might have been such an event in my own life. What was somewhat astonishing for me is that everything I put together to understand this had been well known to me for as long as I'd been an adult. I had never connected the dots. This is a deflective process in me, what Don Stern would have called weak dissociation (D. B. Stern 1997).

As the family story goes, my father was studying for the bar exam and I would not go to sleep. I cried. He couldn't study. My mother could not soothe me. In casual conversation about babies in my family, my mother characterized my infancy as one where I cried for the first two years of my life. Pediatricians had no answers. The solution for my parents was to send me to my maternal grandmother, for a week or more at a time, on the other side of New York, the Bronx. This repeated several times.

Any baby worth their salt would have been enraged at the separations, but my rage would have done no good. I would have experienced the infant equivalent of shame-rage (Lewis 1987b). The child's rage is humiliated by the overwhelming force of the caretaker's actions, and then welded to shame feelings as the child fails to mount a protest and collapses in deeply private pain. The same thing happens to older children and adults in failing to mount an angry or rageful protest to sadistic abuse. This was a rough match for Rachel's story of being left to cry for hours in her crib, something she says she can remember. For her, sleep would likely have been as it was for me—a default of frustration, sadness, and loss. Sleep would have been a welcome part of the script of the scene. Sleep stops time. Perhaps there had been a match of a kind in the transference-countertransference, one that took shape in Rachel long before gross sexual and physical abuse occurred in her life. There was also the event that when Mr. X had abused Rachel by raping her in a confessional at his church, she ended up hiding in a closet nearby, wept silently, and then fell asleep in a fog of dissociative confusion. Sleepiness, in both scenes, held traumatic experience at bay.

I had become increasingly aware of the potential role my difficulty with sleepiness could have in prolonging my patient's negativity. Anna Ornstein has commented: "While listening and responding from the patient's perspective facilitates a sense of safety and the establishment of one of the selfobject transferences, the analyst's increasing importance also increases the patient's narcissistic vulnerability. It is under these circumstances that patients are likely to respond with intense rage to relatively insignificant appearing slights and misattunements" (Ornstein 2013, p. 163). Of course, my behavior was not insignificant. But missing in action was Rachel's rage.

She wasn't angry with me, she said. She had talked about not being able to be angry with her mother because she had compassion for her, something she said I taught her to have. She had told me I taught her to see the abuse by the man who mauled her repeatedly, Mr. X, in the same compassionate way, and so she couldn't be angry with him either. These cognitive distortions seemed impermeable to a shift in view. If my intuition was correct, we were enacting together our worst fears and suffering the humiliation of our rage. It was held aside in a dissociative sleepy place, with me tolerating it in the service of being a good therapist (Searles 1967) and she being a good patient, not angry with me, just as she was not angry toward her mother or Mr. X. This was a pathological accommodation in the transference. She said she didn't want me to have to suffer her anger toward me because I had been so good to her.

I'm getting ahead of myself in the story of Rachel's treatment. It's important to understand the feeling and context of the ongoing work that preceded the understanding above. Though the fact of my sleepiness was occasionally still an intermittent impediment, there was a lot of important work going on and a very strong treatment alliance.

A Fear of Going to Work and a Wish to Die

As we return to the treatment scene, Rachel, a now middle-aged woman with DID, had been having unremitting expressions of negativity about being alive and repeated negative therapeutic reactions that had profound effects on both of us. In the particular session where we rejoin her story, she was struggling with a deeper level of despair than usual. This was some 5 years after she woke me, her "dead" therapist, in a treatment now running longer than 15 years. The frequency was three sessions a week including one invaluable double session that started the weekly sequence. She was still changing, still working.

There were a number of bright spots in her life that were visible to me but apparently not to her. She had gotten a part-time job on her own initiative and accepted my support in the process. She was a highly valued employee. She was a valued babysitter for family members. She was enjoyed by her extended family. But there was no joy for her. She came into this particular session telling me she was exhausted. While she was usually focused on all the various tasks she had to do at the retail store where she worked, on this day she said she was exhausted from all the "switching." I asked her to describe what she had experienced and she said: "I'm just looping around and around. It's like I can't get comfortable. I'm running here, and I'm running there, and nothing feels right; I keep on running from this place to the next."

"Sounds like you are feeling rather frantic, Rachel; would that be a good word to apply to this situation?"

"Yes, that fits perfectly. I am frantic."

"Do you have a sense of why you have this feeling?"

"Nobody tells me what I really need to be doing. All they do is tell me where in the store they want me to work that day. They don't tell me exactly what they want me to do, and I'm terrified that I'm not doing what they want."

"We both know your manager has said she wished they had more employees like you and that you were one of her top three people. She said she wanted to clone you, you were so good."

"I can hear her say that, but it doesn't do anything for me. It means nothing. It doesn't get in. So, as far as I'm concerned I'm frantic because they really don't tell me what they want me to do, and I am thinking I must be doing the wrong thing and they're getting ready to fire me. I'm afraid I'm going to lose my job. I'd rather quit before that happens. So, yeah, I'm frantic."

Focusing on Rachel's emotional state reminded me of her relationship with her mother. Weekends in her childhood were marked by mother keeping Rachel occupied all day long by sending her to the store to buy something like tomato paste, which she dutifully did. Upon her return home, Rachel was confronted by what she experienced as a mother who changed her mind, told her how stupid she was for getting the wrong thing, berated her further, and sent her back to the store to return the item. (This is a good example of "mystification"; Feiner 1970.) This sequence repeated itself for hours. The lack of clear instructions and Rachel's anxiety seemed a neat fit for this relational mother pattern at her retail job.

We had actually talked about her stressful store experiences many times, and yet a working solution seemed outside the capacity of our rational discussions. Her inability to take in any kind of compliment or validation of having any worth was glued to her worldview of herself as incompetent. Rather than repeating the same discussion of psychodynamics we'd had many times over the previous several months, I decided to use a modified EMDR (eye movement, densensitization, and reprocessing) technique (Shapiro 1995) and aim for nonverbal content since the verbal had been unrevealing. Sometimes the focusing (Gendlin 1978) was on an image, sometimes on a sensation, sometimes even on a blankness or emptiness. The work is consistent with sensorimotor psychotherapy (Ogden, Pain, and Fisher 2006) and focuses on bodily states of experience. Somatic experiencing often starts with a focus on bodily states that are consciously available to the patient, and doesn't necessarily rely on the chance emergence of a somatic association that might arise as a by-product of EMDR, for example. Meanwhile, the modified eye sweep and focusing technique can make much more efficient use of clinical time since there is no need to set up a more complex formal EMDR session.[2]

Rachel was about to up the ante in the session, and I was soon glad that I was thinking about going off in a different technical direction as she said: "If we can't fix this frantic thing, then I expect the next time I'm at work I'm going to end up collapsing, just like I've done on every other job in my whole life, and lose this job, too, as the ambulance takes me to the hospital. That's the only way I've ever left a job."

"Can you focus on the feeling of being frantic and follow my fingers please?" I was prepared to hear all about her mother. But that was an error of countertransference optimism. I had barely started to move my hand when she immediately broke off the process and said: "It's Mr. X, he's chasing me around the room. I am frantic. He's going to catch me even though I'm pretty quick. He does catch me. He ties me on the bed. He gets on top of me and he rapes me."

It turned out that the full context of the scene of Mr. X chasing her and then raping her was generalized and extended into the adult work setting because of her associations with his drunken rants about his own work scenes, situations where he was failing and felt unjustly criticized. Neither Mr. X nor Rachel's mother had given clear instructions to Rachel. They had both punished her for her lack of coherent responsiveness to their obtuse commands, a lack they invented. In the case of Mr. X, there was violent sexual and physical abuse over trumped-up accusations that she had told others what he had done to her. Rachel's denials had no effect. Her words didn't matter. (This reality took a great toll on developing a psychotherapy significantly based on words.) Now, when Rachel was at work, she became uncontrollably

---

[2] Whether working hypnotically or with EMDR, these techniques often evoke powerful releases of emotion. Proper clinical training is required to maintain the safety of the patient. Good clinical ideas delivered without proper training are not necessarily good ideas. The American Society of Clinical Hypnosis provides outstanding training in hypnosis; see http://www.asch.net. The EMDR Institute also provides excellent training; see http://www.emdr.com.

anxious about doing the right thing, and she associatively experienced a risk of being beaten, raped, or mindlessly punished as previously unconscious flashbacks of frantically running from Mr. X came closer to awareness. It didn't matter that this was a retail store essentially run by women. The linking perception was that lack of instruction would be followed by punishment. The more we did the work of the therapy and explored, the more "sick" she said she felt. *Sick* was her word that signaled she felt unable to cope and compose herself and was potentially in need of the hospital.

The people who supervised her at work trusted her to do her usual good job and didn't give her specific instructions. Since Rachel found it not believable that she had a mind or could be valued, the idea that her employer thought she had a mind of her own, much less a very good mind, was incomprehensible. If they didn't instruct her, then they didn't value her and were getting ready to fire her and likely hurt her.

The work we did in the 20 minutes subsequent to the revelation of this constellation of tangled old and new experience built on our previous conversations on the subject and ended a significant amount of the related dissociative experience. We worked through the standard collection of behaviors, affects, sensations, and knowledge (Braun 1988), as well as identifying all the self-states that had participated in dealing with Mr. X's abuse in this scene (Kluft 2013). Nothing fancy was required, just regular grounding and reorienting exercises so as to stop the action in the scene in Rachel's mind and get oriented to the present. At the conclusion of the session she stood to leave, and then she surprised me when she asked me how tall I was. I stood up from across the consultation room. I responded to her face to face.

"Well, at my age I can say I used to be 5' 11", but I'm just under 5'10" now. Why do you ask?"

"Oh, I wanted to know because now that I'm standing here getting ready to shake your hand, like we always do, I'm looking at you and I think I'm actually nearly as tall as you are, or a little taller. I don't understand what happened. I feel so much bigger than usual." She had become more embodied as a result of the session.

Whatever Rachel might have gained by staying wedded to her illness can only logically be seen as protection from new abuse because healing meant further time spent in a toxic world, the "stench of adulthood." From Valenstein's (1973) perspective she was attached to painful affects, but from her subjective view, the dissociative distortions of experience left her desperately holding onto the painful past lest she err and be surprised and abused again in the terrifying though logically contorted and misattributed present. This kind of self-protection was only visible from inside her mind, where the terror she felt in a new situation was a good enough match for her specific pattern recognition. She was not so much attached to her suffering as she was haunted by these isolated self-state generated misattributions.

Rachel believed that she must have done something wrong for Mr. X to have abused her so thoroughly: "He must have had his reasons!" I was honestly completely appalled by her saying this. Her mind was still significantly in captivity (Herman 1992). The seeds of the negative therapeutic reaction were an effort by some self-states to warn others of anticipated danger and what felt like continued vulnerability. But the self-protection was way out of proportion to the risk that had been assessed on the basis of past, not on current reality. Reality testing was generally intact, but not in regard to personal safety.

After the session where Rachel had an integrative experience marked by feeling taller, she had two sessions where she felt much better. She was sleeping well for the first time in years, had no anxiety about going to work, and was relatively lighthearted and philosophical about minor conflicts that occurred during the day. By the third session she declared that all had been lost, a negative therapeutic reaction. "I'm not sleeping again, I am afraid to go to work, and my thoughts are going in circles again. I can't get anywhere in my thinking. It's almost impossible for me to think. I'm sick of this. I give up."

When I asked about more details of her experience there were none forthcoming. When we did our EMDR variant (eyesweeps without a formal EMDR protocol) and focused on the frantic feeling, there was a blank. There was nothing. Focusing on the blank left her with an odd feeling in her body. "What is the feeling like?"

"It's like the Devil is inside me!"

"What do you think that feeling is about?"

"It's what I was always told. My mother used to say to me, 'You're a bad child. You never do what you're told. The Devil is in you. Every time I tell you to do something the Devil takes over. One day the Devil is going to find you and kill you if you don't get rid of him. He's going to be the death of you.'"

"You've got to be kidding. She said all that stuff? How often did that happen?"

"It happened every time I did something she didn't want me to do."

"Oh, you mean that if you had a mind of your own and you initiated some course of action different than exactly what she wanted, then she told you the Devil was in you?"

"It wasn't just my mother who did it. Mr. X used to tell me that the Devil was in me and I needed to be punished. Even the priest at church would tell me that Satan was in me and I had to be careful that he didn't get control. It wasn't just my mother. It was like everybody knew how there was a devil in me!"

"There was and is no devil in you, Rachel. What's in you is a heart and soul of your own, a mind of your own, and the history of your childhood when some adults didn't like you having your own mind. If you didn't allow yourself to be completely dominated by them, totally passive and submissive, then they told you this devil and Satan bullshit to scare you. Adults who wanted to dominate you tried to frighten you, and it looks like they succeeded."

"Well, I don't want the Devil to get me. I can't let that happen."

"If I were a betting person, I'd guess that one of the ways in which you avoid feeling vulnerable is to avoid being in your body. It's like if you are in your body then the Devil can find you and kill you. You stay out of your body to stay safe."

"That's right. I'm not going to let him get me." I was privately dismayed at this dynamic root to persistent depersonalization. No wonder it had been such a problem.

By the end of the session, though I was pleased to have found an unexpected source of avoidance of her body, I realized we had stum-

bled on a deep pool of fear and self-loathing that had a long and painful history in her life. As a way to draw things out, I invited her to
write out what she believed the origins of her views about the Devil
inside her might have been about.

In the next session, we reviewed what she wrote about a lifetime
of "parents, God, teachers, and priests telling me about the demons
inside me and the work of Satan within me." "I have demons inside
of me that want me to suffer or die, and I am bad and evil." We then
happened on an additional scene of Mr. X ranting about work issues
and raping her that provided a combination of abuse scenes and reli-
gious issues. Mr. X choked Rachel while telling her, "You are evil, you
are bad, you deserve to die." That was a powerful admonition when
combined with violence.

She was in despair at the end of the session, highly agitated, believing she could not tolerate going to work the next day, and actively
suicidal. I brought her back at the end of the day rather than use
the hospital. By the time of that later session, she had advanced her
understanding of the morning's work to associate it with a previously
unmentioned painful feeling she'd had between her shoulder blades
for the past four or five days, "sort of like somebody hit me with the
branch of a tree. This is the same pain I had when I was 20 and spent a
year in the hospital. Nobody could figure out what the pain was about.
Even the psychiatrist who usually said very little asked me, 'What in
the world could have happened to you to cause you so much pain?'
Nobody figured it out."

We used the modified eye sweep/focused attention technique and
she saw herself at a tent revival or Ku Klux Klan meeting (she wasn't
sure which), her hands tied and being hit in the back by somebody,
but she couldn't see who it was. When they hit her it was like her
breath was taken away with the startle. "I don't believe it. I've never
been to a KKK thing. It's all made up! This is ridiculous. I've just
invented it all."

"Rachel, please don't be so quick to dismiss this harshly. Let's not
prejudge what is in your mind and instead just work with it and see
what happens." Using direct suggestion in a hypnotic fashion, but

without a formal induction, we reviewed the scene by playing it backward, and then playing it forward again, and then zoomed out to get more perspective. As we did this, she suddenly said with utter conviction, "We have to watch the Susan Boyle video on YouTube."

I was somewhat dumbfounded, and I also knew the passion with which she spoke was very important. She seemed insistent and spending time looking at the meaning of her request seemed offensive, given the gravity of her suicidality in this situation. While I'm often completely in the dark about things people watch on YouTube, as well as on television, I recalled that Susan Boyle was a singer discovered on a British talent show. My computer is a highly visible part of my office; we opened YouTube and she stood and watched the show with me. I watched as Rachel wept. Boyle clearly captured the hearts of the audience after an initial dismissiveness of her that was visible in the smirks on the judges' faces. Rachel shook as if she had a fever and chills, continuing to cry as we watched the entirety of the clip.

Through her tears and sniffles, Rachel spoke haltingly: "I love to watch this . . . because they didn't like her . . . and then they did. . . I especially liked . . . how the people apologized to her and then praised her."

"She was so misunderstood, and had been so dismissed, humiliated, just like you, Rachel."

The tears had stopped, and we went back to the feeling of being beaten on the back. This time she said that she could see a long line of people behind her who had punished her, including Mr. X. She clearly now remembered he had hit her in the back with a pool cue, "and there were others who hit me too, but it was mostly the feeling of being misunderstood and punished for no good reason that was so much a part of my earlier life."

"Maybe that was why you saw such a crowd behind you, in your mind, when you first talked about the feeling of being hit between your shoulder blades and losing your breath."

"Yes, I can appreciate that now. It just happened so many times."

Working with the feeling in her body, I asked her to stand, and as if in a play, to turn suddenly, and grab the stick that was about to hit her, telling the person hitting her an emphatic "*No!*"

She went through a series of passionate imaginary exclamations of boundaries and admonitions about not being hurt again as I talked with her about being an adult now. At one point she asked what would happen if somebody actually did hit her. I said, "If somebody hits you, then you protect yourself as best you can and get away from them. Then you call the police. Then the police come and arrest them and they go to jail."

"Don't you think that's a little harsh?"

"No, that's what happens when people assault someone—they go to jail. It's not harsh, it's the law. People know better than to hit other people. It's not okay. It's against the law."

She sat back, looking calm for the first time that day, and said to me, "You know, I really have never minded coming here to talk with you. You are always so kind to me. No matter what I've said to you, or what I've talked about, you've always been kind to me. Thank you."

Finding the Positive in the Negative Therapeutic Reaction

In the management of Rachel's negative therapeutic reaction, the task at hand was to create enough working space for us to explore the past and discover reasons as to why she would believe living in the world was unacceptable. That meant exploring intense emotion that was often grossly isolated and visible only in the action of her life. My speculations about murderous rage toward her mother were met with Rachel's denial. In fact, when I had first raised this thought years before, Rachel had become actively suicidal for several weeks. Now she knew she was angry. How angry?

For the longest period, Rachel was fairly certain that she had no murderous rage within her. She challenged me a number of times on this, and at one point openly proposed that I might have my own "thing about murderous rage" and mistakenly thought it was hers. That was certainly a plausible possibility. The sessions ticked by. In one curious session I began to have the fantasy of her murderous rage again, but said nothing. She was quiet, too. I noticed I had begun to recall several scenes when she had violently begun to hit herself in the head both with the flat of her palms and at times with fists. I told her about my quiet musings. Did she have any sense of what that experience was about?

"It's just automatic, Dr. Chefetz. It's something I do. I've always done it. It's just me, it's nothing out of the ordinary, and it doesn't hurt."

"How could it not hurt?"

"I don't feel it. I'm just doing it." I had a sense of dissociative process being highly active and was more than a little curious about why.

"It might be that it happens fast enough, in reaction to something in your mind, that you don't track what it's coming from."

"Okay, I can imagine that. But I don't know that it has anything to do with what you're talking about. This murderous rage thing just seems to be something you are really stuck on." She giggled a little bit, poking fun at me in an affectionate manner. "It's just something I do, Dr. Chefetz. Don't worry so much about it." Rarely had my curiosity been stoked so much by a series of denials and disavowals.

She was agreeable to exploring it, though. Using the modified EMDR technique in the face of her cluelessness about an association to murderous rage, there was no particular associative link to anything, not even the strong presence of blankness, nor any somatic disturbance that could be focused on, as is often the case when something is motivationally but unconsciously hidden via active dissociative process. I recalled her psychiatrist's comment about her back pain—"Whatever could have happened?"—but I knew what had happened by her own report. I knew about the violence done to her body and her mind. I felt completely stymied. I recalled a modification of EMDR technique that could be accomplished simply, and often effectively, by covering one eye or the other and using visual bilateral stimulation with eye sweeps (Bradshaw, Cook, and McDonald 2011). I didn't understand how it might help, but neither did I understand exactly how a lot of things really worked. So, asking Rachel to focus on the feeling in her body of pounding her head with fists, I repeated the eye sweeps with only one eye open. What emerged immediately were violent scenes of interaction with Mr. X during moments of brutal abuse. In fact, Rachel had tried to resist his beatings and rapes with all the energy that was in her child-sized body. The response that came at her, as reported, was to be thrown across the room against a wall, to have a beer bottle broken over her head, and other nausea-inducing events which she conveyed. Her defiant rage toward Mr. X was out in the open, futile though it had been. But where was the rage at her mother? Touching on that was like a third rail of the treatment; the potential shock felt like it would kill her. No surprise it remained outside awareness.

It was hard for her to stay oriented in time when safety was a concern and thinking about rage toward her mother challenged safety. Here's how she put this orientation problem in a middle of the night phone message: "When we talked in our session about humiliation now and then, what I realized is that right now, anyone, even at work, anyone that downs me or doesn't agree with the way I think, or suggests there's something I did wrong, even myself to myself, all of these are read as I am being violated, thrown against the wall. It's not now, it's then, it's like everything is then, everything is a violation of me and I feel like I'm just going to run down the alley and just strip off all my clothes and lay down and just lay there and maybe I can be alone and safe for a moment."

Rachel emphasized that to whatever extent Mr. X assaulted her body and mind, the chronic repetitive experience of her mother invalidating her thoughts, negating her feelings, and remaking the landscape of Rachel's mind like an out-of-control bulldozer was much, much worse. "I think my mother was jealous that my Dad liked me. I keep going back to the scene of her ignoring my cries when I was in the crib, to the point where I gave up and stopped crying. I keep thinking about the lack of interest in what was going on for me. It wasn't just a kind of neglect. It was that she had interests and I wasn't one of them. She kept on stamping me with the image of who she wanted me to be. She would not tolerate anything else. She was relentless. My mother was in her own world, and she rewrote me and reality as it suited her. To be loved, you had to be as she wished you to be, but that actually regularly changed. She would crush the ideas I had in my own mind. She invalidated who I was, what I believed, to the point where it was only safe to be nothing. Everything about me was sabotaged. My mother didn't want my father to know about my abuse because it would have exposed her inability to manage the family, in his eyes. She couldn't tolerate that idea, and so I had to stay silent."

Ending an Enactment?

Several days after I had digested more of the Wurmser and Jarass book (2013a), I became serendipitously aware of the scenes of abandonment in my childhood that had an eerie similarity to abandonments in Rachel's growing up, as noted in the section on countertransference. My mind was filled with the sense that the single most important factor impeding the work with Rachel was me. I had convinced myself there was an enactment taking place where neither she nor I could consciously know about the humiliated rage we felt, at about the same age, when I was sent to the Bronx and she was neglected in her crib and left for hours, crying and in despair. The script in me was like the one in her, despair leading to sleep. There were no words. Dissociation of our matching humiliated rage from a time prior to coherent narrative formation was unbearable, and only the closing of our eyes and minds was visible at this point in our lives as we repeatedly bumped into and tripped over frustrations beyond our capacity to tolerate. For me, I had buried my anger at her intransigence, as I had done in the case with Alice (see Chapter 1). I was being the good therapist but denying reality; at the same time I was also resonating with her despair from a place of my own. One Monday, as her regular double session started, we exchanged the usual pleasantries of our ritualized checking in and she then told me she had nothing particular on her mind. She was placing the burden of being mindful about her life and difficulties on me. She was in retreat. Perhaps she was waiting for me to show up, awake?

In the previous Thursday session, I had gone off on a several-minutes-long rant of anger toward the people who had hurt Rachel, emphatically challenging her about her idea that she couldn't be angry with them. When that session ended, I had felt somewhat exhausted and also relieved. I could not allow her negativity and lack of felt anger

313

at having been abused go unopposed. After the fact, I was pretty sure I was resonating with the isolated feelings in her and voicing them. However, as I looked at the situation, it seemed to me those feelings needed to be voiced by me if not by her so she could hear it out loud and from somebody who cared about her. I also believed my emotional plea to recognize her anger likely had no salutary effect and was left with a continuing sense of the work being stuck while she sank deeper in despair. Now, on a sunny Monday afternoon, when she said she had nothing to say, I accepted the burden she wanted to hand to me, and I replied with an emphatic, "Well, I certainly do."

"Rachel, you have been very gracious and understanding about my sleepiness. I think you know I've been working on it, and been somewhat successful in curtailing it, but we both know it still happens, and I believe that it really hurts you deeply when it occurs. It's a kind of neglect, me leaving you alone while you hurt and are trying to tell me your story. How could you feel confident of me listening to your hurt if I'm falling asleep? It reminds me of the kind of neglect you described earlier in your life when you were left in the crib, deeply upset, and ignored for hours. I feel that I owe you an apology, and so I'd like to apologize."

"I really appreciate you telling me you're sorry, but I feel that you have worked hard on this and that in my accepting your humanity that you will accept and respect mine. But thank you for telling me. I just don't know exactly what the sleepiness is about."

"I think I've located it in me, and it resonates with your story." I went on and shared the scene of my colicky infancy and imagined humiliated rage in resonance with her crib scene. I went on to say that I thought that despair and fear were more of the picture of what likely was going on behind the scenes of her negativity than a wish for punishment or a fear of getting better. I reminded her of how much fear she had of being real in a real world. She agreed with the formulation.

I thought Rachel would come back to the theme of childhood rage, but she surprised me as she said, "I finally found out which part of me has been guiding all my negativity and making it impossible for me to choose anything or do anything. I know now that it's Lucy. She wasn't belligerent or anything about it. She was just kind of matter of fact. She said that she didn't think she was going to talk about what motivated her because talking about these kinds of things didn't do any good. We told her about therapy, and about what you've told us about talking and getting the story out, but she said she wasn't interested. And she made it pretty clear that if she didn't tell her story she wasn't going to go along with any healing because it would dishonor her and others inside who haven't yet told their whole story. It would be like it was okay to forget them and how they suffered if we went ahead and healed without the stories."

"That's such a surprise, Rachel. I didn't know Lucy had so much anger."

"Oh, yes. I understand now she was the first part of me to be created as I was growing up. She's been around the longest, and so she's the most powerful and I think most angry of them all. All that energy gives her a lot of clout and she pretty much gets her way regardless of what anybody else wants."

"That certainly explains why every part of you has been frustrated about healing, but no one part of you could account for what was going on, just like we've learned checking it out thoroughly many times in the past. Everybody inside was reacting fearfully to Lucy as if your mother was present, angry. May I ask you a question?"

"Sure."

"I'd be interested in talking with Lucy about the things you just told me about. If she doesn't want to talk about more, that's fine, but I'd really like to get into more detail with her about the things you've already described. Would that be okay?"

"Yeah, that's okay with her."

"Lucy, let me know when you're here and ready to begin." There was no apparent transition as Lucy jumped right into the conversation.

"I don't know why you would want to talk with me. I'm evil. I'm dirty. I'm evil, evil, evil, evil, evil, evil. I'm filthy. I'm violated. I'm bruised and raped." I had talked with Lucy several times in the past, but this kind of self-shaming had been invisible behind a major shield of anxiety. Lucy was the cleaner. She was totally obsessional about it.

If she didn't get things perfectly clean, she would be anxious. At work in the retail store it turned out that Lucy was the source of major discomfort about leaving a job incomplete when quitting time arrived. Lucy arranged to clock out and then return to the floor to finish her work to the point where she could tolerate leaving.

"I had no idea you have been carrying all this misery in you. I'm so sorry. Where do you think this comes from?"

"I was my mother's puppet. I was her dress-up doll. I had to be a certain way, just so, or I was accused of doing something wrong, or just being wrong. She never complimented me. I had to be perfect. It's like you'd think that if you did something that was perfect, then she'd notice and you'd get a good feeling back. My mother never did make me feel good. As much as Mr. X hurt me, I have much more anger with my mother. She always was judging me but never understanding me."

"Lucy, what did you think about the conversation earlier when I talked with you about my sleepiness and how I thought it might match your experience of being neglected and left in the crib? What's your understanding of that?"

"I think it's a good match. It's like when I raged in the crib, I just ended up getting no response and it left me in this kind of dazed stupor."

"Is that also connected to scenes with Mr. X?"

"I remember after he raped me I was just so confused. I was upset and shaking. I was confused about what happened. I was in pain, but it wasn't like being dazed like in the crib. Well, maybe some, but it was kind of different, too. But the stuff with my mother was worse. Even when she calls now I feel like I have to be on my best behavior and compliment her and say all kinds of mushy nice things to her so she can feel good about being a mother. I have to be proof that she's okay and a good mother. I'm a robot who compliments her so she doesn't hurt me."

There were two other things that Rachel told me in this session that were highly significant for the further course of her treatment. Lucy was essentially behaving just like her mother in regard to Lucy's relationship with other self-states (treating them as if they had no mind),

and also that she bitterly resented my keeping Rachel alive. This sentiment was delivered as a pressured flood of invective toward me.

"I hate you for having a life that you like and having all these nice
things around you; and I hate you for stopping me from killing myself
and taking pills because that's what I want to do; and nothing will do
any good; and I can't be helped so I don't understand why it is that
I'm not allowed to die and I hate you for it! And I know you've always
tried to help me and you've always been nice to me, but it's my life and
I don't understand why you won't just let me die."

I met her acidity and despair with soft compassionate tones and
telling her that I knew she was in pain, and my response to her pain
was to try and help her heal. "I understand that healing means that
you feel more real and that this is scary for you. I get that. It's just
that I happen to like you and care about you and when that happens
between me and another person, then my response is to try and understand their hurt and help them to tolerate their healing. Either way I'm
relieved that you've been able to tell me how and why you hate me. I
need to know and I appreciate you making the effort to tell me these
feelings so I can be alert to them."

At the end of this session I was actually feeling enlivened and fully
alert, as I had the session before. It was a nice change. Rachel looked
alert, too. She had not withdrawn. As Lucy, she was not hostile, just
needing to tell me her feelings. She surprised me and cheered me
when as she left and we did our ritual handshake of parting, she said,
"Thanks for listening to my feelings. You always have. I appreciate it."

Of course, in the next session, Lucy showed more of her colors,
particularly those that matched the single-minded intransigence of the
mother she was designed to deal with. Still, the tenor of the treatment
had changed.

The Fear of Being Real

The gravity of the negative therapeutic reaction and the negativity with
which it is often associated is understandable as a paradoxical effort to
remain safe and stay the same while still wanting to change but being
terrified that change means being subject to harm. These simultane-

ous contradictory motivations are made possible by their organization in the isolated self-states predicted by Type D infant attachment and their typical not-me organization. In the case of Rachel, incremental increases in coherence for her story congruent with the exploration of what were often enough only sensorimotor tags of old experience slowly led to accumulated growth. That growth was threatening in the context of childhood admonishments to not have a mind, to not assert, to have no agency, to not exist except for the pleasure or the benefit of those who when disappointed invoked fear of the Devil being inside Rachel. None of her growth would have been possible without a safe-enough relationship in treatment. For many years the space in my consultation room had been a transitional space for her, where what she observed was neither part of the world nor part of her past. We had observed that dislocation in time and place periodically, and it had yet to change, though there were moments when it felt like it might. All in all, I was still waiting for my office to be experienced as in the real world with Rachel fully present in it. The emergence of Lucy heralded a shift in her relationship with herself, and palpable movement toward healing.

The presence of self-states in Rachel affected the trajectory of the treatment by requiring that I cross the dissociative gap to isolated thoughts and feelings in self-states like Lucy, using conversation and special techniques at times. Consciousness for the action of dissociative processes was important to ensure an integration of past experience, as we systematically gathered behavior, affect, sensation, and knowledge into a felt coherent whole, as Braun described years ago (Braun 1988) and Kluft more recently (Kluft 2013). This eventually would lead to her feeling real, finally making the transitional space unnecessary and even unattractive. Dissociative time distortion often has complex dynamic roots. To not have access to Rachel's self-states would have made incremental resolution of her negativity more difficult and prolonged her negative therapeutic reactions.

Negativity and negative therapeutic reactions had kept Rachel safe but ill and were draining her soul of the will to live as they recouped power and deflected therapeutic progress from the felt threat of feeling real. We had to tolerate the feelings in each of us and maintain respect for each other as the work evolved. There was a clear need to reframe her behaviors as the self-protection they were, as visible only from inside her mind. To have attributed other motivation would have risked shaming her and would have further undermined clinical progress.

Chapter 10

Object-Coercive Doubting

THE COMPLEXITY OF THE TREATMENT OF PERSISTENT DISSOCIATIVE PROCESS is a given. Reiterative patterns of moving from impasse to impasse, from crisis to crisis, and into and out of negative therapeutic reactions are only some of the challenges awaiting a clinical couple. The work is not impossible, but it's not easy. Alice had certainly taught me that reality. We had learned it together. This chapter describes the first of three sessions in which I first discover a theoretical frame, object-coercive doubting (Kramer 1983), for holding and containing Alice's regular attacks on the treatment, which she delivered at the same time she was trying to figure out how to make the treatment work. In Chapter 11 I illustrate the enactment that followed. Last, I show the emergence from that enactment in Chapter 12.

You will see how Alice and I behaved coercively toward each other, each of us arguing persuasively, under the sway of the enactment dynamics in addition to carrying doubt about our beliefs regarding the other and ourselves. Alice's coercion is subtle, nearly invisible without the broader context of the treatment that I spell out after the first vignette concludes. In essence, though, Alice's desperate need to avoid feeling anger (for fear that she will become a very angry and out-of-control person) creates the need in her to deny and disavow the reality of her internal world. She wages war on reality and does so as skillfully as anybody I've ever known.

Alice's level of argument in the face of a reality that I could see was tantamount to a kind of torture. My mind was challenged to hold on to what was real. As noted in the first chapter, I was figuratively like the girl who is raped by her father at night, only to sit down the next morning to a family breakfast, aching and exhausted, and hear her father announce he had a great night of solid sleep and then ask how everybody else is. What is real? What just happened? In the enactment, Alice and I both feel coerced, behave coercively, and doubt our perceptions.

I was at times really subject to doubting my conclusions and perceptions. It took an effort of will to hold that conflict inside myself and not simply agree with Alice. I wondered if I was wrong. It was a struggle within me. In the enactment, I lost my clinical footing, became emotionally overwrought, didn't listen to Alice, and pushed my own agenda as I struggled to deal with what felt like her ongoing coercion of me and my perception of the reality of her behavior and its meanings. I unconsciously responded in the countertransference to maintain my hold on the reality I had observed in the face of disinformation and dissembling from several of Alice's self-states working behind the scenes. My anger at these attacks on reality was dissociatively detached, isolated in me, and this unconscious denial of my emotional state left me without a conscious marker for what was happening. Neither of us could own our anger, and the enactment was joined.

When we first met Alice earlier in this book, she was on the verge of a handshake at the end of a psychotherapy session. She had been angry with me, and then as we parted she had rather unemotionally said, "I feel like I want to hit you in the face." Her anger had long been a chronic threat to her stability. Talking about hitting me in the face was related to a scene with her father where he had actually hit her in the face. Her reaction was, "I never felt so alive as when he hit me in the face." Yet her anger was hated by her. It had caused her all manner of problems at home and led to repetitious scenes of her parents humiliating her for being angry, for what they called her being in an "angry snit." To my mind these scenes were generative of the shame-rage described by Helen Block Lewis (Lewis 1987a) which I touched on in Chapter 9. Her anger was banished by parental admonishment and remained under pressure, isolated in Alice's mind.

In Chapter 6, an exploration of fear and depersonalization, we again came across Alice's difficulty with anger and how her fear of her anger made it hard for her to think. Bringing anger into her psycho-therapy was essential, and for Alice it was threatening. It could over-turn her whole life, she believed. In fact, it had, several times.

Years before the vignettes that follow, I had noticed that I withheld my own anger from the therapy with Alice. This had given her the implicit message that my anger was not tolerated by me any more than she tolerated her own anger. When I finally expressed my anger toward her, as a result of frustration over her "blinding denial"[1] (Wurmser 2000) and disavowal, I told her, "If I can't bring my anger into our relationship, then how in the world could I expect you to do that?!" She replied, "That's the smartest thing you've said in years." Smart or not, I had since lost touch with that lesson.

Since Alice hated and feared her anger, and since her anger was welded to shame experiences, my approaching her anger was deflected by her with regularity. She didn't want me to "feel into" what she was feeling. This made the task of birthing her anger like rowing a small boat across a busy commercial shipping lane: You spend as much time working hard to save your life as you do in making progress toward reaching the other shore. Of course, Alice's suicidality was always a concern and had been for many years, though less so as our little row-boat got further across the waters.

During the times when Alice was in her own small rowboat, it was as if she believed she sat there with her mother, a woman who would not see large ocean liners approaching if she didn't want to. Reality, for Alice's mother, was negotiable in a manner that Alice had come to appreciate as dishonest, and she was furious with her mother about this. However, her mother couldn't cope with anger coming at her, and Alice feared that consciousness for her own anger might scuttle the boat as a result of an angry outburst. The potential for the loss of the relationship with her mother was felt as nearly equivalent to losing her own life. This was intolerable to Alice and fueled deflective pro-cesses. It was also true that a part of her didn't see dissociative experi-

---

[1] The entrenchment of this level of denial has the quality of a delusion in that it is impervious to any level of modification, regardless of contradictory material presented to the patient (including videotape), in my experience.

ence much better than her mother saw ocean liners. Alice's deflective process was such an active part of her treatment that it was like being lobbied to give up my views about things dissociative. The extent of her active denial and disavowal of what I could plainly see was infuriating as it dragged on for years. It seemed impervious to any logical or emotional intervention.

There were two threads of discussion in Alice's treatment that are woven into the background of our experience together and provide additional context in which the dialogue occurs. First, for many years, on and off, Alice had acknowledged the presence of younger self-states in our sessions, but then, several sessions later, she would deny the significance of those spontaneous revelations and accompanying interactions. This was particularly true about a child self-state, Emily, whom Alice understood as having a strong attachment to me. At this point in the treatment I had heard neither from nor of Emily for several years. Each time we did self-state work there was movement toward acknowledgment of those self-states that I and other clinicians (during hospital stays much earlier in the treatment) had met. Several sessions later, there was denial and disavowal of her recognition of these same self-states, and sometimes this was accompanied in short order by threats to leave treatment because "nothing is happening." I had come to learn that this statement was in fact delivered by another self-state, one who felt at risk of shaming if the multiple self-states accessed became fully conscious to Alice in her everyday Alice-ness. Her mind would be less than what she hoped—damaged.

Second, Alice had given up on medical models for weight loss, an important issue given that she was more than 100 pounds overweight. She was opting for a surgical solution. When this first came up, I felt she was simply too emotionally unstable to follow the strict postoperative regimen of restricted eating. However, a year later, she was much more stable, and I had begun to believe I might be wrong to continue to oppose her wishes for surgery. I was aware that some child-states regularly engaged in eating behaviors as self-soothing, and they were not to be denied that capacity. In addition, there were other psychological origins for the overeating and several patterns for it. Just at the moment I was wavering toward giving my approval, a distressing email came from Alice indicating her suicidality. When I brought this up in the first session after the email, she first had no memory of having sent it, and then recalled it. I took this as an expression of distress about her wish to forge ahead and have surgery, and so I could not sign off on her safety. I felt pushed hard by Alice to do something I felt would place her at risk of suicide. She expressed the sentiment that her life wasn't worth living if she did not have the surgery and lose weight, so she had no concerns about her safety after the surgery. It would either work for her or not; safety was not in her calculus. I was clear that without resolving internal dynamics among self-states about eating, the surgical result would eventually fail.

So it was with some relief when I became aware of Selma Kramer's incisive article about object-coercive doubting (Kramer 1983). Kramer's perspective was forged in the context of several cases that entailed what she believed was specifically a pathological defensive response to maternal incest. Her view, at odds with others of her day, was that deliberate sexual stimulation of a daughter by a mother constituted incest (1983, p.327). She characterized the mother–child symbiosis in these cases as parasitic (1983, p.329). These mothers ordered their children to not know what the mother did, but instead to believe what the mother insisted on in her exhortations about reality. These mothers were harshly punitive. The object of coercion is the one who receives admonitions not to believe what they otherwise might know; initially the target of the admonition is the child, who then doubts the reality of their perceptions. But a feature of this constellation according to Kramer is that the child eventually turns the tables and pesters the mother with doubts about other, more mundane matters; the coerced object is now the mother, with the child doing the coercing.

Akhtar beautifully summarized the moment-to-moment interactions that follow between mother and child as characterized by

> (1) the child engaging the mother in endless arguments in which she is coerced into taking the opposite side of what the child feels is true at a given moment, (2) such coercive

doubting "often ends in orgasm-like fury for both, thus reenacting sexual play between them," (3) the coercion also represents a hostile tormenting of the mother, and (4) the child forces the mother alternately to tell him the truth and set him free from the burden the mother's earlier dishonesty had placed upon him and to continue maintaining earlier denial. (Akhtar 2009, p. 193)

You will see how this summary describes much of the action of the enactment in the later dialogue between Alice and me.

When I read Kramer's contribution, several lights came on in my mind regarding ongoing impasses in several treatments. In fact, one of these patients, stuck in a repetitive doubting situation, brought the article to my attention. Kramer focused on parental denial and disavowal. The perpetrator of incest had coerced the child into agreeing and believing that all was well and that nothing adverse had happened. There were also maternal prohibitions against the over stimulated child masturbating and an insistence on denial of their awakened sexual excitement. This "rendered the child unable to believe his own perceptions and intensified the child's need to seek answers by repetitively questioning himself and the adult world" (Kramer 1983, p. 345). Self–object boundaries had blurred or were nonexistent, as if the child was externalizing the mother's intra-psychic conflict. In the face of the child's questioning, it was as if mother felt tormented by the child, much like the child was tormented by the mother. The child ineffectively implored the mother to tell the truth. Kramer believed this was so as to get free from guilt through maintaining denial and "repression" (1983, p. 346). She saw what today we would call dissociative process, but didn't know that was implicit in her description of the growing child's "pseudo imbecility." She quoted Shengold, who described "the confusion and cloudiness that denote an alteration of consciousness affecting the feeling of identity and inhibiting thinking" (Shengold 1974). Of course, Shengold, following Kohut, thought of this as representing a vertical split, as described in Chapter 6.

The narcissistic exploitation of a child by an adult, together with the adult requiring that the child not know it, constitutes an admonition powerful enough to create object-coercive doubting. Furthermore, the efficacy of object-coercive doubting seems to be predicated on the generation of active dissociative process in the child as a result of intense emotional pressure to conform to the emotional and logical contingencies of the parent's mind. Additionally, it can happen that the child's demand for truth from the adult remains isolated within the child's unconscious because it would be too dangerous to oppose the parent's wishes. Simultaneously, on an implicit level, the child understands that the adult is being dishonest, but is inhibited from consciously noticing or protesting lest they suffer additional humiliation. Even toddlers know emotional dishonesty when it occurs (Fonagy et al. 2003).

Patients often can have an effect on the therapist via a very different kind of coerciveness—intense lobbying to be believed, as identified by Kluft and others (Fraser 1997; Kluft 1990b; H. B. Levine 1990). My own observation, however, is that object-coercive doubting is just as ubiquitous in trauma treatment, and I believe Kluft would agree. In Alice's treatment I eventually realized object-coercive doubting was at the center of the storm. She and I were repeating the dynamics of her family. We were rowing across the harbor, and our progress (or apparent lack thereof) was subject to excoriating attacks by her, resulting in a disjointed rowing effort that made our little boat feel like it was going in circles.

Several sessions before this next scene from her therapy, I pointedly told Alice that if she wasn't going to row as hard as I was, let alone pick up an oar and try to row, even a little bit, she needed to rethink what she was doing in therapy with me. We discussed that, and the work picked up a bit. In the middle of the scene that follows, the content was related to a funeral of a younger man, the husband of a friend. Alice saw a great outpouring of love for him and felt bereft that this did not feel like the response that would occur if she died. She identified the possibility that she would have a shame spiral toward suicidality if that thinking kept up, and she veered off the topic.

Conveying the struggle to emerge from an enactment where object-coercive doubting is a centerpiece of the action requires that I illustrate it. It's not pretty. Yet that's the nature of some of this work. We often work in darkness as dense and foreboding as the muddy waters of a flood. These dissociative waters can be negotiated, but there is some peril. Alice's mind had resources that although isolated and hidden from her were visible to me. She was both allied with the treatment and desperately opposed to it. She was terrified of her anger and knowing the full extent of sexual traumas that occurred during her teenage years. The feeling in the treatment was one of being challenged by a team of different ways of being Alice who did not play by the same rules of discourse.

Given Alice's need to avoid intense emotion, especially anger, any strategy that worked to deflect the treatment was fair game. In fact, she was a brilliant tactician in her efforts to paint me as the bully her father was, a man who in his worst moments beat and kicked her. Even in his best moments he was markedly competitive with Alice. This father-based transference was highly active in the treatment, and I responded to the attacks on the treatment and my ability to perceive the reality of her dissociative productions by becoming insistent in pursuit of her agreement with my perceptions. I inadvertently became the bully she accused me of being. I had stopped being curious. The dynamics of the enactment were activated. The perception of reality and the metabolism of anger were core issues. The conflict in Alice's mind about noticing dissociative experience was externalized into our relationship and became part of the enactment.

Alice had read much of the literature on dissociative disorders, as well as having been something of a student of clinicians who attacked the validity of the diagnosis. Her attacks on the treatment were rather sophisticated. It was as if she had full knowledge of all the arguments detailed in a formal review of those attacks (Brand, Loewenstein, and Spiegel 2014; Dalenberg, Brand, Gleaves, Loewenstein, Cardena, Carlson, and Spiegel 2012), and was using them in her treatment to shut things down. Moreover, every time clinical gains were made, she threatened to leave therapy. Healing was a threat because it increased her access to unacceptable feelings, especially anger, and the unacceptable view that she had DID, a perspective that activated intense shame related to childhood accusations of behaving childishly. This was the dynamic at the center of the negative therapeutic reaction repeatedly encountered in this treatment. At these times she was insistent that she needed a therapist who did not have expertise in understanding dissociation. Sometimes she would quit, leaving treatment for several weeks. She would return for relatively passive and passionless reasons. "My mother and my girlfriend were urging me to return to therapy with you, and so I have." "I really needed somebody to talk to because I was so tense, and there really wasn't anybody I could do that with besides you." Her reasons felt disingenuous, at best, and dissembling at worst—a statement of her reluctance to value the work we were doing, as well as her fear of doing it.

I had been attentive to her wish to deal with her anger so it did not spill out into her relationship with her mother. However, she was dubious about even approaching her anger. In the previous session, she quipped in reply to my wish to go in the direction of her anger, "Surely, you jest." She then played with the enunciation until it became clear she was saying the name "Shirley," as potentially representing a part of her with anger, and we laughed about her mental agility and creativity. However, there was no clear confirmation of her appreciation of a part of her with that name. In the session that follows, we begin where I recall our exchange about Shirley and jesting. I'm speaking about this as we pick up the action of the session. The doubting is visible. At one point, we work with her in a hypnotic state that is therapeutically induced with her permission. We had done that in the previous session as well. Also, invisible until after the hypnotic work is the presence of her pet dog, Buster, who often accompanied her to therapy, with positive effects. He liked me, an unusual thing for this formerly abused dog from a pound. Alice enjoyed Buster's relationship with me.

"You were punning and we had a bit of a giggle over 'Surely, you jest,' and 'Shirley.' I don't know if you've come out in a place where you understand whether you have a sense that there's a part of you with a signifier name of Shirley or if the punning was about something else."

Alice breaks in. "No, I don't know, however. . . [pause] However,

I've always pictured myself as . . . possibly becoming an angry black woman. I mean it, I've always seen this as like, the worst case of me."

"Uhhuh."

"Um . . . And here she is."

"Pardon?"

"And here she is! I mean I always envisioned that, I mean, for years envisioned, I looked at angry black women and say, 'Oh my God, I, you know, I could get that way but I hope I never do.'"

"Huh" (curious).

"And so here I am . . . With that same person inside me."

"Okay. Well, I'd like to pose a question for you that I didn't expect to be posing . . . but I think is on point. Why do you think all these black women have been so angry?"

"Because they're treated like shit and they've been abused their entire life, from a class perspective and a racial perspective and everything else. I mean, they have every right to be angry."

"Bingo!

"But in polite society, you can't show that much anger."

"Well . . ."

"And still expect to be respected."

"Right."

"And to function normally."

"Right. And where . . ."

"And so people get scared because, of being around them, because they don't know when they're going to go off."

"Which is how you feel about you?"

"Right."

"And for quite some time, I've been trying to figure out how to make our relationship safe enough, not perfect, but safe enough, a place for your anger to be present and be heard."

(Long pause) "Well, it's still not here yet."

"Pardon?"

"I mean it. . . . I still feel like I'm talking around the anger. I still think that when I was in hypnosis, I was talking about the anger, and telling you what she was saying, not necessarily her talking with you."

"Right. Shirley didn't speak directly to me."

"No, I think she might have, but she didn't realize that."

"Of course."

"I don't know where to go from here, I have a lot inside."

"Yes you do."

"I was really drastically affected by Sam's memorial service."

"Yes."

She returned to the focus on the memorial service, which then morphed into a discussion about her book club, a deflection interrupted by me when she paused.

"And then there's Shirley."

"Yeah. . . . And so, as soon as you said, 'And then there's Shirley,' I pictured lifting my arm up and throwing this cup of coffee and getting it all over the floor." (She appeared delighted to be saying this as though it was a discovery of some value.)

"Well, what a great symbol of how angry Shirley feels—how you feel . . . Because, what Shirley has is what you have, it's just that Shirley's been the container for it."

Here I paused, waiting for her, but was met with only silence. So I continued. "The container for what felt unmanageable to you."

Thirty seconds of silence followed. Although there were times when I had lost my clinical balance as part of the pressure of the enactment in which we were becoming embroiled, I was conscious of the need to leave room for Alice to struggle internally and eventually speak about what was important to her. Of course, this often involved a double bind when she would admonish me to not be silent: "You know how I hate your being silent!" I was in a no-win situation in trying to respond to her expressed wishes to let her speak and to not leave her in silence. She would become intolerably anxious when there was silence. In retrospect, this double bind may have partially been responsible for me losing some of my clinical balance and speaking much more than I did in other treatments. In this instance, Alice eventually responded, and she took the conversation in a parallel direction, having jumped tracks from the anger in Shirley to considerations of the impact of her anger on other people. She expressed this as a fantasy that nobody would come to her funeral, underscoring her lack of impact on others.

"I've always had a fear that if I died, I'd have a funeral and no one would come. And I still feel that way."

"No one would come because . . . ?"

"I haven't made enough of an impact on anyone's life."

"Well, that would feel very, very sad. I'm not sure it's true, but . . . that feels very, very sad." (A 20-second silence.)

"So this is why it's such a downhill spiral for me, because once I'm at a point where, I'm going to have a funeral and no one's going to come, I may as well kill myself."

"Except . . ."

"I'm not, I'm not really having suicidal thoughts."

"I get that. I get that."

"I'm just saying that's where the . . ."

"That's where the spiral comes in."

"Yes, exactly. Exactly."

"Yeah, because there's this fear that you're not related. That you haven't had an impact on other people. And that fear stands in juxtaposition to what you just told me about, about all the connections with Mabel and Sam and—"

(Breaking in) "But, no, no, no. I mean, it's just, I haven't had enough of an impact. It would be like Mabel and Vivian and Claire, and my mom." (A 20-second silence.)

"What kind of impact would you like to have?" (Another 20-second silence.)

"Really?"

"Yeah."

"Honestly?"

"Yeah."

"I would like to make people feel good about themselves."

"That's just perfect . . . That's absolutely right on! . . . And I think the first order of business in pursuit of that is to welcome Shirley to the therapy and to your life." (There was a 10-second pause.) I was aware that I had returned the conversation to the topic of Shirley, who

I still suspected might be a part of Alice holding a good deal of her anger. I didn't want Shirley to disappear beneath the waves of deflection. This was clearly my agenda, not necessarily Alice's. It seemed to me, consistent with past efforts by Alice to bury knowledge of her anger, that if I didn't raise the subject of Shirley, then she wouldn't either. Regardless, I needed to try and understand her agenda and explore it. If I pursued what I felt needed to be explored, in the face of her deflections, then I would be engaged in the process of the enactment. If I didn't explore her anger and deflections, there was risk that the very things we needed to explore to help her with her eating habits would remain invisible. I was in a double bind but couldn't see it. It was honestly very challenging to figure out what was deflection and what was real that was coming from Alice.

"I'd like to say it a different way for a second, which I think you'll get immediately, and especially because it addresses Cathy's concern." Here I begin talking through and speaking slowly to Cathy, a part of Alice who periodically makes a cameo appearance with a wise admonition about the treatment. Alice has been aware of this part of her, but has retrospectively declared she just invents Cathy as a way to please me. Cathy had spontaneously emerged again in a recent session. Now I said, "Cathy, as much as you are absolutely correct that to help with eating issues, we need to find additional sources of pleasure beyond food, I think it's also true that it would make a real difference to find ways to significantly reduce the pain that's inside you. The pain drains away the pleasure that comes your way . . . and nullifies the positive effects of good things that happen to you." (A 40-second silence follows.)

The idea of pain draining away pleasure is relevant because Alice has been clear that she overeats in large part because that's the only way to soothe herself that she knows. (We've worked on eating issues for years, with intermittent success, but not for a long while.) The idea is to find some other mode of soothing or decreasing the pain that prompts the need for soothing in the first place. But Alice has a hard time with this concept, a surprise to me. She looks at things from a different angle, in terms of not being able to hold onto good feelings, and because that's a worthwhile perspective, I just go with it.

"So you're saying . . .what are you saying? Good things are happening, but I'm not able to appreciate them, or recognize them, or hold on to them?"

"Yeah." (Ten seconds of silence.)

"But I don't know if that's true, because this weekend I had experiences that I really knew were good, I really appreciated them. I wanted more of them. . . . I mean, when I realize that I knew like eight people at the memorial service."

Alice is in pain that is noticeable to me. A single tear rolls down her cheek, but her facial expression is otherwise devoid of painful emotional expression, and so I chose to go with the content, rather than the emotion, the opposite of what I usually do. I'm thinking about how important it could be for her to actually be able to work with the pain inside, directly, and not just incidentally in this moment. A momentary relief could be useful, but we've done that for years, and the baseline problem persists.

"Your tear is noted. . . . What I'm saying is that the good feeling about being known and knowing . . . is something you can recall, but it's not something you can keep in the bank, so to speak. It's like you put it in the bank and then you go to see what's there and . . . there's not so much there, or maybe it feels like there's nothing there. That's what I'm talking about. The pain, that's under pressure, and is disowned, drains away what feels good. . . . It's not a whole lot different from what you're worried about in your mother. The doctors are not relieving her pain [her mother has a painful illness that has resisted efforts at effective management over several months] and that drains away her capacities to live a life. There's physical pain, but there's also mental anguish about it. . . . You can see the effect in her, it's not that much different in you. It's just different effects. I could say, probably with some accuracy, that eating behaviors are a potential antidote to the pain that you carry around inside you already . . . and that pain won't be quieted. Then we can understand the paradox in your therapy, of your losing weight and gaining weight. Because when you heal some, and become aware of how much it hurts inside, paradoxically you end up eating. I think we could have some clarity that if the pain got some relief, the urge to eat and blot it out, would change. . . . And your wish about your life to make other people feel good, to feel happy, would be realized inside yourself. Perhaps as a simple beginning that's also very complex."

"I haven't been able to take in everything you just said, but I certainly can take in the sentiment of it." Alice seemed grateful. She implicitly got the message, but my long summary was too much. This often happens, with short summaries no less than long ones: She appears to switch states while listening, as if she is distracted internally.

"Yeah. May I ask a question?" (Alice nods.) "And I ask this with respect. It's fairly straightforward, and that is I think there is a real need to engage with Shirley today, and we can do that hypnotically, or we can do that without hypnosis, I think. My question is: How would you like to proceed?"

"I don't know, I'm not thinking it's possible and you know, I hate, I hate it when you call out parts." In fact, that's not something I regularly do and haven't done in years, though I do talk through from time to time. I've avoided it specifically because Alice objected. However, although it might have offended her sensibilities, it might still have been useful to her. That was not what I chose, given my emphasis on relationship in treatment and mutual respect.

A skeptic of the treatment of DID will likely take the technique of talking through and making reference to other self-states as me actually calling out parts of Alice. They might argue she has acquiesced to my suggestion that there is a Shirley and a Cathy, and so on. However, there is a contextual issue that is not obvious and deserves clarification. First, Shirley is a name Alice used in a previous session, and she did so creatively. Second, having used that name previously, she then sought to undo it by saying she made it up to please me. It is not obvious, but this is the stuff of object-coercive doubting as she denies and disavows reality, undercutting the experience we've had together and holding me responsible for what she's done, saying she's made these things up to please me. In this organized retreat, she further distances herself from the idea of sequestered intense anger within her, an anger that had felt unmanageable and historically had led her to behave in an out-of-control manner. For example, several years ago in a group therapy for eating disorders, Alice's anger got the best of her, and she spontaneously lambasted another group member in a manner that horrified the Alice who was observing what she was saying but not feeling in control of saying it. She quit the group afterward, unable to deal with the shame she felt over being out of control. This shift in executive control is typical of DID (R. J. Loewenstein 1991). Alice once described driving home from work at night, having the urge to buy ice cream, not wanting to do it, and fighting to keep the car from going up the exit ramp to an ice cream store, a battle she lost. She felt horribly humiliated by buying another half-gallon of ice cream from the same clerk, only a night after she bought the first. What at first glance might seem like me speaking to other ways of being Alice without any clinical justification was not that at all. I did, however, respectfully address her concern by asking permission.

"That's why I asked you the question I asked you. I certainly would not be calling out parts. I would be speaking . . . to you as Shirley, a different way of being you." This might seem like a psychodrama technique, and that's a reasonable way to imagine it.

Alice closes her eyes, leans back on the couch and rests her head on the back of the couch as she regularly does when using hypnosis—I follow along after she takes the lead in entering a hypnotic state, as I regularly do—and after about 20 seconds of her own efforts I start to assist and guide the process.

"Going deeply in trance . . . deeper and deeper with each breath out." (She takes a deep breath.) "Arriving in the deepest places, ready to begin the work in hypnosis, and when that readiness has been achieved, simply let the head nod yes." (There is a 20-second pause and then a head nod.) "Thank you." Then reinitiating a conversation that had once already taken place with Shirley in a previous session, I spoke through to that self-state again. "Shirley, I've been talking about a need to engage with you, to be respectful and engage. . . . If you're willing, I'd like to do that . . . if it's possible."

"You just don't understand anything."She speaks as if I just didn't get it about her.

"Well, I'm open to being taught, educated. Teach me, please."

Alice is now in tears, as if pleading for me to understand. "It is hell. It is pure hell" (crying, heavy breathing, fully embodied emotion). "To have to live like this" (gasping a deep breath, and then breathing deeply several times as if out of breath).

"Tell me about it, please." I don't know the reference in terms of what is "pure hell." Is she speaking from the perspective of Alice about something related to parts being called out? Is she speaking about the relationship between Alice and Shirley? Is she speaking about Shirley's anger being bottled up and unwanted? Not knowing the reference, I ask her to tell me about it. This is a permissive approach to working hypnotically and drawing out the content without directing it.

Alice is still breathing deeply. She establishes the context of the hell she's in."I feel like nothing I ever do is right, and I can't please anybody and people want things that I can't give them." She exhales, forcefully. "They don't want me to be angry and my mother says that showing any pain, even though she's been in extraordinary pain for four months, is just the worst thing in the world, it's just so tacky, and she probably thinks since I wear my pain on my sleeve that I'm a horrible person. You know, fuck her. I don't really care." A 15-second pause. "I don't know what to do to make it better, it's been all, it's been like this since always, since always I can remember."

"What's an early version of it? An early time where it was like this?" I continue to be nondirective, exploratory, and making an effort to be alert for material in the transference.

She breathes deeply again."I mean, I remember being in first grade and . . . I wouldn't climb the rope" (exhales, sniffs). "Everybody made fun of me." Alice was overweight at that age and could not lift her disproportionately heavy body.

"It's humiliating."

"So I'm just like, Fuck you to everybody. (angrily) Fuck you, fuck you, fuck you. To everybody. Because everybody I've ever dealt with has hurt me. . . . Everybody I've ever had anything to do with in my whole life has hurt me."

"There's been so much pain..."

"I don't know why people expect me to be nice. I'm not nice. I'm pissed off!...I feel like I'm getting beaten up every single day. . . . I don't even know if I want to have friends, because friends always hurt you. What am I'm going to do, I've dug myself a hole so deep?"

"Well . . . "

"I don't know how to get out of it."

"I think . . . "

"And then all I want to do if I have a shovel in my hand is hit people and hurt them with a shovel." Alice is aware that when she's very angry it spills out and she hurts people. She doesn't know how to control it. She wants that control, and she is speaking from the perspective of both Shirley and Alice here. This is one of the curiosities of DID: There are moments of emotional intensity where there is co-presence of self-states, and an observer can only guess at what's going on. Only in retrospect might a patient report what they experienced and the meaning of it. I go with the emotion, validate her anger, and she produces a memory of being invalidated.

"Well you're angry, look what's happened to you. Look how often you've been hurt. Of course you're angry. My God."

"But mother says I'm overly sensitive."

"Well Jesus H. Christ! Anybody who's been hurt as often as you have would have some raw and tender spots, my God. They would be sensitive, like duh. I guess she doesn't appreciate how you've been hurt. And maybe she doesn't know, doesn't remember. . . Maybe she has a way of making her own hurt disappear."

"She asked me recently if I was bullied in school and I wanted to just explode at her."

"She didn't remember?"

"No."

"She didn't remember all the times that you came home upset?"

"No."

"You're kidding."

"Nope, no."

"Not remembering it?" Here my voice tones rise in disbelief. "My God."

"Not a one."She sighs.

"She didn't remember what happened between you and your father? How he hurt you?"

"No, we didn't bring up my father."

"Oh my. She didn't remember what it was like for you to have your father and brother go at it?"

"We didn't talk about that, we were talking about bullying in school."

"Yeah. But I mean it's like, you know, she doesn't have a clue as to why you might be hurt. Why you might be angry."

"No, no." She sniffs.

"That's infuriating." Shirley is fully engaged in the discourse now as I pace her emotional state. She really gets into the feeling with this permission to be emotional.

"Really pissed me off! We just wanted to explode at her 'cause she could have helped me and she didn't. And that's how I feel about you sometimes, you could have helped me and you didn't. And so now you're talking about all these fancy things to all these other people but you're not helping me." She started the session with small talk about Googling me and learning about my speaking engagements. Shirley is upset that I hadn't engaged with her before, and she seems to be oblivious to several years of effort I had made to encourage Alice to allow access to her anger. I try to speak to that and openly attune both to the state in which Shirley was angry, and the state in which Alice was fearful of anger, linking them together (Putnam 1989).

"Well Shirley, I couldn't get to you. . . . God knows I've tried. I think it's just been really frightening . . . for Alice to know about the anger that you've been holding for her. I think it really scares her. I think she can sense the violence in you. The protest. I think she's been afraid to approach you, or even know you."

"I think I could kill somebody."

"Well, yeah. You've been furious, murderously rageful, at times.

I'm just glad you haven't killed anybody. . . . But that's a feeling. . . . It's different than an action, but it's a feeling, it's a real one. . . . Alice has been worried, Shirley, that if you come to therapy, that she's going to end up letting your mother have it, and have a big angry to-do."

"Bitch deserves it!"

"There's no doubt that your mother has disappointed you, to say the least." (Thirty-second silence.)"What's it like talking with me, Shirley?"

"Um . . . Trying to go deeper."

"Pardon?"

"I'm trying to go deeper and get away from Shirley."

"Why?"

"I'm scared of her."

"Why?"

"She might hurt me."

"Do you think she . . . wants to do that?"

"Nope."

"You know, maybe one of the things that's missing in the picture is that Shirley feels rejected by you . . . dissed by you." (Ten-second pause.) "Seems to me that as angry as Shirley is, even Shirley could use a hug from you . . . rather than being treated like a pariah . . . 'cause she's not. She's just holding hurt that happened to you."

"I just ate butter." Spoken as if surprised.

"Well, maybe that's a way of getting rid of the pain that we're talking about. Maybe you eat butter to help with the pain that Shirley holds and that Alice doesn't want. . . . Is that a possibility?"

"I don't know, it just came in my head."

"Uhhuh. Well, I appreciate you telling me very much."

"I want to come out now."

"How do you mean? Do you want to talk with me or do you want to come out of hypnosis?"

"No, I want to come out of hypnosis."

"Okay. Well, I think you have done some very, very good work just now, and we've learned some really important things. And you got to tell me about the feeling of just eating butter, and Shirley's gotten to tell me how angry she is, and Alice has gotten to talk about how she wants to distance herself from Shirley, how afraid she is of all the anger still. And we've talked about how Shirley might need a hug and to be respected by Alice, even though there's fear. . . . And I really appreciate all of the good work. And is there anything else that wishes to be said before we finish our work in hypnosis this morning?"

"No, I don't think so."

"Okay, thank you." At this point I speak quickly, but conversationally. What follows is ritual in our hypnotic work: "In a few moments, I'm going to count back from three to one, and then say that word that signifies the end of work in trance, that word at that time being the word 'open,' at which time you will be here fully alert in your normal waking state, and bring back with you, as best you can and as tolerated, your understanding and appreciation of the meaning of the conversation we've had . . . As I begin to count."

"Mmhmm" (agreeing).

(Slowly) "Three, two, one, open."

Alice exhales.

"Three, two, one, open. All the way back. Get yourself oriented. Here's Buster sitting right next to you with his head on your leg. He's been very attentive to you. He's taking a break now that you're back out of trance."

"Not quite."

"Well, I can see that now. You still have a sort of shell-shocked look, a little bit zoned out. All the way back." Loudly, as a command: "Three, two, one, open." She stretches as if waking from a deep sleep. Slight disorientation after being in trance and absorbed in another emotional state is normal and requires a clinician's attention to relieve it. It's important to completely alert and orient a person after hypnotic work.

Alice exhales.

"Back in your body. All the way connected."

She exhales again. "Buster! Do you know it's me?" Alice is now animated like a mother talking to a child she's missed while being away.

"He knows all the different ways of being you."

"I'm feeling sad."

"What'd you learn?"

She inhales, exhales. "I'm feeling, I think I'm feeling some of the pain."

"Yeah?"

"That truly feels."

"Yeah."

"He licked my head." She was distracted by Buster licking her and so I add context about her expressed feelings, but she doesn't go with that.

"Some of the sadness and frustration about having to have been sort of bottled up inside you."

Alice exhales again.

"And what about the feeling of eating butter?" She's not interested in talking about the feelings, as is typical, and so I shift to curiosity about eating butter.

"Where did that come from? It was actually liquid butter . . . I don't know what that was." Alice seems baffled as she tries to explain why she made the statement.

"Well it sounds like forbidden fruit. Liquid butter is code for instant fat." These are my associations, not hers. This undermines the free flow of the material and needs to be corrected. I do that in the next session (Chapter 11). I added the metaphors about forbidden food from our discussions of her childhood and about fat as insulation from her feelings and her way of being in the world. But it's not useful at this juncture. It's off point, and she doesn't take it anywhere.

"That's true."

"It's like sipping on insulation." I am still making suggestions that are not useful.

"I know we need to finish, but we have to talk about the surgery." She breaks off the conversation and switches topics to having bariatric surgery. To the casual listener, it sounds like she is coordinating dates for a surgical procedure. To me, I hear it as an end run around the intensity of feelings of anger residing in a self-state she's dubbed as Shirley that are linked to eating behaviors. The eating butter state-ment that spontaneously arose was important. In the past, Alice has regularly brought up surgery and argued about it as she attacked the treatment as worthless. What seems like scheduling time to talk about surgery is not-so-subtle coercion. She has essentially been lobbying to use surgery to bypass exploration of her emotional states. She's also written me an email letting me know that if the surgery fails she'll likely be so distraught as to kill herself. But Alice now fully denies this is the case. Now she is not consciously concerned about suicide risk at all. We conclude the scheduling discussion. She still had information to gather before anything might be scheduled, and I check in on her orientation.

"Back in the saddle?"

"Think so."

"Okay, good."

"We have a lot of feelings, so. . . ." It's not lost on me that she says we have a lot of feelings. But I don't note it out loud since I know she'll object and that will create a fuss.

"Yeah! That's not a bad thing. . . . I don't think feeling sad was on your list of what it might be like to really be in touch with Shirley, be in touch with your anger . . . and all the frustration you've had through the years . . . and the lack of validation from your mom. And I think that one thing we can say for sure and take to the bank, as little as she has validated your anger, she has done the same thing to herself."

"That's true."

"That is part of what creates the kind of reactivity she has for her pain. Because bottled up inside your mother is a reservoir of pain that she can't go near, but when her body hurts, the barrier between her consciousness and the pain begins to erode, and she has a hard time."

"Yep; do we stop here?"

"Would you like to?"

"You say that it's time to stop?" Alice is lobbying to stop the ses-sion, and at the same time I'm sensing she's in a lot of pain and would benefit from being able to acknowledge it. I've talked about her mother, but the language applies to Alice, too. My intuition is on target.

"Yeah, but we were having a conversation. Trying to knit things together, close things down."

"I'm really hurting."

"I know. I know."

"I'm really hurting."Alice bursts into tears and begins crying.

"Yeah, I know, I'm not happy that you're really hurting, but I'm thrilled for you that you've been able to make contact with Shirley." Alice's nonverbal movements tell the story here. There is intimacy in the interaction. In a treatment that did not involve multiple self-states, I would opt to simply stay with the feeling. For this work with Alice, there is a need to make the effort to link the feeling to self-states that have been present in the session as well.

Alice is crying; she exhales, sniffs, exhales, and then there is more breathing and crying.

"I'm so glad the pain can come out some," I say.

Alice continues to inhale and exhale audibly.

"Buster wants you to feel better, too."

More sniffs, then she inhales, exhales.

"But he may understand, like I do, that it's not a bad thing that this pain is coming out, it's actually a good healing pain . . . and it just hurts . . . and it's sad."

Alice inhales and exhales, repeats that twice more, then sniffs. "Uhh" (gasping in relief).

"He knows. Dogs are people, too."

Alice exhales, then blows her nose. "All right, I think I'm okay now. I have to drive so I think by the time I get to work, I'll be okay."

In this vignette the initial conversation was composed of the details of Alice's relationship with her friend, whose husband's funeral Alice attended. At first seeming like deflection, it actually was filled with painful emotional content that eventually pointed toward feelings of worthlessness in Alice. She held a sense of shame that her life was not filled with the relatedness someone with her basic wish to help other people would deserve in response to that sensibility. When I reminded her, she seemed more bemused than curious as to what had happened in the previous session regarding the name she introduced,

Shirley, imagined as an angry black woman who had been mistreated her entire life. Beyond that she was dubious about the meaning of her experience in the previous session and was uncertain about whether Shirley was a self-state or a symbol, once more conjuring up the doubt that plagued her. Her doubt, however, was a prelude to doing work in this session that she ended up feeling good about, work that confirmed dissociative experience, although she then turned around again in a subsequent session and began doubting it, challenging my recollections and perceptions. All of which left hanging the exact meaning of Shirley, for both me and her. After years of trying to talk directly with the angry part of her and not succeeding, I did not want to lose track of Shirley. But Alice did. The next chapter, following up on this session several weeks later, vividly shows the kind of doubting she evoked. In this chapter, the reader has seen part of the context of my contribution to the full-blown enactment to be illustrated, based in part on the content of this session.

Alice also articulated her resentment over my potentially "calling out" alters, something she had heard of outside of treatment and had only experienced with me in the past. Of course, my clear observation, and that of others, was that she demonstrated switches to other self-states on her own; this was later finessed toward meaninglessness by her statement that she does those things to please me. The echo of her feeling coerced into that behavior is clear. Did she really feel coerced by me? To what extent was she living in the transference and ascribing to me that my intent to help her make conscious of her dissociative experience was actually coercion? Regardless, at least part of her felt that way in her subjective experience of me. My intent in speaking with Shirley was to build the basis for further relating and normalize her anger as well as to welcome her and the anger sequestered in her. When I got too close, Alice took charge of the trajectory and tried to deepen the trance. That was the end of Shirley's presence. Alice feared Shirley would hurt her, and this is a statement in the context of the delusion of separateness. It also relieves the conversation of the task of understanding if Shirley was symbol or self-state, based on Alice's internal experience. From Alice's productions,

Shirley had the quality of a state, one that spontaneously and passionately expressed her anger with an outpouring of feeling unheralded in more than a decade of treatment. One could argue that it occurred in hypnosis and so who would know what this was? The science of hypnosis, suggestion, and memory is spelled out in a lovely document by an extraordinary group of respected senior clinicians (Hammond et al. 1994). What's most important to understand is that the permissive approach to hypnosis which I use does not create memory, nor does it create experience. The wild card here is that hypnosis will create a sense of conviction about the validity of what is experienced in trance. Apparently, Alice has her own way to counter this, a way that is more consistent with the theme of object-coercive doubting. Over many sessions of difficult work, it had become clear to me that Alice used denial and disavowal to coerce her own sense of disbelief. This activity took the form of a self-state related to her father's attitudes, and this self-state bullied other states internally. There was also a self-state related to her mother that separately coerced disbelief and doubting. Both were affect-regulating states, but with paradoxically suppressive tactics. The fear of losing the relationship with mother if anger emerged was a large motivating factor that predicted Alice's retreat from knowing Shirley.

An intervening experience was the surprise internal "experience" that she had eaten butter. Hypnotic technique could never have predicted this experience. This is what I think of as a cameo appearance of a self-state. When we talked about the experience in the session, I was advised by her that this was liquid butter. I erred in pushing the idea that there was a connection to overeating. The fact that it was liquid was likely significant, but I failed to explore it. Alice had an old history of eating a half-gallon or more of ice cream in an evening. Her method of consuming it was idiosyncratic. She would find the biggest spoon she could, stir the ice cream into liquid, and then often sloppily try to get the ice cream into her mouth. She had astonished herself when replying to my inquiry about why such a big spoon was required by saying it had to be the "size of a penis." Thus, liquid butter certainly is food, but it also might, like ice cream, have been a stand-in for ejaculate. In fact, when I explored this with Alice in the next session, she told me for the first time about a teenage scene of feeling obligated to perform fellatio or lose a relationship. The connection with anger was part of the context, but that was not specifically discernible. Was it somehow a veiled reference to the feeling of Shirley becoming visible in the treatment in the face of conflict with some ways of being Alice who opposed this?

If Alice was so opposed to identifying self-states, then what made it so clinically important to pursue them? The isolation of self-states—one from the other as well as from the usual presenting self-state of a person—creates many liabilities for living. Chief among those problems created by persistent dissociation when there are isolated self-states is what results from truncated capacities to feel emotion, feel connected to a body, understand and predict behavior, and maintain a full fund of personal and social knowledge. These are the general lines of cleavage often seen when there is active dissociative process (Braun 1988). Linking self-states together (Putnam 1989) is a central task of treatment and often begins through the relational link between individual self-states and the therapist. Gradually, the coordinates of experience in Braun's BASK model become linked and shared throughout the system of self-states. Eventually, distinctions between states are lost through shared experience. A situation of integration of self-states occurs where one self-state may feel nearly indistinguishable from another. Thus, defining the similarities and differences between self-states is a central task of treatment on the road to integration and living a life fully.

The internal experience of having multiple self-states typically moves from argumentative to cooperative, from feared to accepted, from adversarial to collaborative, from young or old to age-appropriate. The moment-to-moment subjective experience of an unintegrated scene of multiple self-states varies from chaotic to rigid and sometimes a bit of both. The experience is highly idiosyncratic. Alice often just experiences a thought coming to mind that may take her by surprise when she experiences the influence of another self-state. During a video of a session some years ago, we both became aware of her having an experience of seeing a younger self-state from an inside-her-mind perspective. This was immediately after that younger aspect's appearance in the session; she had then switched to an adult state. I asked her if she had been aware of the child-like state having been present, and in response she looked over to her side, as if she was going to check to see if that state was still there, with "there" being where she had seen her in her mind. Some people have a physiological experience of being able to touch or hug self-states. For people who become aware of these kinds of self-state experiences when they are children, it can be confusing to distinguish inner reality from experience in the world. This is where psychic equivalence and pretend modes of thinking (see Chapter 3) in a dissociative transitional space play a prominent role.

There are two other factors visible in the work with Alice that are worth mentioning at this point. First, she is extraordinarily intelligent, has studied dissociative disorders and relational psychoanalysis, and has made a special point of using psychoanalytic terminology when commenting about her treatment. She uses these terms correctly. While I try and stick to plain English in my discourse, not responding in kind to Alice would be disrespectful. It may be jarring to note the use of the words *transference* or *enactment* in the clinical dialogue. Second, as part of my agreement with Alice, I have shown her the chapters in which our work is depicted. Though Chapter 12 is sequentially several months after the work in Chapter 10, our discussion then included references back to the content of this chapter, which she had already read. This juxtaposition may leave the reader feeling as if they are in a house of mirrors. If it does, then rest assured it has been rather difficult for me to maintain coherence for the sequence of events and the content of discourse in a long and sometimes contentious treatment.

A mother I know reported her healthy child to have articulated an emotional conflict recently with these words: "I'm angry, and I know I'm not angry, but I feel angry. Make it stop." Luckily for this little person, she had both the strength and active permission to verbalize her feelings. Such was not the case with Alice, who was clear her mother would not permit expressions of emotion related to pain. Although this does not fit the letter of Kramer's defining scenes for object-coercive doubting in maternal incestuous situations, it fits the psychodynamics exactly.

In the next chapter, we pick up several weeks after this session and can see the dynamics of object-coercive doubting in action. There's more to say and more to learn about this kind of entanglement, which certainly fits the tenor of the Chinese curse that many people know: "May you live in interesting times."

Chapter 11

In the Throes of an Enactment

ONE OF THE NOT-SO-HIDDEN BENEFITS OF WRITING UP CASEWORK (ESPECIALLY doing it from audio recordings) is that I get to hear how I sound, the nuances of it all. I also get to notice when I am wholly wrong, when I am trying to get in the boat with my patient but fall off the dock and into the water. It's humbling to think you are going to see and hear one kind of thing only to find you've missed the boat, fallen in the water, and are all wet. Near drowned or not, I find that there is work to be done and new things to be learned about countertransference in action, my very own performance art.

Part of the magic of psychotherapy is that with a strong enough relationship both patient and therapist can be rather forgiving about their errors in judgment and inherent blindness. What's required is the constant good will of each person in the service of healing. We often think this primarily comes from the therapist. Not so. Good will needs to be invested in a treatment by both parties in an individual psychotherapy. It's certainly visible in the transcript that follows as Alice tries to help me see what I'm doing. This need for mutual support of the treatment was especially critical in the complicated enactment that was being played out. It's not that Alice wasn't also occupied in an unconscious effort to hide her mind. What mattered most was that we both needed to become aware of the conflicts and tensions inside us rather than externalize those conflicts into our relationship. Her externalization could not be reined in, nor could it become visible to her, no matter how much I interpreted and confronted her about her unconscious process, until I stopped making my own contribution to the scene.

Thus, this chapter is about being in the throes of the enactment. I learn from it, and so does Alice, but only after I do. To be fair and to honor her dedication to the treatment, even as she fought to keep her mind hidden, she had several times announced to me that she thought there must be something going on between us because things seemed to be stuck. We were in agreement on that, but the essence of it was elusive. She had even said that there must be some kind of enactment, making use of her self-taught knowledge of psychotherapy. In fact, I had agreed with her, in general, but, like her, I had not been able to see what had been going on.

Enactment Under the Sway of Dissociative Process

Gorkin (1987) has introduced a distinction between the subjective and the objective countertransference that has great bearing here. The objective countertransference is what any clinician likely would have evoked in them by the patient, while the subjective version brings to life in the clinician what is idiosyncratic to their own psychology. I am proposing that enactment is a subjective countertransference phenomenon. Unfortunately, knowing about my tendencies is not an inoculation that can prevent enactment. When we heal from our hurts, old patterns fall into disuse; they are not erased entirely. We develop additional ways of thinking, feeling, and being, but we don't delete the past from our neural pattern libraries. In enactment, these patterns can be blindly enlisted to skew clinical formulation and assign responsibility for the pattern of a treatment as if it wholly belonged to a patient. This can be therapeutic tyranny if it goes unchecked. The importance of the concept of enactment is that it speaks to the necessity that sometimes this tyranny must occur, at least for a while, if certain unspeakable and unknowable aspects of a patient's life are to enter awareness. It's the same for the patient's transference; it must be allowed to occur and unfold. If enactment goes on too long, however, or if nothing else is changing, then it can precipitate the end of a treatment or lodge itself at the center of a stalemate. Consciousness that something is off is essential. Sometimes the clinician blows the whistle, and sometimes the patient does. Sometimes both are blowing whistles, but nobody can figure out what's wrong. Harmony is lost. That's the story here.

I wish it were only this complex. In the treatment of persistent dissociative process, there is also a phenomenon I've come to think of as nested transference. One transference constellation nests inside another, like Russian matryoshka dolls, nested one inside the other, the larger holding the smaller. In some ways, this is the transference and countertransference version of the principle of multiple function (Waelder 1936).

Because self-states often have the quality of being semi-autonomous centers of initiative, transferences are activated at multiple levels and with similar intensity across a self-state system. Thus, in the person with a dissociative structure of self-states, these transference modes influence the treatment seemingly all at once or in rapid-fire succession, whereas for the activity of self-states in the more integrated mind of a neurotic individual, there would be a more measured sequence to transference pattern activation. There would not be the quality of near simultaneity of experience as there can be in DID.

Alice activated patterns of transference that impacted me and the treatment like bullets from a well-oiled machine gun. The rapid-fire changing of perspectives often left me stunned, and I am quite experienced with this kind of shifting. I reacted at times with some desperation to stay oriented. I was unaware of the conflicts inside me about my own confusion as to what I was seeing in Alice. This conflict led me to adhere to my certainty about what was going on, a misuse of clinical authority if there is such a thing in the era of the two-person psychology. A healthy sense of ambiguity was not to be found in my mind.

The object-coercive doubting at the center of the enactment in Alice's treatment was based on her feeling in the transference that I was pressuring her to believe something that made no sense to her, just as she capitulated years before to her parents' negative beliefs about her in regard to her anger. She refused to be tricked by me, a direct attribution of characteristics taken from her father. My contribution to the enactment was related to her behaving toward me like her parents behaved toward her and trying to convince me that I was a mistaken and misguided therapist who could only see things dissociative. I was angry about this, but it was so routine in our conversation that I missed the build-up of anger and its significance. "I don't know what my problem is exactly," she would say, "and while I have dissociation, so does everybody else. So, I'd be better off working with somebody who isn't an expert in dissociation." When I didn't get angry with her over her bland denials, but tried to reason with her, she couldn't believe what I was saying because I wasn't being real with her about how she was behaving. My denial and disavowal of my anger fueled the enactment.

After Alice read Chapter 10, we talked about it and made it part of the therapy. She told me at one point that my depiction of her was "not very flattering." I told her I could appreciate that. I also told her that she hadn't yet read this chapter, which was largely already written and was not very flattering of me. I said I wasn't sure how much of it would survive the editorial process of what would be included in the book given that showing people work that doesn't really pass muster might be ill-advised. But, I noted, I was inclined to include it with a view to showing what's real about the work and how two people can work through hard issues and come out the other side. She thought I should do it, and I have agreed with her.

I am talking about what happens during the discovery of the presence of an enactment (Bromberg 2006; Chused 1991; McLaughlin 1991; D. B. Stern 2004). The concept reflects a naturalistic evolution in the context of theoretical change from a one-person to a two-person psychology in dynamically informed psychotherapy (Ghent 1989). Like other kinds of transference–countertransference expressions of mind, enactment is what you discover, if you're lucky, after it's started growing and taken root. Just like life, enactment happens when you are looking the other way, perhaps distracted by something else. In the view of Philip Bromberg, enactment occurs especially when both patient and clinician are intolerant of some emotional content in each of their own minds, often in affective resonance, and this content is isolated as part of dissociative process in action (Bromberg 2003,

2006). When language and conscious thought are not available, action takes the stage, and implicit knowledge and unconscious dynamics direct the flow of the drama.

I am not unfamiliar with this way of looking at things (Chefetz 2003). Being familiar with it is not an antidote for being human, nor could it be, given that the story of a life cannot always be told in words. The person on the receiving end of an untellable story may begin to generate their own unconscious resonating performance art when they, too, are intolerant of their emotionally matching experience. While a theorist could invoke the lore of projection and processes of projective identification to explain enactment, my view is that a therapist "doth protest too much" about what is already deeply inside his or her own mind when he or she does that. Nothing toxic is put into a clinician's mind; it's already there. A clinician needs to do what we ask our patients to do: speak about what is real in their heart and mind and own their behavior. This is all in the service of becoming conscious of what has been unconscious, or implicitly held outside awareness. There is little room for thinking you can finesse countertransference enactment by not calling attention to it, or for believing in the self-aggrandizing stance of being able to track one's countertransference. That is folly, at best. Neither is there much room for self-flagellation about having participated in an enactment. There is no room for a not-me stance (Chefetz and Bromberg 2004) in this context. Awe is more appropriate in being able to appreciate the work of an unconscious mind.

When a clinician can finally put to work the understanding of an enactment, it's sobering to see where and how far all the tentacles reach. I wholeheartedly agree with Bromberg that when enactment is in its glory, threatening to sink a treatment, acknowledgment of it and the mutuality of it by the therapist may be essential to the work of the treatment (Bromberg 2006; Levenkron 2006), perhaps even required (Bromberg 2011). This is one of Bromberg's exquisitely important contributions to clinical work. It certainly levels the clinical playing field and makes the clinical pairing real partners in the work, a point well articulated by Donnel Stern (2010).

An Introduction to the Clinical Protocol

In listening to the recording and reading the transcript, I found what seemed to be the work of a newbie clinician. It was as if I was so enamored of my own ideas that I not only lectured Alice but didn't really let her speak at times, interrupted her regularly, and appeared to be hell-bent at having her see the dissociative process at work. If you could have heard her voice tones, you would have been struck by how she sometimes took on the role of therapist, clarifying, being curious, and trying to understand what was being said to her. She specifically noted that neither she nor I had changed positions vis-à-vis her insistence that she didn't have a dissociative disorder, and I didn't listen to that language either. It was more than a hint that I had indeed taken a position and had stopped being curious. I continued to aggressively pursue consciousness in Alice for things dissociative as she continued to deny, disavow, and dissemble. She never seemed to know she was doing it, nor would she acknowledge that she herself was curious about it. She seemed to give in quickly to her deflective processes. She sometimes hinted that she privately was curious, but she either couldn't or wouldn't provide me with her musings. Of course, even this perspective reflects my feeling shut out from Alice's mind as much as she herself was shut out. Importantly, when she hinted she might get curious under the right conditions, I didn't hear that either.

Alice's conviction that she was working hard in the therapy was honest. I also believed my observations of her deflecting the work were accurate. There was an interesting explanation for some of this experience. As the enactment resolved, her dedication to the treatment became visible in an email she wrote about how both our perceptions might have been accurate.

> I think I just got what you have probably said to me literally 1000 times. I am just one way of being me. When I am in strong denial about the DID and you would say that's not how all of you feels, but I really thought it was the true me who was talking to you. But now I can almost

see that there are many true me's and when each of them
is forward they have no conception of not being the
real Alice. And that is where the identity confusion and
maybe even amnesia come in.

Some Clinical Background

I could see and hear that there were well defined self-states at work
in Alice's mind, sometimes with the aid of hypnosis and sometimes
naturalistically. I was not alone in my opinion. During several hospitalizations, the diagnosis was confirmed. I also had videotape of Alice
changing from a child state to an adult state, which was an example of
classic switching phenomena, a change in state that she confirmed on
tape. Moreover, she had extensive state-of-the-art psychological testing by a recognized expert in the evaluation of dissociative disorders
who also confirmed the diagnosis. What that examiner told me was
a harbinger of what was to come: characterological problems were
going to significantly drive the treatment trajectory. Since the character issues were being driven by isolated self-states and fear, this meant
that Alice was going to be a very challenging patient. It also meant that
as her fear abated and her self-states became conscious and collaborative, her personality disorders would significantly melt away.

Alice had recently begun to understand that she used dissociation
regularly. She dismissed its significance by saying it was normal, that
she performed dissociatively to please me and to maintain our relationship. Actually, to be perfectly accurate, for years after her diagnosis, she insisted she did not have any dissociation. Eventually there
came a point where it became so difficult for her to maintain her denial
that she began to say she did have dissociation—but dissociation was
normal in everyone.

Thus, part of what was so challenging and infuriating about working with Alice was that she both knew and didn't know about dissociation and her self-states. She had amnesia for what she had learned,
and she had amnesia for this loss of memory. She didn't know she'd
forgotten (R. J. Loewenstein1991). It was sometimes as if she had

never known about other ways of being Alice. Most important, she was afraid, on a level approaching terror, that if she allowed herself to know about the organization of her mind, she would lose control of her mind altogether. She was especially fearful of regressive behavior she had experienced in her first hospitalization, of which she was deeply ashamed.

In spite of Alice's desperate need to keep what was in her mind hidden from herself, she did change over the years. She became less suicidal. Profound depersonalization ended. She was more tolerant of her emotions. She joined several social groups, went on regular outings with other women, and was part of a book group. She increasingly became able to tolerate frustration in her sessions, and rather than storm out of the room, threatening suicide, she could better tolerate the dissonance inside her mind and talk with me about what she was feeling and thinking. At one point in the treatment, she offered that the psychiatrist I was, whom she didn't like, and the person I was, whom she cared about and knew cared about her, could not be kept separate in her mind any longer, and the two versions of me to which she had related had intersected. This was a cause of real distress for her. It prompted threats of leaving treatment. Historically, these threats tended to occur in January, or sometimes before or after my late August or September vacation. She regularly denied that vacation disruptions in our routine had any meaning to her.

I had a recurrent feeling that Alice was baffled by her own behavior, but that she was unwilling to acknowledge the extent to which she felt out of control because it would confirm what I was saying about her mind. She could not seem to tolerate that idea. My frustrated response to all this became a hand-in-glove fit with the profile of the parent who doesn't listen to their child and simply tries to impose their view on the child, telling them what they must think and feel. I didn't do that, specifically, but my "position" was clear enough and felt like, as Alice put it, "You are trying to stuff this dissociation thing right down my throat!" Basically, any mention of something dissociative, by me, constituted stuffing. This is right out of the playbook of scripts for coercive doubting as summarized in Chapter 10 by Ahktar (2009).

The emotional constellation was further fueled by Alice's amnesias for the content of her sessions. (Recently she takes home a recording of the sessions because she often has no memory for salient events in them, though she disputes this at times). I had also repeatedly observed self-state bullying and distortions of reality by a combination of a father state and mother state, respectively. When a child-like self-state emerged once and was weepy, Alice quickly switched to a father-like state and spoke aloud as if lecturing a child, "There'll be no more of that here!" She was rather startled by the sequence. In regard to amnesia, she said that she didn't have amnesia, she wasn't an Alzheimer's-like patient. She joked that she had "half-heimers," and then went on to say she didn't have amnesia, but she had problems forgetting things. This put me in mind of *Alice in Wonderland*: "'When *I* use a word,' Humpty Dumpty said, in rather a scornful tone, 'it means just what I choose it to mean—neither more nor less'" (Carroll, 1960).

The contempt with which Humpy Dumpty regards Alice in Wonderland about the meaning of words and his mastery thereof is reminiscent of what I experienced in being coerced by Alice's denial and disavowal, a mother-like strategy in Alice. There was also a parallel with Alice's experience of doing crossword puzzles in competition with her father, who could not tolerate her intelligence. He insisted on *his* words.

For years I heard that what I observed in session was meaningless and distortions of my own doing. According to Alice I didn't see the little curls, I imagined them. She said I was preoccupied by dissociation and couldn't think any other way. She was aggressive in her accusations: "I need a therapist who doesn't know about dissociation." In the throes of the enactment, neither of us was entirely wrong with what we perceived of the other, and neither of us was completely right about what we perceived of ourselves and our own contributions to the enactment of aspects of her relationship with her mother and father.

As noted in the previous chapter, of critical importance was that Alice had been overeating for a long time, and was more than 100 pounds over a healthy weight. I was concerned about the degree of dissociative process in Alice, and it was slowly killing her in regard to her morbid obesity and the medical complications that created for her. I knew from past discussion that her child self-states ate to self-soothe. But access to child-like states was prohibited, and her eating remained out of control. Though her weight was currently stable, her body was suffering, and she was living in it. She was understandably desperate to do something about it.

The Clinical Protocol

In presenting this work I am attempting to illustrate the complexity of these treatments. If the reader is of a critical mind, he or she will have plenty to work with, but that's not the point. The intent here is to learn from mistakes and from unavoidable clinical process that must happen and be deciphered and understood for a treatment to advance when old wounds are only known implicitly. I could present the material more as a synopsis, but that would fail to make the experience alive. The following transcript is from a session nearly two months after the one in Chapter 10, though it contains references to Shirley and other content from that session. Alice had avoided listening to the recording of that session for weeks. When she initially reported on listening to just part of the recording, she said it had an "odd" but powerful effect. She was going to tell me about it, but never did, and it was lost by the next week. She had no memory for the "odd" experience. I had subsequently given her the transcript, but she hadn't read that either. In what follows, Alice starts the action in response to my latest assertion that she treats her inner world as if it's not real. We pick up at the point where she once more asserts her view of the original experience of Shirley. My comments are in parentheses. I have endeavored to provide the reader with my thoughts during the session, on the fly, as well as some of what I came to understand afterward.

"I do tell myself it's not real . . . but I don't believe I have a personality inside me named Shirley, who holds all the anger. I don't believe that all, zero . . ."

"Oh, did you listen to the tape?"

"Yeah."

"To the recording?"

"Yeah."

"So what's that about?"

"I'm making it up."

"Wha—. . . Well why would you?" (My voice tones are ones of disbelief and my frustration is barely contained.)

"This is what doesn't make sense." (She is hinting that she agrees with me, but I don't give her room to consider it or even to ask her what she means. I am caught up in my frustration.)

(Now, I speak with almost complete exasperation; I've lost my footing.) "Well it doesn't make sense that you would make it up . . . not at this point. I mean, you, who are livid about the whole thing and tell me nothing's happening here and that you're just making these things up, why the hell would you do that? Why would you do that? Why would you make it up? You wouldn't do that. It's not . . ."

"Just to have fun." (As I read this simple statement, yet again, it is hard to know if it is a taunt, while I helplessly flounder around on the deck, a fish out of water, a clinician who unlike her father won't literally fight her, and she might just know that.)

"No, you wouldn't. Why the hell would you do that? What are you doing, trying to torture yourself?" (I can remember saying this and quickly editing my verbal comment and not adding a comment about "torturing me." That would have been more to the point, and was certainly part of the enactment, acknowledged or not. If I had acknowledged it, things might have gone better.)

"No. I'm trying to . . ."

"You're trying to spend . . ."

". . . make things work between us."

(I'm agitated, and with lots of energy.) "No, I don't think so. You want to leave. You want to leave." (She had been threatening to leave the treatment because I won't sign off on her having bariatric surgery.) "You're telling me this bullshit that you want to leave and so, you know, why would you make it up? If you want to leave and there's nothing happening and I've had my chance, why would you make it up? Why would you waste your time? Why would you belabor the point?"

"'Cause I didn't want to leave then."

"Well, see, the thing is . . ."

"I want to do, do the hypnosis and do the work and I guess I just fake the work."

"No. See, you're not faking it. You won't believe it. You don't want to believe it, just like your mother wants to believe what she wants to believe. That's the position you're in. You're occupying your mother place and using father strategies. It's really interesting." (I've managed to calm down enough to respond on point, but I'm still off-balance. I don't hear Alice's uncertainty about faking the work. That's a lost opportunity. She's trying to break out of the enactment, and I'm apparently not ready emotionally, even though intellectually I thought I was prepared with my new knowledge of object-coercive doubting. I might have simply asked: "How do you manage to fake it?" If I had done that, then we could have explored her fantasy that she faked it. I say "fantasy" because I already had seen Alice switch from state to state at other times in her treatment, times when she herself con-firmed the switch, but then later denied it.)

"Yes, I had a vision of my mother trying to do hypnosis for pain, and it looked very much like I look." (I could have explored this but didn't. If I had been on my game I would have noticed she previously had told me that when doing hypnosis she might, at times, be in a mother-related state. I missed this back-reference entirely. From here, the conversation moves on to the subject of her actual mother, and her illness, and then gradually comes back to the work at hand with Alice trying to focus the conversation.)

"Okay, so you feel like one of the reasons I'm scared of getting inside of my own head is that I would feel shame about it."

"You've told me that, Alice, not today, but you've told me that. And you've essentially said that you didn't think I would like you any-more if I learned how things really are inside you." (I'm trying to get some traction. However, my emphasis on having been told that before undermines what might have been helpful. She lets me know that,with hostility and dismissiveness in her voice tones, and with a manner that is uncharacteristic of her, perhaps representing a switch. But she's cor-rect that I'm not listening. Regardless, she opens an important theme.)

"Nah, I don't think you'd listen anyway."

"Pardon?" (I'm dumbfounded.)

"I don't believe you'll listen anyway. You still think part of being a good psychiatrist is being super-supportive of me even when I'm not good, so . . . It's the same thing I get from my parents . . ." (My support invalidates the reality of her behaving badly, for her, and when I do that, she feels not heard. This is the stuff of the attackment relationship. It's like she's hit me and I don't even say "ouch," but keep talking about dissociation and being nice to her. The potential effort to get me to behave like her father and hit her in the face is in the air. If I become enraged, hit her, then she would have evidence that we were related. One solution here would have been to announce the double bind in my mind regarding unbridled reactivity versus a simple intellectual response. An emotionally alive statement of the bind and the wish to be real in the relationship was required, while still being responsible for the work of the psychotherapy.)

"That I would—," I start.

"My parents were always very supportive," she breaks in. "My parents were very supportive."

"Yeah."

"But it was very artificial, so I didn't believe any of it because they were supportive when I did good stuff and they were supportive when I did bad stuff."

"Oh, well, was my telling you that you needed to work harder in therapy supportive? That it didn't make sense that I was working harder than you were apparently? You took stock of that. That's not a generally supportive thing to say, that's just rather confrontational, though." (This is nothing like working in the transference, being role responsive [Sandler 1976], or wearing the attributions [Lichtenberg et al. 1996]. I ought to have responded with something like, "So, when I don't recognize the behavior you call bad, as you see it, then would it be true you feel somewhat invisible, as if I don't see you?")

"But I didn't find it like that." (She's alluding to the paradox of what I said actually being invalidating of how she knew she was behaving, i.e., badly.)

"Well you said that you were first really angry and then you finally realized that it was true and you agreed, and then you started to become anxious about whether if you didn't show up regularly for therapy I'd throw you out, kick you out of therapy."

"Maybe that's what I'm trying to do." Here we go around in circles again, for a short while, and then she pulls out a theme she's raised many times before: attacking the treatment and ridiculing it. A skeptic about DID would be having a field day with this protocol.

"Do you want me to believe that UFOs abducted me and I can't do that."

"I'm sorry, could you . . . Do you want me . . .?"

"You want me to believe that UFOs abducted me, basically. Well, I don't believe that and there's no getting around it."

"Um . . ." (dumbfounded).

"I didn't come see you because I had a dissociative disorder. I wasn't referred to you because I had a dissociative disorder. If your name was Smith I never would've seen you." (I was on her insurance panel back in the days when I participated. She complained of anxiety.)

"I want you to believe that what you notice in your mind has meaning. I want you to take yourself seriously and not dismiss what you perceive as of no value."

"Ironically, I've . . . been told so many times not to take myself so seriously."

"By whom?"

"By people and friends."

"Well, and I think your parents both told you not to believe in what you were perceiving about how you behaved or what you thought . . . or certainly about how they behaved. They repeatedly pressured you into doubting yourself, and that's part of what is being played out and enacted between us, the thematic content of your experience of them relentlessly, repeatedly, endlessly pressuring you to doubt what you've perceived, and that's why this shows up the way it does in our relationship." (I'm trying to make use of coercive doubting theory, but there's still pressure in my voice.)

"Well that makes logical sense. I don't . . . I'm not sure I agree with it, but it makes logical sense." The discussion stalled for a moment, and I tried to pick up the coercive doubting theme that felt logical for Alice but didn't generate an emotional response that was visible.

"You know, I was just thinking about . . . how it is that you might teach me about what you only implicitly know that feels intolerable for you. And I could imagine that part of what might feel intolerable for you right now in your life is the relentlessness of the way in which your parents pressured you and coerced you into not believing what was in your own mind. And what you perceived about their behavior, or what was going on in the family, and all kinds of other stuff and the tactics they used that were humiliating and belittling and ridiculing, not just on you, but also on your brother, especially. How tiring that would be. How exhausting that would be to try and get them to, to see that there was another way to see things."

"So I stopped." Alice confirms the coercion in her family. She's engaging.

"You gave up."

"I gave up." Alice is visibly sad, gets distracted for a moment, becomes aware it is near the end of the session, and then comes back into focus with another father strategy. She attacks the treatment again, more coercion. I've relaxed now that reality is being validated. But almost as if that is too much for her to tolerate, there's the I-don't-have-a-trauma-history theme. I didn't see it as part of the coercion in that moment.

(She continued.) "We need to emphasi— . . .I know we have to finish up, but I have one more thing I really need you to get. And I told you this so many times before and you just seem to forget and you just implied a min— . . . not, not a moment ago, about 10 minutes ago . . . I don't have these hidden things that I haven't told you about. There's no big secret that's going to come out and explain everything. This isn't a vignette in a Bromberg book." (She enjoys his work and has read most of it.)

"I couldn't agree with you more. This isn't a vignette in a Bromberg book. It's much more than that and, um . . ."

"Well that's not going to send . . . I mean, it's not like I'm going to suddenly pop out and say my father sexually abused me. That's not happening."

"That's not in my mind. That's in your mind. That's not a thought I have."

"But you keep on thinking there's more in my mind that I'm not telling you." (Alice is absolutely correct, and the "more" has to do with what feels like a strategic hiding of an acknowledgment of what she sometimes shows and acknowledges and then denies has existence or meaning, her multiple self-states.)

"Actually, what I think is that your mind first learned how to hide from your parents and then simultaneously from you . . . and also partially from itself . . . and that's the thing that is slowly becoming visible to you, I believe. And I think needs to be visible in order for you to heal from what hurts and to have the kind of life you want, your mind will slowly come out of hiding. The beating your mind took emotionally . . ."

"There's nothing there! There's nothing there . . ."Alice voices this in an insistent manner, as if in despair. She's insistent there's no trauma history that's secretly held in her mind. She behaves as if I am bullying her; it is a variation of coercion. She is working from the memory of years of pleading with me to think that she has no trauma history, but she does. Why she doesn't hold it in her mind as accessible to her is a mystery. When I don't agree with her, she feels bullied. In fact, there are times when I don't gently remind her that she does have a trauma history. That's not the case here. I have no idea if there is or isn't something that's secret. But it's understandable that she feels like she's being bullied, from her amnesic perspective. The pressure in the enactment is real. She seems regularly to lack access to information about the past, though she would deny this, so I spell out some of what I know with certainty, confirmed over the years, and I do so in an impassioned manner. Although my energy in the enactment is overwrought, here it is on her side and she knows it. What she then produces is more detail about being physically abused in childhood. The complexity of our interaction is interesting and would be more so if it weren't so tangled up in the enactment. I continue.

"Your mother . . . Your mother and father ridiculed you, bullied you, pressured you, coerced you into not believing in yourself for years and years. What was your mother doing sticking her finger in your belly and saying, "Tuck-tummy-in?" What the hell was that? What was your father doing punching you in the face, kicking you while you were on the ground? What was your mother doing not protecting you, not protecting your brother? It's not that there's nothing there, it's just that it's so big and so close that it can't be seen and it's like a surface that's huge and so the full scope of it is hardly visible because you're so close to it."

Here there occurs a voice change in Alice: she's speaking in softer tones, suddenly, nearly gently; it is a rather dramatic shift, from my perspective, perhaps a state change, but I leave that aside. She drops her denial completely and joins me. I've never before heard what she now says about her father.

"Sometimes he would pull his belt out and beat us with his belt, and it wasn't just the belt that hurt, it was the amount of anger he had, that he showed while he was doing this. It was a . . . like a hatred. It was like when my mother punished us, she punished us like with a ping- . . . not a Ping-Pong paddle, that little paddle that had the red ball on it, you know, that's what she used and . . . she believed we needed to be punished for something we did. I believe my father used to punish us for who we were."

"That's the essence of shame experience, being punished for who you are."

"The shame is who I am."

"That's part of why there feels, I think for you, so much risk in not hiding any longer and in believing in yourself, which is sort of what I'm asking you to do. It goes completely against the grain of your experience with your father, who punished you for being you and I think that you expected if you are yourself with me, then I, too, will punish you somehow."

"Great, so now I'm going to walk around all day with that, a picture of this in my head."

"Pardon?" (I don't understand what she's saying. She has shifted context some, and is speaking from a different perspective, as if saying to me, and perhaps another part of herself, "Now look at the mess you've made!")

"I'm going to walk all around . . . uh . . . I'm going to walk around all day with this vision of my father gleefully hitting me with a belt." (There has been a switch, and she's no longer attacking the treatment, but finally talking about what's in her mind.)

"I'm so sorry, Alice, it's such a horrible image. I bet you can really just see him now." (With her attacks on reality gone, I'm able to more easily empathically attune.)

"And I used to say, 'Dad, what's wrong with you?' This was before I took my first sociology course and learned about alcoholism. I didn't really know, but I certainly knew when I took my first sociology course and I understood then that he was an alcoholic. Okay (sighs) . . . Don't look at me like that."

"How am I looking at you?"

"The way that's going to make me cry more."

Alice and I were finally engaged on an emotional level, and the work was flowing. The shift in the tone of the interaction was palpable, and there was certainly a feeling that there was another way of being Alice engaged in conversation with me. Identifying and working with self-states is important (Kluft 2006; R. J. Loewenstein 2006; Putnam 1992). Without access to isolated emotion, the resolution of problems like overeating in a highly dissociative person is unlikely to occur, in my experience (Torem 1990). I've tried other approaches. They haven't worked.

The session ended, and as is our routine, I took Alice's digital recorder to my computer and downloaded the session file. After I transferred the file, I gently handed the recorder to Alice, and she packed it away in her pocketbook, as she usually did. She had brought her dog, Buster, to the session, as was typical, and after he came over to me to be petted, and then back to Alice to be connected to his leash, Alice and I stood face to face, again on the verge of a handshake. We started to shake hands, and with her hand still in mine she stopped the process and asked: "Is it okay if I feel your hand?"

I didn't understand what was happening, but it seemed wrong to deny her simple request and that she would be shamed if I said no. I said, "Okay, Alice." And she then went and felt my hand as if she were blind and wanted to know what my hand was like, patting it on the back, on the palm, and around the fingertips in a curious 10-second interlude.

"What was that about, Alice?"

"I don't know why I did that."

"Sounds like it was a bit of a surprise."

"Yes, it was." She smiled. "Time to go." I had a sense that I had just been visited by a part of Alice who felt safe enough to come and meet me, but didn't want to be known to Alice, who didn't know why she behaved the way she did. Eating, at times, is likely no different. She didn't know why and wasn't in executive control of her body.

In the next session, Alice makes reference to finally reading the entire transcript I gave her of the session she long avoided listening to, the one where Shirley does some work (Chapter 10). I found her behavior in regard to the session curious because she usually did listen to sessions afterward. Did she avoiding learning about Shirley, still fearful of being hurt by her? I also had broached the subject of object-coercive doubting with her, and in the session she's able to see the parallels in her life and our relationship. The storm of the enactment is losing energy, but it's not over. I'm more relaxed, aware of the denial of my anger, aware of the coercion dynamics, and working. We pick up the session after she notes the object-coercive dynamics to me.

"Well, it's interesting how the process here with you and I parallels the process there with you and your mom, Alice."

"It is interesting, but is it true?"

"That's a good question." (I'm handing the problem of discerning reality back to Alice, and not fighting her or lobbying her to accept what I think is real.)

"I think it is, but I'm not sure. Had you been saying things because you believed them?" (She pauses and then seems to catch on to the dynamic.) "Yeah, actually, it is more than I realized because I think part of what you're saying is that you're doing what my mom was doing, which is fitting me into your picture rather than listening to me and then letting me fit into my own picture."

"Mmhmm [affirmatively], so there's a process where one person is insistent and the pressure that they aim at the other person is coercive. And it's the dynamic that you grew up in the middle of, your mother coercing you with her perspective, your father coercing you with his perspective, and the two of them both in lockstep agreement and colluding to maintain those perspectives. You didn't stand a chance against that united wall of distortion of reality, and they would acknowledge little in you of the reality that you experienced with them."

"I read the transcript you made recently, like over the weekend, and when I came to the part about my mother not remembering . . .Oh no, that's not even it. It's not that my mother didn't remember that I was bullied in school. It was that she never reacted to me as if I were being bullied in school, even though I came home repeatedly crying, talking about all the names that people had called me, talking about how I was snubbed for this or that. I was the only one that didn't get any Valentines or, you know, I always thought that it was this more of not knowing what's real and what wasn't real."

"Yeah."

"Because then I was thinking, well, was I really bullied in school, knowing full well that I was, but yet here was my mom who I trust telling me that it didn't happen or that she had no recollection of it."

"Right. Go figure. How were you as a child supposed to sort out what you were hearing from her and what you were experiencing at school?"

"Luckily I had my brother and sister who both saw what was going on. My brother actually defended me against my dad a few times, more than a few times."

"You were very grateful for that."

"That was the problem."

"Your father took it out on him."

"Yeah."

"Big time."

" My brother got really screwed up."

"He was very angry."

"Yeah, he's not . . . He's had more anger than I've ever seen in anybody. I've seen myself that angry, but I haven't been that angry. Actually, that's not true. I've been that angry recently. I don't remember what prompted that. I think when it was, I was trying to get a medication, and after an hour on the phone with various people, I just got real, I got angry at my doctor's receptionist because they don't 'electronically prescribe.'"

(Alice continues.) "And I was just, 'Oh my God,' so I had to call back, you know, I had to call back the company, have them fax, all this shit, so and I just, I was so pissed, and I definitely still have med issues.I need to just sit down and take care of them. I don't have all my medications right now. I have all the psych medications, but I don't think I have any, I don't think there were any prescriptions on . . ."

"On file?"

"On file."

"So there's this thing about what's real and what can you believe about what you perceive, and there's this thing you do to yourself about accusations that you make things up."

"Just by using the word accusations you're, you're taking a position you don't need to take." Alice's sensitivity to language is extraordinary. Here I am making reference to one part of her saying she makes things up, and she copies and pastes that right into our relationship. On the other hand, it might be that the part of her saying another part of her made something up is unaware of shaming and coercion dynamics. I set about the task of understanding the meaning.

"Okay. What would you, uh, I'm, I'm open to . . ."

"I think you, even just saying you believe, I mean *accusations* sounds like such a punitive word and . . ."

"Okay."

"If you just use the words like 'I believe that I was making things up,' that might soften it a lot and not put me on the defense."

"Okay."

"The other thing about *accusations* is you're talking as if you know what's inside my head when part of me is accusing another part of me of making things up."

"Hmm. Well, I think you're right. I think I do have that feeling."

"And I guess when I think of the word *accusation*, I think of wrong-doing. It's always an accusation of a wrongdoing. Therefore, you're telling me I'm wrong just by using that word."

"Actually, I've had the feeling that you're telling me that I'm doing something bad to you."

"I have been telling you that."

"Yeah."

"'Cause that's how I felt."

"Right."

"And when I ask inside whether or not I made this stuff up, I just have no idea." This remark changes the level of the playing field from her saying she makes things up to please me to a more considered ambiguity. Unfortunately, the sway of the enactment leads me to defending myself about the use of hypnosis rather than asking her what it's like to try and do this work and not have any idea what it's like to know if the sentiment of making things up is true. In retrospect, I'm not sure she could have taken it anywhere, but the pressure on her would have been significantly removed, and that would have been useful.

I say, "Yeah. I mean if we were to go back and go through recordings line by line at the time we do hypnotic work . . ."

"Mmhmm" (affirmative).

"I have been so scrupulously conscious of the need to be nondirective . . ."

"Right."

"That if I were any less present, nothing would happen."

"What do you mean 'nothing would happen'?"

"Well, I wouldn't be there."

"Oh."

"I wouldn't be repeating your own language. I wouldn't be referencing things that you had just told me in a nonhypnotic state, and then being curious about the potential meanings and so on. 'Cause that's how I've been working with you for a very long time, just acutely aware of this issue, so when you then say that you're making it all up to please me, I hear you say, 'Why are you doing that to me?' Why am I making you do these things?"

"That's actually a pretty strong statement," Alice says.

"Which?"

"'Why are you making me doing these things? Why are you making me do these things?'" (What I didn't hear then in my own language is the standard ploy of the perpetrator of abuse who asks their victim, "Why are you making me do this to you?")

"Excuse me. That is how I feel," I reply. (I am verifying to Alice that's the feeling in me.)

"Yeah, that's what I heard. There's one thing that may or may not be in your experience but I certainly have gotten it from being online, and that's the 'calling out of alters'. . ."

"Uhhuh" (affirmative).

"Or the calling out of parts."

"Uhhuh" (affirmative).

"It just totally screws a lot of people up, so when you use a name or say 'I'd really like to speak to Shirley' or 'I'd like to invite her to come to therapy,' it just freaks me out."

"You know, I don't think I've actually said either one of those things." (Here I'm being defensive. What she has said is close enough to what I did say that I ought to acknowledge it.[1] In my lack of acknowledgment, in my feeling that I've been accused of doing something bad to her, I re-create the potential to reenter the enactment. She becomes doubtful, as a result, and that's where the conversation resumes. If I had asked her, "Why does it freak you out?," then we'd

---

[1] I did say to her: "I think the first order of business in pursuit of that is to welcome Shirley to the therapy and to your life." I also said, "I think there is a real need to engage with Shirley today, and we can do that hypnotically, or we can do that without hypnosis, I think . . . And my question is: How would you like to proceed?" This was not a calling out of Shirley, on command, as Alice was implying. This is a reasonable example of how Alice preserved the general gist of a memory, my interest in Shirley, and then adapted the context to match the feeling of threat in her mind about the work. Her anger had indeed caused trouble.

have been on solid ground. However, it's also true that I don't roughly call out parts. For Alice, any mention of parts of her mind is tantamount to an assault on what she prefers to keep hidden. Having spoken to different ways of being Alice, on and off, for years, I don't have a doubt about the reality of what I've seen, heard, and captured on video. The discrepancy between what I observe and what she reports as her subjective experience seems unresolvable. In my response to Alice's doubting, I try to reestablish the context of the conversation about Shirley. I am momentarily in the enactment, defending both my perception of reality and the respectful intent of my previous interactions with Alice.)

"I don't know." Alice becomes noncommittal as to what happened.

"I know I have said, referencing to conversation we had where you were joking and jesting about 'Surely you jest.'"

"Right."

"And sort of bridging on that, I'm curious . . ."

"I'm thinking if it was the session right after that."

"Yeah, because I was referencing the previous session, and then there was a spontaneous shift and really powerful expressions of anger and resentment and real clarity about why you were so angry and how that matched your sense of why black women are so angry."

"Yes, that was in the session that you did the transcript of it."

"Yes, so that would be one of those things that you would be saying that you make up."

"Yeah."

"And that you only say those things to please me and to . . ."

"Yeah."

"To massage my ego."

"No, I don't, I didn't say it was only massaging your ego."

"Well, to . . ."

"It's that I try to make things work between us . . ."

"Right."

"By playing along." (Alice is in her "I make it up" position. On one hand her sentiments are coherent and consistent, one after the other. On the other hand, in the context of her assaults on reality, we

hear about the world according to Alice. If I go with what she is saying as both subjective and objective reality, then there is no treatment
and my observations are of no value. She is close, however, to talking
about some degree of uncertainty in her mind, in addition to making
statements like she makes things up to play along. I take a moment to
remind her about the experience with Shirley.)

"Right and of course when I hear you say that, I think, 'really?' You
spoke with that kind of energy, and conviction, and frustration, and
anger to play along? That's not how you really feel?'Cause you . . ."

"But it might be how I really feel."

"Well, see, that's the problem right there. That's perfect."

"But it's not because it's not a case in which somebody named
Shirley—"

"Well, but here's the thing, Alice. On the one hand, you're telling
me you're playing along. On the other hand you're saying, 'That might
be how I really feel,' both things potentially being true."

"Mmhmm" (affirmative).

"Then there's the example of you being just like that when you
were talking with your internist's secretary, receptionist, whoever it
was, because of frustrations over medication, so this is the dilemma
you see in your mother. What's real?"

"Well, then we have to look at why my mother is so scared of
admitting what's real . . ."

"Yes."

"Versus why I might be . . ."

"So scared of admitting what's real, and why might you be so
scared of admitting what's real?"

"Because I'm scared of becoming an angrier person than I am now."

"I can phrase that in a slightly different way, Alice, which I think
would make sense to you, that you're afraid that you'll really feel
angry and know it, really know it, really be real in your anger. And
experience a kind of intensity and verification that might feel overwhelming to you or might place you at some kind of risk if you were
that angry. I suspect that as a child, when you were that angry with
your parents, their reaction was swift and draconian." (I'm still in the

enactment, not listening, and pursuing my own line of thinking. Nevertheless, Alice isn't put off. I've activated a memory.) "They crushed and humiliated. You were ugly. You were bad. You were sent . . ."

"But I was. I mean one time when I was 13 and I knew we were going to move to . . . Maybe I was 14. I was 13, almost 14, and I got so angry I think about that, about something they said but about probably really about the move. I pulled everything off the shelves in my room and . . . I mean I was 13 years old."

"Yeah."

"And I just had a fit."

"Yeah."

"I pulled everything off."

"In your room."

"In my room."

"Not in the living room."

"No, my room, and my father came in and hit me, and then pushed me to the floor; and I landed on my knee, which I injured ice skating a couple of weeks before, and my God, I don't even know what it's really called, but I got water on the knee. Um, and it was very painful. It got me out of gym for a month but I just had a memory of that recently 'cause that was probably the most out of control I've ever been."

"Yeah. Well, so you're, you're telling me that you were bad. You were ugly."

"I am."

"Now could you imagine having a father who hears the ruckus of things hitting the floor, comes in the room, and looks astonished at what's happened, and realizes you feel out of control with anger and upset to the point where you've raged and just cleared stuff out of frustration, and stopped and said, 'Oh my God, I'm so sorry. I really had no idea what this move would do to you and what it would mean to your whole life, the whole structure of your teenage years is being disrupted and thrown away. It's such a tragedy. I'm so sorry. I didn't know,' and put his arms around you and cried with you?"

"We need to stop. I need to change the subject." (This is an old habit, deflecting when she's uncomfortable. But she sticks with the subject after encouragement.)

"Rather than using a guillotine to stop your reaction, please take a moment to react and be real with me and you."

"I feel so cheated."

"I see the upset in your body. You were cheated."

"And then I flashed on my best friend Jennifer's father, and I could never . . .I could see him doing exactly what you're talking about."

"Apologizing and saying, 'I'm so sorry. I didn't realize.' I saw in you such tears a moment ago, such a grief, and recall several minutes ago you saying, 'I was bad. I was ugly. This is the example, let me tell you.' Not so. You were desperate to be heard."

"I was desperate to be heard, and in the psychotherapy quite often I felt desperate to be heard as well."

"Yes. the back-and-forth coercion that got played out in our relationship for so long and was labeled as, just like you were saying, "But I was bad," and things that went back and forth between us where reality was taking a hit in both directions, and my tendency to hold my anger rather than tell you that you're torturing me with denials and disavowals, it didn't help. It only fueled the possibility. Rather than me being kind and compassionate by holding my anger, I was depriving you of the signal you needed to allow you to feel more real and to risk being real with me, like you're risking today being real."

"I feel wiped out."

"It's exhausting to have so much feeling."

"I mean, you pointed out to me for the first time that there could have been a different outcome, and I didn't even think . . . I never, it never crossed my mind. I never played that scene out differently. I just played out what happened. I never even fantasized that there could be a different outcome, and obviously I've been looking at a lot of the interactions with my parents that way." (Ten-second pause.) "I just want to clarify one thing."

"Oh."

"Vis-à-vis my being real with you."

"Yeah?"

"Um, I'm not not being real with you. I never feel I'm not being real with you."

"That's . . ."

"You may think it, but I don't think it."

Alice has done her best to try and give me a picture of the state of her mind, her view of how her mind works. It's hard to feel real. The fog of dissociation was starting to lift, but that was threatening.

At the beginning of this chapter I talked about the experience of listening to audio recordings of these sessions and discovering I had been wrong about my assessment of what was going on. I made a discovery, in the best sense of the word: I had partly become the bully in the relationship with Alice. I finally heard, and then saw in the words of the transcript, my insensitivity to Alice as a person. For a clinician who takes pride in being sensitive to shaming dynamics and other similar processes, I was horrified and dismayed. What had I done? Why had I behaved so poorly?

I have come to understand that the coercive process was in me as much as it was between me and Alice. She only activated it by my resonance with the process between us and by her insistence that I accept the reality she offered me, a reality I believed was skewed. At the end of the day, I had come to honestly doubt my fantasies of being the good therapist (Searles 1967), dedicated to the task of helping Alice better see what was real. Instead, I had to learn that what had been my good will had been rigidified into a "position," as Alice called it. I did not have the ability to tolerate doubting my good will, and I believe that was because I could not manage to know how angry I was with Alice and what felt like her coercion. I can't know for sure, but it still feels to me, after considerable effort, that this relates to old family dynamics where my anger was experienced by me as not allowed, lest it destroy relatedness. I protected Alice from that. I also believed I kept me and my anger from destroying her and the therapy. (Sound familiar? The same dynamic was between Alice and her mother.) She would have quit if I'd been angry, I imagined, given all the threats to quit she had made, and all the affective lability she had demonstrated.

The coercive doubting was both present and a screen behind which neither Alice nor I felt safe enough in our own eyes, or in the eyes of the other, to show our anger. I had to see myself reflected from Alice's perspective and have healthy doubt about who and how I was. She had to see herself from my perspective and have healthy doubt about who she was. I needed to set the example. I did it privately, and she could feel it. I also did it in her presence, and she could know it.

I had to achieve the healthy doubting of my own intentions before the coercion could stop coming from me, and before I could feel emotionally quiet enough to see what was really coming at and from me. Then I had to forgo knee-jerk reactions to protect myself from Alice's efforts to convince me of her views. I had to respond with noticing what was happening, a clinician's response in addition to the human response. I was intolerant of the potential for ambiguity and doubt. I had become too smart.

Coercive doubting ran in Alice's family and mine, though to a lesser intensity. The dynamic was there. Behind it was the fear of intense affectivity, the emotion of anger, and beyond that was the risk of mortifying shame and fears of annihilation, a Kohutian constellation (Kohut 1971) wherein the rigidity of the position I took reflected grandiosity, the Kohutian bipole. You will see how that plays out in both me and Alice as Chapter 12 draws to a close. There, Alice and I work hard together to advance our understanding of what happened between us and in each of us. I provide some asides to the reader in regard to some of what was evolving as we talked, but the chapter has no other commentary.

I think Chapter 12 is a fitting way to end this book. Visible is the hard work of two imperfect people, talking about what neither of us really started out wanting to talk about, and listening hard to what neither of us thought we might ever want to hear (Chefetz 1997). Nevertheless, we agreed to do the work and tolerate our hurts in the service of Alice's request for help from me. Lucky man that I am, I have grown in the process, too, a hidden benefit of the growth that is possible with the full immersion in human relatedness that has been called intensive psychotherapy. Thank you, Alice.

Chapter 12

Emerging from an Enactment

"SO I WAS JUST LISTENING TO THE SESSION AND I HAD FORGOTTEN WHAT WE talked about, 'cause I was focusing on the paper in the other sessions and I guess I had fallen behind in my own work." (Alice begins the session. After I had invited her into my office, she sat down on the couch, and I stepped out for a brief moment. When I returned she had her recorder up to her ear and was listening to the previous session, Thursday of the week before. It was Wednesday afternoon, and she had overslept and missed Tuesday's session. She had asked for the first available time I might meet with her so she didn't have to wait until her regular Thursday session.)

"So you were very eager to meet this week after missing yesterday."

"Yeah, I had the same thing happen this morning, although I woke up at . . . I eventually woke up at 6:30, so there's something's wrong with my alarm. I've got to . . . figuring it out. And then it took me almost two hours to get to work. It's so frustrating."

"Traffic?"

"Yeah, and I went a whole different way today thinking it might be easier. I drove the opposite way around the beltway, but at least I got up. So there's a lot of this stuff going on between us right now and a lot of stuff inside of me. The biggest thing I need to clarify, which you've said many times and I've never said this, um, that I'm not having bariatric surgery in lieu of doing the work inside myself. I'm having bariatric surgery because I've been seeing you for 16 years and the work hasn't gotten done, so I'm not holding my breath anymore. I have no, I'm not saying I have objection, yes or no, to doing the work, but I've never said that I'm having the surgery in lieu of doing the work. That's just not true. I've never implied that or anything else. I have never said I shouldn't do the work, but I don't know where you've gotten an impr—, I think that impression is just something that's gotten inside you and it's part of your prejudice against the bariatric surgery, 'cause you assume, maybe you're assuming that that's the case, but in fact we've had plenty of discussions on this. I've made it clear that I'm not trying to avoid the work for that reason. I may be inclined to avoid the work for other reasons, but I'm not trying to avoid the work . . . I'm not trying to have bariatric surgery in order to avoid the work."

"Okay. That's pretty clear." (She is fishing for the dynamic of the enactment and I'm noticing the bait in the water, but not biting. She let's go and moves on to anger.)

"And ever, as I said, there might be other reasons, like I'm scared of my anger, you know. Here we are working on anger and then my administrative assistant quit because I was frustrated with her. So you know, I'm feeling pretty bad about the anger right now. I'm feeling like yeah, we worked on it. It came out and I couldn't put it back in and it came out at somebody in a way that I usually don't let it show, and she quit. So now I'm having to do her job and my job and on top of that, my boss spoke to the man who's been doing my extra work for the last few months, he spoke to him without me, so obviously he has some idea of where he wants to go, but he hasn't bothered to talk to me. So I don't . . . for all I know, he's telling him that he's, you know, he expects me to go part-time and they'll insist I do that and, I mean, I feel like I'm working and I'm getting my work done."

"You had been talking here about going part-time." (I'm staying with what she's said.)

"Yeah, but I realized if I go part-time, I really can't afford to see you. In fact, I really, until things are a little more stable, I really am not sure that I want to do that. I really don't think I could afford to see you if I went part-time. I mean, that's, you know, part of the income that is superfluous to me for my living needs and if I have my income, I would only . . . and the other part, I save, and so if I'm . . . why would I work just to get by and I don't, I don't know . . . I mean, I have enough money to get by, so I could just live on . . . I would either, I mean, I don't know. And I don't completely understand the object-coercive doubting. I read Kramer's article. I've read Shengold's article. I've read Kluft's article. I've read quite a number of others, but they don't . . . you know, part of the problem is, especially with Kramer's article, is that she's so focused, and I don't know why, on maternal incest as being the cause of this. I don't know if she's coming from like trying to explain this specific Freudian perspective or not, but it gets in the way and my disgust for the act gets in my way of thinking about what she's saying that doesn't apply to incest."

"Sure."

"Does, does that make sense?"

"Oh, yeah, yeah."

"And instead of disgusted by what she's talking about though, I can't really get the, you know, get the words and the concepts."

"Right."

"So I've read the article several times, about five times. I spent more time listening to the last session, because the last session was really important to me. I just listened to it."

"What was important?"

"The nature of the blockage and why I haven't been able to do therapy with you."

"Okay."

"That's really important to me."

"Yeah. Yeah, I'm glad."

"You asked toward the end of the session something about it and then you said I really should be curious and then I realized I really am curious. I think you wanted me to say that basically the blockage was coming from another way of being me, a separate consciousness, or separate constellation and as I said previously, I wasn't willing to go that far. Especially, I especially can't do that because it would have to be . . . if it's a 'constellation' that implies there are other feelings and facts and history and everything else that goes along with it, and I don't know what that is, you know. The fact, is it an unconscious block? Well, it's not a conscious block, so I mean, I'm not consciously blocking. I'm really wanting the therapy to succeed." (Her voice has risen and she's signaling her upset and need to find out what's wrong.)

"Right."

"Am I scared of my anger? Yes, I'm very scared of my anger. Do I have reason to? Yes, my admin just quit, for God's sakes. We started working on my anger and my admin quit and my partner's plotting behind my back, probably to force me out, so I'm a little upset."

"Do you have some speculation about what's going on about the blockage?"

"I don't know, but for some reason, all of a sudden I got sexually aroused. That very much surprised me. [Twenty-second pause] Obviously it made me think of Emily, as it did you. But putting Emily with the blockage doesn't make any sense to me . . . at all." (Emily is a child self-state well known to me and Alice. All of a sudden she has brought in her own data about self-states.)

"What are you considering as you try to put that together?"

"I'm trying to figure out why she would show up now as soon as I started talking about blockage."

"What are your ideas about Emily?"

"I don't have any ideas about Emily. I haven't thought about Emily in probably years."

"How do you think of her?"

"I don't. I just . . ."

"I mean right now, when you brought her up."

"I think of her as . . . a younger part of me."

"With some sexual arousal?"

"No, it was only that the sexual arousal, my sexual arousal, was always an indicator of a presence."

"Of Emily. But you don't connect Emily with sexual arousal. [Ten-second pause] Well, if your mind is guiding you, then perhaps there's something to it in regard to your thinking about what could the blockage be about, and you're speaking in angry tones about the things that happened at the office, and then having the sexual arousal feeling, thinking of Emily."

"I'm just not getting it together. [Twenty-second pause] I'm just not getting it together. I'm totally losing my train of thought. My mind's going elsewhere."

"So, when you think of Emily . . ."

"My mind started going to like where, what am I gonna do when I get home. So I need to pull it back."

"Yeah...yeah, your anger was seemingly a gateway to these thoughts."

"Now I want to walk out 'cause now I feel guilty for being here in the middle of the afternoon. Or maybe I'm just trying to avoid it. I don't know. I can't tell."

"That was one of the problems that you identified in the last session, not being able to tell."

"Yes, that's correct."

"That's got to be terribly frustrating."

"And as you said, nobody else can get in my mind, but I can't even get in my mind."

I tried to summarize for Alice. "That's the 'I can't get into my mind, I can't get in touch with what's tugging me and pulling me,' that's a blockage issue and that's the thing to be curious about, of what in the world could that be about?"

"I just feel like we're going around in circles again." Alice was correct. I did circle around. It didn't help. Then I took another route to explore.

"What's your experience of bumping into the difficulty? What do you experience when you can't decide, when you find yourself blocked?"

"I just go on to something else. It lies there and festers."

"So you started looking and your mind goes elsewhere?"

"Mmhmm" (affirmative).

"Even when you don't want it to."

"I guess . . . I mean, I wasn't trying to think of what I need to do as soon as I get home, but . . ."

"But that kinda happened."

"Yep. And now I'm like completely focused on it."

"So then what happens to the feeling of being here when you're completely focused on what you need to do when you get home?"

"I don't even have the concept of being here."

"That's just sorta gone?"

"Mmhmm" (affirmative).

"And then you feel guilty about being here."

"Well, yeah, 'cause I took off in the middle of the day to come here, even though I got to work a couple of hours earlier than usual."

"Mmhmm" (affirmative).

"I don't know. It's just not flowing for me today and I was really hoping it would. It's not like I expected it to, but for some reason after I listened to that session, I got angry and I haven't quite listened to the very end, but I start saying I'm angr—, how I felt. You know, also reading the chapter that you wrote about me has been difficult [Chapter 10]. It's not very flattering."

"What did you discern? What's your sense of what I was saying?"

"Well, it's not what I discerned you were saying, but it was my view of myself as just a snivelly little brat. I mean, I think I'm just the worried well, except that I want to commit suicide with some regularity."

"That certainly doesn't go together."

"I realize that. I guess I fear gr—, like we can't figure out what's wrong with me so there must be nothing wrong with me."

"If you were the worried well, would your thoughts go in this direction?"

"What?"

"Pardon?"

"I don't understand what you're saying."

"Well, I mean, you're talking about things of some real gravity when you're talking about suicide. It sounds as if . . ."

(Irritated) "No, I'm just saying if we can't figure out what's wrong, if I can't figure out what's wrong with me, after all these years of seeing a psychiatrist and therapist, then there must be nothing wrong with me. So maybe I just need to start sucking it up and acting like there's nothing wrong and everything will go away."

"Isn't that sort of what your parents told you to do?"

"Yes, and maybe it's time to try it."

"I guess this is the place to where the coercive doubting comes in."

"Well, explain it to me better in a way that I can understand and apply it to the therapy in a way that I can understand it" (openly curious).

"Well, let's start with your parents."

"Okay."

"Okay. When we talked about this before, we talked about the idea that if you were angry with them, they basically said to you, 'Why would you be angry with us? You're being bad. You're being angry with us. Go to your room.'"

"Yes, and what came to my mind is them saying, 'What's wrong with you?'"

"Yeah. The shaming."

"Yes."

"And that's the coercion. Instead of saying, 'What do you feel we've done to hurt your feelings? Why would you be angry?' they basically pressured you to give up your anger and sent you to your room after which you would emerge and beg them to forgive you."

"Yes, that's right."

"Believing that you were bad . . . for having been angry with them."

"Well, there's a good question. Did I really believe I was bad for being angry with them? I guess I did because I was young and they were telling me and they were my parents so, yes."

"And they were insistent. That's the coercion. So the coercion has to do with the person or persons being insistent on their view and trying to make someone else agree, coercively."

"So you're saying this is what I've been doing to you?"

"Yes, and that the joining of the problem has been that in my observations of your behavior over a number of years, and putting those together with observations of other people who have worked with you in the hospital and out, I have certain impressions and certain observations."

"Don't use euphemisms" (demanding).

"My observations have been that there are different ways of being you and you have been insistent that the idea of somebody like your-self having another part of yourself named Shirley who's angry, is tantamount to me wanting you to believe in UFOs and abductions."

"Right."

"So the ways in which you insist on having your own mind and your own impressions in a lot of ways is understandably reactive to what you experienced with your parents and not to be influenced by anybody else. Again, not to be tricked or misled or cajoled or anything like that. Similarly, given my observations and my careful study, uh, when I see something, I see what I see. You can disagree with me, but in the ways that you've disagreed and the forcefulness of your disagree-ment, there is a way in which I got caught up in the argument with you rather than the two of us being able to talk about your experience of yourself—like we were doing a couple minutes ago. So back and forth we went, each of us trying to, as you say, maintain the position, and neither of us interested in being coerced or being bullied by the other, and part of, I think, what would have been, um . . . What's interesting is to think about the sense to which the anger that I felt about some of the ways in which you lobbied your position, I held back . . ."

"Well, it's interesting you say that because I even asked you specifi-cally if this was as frustrating for you as it was for me and you insisted it wasn't, and that frustrated me even more."

"Right. I can't remember where it was in the work, but we both have a recollection and some clarity of in the past, how if I'm angry with you, but don't acknowledge it . . ."

"Yes."

" . . . it leaves you in this place of unreality and feeling not recog-nized and then feeling that my support or whatever it is that I'm doing is unreliable because if I'm not angry with you when you're doing things that ought to evoke or provoke anger . . ."

"Yes. Yes, 'cause that's my mom."

" Then how can you believe me? Right. I have been angry. It's been very frustrating."

"Then why do you still work with me?"

"I work with you because from time to time, you don't do what you've been doing recently in terms of trying to tell me that you don't have dissociative experiences that are meaningful. And you honestly, from my perspective, work . . . and grow . . . and change. When you do that, I cheer because I see you growing and changing and there are times where in a way that I would never have expected, but just sort of things that happened suddenly and surprisingly, you have experiences that clearly come from some place you don't understand, and we talk about them, and these are spontaneous things. Like when you talked about Emily a couple minutes ago as being a younger part of you. That's certainly been my experience of you and I've talked with Emily, and we've talked about her in the past. You haven't done so recently." (Thirty-second pause.)

"But when I'm talking to you or Shirley, there's a part of my mind that says am I actually going to speak as a black woman with an accent? You know, like a ghetto accent and be angry like that?"

"Right."

"And . . ."

"Well, you didn't."

"Well, I did the previous session, the first one she came out, a little bit. In my mind I did, so maybe I didn't."

"Well, but out loud you didn't."

"Maybe out loud I didn't."

"Yeah."

"But it was something that was consciously in my mind and um . . ."

"Sure."

"So I'm thinking that if that was in my mind, then she couldn't possibly be real because she would just speak the way she was."

"Well, that's part of some of the mystery of what it is that happens when a person has, uh, different aspects of themselves because sometimes, in a desperate way to convey meaning, somebody behaves differently or uses an accent or so on. You know, I know there aren't other people living inside you. I know there's no black woman living inside. You know that, too, but it's a metaphor in the sense of 'like an angry black woman.'"

"I know and I was just sitting here a few minutes ago, about three minutes ago, and looking around thinking, 'my God have I just like walked over a step that I can't come back from in accepting the dissociation?' Because it doesn't freak me out to talk about Emily or Shirley?"

"Tell me some more about what you're saying."

"Well, I realized I didn't have the visceral reactions I normally do to your talking about parts of me, that I didn't just throw up my hands and roll my eyes and go, 'Oh, not again.' I didn't do those things, so maybe I was looking for an a-ha moment and I never got it and things just changed without my realizing it."

"People more often change and look back and say, 'Huh, I've changed. When did that happen?' then they have a-ha moments, in my experience. But tell me more about what's going on inside you. What do you sense about this?"

"You're asking me for things I don't know, what the answers are."

"Well, I'm asking you for more reaction to what you're saying about uh, have you changed your views?"

"Well, it's interesting because here I am thinking I just gave you a mile and you're trying to take 10 miles. That's how I feel right now."

"Okay. Well, I'm . . ."

"I gave you an inch and you're trying to take a mile, so here I am saying, 'wow, you talked to me about the searching for process and they didn't freak out' and now you're trying to get me to go farther, which is not the best thing to do right now."

"Well, I . . ."

"Because here I am, being vulnerable . . ."

"Yeah."

" . . . and I feel like you're trying to take advantage of it."

"Well, okay, I can understand where you're coming from, uh, and this is an interesting place because . . ."

"Because actually if I were in your position, I'd do what you're doing."

"Yeah, 'cause I'm sensitive to not wanting to do anything that at all resembles coercion, you know, and I appreciate your nodding your head that you understand that. And so if I'm not gonna ask you some-thing new, then I can . . . perhaps rely on you telling me about your experience, which is not coercion, it's just asking you to tell me about your experience.

"And my position is I just told you and that's all there was. There isn't any more."

"Right [laughs].Right, so . . ."

"I have these thoughts and they happened and they're over and that was it."

"Yeah?"

"Now, if you'd like to take that further, I guess we can think about that, we meaning you and me." (I remember smiling here.)

"Well, I wondered if you'd hear that, the 'we.'"

"I'm drinking a latte. I've never had a latte before. I'm sure every-body else in the world has had a latte, but you don't drink coffee so maybe not. I think it's disgusting."

I laugh.

"I can't believe Starbucks is selling all these lattes and it's awful."

"Why in the world did you buy it?"

"Well, 'cause they had . . . the coffee that they had had had lemon in it and I, I'm al—, I react."

"Oh."

"Lemon doesn't sit well with me."

"Oh."

"And I didn't want regular coffee 'cause I don't like the taste of it so I figured I'd just have them put milk in it and maybe it'd be okay."

"So, can I ask you something about the contents of the paper . . ."

"Yes."

" . . . that might advance our discussion?"

"Yes."

"The other day when you were here, I guess it was last Thursday . . ."

"Mmhmm" (affirmative).

"I gave you the paper . . ."

"Mmhmm" (affirmative).

" I read something to you from the paper. Do you recall?"

"Yes, I recall. I just listened to it."

"Right. I read a section . . ."

"And you had to have been really close to me when you read it because it w—"

"Very loud."

" It was . . . no, it sounded like you were really close to the microphone."

"I was only about a foot away from . . ."

"Yeah."

" . . . the ottoman there with a microphone, and 'cause I put the paper down on the ottoman to read it. I read you a section about talking about you being angry with your mother."

"Mmhmm (affirmative).

"And you began to cry."

"I don't think I picked that up."

"Well, it wouldn't necessarily be on the recording, but I recall you were very upset and it, my recollection isn't 100 percent clear, but I think I went on to read about the end of that sequence in my talking with Shirley . . ."

"Yes."

" . . . where . . ."

"That's the part I remember from."

" . . . where you went deeper in trance and I asked you why, essentially . . ."

"Yeah, I don't recall it going that far though."

" . . . and you said to get away from her."

"Yes."

"And the . . ."

"And I talked about whether she was going to hurt me and I really believe I misspoke at that point and I said I thought she would hurt me, and I don't think that's the case at all. I think she would enable me . . . *enable*'s not the right word . . . *force* is not the right word . . . to hurt other people. I think letting Shirley have her way would make me hurt other people. I already have. Look at this. Look at my life. It's fallen apart since the last time I was here. Whoops. [Buster slipped off the couch next to Alice.] You can get back up."

"There's a general rule of thumb about isolated self states."

"Mmhmm" (affirmative).

"Since we're talking about parts-of-self and dissociation today, the rule of thumb about an isolated self-state is that if that state has, if that part of you has a lot of energy related to a particular feeling, then keeping that part of you at a distance creates a kind of . . ."

"Yeah."

" . . . permission for that part to behave as they please. Or another way to think about it is that . . ."

"The more I stuff them down, the more they want to come out."

"The more you deny their reality . . ."

"Am I denying her reality?"

"Well, in relation to you, yeah."

"Really?"

"Well, you said you believe that you have a part of you named Shirley with anger as much . . . that was zero, the extent you believe that. That was the word you used and that that was tantamount to UFOs."

"Yeah, but I think I might be changing my mind."

"Okay, what's your mind changing to?"

"What I talked about 10 minutes ago" (annoyed with me asking).

"That you're more accepting of Shirley than Emily."

"Yes."

"Okay, so if you're changing . . ."

"Or thinking about myself as having different ways of being myself."

"Okay. So to avoid scenes like you're talking about with your employee, who to add additional context, was really screwing up and was causing you to be really upset about her screw-ups, and you might have ended up firing her anyhow at some point, right?"

"Mmhmm" (affirmative).

"Because of how she was behaving and working. Didn't sound like she was quite competent."

"She was competent. She was just not . . . it was not in, not in the job that she was in."

"Yeah. So you got angry and hypothetically, if at that time, you had a kind of inner relationship with Shirley, one where you didn't try to escape her . . ."

"Mmhmm" (affirmative).

" . . . but instead tried to get to know her, then in a way she might have consulted with you or you might have been tuned in to her wish to burst out, and been able to have some self talk, just like anybody talks to themselves about their behavior. Like the other day, I was [laughs] I was . . . this was so stupid of me. I was sweeping some stuff. I don't even remember where and I turned my head and I swept the broom at the same moment and poked myself in the eye!"

"I've actually done this, yes."

"And I said, out loud, under my breath, 'That was stupid. Don't do that again.' That's self talk. Now, it's not the same as engaging with a state of mind, but I was actually doing something kind of mindlessly, on autopilot, and then I tried to do something else without checking in with myself about what I was doing, that's when I poked myself in the eye. One part of my mind was sweeping and I went off in another place in my mind to do something else . . ."

"I know, but when you talk about you, you think it's normal, but when you talk about me, you think it's not normal."

"The not-normal piece has to do with the extent to which the action occurs unbridled, ungoverned, or as a surprise. Do you recall at the conclusion of the session not too long ago, we were shaking hands and you stopped me and asked if you could feel my hand?"

"Mmhmm" (affirmative).

"At that moment, I thought, 'geez, I don't know what this is about' . . ."

"Nor did I."

" . . . but if I say no, I'm going to shame Alice and I don't want to do that, so I said, pretty quickly, 'okay.' Do you recall what you did?"

"I felt your hand, I guess." (Alice knows this happened, but there is no clear memory of it.)

"Yes."

"The palm of your hand."

"Well, not just the palm."

"Oh, really?"

"Yeah, all over, just like you were patting my hand down, trying to see what the landscape was, and then you stopped, and I said, 'What was that?' and you said, 'I don't know.' I said, we had been talking about surprises in this session, and I said, 'I guess that was a surprise,' and you said something like, 'I guess so,' and then . . ."

"I left."

" And then you left. That is a curiosity and that is an unbridled, unexpected behavior that feels to me like it came from a center of initiative in your mind that you were unaware of and still are."

"See, when you say things like that, I just feel flattened."

"By?"

"I feel like back in space alien territory."

"That's so interesting because you don't feel that way about Shirley."

"No, but when you talk about some random some . . . no, because I've enabled her, listen to her words and read her words that were mine . . ."

"Yes."

" . . . and how could I possibly think she's not real?"

"Yes."

"But now you're talking about something that happened and you're sort of, by default, backing into the fact that it must have been from some other center of initiative."

"Well, th—"

"That we don't know."

"From some other part of you. I mean, you didn't know, you didn't understand what was going on. I mean, you just said you didn't know why you did that."

"Well, I do know why I did that."

"Why'd you do that?"

"I think, I think I actually do."

"Okay."

"I think that I knew you had boundaries so you weren't going to give me a hug, but I really felt the need to be closer to you . . ."

"Okay."

" So I think that's why I asked to touch your hand."

"Okay."

"I don't know that that's correct, but I mean, I think that's what it was." (This sounds to me like rationalization for surprise action that intuitively involved her behavior in a child-like manner. Alice is really uncomfortable and trying to rationalize away the state change data. I made an active choice to avoid the enactment.)

"Okay. Well indeed that may be what it was" (not going to challenge, but trying to draw out her curiosity).

"So I didn't say, 'Would you give me a hug?' because I knew that you would say no, and . . . but I really needed more from you. I needed more . . . I needed to feel closer to you in some way that satisfied me, that I thought you might be able to tolerate."

"Right, and what's your sense of why you felt you wanted to be closer to me at that moment?"

"I don't know the answer to that, because I don't remember which session that went with, but it was either because I felt distant from you or because I felt close to you and I don't know which one it was."

"You have a guess?"

"I don't, 'cause I would do exactly the same thing . . ."

"For either . . ."

" . . . for either one."

"Oh. So, sounds like what you're saying is, having listened to the recording and read the transcript and the chapter, in regard to Shirley, that there's a way in which you appreciate that Shirley is another part of you."

"Yes."

"And I guess the same for Emily, even though Emily hasn't been to therapy for a while."

"Yes."

"Well, that's pretty cool. I really appreciate your willingness to say that."

"But it doesn't get me past the blockage." (Alice's voice tones in this exchange are calm, collegial, curious, seeking coherence, and not energized by a feeling of being coerced.)

"Well, it might get you closer to moving through it and certainly will benefit you in regard to your anger 'cause there's a lot of work to do with your anger that you and Shirley can work out. Imagine how she's felt about being dissed by you, given how angry she gets."

"Yeah, I can actually physically feel that."

"I mean, Shirley is not a UFO, so to speak. She's another way of being you."

"I guess I'm saying I understand that."

"I'm so glad. It's been so hard [with feeling]. You've really struggled with this. And I've really wanted to support your struggle at the same time there's been a need to hold on to my observations."

"Well, I hope I'm not going to go home now and instead of working I'm going to feel the need to finger paint." (This is a rather dismissive and shaming statement aimed internally.)

"Well, tell me what you're thinking when you say that."

"What I'm thinking is that . . . about everybody who says they have DID and has Littles and the Littles take control of their life and do what they want to do, they want different things than the other parts of them."

"Well, um . . ."

"Like I don't feel the need to buy a teddy bear."

"Right. Nor do I."

"Nor do I feel the need to bring one into therapy."

"Yeah, and why should you?"

"Well, because I have these younger ways of being me. Wouldn't they like to have a teddy bear?"

"I don't know. "

"Then you're going to tell me I have to ask inside."

"Well, I could, I could certainly do that, but that's not my inclination at the moment. I have a different inclination and that is to ask you if you recall how I've spoken to and treated younger ways of being you when they've been present in sessions?"

"You expect me to remember ways of being me as if you were speaking to somebody younger."

"Okay, and what kind of language do I use?"

"I don't know. You used regular language but . . ."

"That's right.

" . . . used regular language . . .

"That's right."

" . . . that is clearly aimed . . . the tone of your voice is different."

"Yes, why?" (quickly and emphatically agreeing).

"It's gentler."

"Yes, why?"

"Because that's how you would speak to a child."

"That's how I speak to a person who is taking a bath in shame, reeling from shame. Very gently and softly, just like I'm doing right now because it hurts so bad to feel that way and I speak to adults in the same tender voice. It's not about children. It's about feelings, it's about tenderness. It's about respect for the hurt."

"I'm having a moment of self-consciousness here."

"Okay."

"Of you saying that just so you can write it."

"Honest to God, if I . . ." (disbelieving and then silent, catching myself from veering off into the enactment).

"I'm not accusing you of doing that. I'm just saying that's what I'm feeling is . . ."

"But I . . ."

" . . . it hasn't, uh, nothing's even remotely fazed me or made me think about it or anything up until this moment."

(Alice recognizes my effort to contain and respects it. In fact, she lets go of the effort to deflect through making an accusation. I pick up on her self-consciousness and go back to that.) "Do you think that in my talking to you about shame in that way, that it makes you uncomfortable in some way?"

"It was, you talking about shame that way made me extremely uncomfortable."

"What's your experience of it? I mean, why so uncomfortable? What . . . and I can imagine why, but from your perspective, why? Why so much discomfort?"

"I'm so sick of questions. Because honestly, it's because you're talking another part of me, of another place where the shame is."

"And you're reacting from . . ."

"And that part is causing me distress."

"Distress? You feel uncomfortable with the resonation with that part of you and the shame experience?"

"Mmhmm" (affirmative).

"So you do, yeah."

"No, no, wait, that's not quite it. They make me feel uncomfortable. I am, I know I'm filled with shame. I mean, I'm walking out the door dragging it on my shoe, like toilet paper."

"Yeah.

"So I know it's there."

"What a painful image. You know, Alice, you, you're . . ."

"And I know it's time to go. I don't . . . I can't even . . . I know it's time to go, so I'm trying not to freak out."

"I'd like to say one thing to you and then let's try to close. Okay?" (She nods her head.) "You're not bad. You've just been hurt." (Thirty-second pause.)

"I'm just trying to imagine what if I'm not bad."

"It's like the different outcome that we talked about several sessions ago with your friend and her father, and the scene where you had, as a 14-year-old or 13-year-old, pulled everything off the shelves, and your father came in."

"I don't . . . I'm unclear what you're talk- . . . [suddenly recalling] Yes! I recall talking about that, but what does that have to do with . . . oh then I said I couldn't imagine my friend and her father having an interaction."

"Like your father . . ."

"Yeah."

"And I spelled out what it would be like for the father to come in the room and say . . ."

"Oh, my God, don't do this." (About to burst into tears) "No, I can't let you do this."

"Let me do what?"

"Can't . . . I can't let you talk about that."

"Because?"

"Because I'll fall completely apart."

"A lot of feelings."

"A lot of feelings" (confirmatory). (Alice is working in treatment and there is an emotional release. The shame under the anger is visible. We're outside the enactment.)

"Yeah. You have a lot to be proud of for the hard, hard work you did today."

"So I guess it was a good thing that I took off in the middle of the day."

"I certainly am glad for it."

"Well, it all depends on whether we, tomorrow's an entire waste or not."

"Well, I think we're a pretty good team and the work isn't easy . . . but it's doable."

"Now I'm definitely stuck in transference with you and my father."

"How's that?"

"Because what you were going to tell me about was a normal father would have seen his daughter do what I do and gone to her saying, 'Oh, my God, my poor thing, you must be really hurting inside to have done that,' and I can't tell if that's you or my father talking now. It's not my father talking, but am I explaining myself or do you . . ."

"You're quoting me . . . from what I told you several sessions back."

"Okay." (Alice seemed at first stunned, and then able to recollect the interaction, at which point she said "Okay.")

"Shall we stop here?"

"Yes."

References

Adolphs, R. (2002). Recognizing emotion from facial expressions: Psychological and neurological mechanisms. *Behavioral and Cognitive Neuroscience Reviews*, 1(1), 21–62.

Ainsworth, M. D. S., Blehar, M. C., Waters, E., and Wall, S. (1978). *Patterns of attachment: A psychological study of the strange situation*. Hillsdale, NJ: Lawrence Erlbaum.

Akhtar, S. (2009). *Comprehensive dictionary of psychoanalysis*. London: Karnac Books.

Almond, R. (1997). Omnipotence and power. In C. Ellman and J. Reppen (eds.), *Omnipotent fantasies and the vulnerable self* (pp. 1–37). Northvale, NJ: Jason Aronson.

American Psychiatric Association. (2000). *Diagnostic and statistical manual of mental disorders, fourth edition, text tevision* (DSM-IV-TR). Washington, DC: American Psychiatric Association.

American Psychiatric Association. (2013). *Diagnostic and statistical manual of mental disorders*, 5th ed. Washington, DC: American Psychiatric Press.

Antonovsky, A. (1996). The salutogenic model as a theory to guide health promotion. *Health Promotion International*, 11(1), 11–18.

Anzieu, D. (1986). Paradoxical transference—From paradoxical communication to negative therapeutic reaction. *Contemporary Psychoanalysis*, 22, 520–547.

Armstrong, J. G., and Loewenstein, R. J. (1990). Characteristics of patients with multiple personality and dissociative disorders on psychological testing. *Journal of Nervous and Mental Disease*, 178, 448–454.

Auerbach, S. M., Kiesler, D. J., Strentz, T., Schmidt, J. A., and Serio, C. D. (1994). Interpersonal impacts and adjustment to the stress of simulated captivity: An empirical test of the Stockholm syndrome. *Journal of Social and Clinical Psychology*, 13(2), 207–221.

Aybek, S., Nicnolson, T. R., Zelaya, F., O'Daly, O. G., Craig, T. J., David, A. S., and Kanaan, R. A. (2014). Neural correlates of recall of life events in conversion disorder. *Journal of the American Medical Association Psychiatry*, 71(1), 52–60.

Baker, S. (1997). Dancing the dance with dissociatives: Some thoughts on countertransference, projective identification, and enactments in the treatment of dissociative disorders. *DISSOCIATION*, 10(4), 214–223.

Bandler, R., and Grinder, J. (1975). *The structure of magic*. Palo Alto, CA: Science and Behavior Books.

Bardy, B., and Mottet, D. (2006). Enactive/06: Enaction and complexity. Paper presented at the Third International Conference on Enactive Interfaces, Montpelier, France.

Bateman, A., and Fonagy, P. (2006). *Mentalization-based treatment for borderline personality disorder*. Oxford: Oxford University Press.

Bauer, P. (1996). What do infants recall of their lives? Memory for specific events by one-to-two year olds. *American Psychologist*, 51(1), 29–41.

Beah, I. (2007). *Along way gone: Memoirs of a boy soldier*. New York: Farrar, Strauss and Giroux.

Bechara, A., and Damasio, A.R. (2005). The somatic marker hypothesis: A neural theory of economic decision making. *Games and Economic Behavior*, 52, 336–372.

Beck, A. T., Steer, R. A., and Brown, G. K. (1996). *Manual for the Beck depression inventory—II*. San Antonio, TX: Psychological Corporation.

Beebe, B., Lachmann, F., Markese, S., and Bahrick, L. (2012). On the origins of disorganized attachment and internal working models: Paper I. A dyadic systems approach. *Psychoanalytic Dialogues*, 22(2), 253–272.

Bermond, B., Vorst, H. C. M., Moorman, P. P. (2006). Cognitive neuropsychology of alexithymia: Implications for personality typology. *Cognitive Neuropsychiatry*, 11(3), 332–360.

Bernstein, E. M., and Putnam, F. W. (1986). Development, reliability and validity of a dissociation scale. *Journal of Nervous and Mental Disease*, 174, 727–735.

Berridge, C. W., and Waterhouse, B. D. (2003). The locus coeruleus–noradrenergic system: Modulation of behavioral state and state-dependent cognitive processes. *Brain Research Reviews*, 42, 33–84.

Bion, W. R. (1959). Attacks on linking. *International Journal of Psychoanalysis*, 40, 308–315.

Blanke, O., and Arzy, S. (2005). The out-of-body experience: Disturbed self-processing at the temporo-parietal junction. *Neuroscientist*, 11(1), 16–24.

Blizard, R. A. (1997). Therapeutic alliances with abuser alters in DID: The paradox of attachment to the abuser. *DISSOCIATION*, 10(4), 246–254.

Bollas, C. (1987). *The shadow of the object: Psychoanalysis of the unthought known*. New York: Columbia University Press.

Boon, S., Steele, K., and van der Hart, O. (2011). *Coping with trauma-related dissociation: Skills training for patients and therapists*. New York: Norton.

Bowlby, J. (1982). *Attachment*, 2nd ed. New York: Basic Books.

Bowlby, J. (1980). *Attachment and loss: Volume III. Loss: Sadness and depression*. New York: Basic Books.

Bowman, E. S., and Markand, O. N. (1996). Psychodynamics and psychiatric diagnoses of pseudoseizure subjects. *American Journal of Psychiatry*, 153(1), 57-63.

Bradshaw, R. A., Cook, A., and McDonald, M. J. (2011). Observed and experiential integration (OEI): Discovery and development of a new set of trauma therapy techniques. *Journal of Psychotherapy Integration*, 21(2), 104–171.

Brand, B. (2001). Establishing safety with patients with dissociative identity disorder. *Journal of Trauma and Dissociation*, 2(4), 133–155.

Brand, B. L., Armstrong, J. G., and Loewenstein, R. J. (2006). Psychological assessment of patients with dissociative identity disorder. *Psychiatric Clinics of North America*, 29(1), 145–168.

Brand, B. L., Loewenstein, R. J., and Spiegel, D. (2014). Dispelling myths about dissociative identity disorder in treatment: An empirically based approach. *Psychiatry*, 77(2), 169–189.

Brand, B. L., McNary, S. W., Myrick, A. C., Classen, C. C., Lanius, R., Loewenstein, R. J., . . . Putnam, F. W. (2012). A longitudinal naturalistic study of patients with dissociative disorders treated by community clinicians. *Psychological Trauma: Theory, Research, Practice, and Policy*, 5(4), 301–308.

Brandchaft, B. (2007). Systems of pathological accommodation and change in analysis. *Psychoanalytic Psychology*, 24(4), 667–687.

Brattberg, G. (2006). PTSD and ADHD: Underlying factors in many cases of burnout. *Stress and Health*, 22, 305–313.

Braun, B. G. (1984). Towards a theory of multiple personality and other dissociative phenomena. *Psychiatric Clinics of North America*, 7(1), 171–193.

Braun, B. G. (1988). The BASK model of dissociation. *DISSOCIATION*, 1(1), 4–23.

Braun, B. G., and Sachs, R. G. (1985). The development of multiple personality disorder: Predisposing, precipitating and perpetuating factors. In R. P. Kluft (ed.), *Childhood antecedents of multiple personality*. Washington, DC: American Psychiatric Press.

Bremner, J. D., Vythilingam, M., Vermetten, E., Southwick, S. M., McGlashan, T., Nazeer, A., . . . Charney, D. S. (2003). MRI and PET study of deficits in hippocampal structure and function in women with childhood sexual abuse and posttraumatic stress disorder. *American Journal of Psychiatry*, 160, 924–932.

Bretherton, I. (1992). The origins of attachment theory: John Bowlby and Mary Ainsworth. *Developmental Psychology*, 28(5), 759.

Breuer, J., and Freud, S. (1895/1955). *Studies on hysteria* (trans. J. Strachey),vol. 2. London: Hogarth Press.

Bromberg, P. M. (1996). Standing in the spaces: The multiplicity of self and the psychoanalytic relationship. *Contemporary Psychoanalysis, 32,* 509–535.

Bromberg, P. M. (1998). *Standing in the spaces*. Hillsdale, NJ: Analytic Press.

Bromberg, P. M. (2003). One need not be a house to be haunted: On enactment, dissociation, and the dread of "not-me." *Psychoanalytic Dialogues,* 13(5), 689–710.

Bromberg, P. M. (2006). *Awakening the dreamer: Clinical journeys*. Mahwah, NJ: Analytic Press.

Bromberg, P. M. (2011). *The shadow of the tsunami and the growth of the relational mind*. New York: Routledge.

Brown, D. P., and Fromm, E. (1986). *Hypnotherapy and hypnoanalysis*. Hillsdale, NJ: Lawrence Erlbaum.

Bucci, W. (1997). *Psychoanalysis and cognitive science*. New York: Guilford Press.

Bucci, W. (2009). Identifying impasse and opportunity in the therapeutic interaction: The referential process in research and practice. Keynote address, Spring Meeting, Division 39, American Psychological Association, San Antonio, TX.

Bucci, W., and Maskit, B. (2007). Dissociation from the perspective of multiple code theory: Part I: Psychological roots and implications for psychoanalytic treatment. *Contemporary Psychoanalysis,* 43(2), 165–184.

Cannon, W. B. (1914). The interrelations of emotions as suggested by recent physiological researches. *American Journal of Psychology,* 25(2), 256–282.

Cao, S. G., Wu, W. C., Han, Z., and Wang, M. Y. (2005). Effects of psychological stress on small intestinal motility and expression of cholecystokinin and vasoactive intestinal polypeptide in plasma and small intestine in mice.*World Journal of Gastroenterology,* 11(5), 737–740.

Carlson, E. B., and Putnam, F. W. (1986). Development, reliability, and validity of a dissociation scale. *Journal of Nervous and Mental Disease,* 174(12), 727-735.

Carroll, L. (1960). *The annotated Alice: Alice's adventures in Wonderland and through the looking glass*. New York: Potter.

Carter, R. (1999). *Mapping the mind*. Berkley: University of California Press.

Chaperon, F., Fendt, M., Kelly, P. H., Lingenhoehl, K., Mosbacher, J., Olpe, H. R., . . . Gee, C. E. (2012). Gastrin-releasing peptide signaling plays a limited and subtle role in amygdala physiology and aversive memory. *PloS One,* 7(4), E34963.

Chefetz, R. A. (1997). Special case transference and countertransference in the treatment of dissociative identity disorder. *DISSOCIATION*, 10(4), 255–265.

Chefetz, R. A. (2000). Disorder in the therapist's view of the self: Working with the person with dissociative identity disorder. *Psychoanalytic Inquiry*, 20(2), 305–329.

Chefetz, R. A. (2003). Healing haunted hearts—Toward a model for integrating subjectivity: Commentary on papers by Philip Bromberg and Gerald Stechler. *Psychoanalytic Dialogues*, 13(5), 727–742.

Chefetz, R. A. (2004). The paradox of "detachment-disorders": Binding-disruptions of dissociative process, commentary on "Cherchez la Femme, Cherchez la Femme: A paradoxical response to trauma (Penelope Hollander)." *Psychiatry*, 67(3), 246–255.

Chefetz, R. A. (2006). "I wish I didn't know now what I didn't know then": Interpreting implicit processes in the psychoanalytic exploration of mind. In J. Petrucelli (ed.), *Longing: Psychoanalytic musings on desire*. London: Karnac.

Chefetz, R. A. (2008). Nolens volens out of darkness—From the depersonal to the "really" personal. *Contemporary Psychoanalysis*, 44(1), 18–40.

Chefetz, R. A. (2009). Waking the dead therapist. *Psychoanalytic Dialogues*, 19(4), 393–403.

Chefetz, R. A. (2010). Life as performance art: Right and left brain function, implicit knowing, and "felt coherence." In J. Petrucelli (ed.), *Knowing, not knowing and sort-of-knowing: Psychoanalysis and the experience of uncertainty* (pp. 258–278). New York: Karnac.

Chefetz, R. A. (2013). A fluctuating capaicty to mentalize: Affect scripts and self-state systems as (not so) "strange attractors": A discussion of Margy Sperry's "Putting our heads together: Mentalizing systems." *Psychoanalytic Dialogues*, 23(6), 708–714.

Chefetz, R. A., and Bromberg, P. M. (2004). Talking with "me" and "not-me": A dialogue. *Contemporary Psychoanalysis*, 40(3), 409–464.

Chu, J. A. (1998). *Rebuilding shattered lives: The responsible treatment of complex post-traumatic and dissociative disorders*. New York: Wiley.

Chused, J. F. (1991). The evocative power of enactments. *Journal of the American Psychoanalytic Association*, 39, 615–639.

Compton, A. (1972). A study of the psychoanalytic theory of anxiety. I. The development of Freud's theory of anxiety. *Journal of the American Psychoanalytic Association*, 20, 3–44.

Cortina, M. (2003). Defensive processes, emotions and internal working models: A perspective from attachment theory and contemporary models of the mind. In M. Cortina and M. Marrone (eds.), *Attachment theory and psychoanalytic process* (p. 490). Phildelphia: Whurr.

Courtois, C. (1999). *Recollections of sexual abuse: Treatment principles and guidelines.* New York: W. W. Norton & Co.

Cozolino, L. (2002). *The neuroscience of psychotherapy: Building and rebuilding the human brain.* New York: Norton.

Critchley, H. D., Wiens, S., Rotshtein, P., Ohman, A., and Dolan, R. J. (2004). Neural systems supporting interoceptive awareness. *Nature Neuroscience,* 7(2), 189–195.

Dalenberg, C., Brand, B., Gleaves, D., Dorahy, M., Loewenstein, R., Cardena, E., Carlson, E.,and Spiegel, D. (2012). Evaluation of the evidence for the trauma and fantasy models of dissociation. *Psychological Bulletin,* 138(3), 550–588.

Damasio, A. R. (1996). The somatic marker hypothesis and the possible functions of the prefrontal cortex. *Philosophical Transactions of the Royal Society B,* 351, 1413–1420.

Damasio, A. R. (1999). *The feeling of what happens: Body and emotion in the making of consciousness.* New York: Harcourt Brace.

Danielyan, A., Pathak, S., Kowatch, R. A., Arszman, S. P., and Johns, E. S. (2007). Clinical characteristics of bipolar disorder in very young children. *Journal of Affective Disorders,* 97, 51–59.

Dantas, A. D. S., Luft, T., Henriques, J. A. P., Schwartsmann, G., and Roesler, R. (2006). Opposite effects of low and high doses of the gastrin-releasing peptide receptor antagonist RC-3095 on memory consolidation in the hippocampus: possible involvement of the GABAergic system. *Peptides,* 27(9), 2307–2312.

Darwin, C. (1877). I.—A biographical sketch of an infant. *Mind,* 7, 285–294.

Darwin, C. (1998). *The expression of the emotions in man and animals,* 3rd ed. Oxford: Oxford University Press.

Davidson, R. J., Abercrombie, H., Nitschke, J. B., and Putnam, K. (1999). Regional brain function, emotion, and disorders of emotion. *Current Opinion in Neurobiology,* 9, 228–234.

Davies, J. M. (1996). Linking the "pre-analytic" and the postclassical: Integration, dissociation, and the multiplicity of unconscious process. *Contemporary Psychoanalysis,* 32, 553–576.

Davies, J. M., and Frawley, M. G. (1992). Dissociative processes and transference-countertransference paradigms in the psychoanalytically oriented treatment of adult survivors of sexual abuse. *Psychoanalytic Dialogues,* 2, 5–36.

Davis, M. (1998). Are different parts of the extended amygdala involved in fear vs. anxiety? *Biological Psychiatry,* 44(12), 1239–1247.

Demos, V. (ed.). (1995). *Exploring affect. The selected writings of Sylvan S. Tomkins.* New York: Cambridge University Press.

Denton, D. A., McKinley, M. J., Farell, M., and Egan, G. F. (2009). The role of primordial emotions in the evolutionary origin of consciousness. *Consciousness and Cognition*, 18, 500–514.

Dodes, L. (1990). Addiction, helplessness, and narcissistic rage. *Psychoanalytic Quarterly*, 59, 398–419.

Dodes, L. (1996). Compulsion and addiction. *Journal of the American Psychoanalytic Association*, 44, 815-835.

Dudai, Y. (2003). Neurobiology: Fear thou not. *Nature*, 421(6921), 325–327.

Duffy, A. (2012). The nature of the association between childhood ADHD and the development of bipolar disorder: A review of prospective high-risk studies. *American Journal of Psychiatry*, 169(12), 1247–1255.

Eich, J. E. (1987). Theoretical issues in state-dependent memory. In H. L. Roediger and F. I. M. Craik (eds.), *Varieties of memory and consciousness: Essays in honour of Endel Tulving* (pp. 331–354). Hillsdale, NJ: LawrenceErlbaum.

Eich, J. E. (1995). Searching for mood dependent memory. *Psychological Science*, 6, 65–75.

Emde, R. N. (1983). The prerepresentational self and its affective core. *Psychoanalytic Study of the Child*, 38, 165–192.

Emde, R. N. (1991). Positive emotions for psychoanalytic theory: Surprises from infancy research and new directions. *Journal of the American Psychoanalytic Association*, 39(Supplement), 5–44.

Enright, A. (2007). *The gathering*. New York: Black Cat, Grove/Atlantic.

Esch, T., and Stefano, G. B. (2004). The neurobiology of pleasure, reward processes, addiction an their health implications. *Neuroendocrinology Letters*, 25(4), 235–251.

Eth, S., and Pynoos, R. (1985). Developmental perspective on psychic trauma in Childhood. In C. R. Figley (ed.), *Trauma and its wake* (pp. 36–52). Bristol, PA: Bruner/Mazel (Taylor and Francis).

Eysenck, H. J. (1997). Addiction, personality, and motivation. *Human Psychopharmacology*, 12, S79–S87.

Fairbairn, R. (1952). Schizoid factors in the personality. In *Psychoanalytic Studies of the Personality*. London: Tavistock.

Fairbairn, W. R. D. (1941). A revised psychopathology of the psychoses and psychoneuroses. *International Journal of Psychoanalysis*, 22, 250–279.

Fairbairn, W. R. D. (1944). Endopsychic structure considered in terms of object-relationships. *International Journal of Psychoanalysis*, 25, 70–92.

Faramarzi, M., Azadfallah, P., Book, H .E., Tabatabaei, K. R., Taheri, H., and Shokri-shirvani, J. (2013). A randomized controlled trial of brief psychoanalytic psychotherapy in patients with functional dyspepsia. *Asian Journal of Psychiatry*, 6, 228–234.

Feiner, A. H. (1970). Toward an understanding of the experience of inauthenticity. *Contemporary Psychoanalysis*, 7, 64–83.

Ferenczi, S. (1933/1955). Confusion of tongues between adults and the child. (Original title: "The passions of adults and their influence on the sexual character development of children). In *Final contributions to the problems and methods of psychoanalysis* (pp. 155–167). New York: Basic Books.

Figley, C. R. (1985). *Trauma and its wake, Volume I: The study and treatment of post-traumatic stress disorder.* Bristol, PA: Brunner/Mazel (Taylor and Francis).

Fine, C. G., and Berkowitz, A. S. (2001). The wreathing protocol: The imbrication of hypnosis and EMDR in the treatment of dissociative identity disorder and other dissociative responses. *American Journal of Clinical Hypnosis*, 43(3).

Flax, J. (1996). Taking multiplicity seriously. *Contemporary Psychoanalysis*, 32, 553–576.

Foa, E. B., and Kozak, M. J. (1986). Emotional processing of fear: Exposure to corrective information. *Psychological Bulletin*, 99, 20–35.

Fonagy, P. (2000). Attachment and borderline personality disorder. *Journal of the American Psychoanalytic Association*, 48(4), 1129–1146.

Fonagy, P., Gergely, G., Jurist, E. J., and Target, M. (2003). *Affect regulation, mentalization and the development of the self.* New York: Other Press.

Fonagy, P., and Target, M. (1996). Playing with reality: I. Theory of mind and the normal development of psychic reality. *International Journal of Psychoanalysis*, Pt2, 217–233.

Fonagy, P., and Target, M. (2000). Playing with reality: III. The persistence of dual psychic reality in borderline patients. *International Journal of Psychoanalysis*, 81, 853–873.

Ford, A. C., Talley, N.J., Schoenfeld, P.S., Quigley, E. M. M., and Moayyedi, P. (2008). Efficacy of antidepressants and psychological therapies in irritable bowel syndrome: systematic review and meta-analysis. *Gut*, 58, 367–378.

Frankel, A. S., and O'hearn, T. C. (1996). Similarities in responses to extreme and unremitting stress: Cultures of communities under siege. *Psychotherapy*, 33(Fall), 485–502.

Fraser, G. A. (1997). *The dilemma of ritual abuse: Cautions and guides for therapists.* Washington, DC: American Psychiatric Publishing.

Fraser, G. A. (2003). Fraser's "Dissociative Table Technique" revisited, revised: A strategy for working with ego states in dissociative disorder and ego-state therapy. *Journal of Trauma and Dissociation*, 4(4), 5–28.

Fratta, W. (2006). Neurobiology of reward. Paper presented at the 6th IMS Workshop: Menopause and Aging, Quality of Life and Sexuality, Pisa, Italy.

Freeman, M. P., Freeman, S. A., and McElroy, S. L. (2002). The comorbidity of bipolar and anxiety disorders: Prevalence, psychobiology, and treatment issues. *Journal of Affective Disorders*, 68(1), 1–23.

Freud, S. (1894). *The neuro-psychoses of defense* (vol. 3). London: Hogarth Press.

Freud, S. (1895). Project for a scientific psychology. In J. Strachey (ed.), *Standard Edition* (vol. 1, pp. 281–391). London: Hogarth Press.

Freud, S. (1900). The interpretation of dreams. In J. Strachey (ed.), *Standard Edition* (vols. 4 and 5). London: Hogarth Press.

Freud, S. (1905). Three essays on the theory of sexuality. In J. Strachey (ed.), *Standard Edition* (vol. 7). London: Hogarth Press.

Freud, S. (1909). Notes upon a case of obsessional neurosis. In J. Strachey (ed.), *The Standard Edition* (vol. 10). London: Hogarth Press.

Freud, S. (1914). Remembering, repeating and working-through. In J. Strachey (ed.), *Standard Edition* (vol. 12, pp. 145–156). London: Hogarth Press.

Freud, S. (1915). Mourning and melancholia. In J. Strachey (ed.), *Standard Edition* (vol. 14, pp. 237–258). London: Hogarth Press.

Freud, S. (1917). Introductory lectures on psychoanalysis 15 and 16. In J. Strachey (ed.), *Standard Edition*. London: Hogarth Press.

Freud, S. (1920). Beyond the pleasure principle. In J. Strachey (ed.), *Standard Edition* (vol. 18, pp. 147–156). London: Hogarth Press.

Freud, S. (1923). The ego and the id. In J. Strachey (ed.), *Standard Edition* (vol. 19, pp. 12–68). London: Hogarth Press.

Freud, S. (1926). Inhibitions, symptoms, and anxiety. In J. Strachey (ed.), *Standard Edition* (vol. 20, pp. 77–178). London: Hogarth Press.

Frewen, P. A., Lane, R. D., Neufeld, R. W. J., Densmore, M., Stevens, T., and Lanius, R. (2008). Neural correlates of levels of emotional awareness during trauma script-imagery in posttraumatic stress disorder. *Psychosomatic Medicine*, 70, 27–31.

Frewen, P. A., and Lanius, R. A. (2006). Neurobiology of dissociation: Unity and disunity and mind-body-brain. *Psychiatric Clinics of North America*, 29, 113–128.

Freyd, J. J. (1996). *Betrayal trauma: The logic of forgetting childhood abuse*. Cambridge, MA: Harvard University Press.

Fried, I., MacDonald, K. A., and Wilson, C. L. (1997). Single neuron activity in human hippocampus and amygdala during recognition of faces and objects. *Neuron*, 18, 753–765.

Friedman, K. (2006). Live without me. I'll understand. *New York Times*. Retrieved from http://www.nytimes.com/2006/12/17/fashion/17love.html?pagewanted=alland_r=0.

Frischholz, E. J., Lipman, L. S., Braun, B. G., and Sachs, R. G. (1992). Psychopathology, hypnotizability, and dissociation. *American Journal of Psychiatry*, 149, 1521–1525.

Gallese, V. (2001). The "shared manifold" hypothesis: From mirror neurons to empathy. *Journal of Consciousness Studies*, 8(5–7), 33–50.

Gallese, V., Eagle, M. N., and Migone, P. (2007). Intentional attunement: Mirror neurons and the neural underpinnings of interpersonal relations. *Journal of the American Psychoanalytic Association*, 55(1), 131–176.

Gazzaniga, M. (1995). Consciousness and the cerebral hemispheres. In M. Gazzaniga (ed.), *Cognitive neuroscience*. Cambridge, MA: MIT Press.

Gazzaniga, M. S., Bogen, J. E., and Sperry, R. W. (1962). Some functional effects of sectioning the cerebral commisures in man. *Proceedings of the National Academy of the Sciences*, 15(48), 1765–1769.

Gendlin, E. T. (1978). *Focusing*. New York: Bantam.

Georgiadis, J. R., Kortekaas, R., Kringelbach, M. L., and Berridge, K. C. (2009). The sweetest taboo: Functional neurobiology of human sexuality in relation to pleasure. In *Pleasures of the Brain* (pp. 178–201). Oxford: Oxford University Press.

Gergely, G., Nadasdy, Z., Csibra, G., and Biro, S. (1995). Taking the intentional stance at 12 months of age. *Cognition*, 56, 165–193.

Gergely, G., and Watson, J. S. (1996). The social biofeedback theory of parental affect-mirroring: The development of emotional self-awareness and self-control in infancy. *International Journal of Psychoanalysis*, 77, 1181–1211.

Ghent, E. (1989). Credo: The dialectics of one-person and two-person psychologies. *Contemporary Psychoanalysis*, 25(2), 169–211.

Giles, G. R., Mason, M. C., Humphries, C., and Clark, C. G. (1969). Action of gastrin on the lower oesophageal sphincter in man. *Gut*, 10(9), 730–734.

Ginot, E. (1997). The analyst's use of self, self-disclosure, and enhanced integration. *Psychoanalytic Psychology*, 14(3), 365–381.

Gold, S. N. (2000). *Not trauma alone: Therapy for child abuse survivors in family and social context*. Philadelphia: Brunner/Routledge.

Gold, S. N., and Heffner, C. L. (1998). Sexual addiction: Many conceptions, minimal data. *Clinical Psychology Review*, 18(3), 367–381.

Gold, S. N., and Seifer, R. E. (2002). Dissociation and sexual addication/compulsivity: A contextual approach to conceptualization and treatment. *Journal of Trauma and Dissociation*, 3(4), 59–82.

Gonzalez, N., Moody, T. W., Igarashi, H., Ito, T., and Jensen, R. T. (2008). Bombesin-related peptides and their receptors: Recent advances in their role in physiology and disease states. *Current Opinion in Endocrinology, Diabetes, and Obesity*, 15(1), 58–64.

Goodman, A. (1998). *Sexual addiction: An integrated approach*. Madison, CT: International Universities Press.

Gorkin, M. (1987). *The uses of countertransference*. Northvale, NJ: Jason Aronson.

Grams, M. (2008). *The Twilight Zone: Unlocking the door to a television classic*. Churchville, MD: OTR Publishing.

Grandin, T. (1995). How people with autism think. In E. Schopler and G. B. Mesibov (eds.), *Learning and cognition in autism*. New York: Plenum Press.

Gratz, K. L. (2007). Targeting emotion dysregulation in the treatment of self-injury. *Journal of Clinical Psychology: In Session*, 63(11), 1091–1103.

Green, A. (1997). The intuition of the negative in "playing and reality." *International Journal of Psychoanalysis*, 78, 1071–1084.

Greenberg, L. S. (2004). Emotion–focused therapy. *Clinical Psychology and Psychotherapy*, 11(1), 3–16.

Greenberg, L. S., and Paivio, S. C. (1997). *Working with emotions in psychotherapy*. New York: Guilford Press.

Gregory, R., and Musttata, G. T. (2012). Magical thinking in narratives of adolescent cutters. *Journal of Adolescence*, 35, 1041–1051.

Grinker, R. R., and Spiegel, J. P. (1945). *Men under stress*. Philadelphia: Blackinston.

Gross, C., and Hen, R. (2004). The developmental origins of anxiety. *Nature Reviews*, 5(July), 545–552.

Grunert, U. (1979). The negative therapeutic reaction as a sign of disturbance in the separation-individuation process. *Psyche*, 33, 1–28.

Guntrip, H. (1969). *Schizoid phenomena, object relations and the self*. New York: International Universities Press,.

Guthrie, E., Creed, F., Dawson, D., and Tomenson, B. (1991). A controlled trial of psychological treatment for the irritable bowel syndrome. *Gastroenterology*, 100, 450–457.

Hamann, S., and Mao, H. (2002). Positive and negative emotional verbal stimuli elicit activity in the left amygdala. *NeuroReport*, 13, 15–19.

Hammond, D. C. (ed.). (1990). *Handbook of hypnotic suggestions and metaphors*. New York: Norton.

Hammond, D. C., Garver, R. B., Mutter, C. B., Crasilneck, H. B., Frischholz, E., Gravitz, M., . . . Wester, W. (1994). *Clinical hypnosis and memory: Guidelines for clinicians and for forensic hypnosis*. Bloomingdale, IL: American Society of Clinical Hypnosis Press.

Hauser, W., Kosseva, M., Uceyler, N., Klose, P., and Sommer, C. (2011). Emotional, physical, and sexual abuse in fibromyalgia syndrome: A systematic review with meta-analysis. *Arthritis Care and Research*, 63(6), 808-820.

Hefez, A. (1987). Long-term effects of extreme situational stress. *American Journal of Psychiatry*, 1, 44.

Herman, J. L. (1992). *Trauma and recovery*. New York: Basic Books.

Hilgard, E. R. (1986). *Divided consciousness: Multiple controls in human thought and action*. New York: Wiley.

Holmes, E. A., Brown, R. J., Manselld, W., Fearon, R. P., Hunter, E. C. M., Frasquilho, F., and Oakley, D. A. (2005). Are there two qualitatively distinct forms of dissociation? A review of some clinical implications. *Clinical Psychology Review*, 25, 1–23.

Horney, K. (1936). The problem of the negative therapeutic reaction. *Psychoanalytic Quarterly*, 5, 29–44.

Horowitz, M. J. (1986). *Stress response syndromes*. New York: Jason Aronson.

Horowitz, M. J., Fridhandler, B., and Stinson, C. (1991). Person schemas and emotion. *Journal of the American Psychoanalytic Association*, 39(Supplement), 173–208.

Howell, E. F. (2005). *The dissociative mind*. Hillsdale, NJ: Analytic Press.

Howell, E. F. (2011). *Understanding and treating dissociative identity disorder: A relational approach*. New York: Routledge.

Hurvich, M. (2003). The place of annihilation anxieties in psychoanalytic theory. *Journal of the American Psychoanalytic Association*, 51(2), 579–616.

Iacobani, M. (2009). Imitation, empathy, and mirror neurons. *Annual Reviews of Psychology*, 60, 653-670.

IJzendoorn, M. H. von. (1995). Adult attachment representations, parental responsiveness, and infant attachment: A meta-analysis on the predictive validity of the adult attachment interview. *Psychological Bulletin*, 117(3), 387–403.

IJzendoorn, M. H. von, and Schuengel, C. (1996). The measurement of dissociation in normal and clinical populations: Meta-analytic validation of the dissociative experiences scale (DES). *Clinical Psychology Review*, 16(5), 365–382.

International Society for the Study of Trauma and Dissociation. (2011). Guidelines for Treating Dissociative Identity Disorder in Adults, Third Revision. *Journal of Trauma and Dissociation*, 12(2), 115-187.

Janet, P. (1901). *The mental state of hystericals*. New York: Putnams.

Janet, P. (1907). *The major symptoms of hysteria*. New York: Macmillan.

John, C. N., and Lambert, M. J. (2011). Psychotherapy relationships that work II. *Psychotherapy*, 48(1), 4–8.

Johnson, S. E., Hunsley, J., Greenberg, L., and Schindler, D. (1999). Emotion focused couples therapy: Status and challenges. *Clinical Psychology: Science and Practice*, 6(1), 67–79.

Jones, J. M. (1995). *Affect as process: An inquiry into the centrality of affect in psychological life*. Hillsdale, NJ: Analytic Press.

Karlehagen, S., Malt, U. F., Hoff, H., et al. (1993). The effect of major railway accidents on the psychological health of train drivers—II. A longitudinal study of the one-year outcome after the accident. *Journal of Psychosomatic Research*, 37, 807–817.

Karpman, S. B. (1968). Fairy tales and script drama analysis. *Transactional Analysis Bulletin*, 7(26), 39–43.

Kass, J. H. (1997). Topographic maps are fundamental to sensory processing. *Controversies in Neuroscience*, 44(2), 107–112.

Kavaler-Adler, S. (1992). Mourning and the erotic transference. International *Journal of Psychoanalysis*, 73, 527–539.

Keinänen, M. (2006). *Psychosemiosis as a key to body-mind continuum: the reinforcement of symbolization-reflectiveness in psychotherapy*. New York: Nova Science Publishers.

Kellner, M., Wiedemann, K., Yassouridis, A., Levengood, R., Guo, L.S., Holsboer, F., and Yehuda, R. (2000). Behavioral and endocrine response to cholecystokinin tetrapeptide in patients with posttraumatic stress disorder. *Society of Biological Psychiatry*, 47, 107–111.

Kelly, K. (2013). Inspired by Denise. *New York Times*, September 17.

Kernberg, O. (1975). *Borderline conditions and pathological narcissism*. New York: Jason Aronson.

Kluft, R. P. (1983). Hypnotherapeutic crisis intervention in multiple personality disorder. *American Journal of Clinical Hypnosis*, 26(2), 73–83.

Kluft, R. P. (1984). An introduction to multiple personality disorder. *Psychiatric Annals*, 14(1), 19–24.

Kluft, R. P. (ed.). (1985). *Childhood antecedents of multiple personality*. Washington, DC: American Psychiatric Press.

Kluft, R. P. (1987). First-rank symptoms as a diagnostic clue to multiple personality disorder. *American Journal of Psychiatry*, 144(3), 293–298.

Kluft, R. P. (1989). Playing for time: Temporizing techniques inthe treatment of multiple personality disorder. *American Journal of Clinical Hypnosis*, 32, 90–98.

Kluft, R. P. (1990a). An abreactive technique. In D. C. Hammond (ed.), *Handbook of Hypnotic Suggestions and Metaphors*. New York: Norton.

Kluft, R. P. (1990b). Dissociation and subsequent vulnerability: A preliminary study. *DISSOCIATION*, 3(3), 167–173.

Kluft, R. P. (2000). The psychoanalytic psychotherapy of dissociative identity disorder in the context of trauma therapy. *Psychoanalytic Inquiry*, 20(2), 259–286.

Kluft, R. P. (2006). Dealing with alters: A pragmatic clinical perspective. *Psychiatric Clinics of North America*, 29, 281–304.

Kluft, R. P. (2013). *Shelter from the storm: Processing the traumatic memories of DID/DDNOS patients with the fractionated abreaction technique.* North Charleston, SC: CreateSpace.

Kluft, R. P., and Fine, C. G. (eds.). (1993). *Clinical perspectives on multiple personality disorder*. Washington, DC: American Psychiatric Press.

Kohut, H. (1971). *The analysis of the self: A systematic approach to the psychoanalytic treatment of narcissistic personality disorders* (vol. 4). Madison, CT: International Universities Press.

Kohut, H. (1979). The two analyses of Mr. Z. *International Journal of Psychoanalysis*, 60, 3–27.

Kramer, S. (1983). Object-coercive doubting: A pathological defensive response to maternal incest. *Journal of the American Psychoanalytic Association*, 31S, 325–351.

Krystal, H. (1988). *Integration and self healing: Affect, alexithymia, and trauma.* Hillsdale, NJ: Analytic Press.

Kubzansky, L. D., Bordelois, P., Jun, H. J., Roberts, A. L., Cerda, C., Bluestone, N., and Koenen, K. C. (2014). The weight of traumatic stress: A prospective study of posttraumatic stress disorder symptoms and weight status in women. *Journal of the American Medical Association Psychiatry*, 71(1), 44–51.

Lampl-De Groot, J. (1967). On obstacles standing in the way of psychoanalytic cure. *Psychoanalytic Study of the Child*, 22, 20–35.

Lane, R. D., and Nadel, L. (2000). *Cognitive neuroscience of emotion.* New York: Oxford University Press.

Lane, R. D., Quinlan, D. M., Schwartz, G. E., and Walker, P. A. (1990). The levels of emotional awareness scale: A cognitive-developmental measure of emotion. *Journal of Personality Assessment*, 55, 124–134.

Lane, R. D., and Schwartz, G. E. (1987). Levels of emotional awareness: A cognitive-developmental theory and its application to psychopathology. *American Journal of Psychiatry*, 144, 133–143.

Lanius, R. A., Vermetten, E., Loewenstein, R. J., Brand, B., Schmahl, C., Bremner, J. D., and Spiegel, D. (2010). Emotion modulation in PTSD: Clinical and neurobiological evidence for a dissociative subtype. *American Journal of Psychiatry*, 167, 640–647.

Lansky, M. R. (1992). *Fathers who fail: Shame and psychopathology in the familiy system.* Hillsdale, NJ: Analytic Press.

Laplanche, J., and Pontalis, J.-B. (1967). *The language of psychoanalysis* (trans. D. Nicholson-Smith). New York: Norton.

Lapointe, A. R., Crayton, J. W., DeVito, R., Fichtner, C. G., and Konopka, L. M. (2006). Similar or disparate brain patterns? The intra-personal EEG variability of three women with multiple personality disorder. *Clinical EEG and Neuroscience*, 37(3), 235–242.

Lazarus, R. S. (1984). On the primacy of cognition. *American Psychologist*, 39(2), 124–129.

LeDoux, J. E. (1995). Emotion: Clues from the brain. *Annual Review of Psychology*, 46, 209–235.

LeDoux, J. E. (1996). *The emotional brain*. New York: Simon and Schuster.

LeDoux, J. E. (2012). Searching the brain for the roots of fear. *New York Times*, January 22. Retrieved from http://opinionator.blogs.nytimes.com/2012/01/22/anatomy-of-fear/?scp=1&sq=ledoux&st=cse&_r=0.

Leknes, S., and Tracey, I. (2008). A common neurobiology for pain and pleasure. *Nature Reviews*, 9(April), 314–320.

Lemche, E., Anilkumar, A., Giampietro, V. P., Brammer, M. J., Surguladze, S. A., Lawrence, N. S., . . . Phillips, M. L. (2008). Cerebral and autonomic responses to emotional facial expressions in depersonalisation disorder. *British Journal of Psychiatry*, 193, 222–228.

Lemche, E., Surguladze, S. A., Giampietro, V. P., Anilkumar, A., Brammer, M. J., Sierra, M., . . . Phillips, M. L. (2007). Limbic and prefrontal responses to facial emotion expressions in depersonalization. *NeuroReport*, 18, 473–477.

Levenkron, H. (2006). Love (and hate) with the proper stranger: Affective honesty and enactment. *Psychoanalytic Inquiry*, 26(2), 157–181.

Levine, H. B. (1990). *Adult analysis and childhood sexual abuse*. Hillsdale, NJ: Analytic Press.

Levine, P. (1997). *Walking the tiger: Healing trauma*. Berkeley, CA: North Atlantic Books.

Lewis, H. B. (1987a). *The role of shame in symptom formation*. Hillsdale, NJ: Lawrence Erlbaum.

Lewis, H. B. (1987b). Shame: The "sleeper" in psychopathology. In H. B. Lewis (ed.), *The role of shame in symptom formation* (pp. 1–28). Hillsdale, NJ: Lawrence Erlbaum.

Lewis, M., and Haviland, J. M. (eds.). (1993). *Handbook of emotions*. New York: Guilford Press.

Lichtenberg, J. D. (1989a). Model scenes, motivation, and personality. In S. Dowling and A. Rothstein (eds.), *The significance of infant observational research for clinical work with children, adolescents, and adults* (pp. 91–107). Madison, CT: International University Press.

Lichtenberg, J. D. (1989b). *Psychoanalysis and motivation*. Hillsdale, NJ: Analytic Press.

Lichtenberg, J. D. (2013). Foreword. In J. D. Lichtenberg (ed.), *Nothing good is allowed to stand: An integrative view of the negative therapeutic reaction* (pp. xiii–xviii). New York: Routledge.

Lichtenberg, J. D., Lachman, F. M., and Fosshage, J. L. (1992). *Self and motivational systems: Toward a theory of psychoanalytic technique*. Hillsdale, NJ: Analytic Press.

Lichtenberg, J. D., Lachman, F. M., and Fosshage, J. L. (1996). *The clinical exchange: Techniques derived from self and motivational systems*. Hillsdale, NJ: Analytic Press.

Linehan, M. M. (1993). *Cognitive-behavioral treatment of borderline personality disorder*. New York: Guilford Press.

Liotti, G. (1999). Disorganization of attachment as a model for understanding dissociative psychopathology. In J. Solomon and C. George (eds.), *Attachment Disorganization* (pp. 291–317). New York: Guilford Press.

Loewenstein, R. J. (1991). An office mental status examination for complex chronic dissociative symptoms and multiple personality disorder. In R. J. Loewenstein (ed.), *Psychiatric clinics of North America* (vol. 14, pp. 567–604). Philadelphia: Saunders.

Loewenstein, R. J. (1993). Post-traumatic and dissociative aspects of transference and countertransference in the treatment of multiple personality disorder. In R. P. Kluft and C. G. Fine (eds.), *Clinical perspective on multiple personality disorder* (pp. 51–85). Washington, DC: American Psychiatric Press.

Loewenstein, R. J. (1994). Diagnosis, epidemiology, clinical course, treatment, and cost effectiveness of treatment for dissociative disorders and multiple personality disorder: Report submitted to the Clinton administration task force on health care financing reform. *DISSOCIATION*, 7, 3–11.

Loewenstein, R. J. (2006). DID 101: A hands-on clinical guide to the stabilization phase of dissociative identity disorder treatment. *Psychiatric Clinics of North America*, 29, 305–332.

Loewenstein, R. M. (1957). A contribution to the psychoanalytic theory of masochism. *Journal of the American Psychoanalytic Association*, 5, 197–234.

Longo, M. R., Azanon, E., and Haggard, P. (2009). More than skin deep: Body representation beyond primary somatosensory cortex. *Neuropsychologia*, 48(3), 655–668.

Luyten, P., Blatt, S. J., and Fonagy, P. (2013). Impairments in self structures in depression and suicide in psychodynamic and cognitive behavioral approaches: Implications for clinical practice and research. *International Journal of Cognitive Therapy*, 6(3), 265–279.

Lyons-Ruth, K. (2003). Dissociation and the parent-infant dialogue: A longitudinal perspective from attachment research. *Journal of the American Psychoanalytic Association*, 51(3), 883–911.

Lyons-Ruth, K. (2008). Contributions of the mother-infant relationship to dissociative, borderline, and conduct symptoms in young adulthood. *Infant Mental Health Journal*, 29(3), 203–218.

Lyons-Ruth, K., Bronfman, E., and Parsons, E. (1999). Maternal frightened, frightening, or atypical behavior and disorganized attachment patterns. In J. I. Vondra and D. Barnett (eds.), *Atypical attachment in infancy and early childhood among children at risk* (vol. 64, no. 3, pp. 67–96). Chicago: University of Chicago Press.

Lyons-Ruth, K., Dutra, L., Schuder, M. R., and Bianchi, I. (2006). From infant attachment disorganization to adult dissociation: relational adaptations or traumatic experiences? In R. A. Chefetz (ed.), *Dissociative disorders: An expanding window into the psychobiology of mind* (vol. 29, pp. 63–86). Philadelphia: Saunders.

Lyons-Ruth, K., Yellin, C., Melnick, S., and Atwood, G. (2005). Expanding the concept of unresolved mental states: Hostile/helpless states of mind on the Adult Attachment Interview are associated with disrupted mother–infant communication and infant disorganization. *Development and Psychopathology*, 17(01), 1–23.

Main, M. (1993). Discourse, prediction, and recent studies in attachment: Implications for psychoanalysis. *Journal of the American Psychoanalytic Association*, 41, 209–242.

Main, M. (1995). Recent studies in attachment: Overview, with selected implications for clinical work. In S. Goldberg, R. Muir, and J. Kerr (eds.), *Attachment theory: Social, developmental, and clinical perspectives* (pp. 407–474). Hillsdale, NJ: Analytic Press.

Main, M. (2000). The organized categories of infant, child, and adult attachment: Flexible vs. inflexible attention under attachment-related stress. *Journal of the American Psychoanalytic Association*, 48, 1055–1095.

Main, M., and Hesse, E. (1990). Parents' unresolved traumatic experiences are related to infant disorganized attachment status: Is frightened and/or frightening parental behavior the linking mechanism? In M. T. Greenberg, D. Ciccheti,and E. M. Cummings (eds.), *Attachment in the preschool years: Theory, research, and intervention* (pp. 161–182). Chicago: University of Chicago Press.

Main, M., and Morgan, H. (1996). Disorganization and disorientation in infant strange situation behavior: Phenotypic resemblance to dissociative states. In L. K. Michelson and W. J. Ray (eds.), *Handbook of dissociation: Theoretical, empirical, and clinical perspectives* (pp. 107–138). New York: Plenum Press.

Manni, E., and Petrosini, L. (2004). A century of cerebellar somatotopy: A debated representation. *Nature Reviews: Neuroscience*, 5(March), 241–249.

Mantovani, A., Simeon, D., Urban, N., Bulow, P., and Lisanby, S. (2011). Temporo-parietal junction stimulation in the treatment of depersonalization disorder. *Psychiatry Research*, 186(1), 138–140.

Marvin, R. C., Cooper, G., Hoffman, K., and Powell, B. (2002). The Circle of Security Project: Attachment-based intervention with caregiver-preschool child dyads. *Attachment and Human Development*, 4(1), 107–124.

McCullough, L., Kuhn, N., Andrews, S., Kaplan, A., Wolf, J., Hurley, C. L., and Hurley, C. (2003). *Treating affect phobia: A manual for short-term dynamic psychotherapy.* New York: Guilford Press.

McFarlane, A. C. (1988). The longitudinal course of posttraumatic morbidity. The range of outcomes and their predictors. *Journal of Nervous and Mental Disease*, 176, 30-39.

McLaughlin, J. (1991). Clinical and theoretical aspects of enactment. *Journal of the American Psychoanalytic Association*, 39, 595–614.

Meares, R. (1999). The contribution of Hughlings Jackson to an understanding of dissociation. *American Journal of Psychiatry*, 156(12), 1850–1855.

Mellman, T. A., Bustamante, V., Fins, A. I., Pigeon, W. R., and Nolan, B. (2002). REM sleep and the early development of posttraumatic stress disorder. *American Journal of Psychiatry*, 159(10), 1696–1701.

Menon, V., and Uddin, L. Q. (2010). Saliency, switching, attention, and control: A network model of insula function. *Brain Structure and Function*, 214, 655–667.

Metcalfe, J., and Jacobs, W. J. (1996). A "hot-system/cool-system" view of memory under stress. *PTSD Research Quarterly*, 7, 1–3.

Michal, M., Beutel, M. E., Jordan, J., Zimmerman, M., Wolters, S., and Heindenreich, T. (2007). Depersonalization, mindfulness, and childhood trauma. *Journal of Nervous and Mental Disease*, 195, 693–696.

Michal, M., Koechel, A., Canterino, M., Adler, J., Reiner, I., Vossel, G., . . . Gamner, M. (2013). Depersonalization disorder: Disconnection of cognitive evaluation from autonomic responses to emotional stimuli. *PLoSOne*, 8(9), e74331 (74331–74312).

Middleton, W. (2013). Parent–child incest that extends into adulthood: A survey of international press reports, 2007–2011. *Journal of Trauma and Dissociation*, 14(2), 184–197.

Milad, M. R., Pitman, R. K., Ellis, C. B., Gold, A. L., Shin, L. M., Lasko, N. B., . . . Rauch, S. L. (2009). Neurobiological basis of failure to recall extinction memory in posttraumatic stress disorder. *Biological Psychiatry, 66*(12), 1075–1082.

Milad, M. R., Rauch, S. L., Pitman, R. K., and Quirk, G. J. (2006). Fear extinction in rats: Implications for human brain imaging and anxiety disorders. *Biological Psychiatry, 73,* 61–71.

Mitchell, S. A. (1991). Contemporary perspectives on self: Toward an integration. *Psychoanalytic Dialogues, 1,* 121–147.

Monsen, J. T., and Monsen, K. (1999). A psychotherapy model integrating Silvan Tomkin's affectand scripttheory within the framework of self psychology. *Progress in Self Psychology, 15,* 287–306.

Monsen, J. T., Eilertsen, D. E., Melgard, T. and Odegard, P. (1996). Affect and affect consciousness: Initial experiences with the assessment of affect integration. *Journal of Psychotherapy Practice and Research, 5,* 238–249.

Moore, B. E., and Fine, Bernard D. (1990). *Psychoanalytic terms and concepts.* New Haven, CT: Yale University Press.

Morrison, A. P. (1989). *Shame: The underside of narcissism.* Hillsdale, NJ: Analytic Press.

Napier, N. J. (1994). *Getting through the day: Strategies for adults hurt as children.* New York: Norton.

Nash, M. R., Hulsey, T. L., Sexton, M. C., Harralson, T. L., and Lambert, W. (1993). Long-term sequelae of childhood sexual abuse: Perceived family environment, psychopathology, and dissociation. *Journal of Consulting and Clinical Psychology, 61*(2), 276–283.

Newbury, M. (1967). *Just Dropped In (To See What Condition My Condition Is In).* Sony/ATV Music Publishing LLC.

Nijenhuis, E. R. S. (2000). Somatoform dissociation: Major symptoms of dissociative disorders. *Journal of Trauma and Dissociation, 1*(4), 7-32.

Nolen-Hoeksema, S., and Morrow, J. (1989). A prospective study of depression and posttraumatic stress symptoms after a natural disaster: The 1989 Loma Prieta earthquake. *Journal of Personality and Social Psychology, 61,* 115–121.

Novey, S. (1959). A clinical view of affect theory in psycho-analysis. *International Journal of Psychoanalysis, 40,* 94–104.

Novick, K. K., and Novick, J. (2003). Two systems of self-regulation and the differential application of psychoanalytic technique. *American Journal of Psychoanalysis, 63*(1), 1–20.

Novick, K. K., and Novick, J. (2004). The superego and the two-system model. *Psychoanalytic Inquiry, 24,* 232–256.

Oatley, K., Keltner, D., and Jenkins, J. M. (2006). *Understanding emotions*. Malden, MA: Blackwell.

Ogawa, J. R., Sroufe, L. A., Weinfield, N. S., Carlson, E. A., and Egelend, B. (1997). Development and the fragmented self: Longitudinal study of dissociative symptomatology in a nonclinical sample. *Development and Psychopathology*, 9, 855–879.

Ogden, P., Minton, K., and Pain, C. (2006). *Trauma and the body: A sensorimotor approach to psychotherapy*. New York: Norton.

Ogden, P., Pain, C., and Fisher, J. (2006). A sensorimotor approach to the treatment of trauma and dissociation. *Psychiatric Clinics of North America*, 29(March), 263–279.

Olinick, S. L. (1964). The negative therapeutic reaction. *International Journal of Psychoanalysis*, 45, 540–548.

Orgel, S. (2013). On negative therapeutic reaction. In L. Wurmser and H. Jarass (eds.), *Nothing good is allowed to stand: An integrative view of the negative therapeutic reaction* (pp. 57–66). New York: Routledge.

Orne, M. T. (1959). The nature of hypnosis: Artifact and essence. *Journal of Abnormal and Social Psychology*, 58, 277–299.

Ornstein, A. (2013). The negative therapeutic reaction revisited. In L. Wurmser and H. Jarass (eds.), *Nothing good is allowed to stand: An integrative view of the negative therapeutic reaction* (pp. 160–169). New York: Routledge.

Paivio, S. C., and Nieuwenhuis, J. A. (2001). Efficacy of emotion focused therapy for adult survivors of child abuse: A preliminary study. *Journal of Traumatic Stress*, 14(1), 115–133.

Panksepp, J. (1998). *Affective neuroscience: The foundations of human and animal emotions*. New York: Oxford University Press.

Panksepp, J. (2004). Affective consciousness: Core emotional feelings in animals and humans. *Consciousness and Cognition*, 14(1), 30–80.

Panksepp, J., and Biven, L. (2012). *The archaeology of mind: Neuroevolutionary origins of human emotions*. New York: Norton.

Papolos, D. F., Veit, S., Faedda, G. L., Saito, T., and Lachman, H. M. (1998). Ultra-ultra rapid cycling bipolar disorder is associated with the low activity catecholamine-O-methyltransferase allele. *Molecular Psychiatry*, 3(4), 346–349.

Pascual-Leone, A., and Greenberg, L. (2007). Emotional processing in experiential therapy: Why "the only way out is through."*Journal of Consulting and Clinical Psychology*, 75(6), 875–887.

Paulus, M. P., and Stein, M. B. (2010). Interoception in anxiety and depression. *Brain Structure and Function*, 214, 451–463.

Peleg, T., and Shalev, A. Y. (2006). Longitudinal studies of PTSD: Overview of findings and methods. *CNS Spectrums*, 11(8), 589–602.

Peri, T., Ben-Shakhar, G., Orr, S. P., and Shalev, A. Y. (2000). Psychophysiologic assessment of aversive conditioning in posttraumatic stress disorder. *Biological Psychiatry*, 47, 512–519.

Phan, K. L., Wager, T. D., Taylor, S. F., and Liberzon, I. (2004). Functional neuroimaging studies of human emotions. CNS Spectrums, 9, 258–266.

Phelps, E. A. (2004). Human emotion and memory: Interactions with the amygdala and hippocampal complex. *Current Opinion in Neurobiology*, 14, 198–202.

Phelps, E. A., O'Connor, K. J., Gatenby, J. C., Gore, J. C., Grillon, C., and Davis, M. (2001). Activation of the left amygdala to a cognitive representation of fear. *Nature Neuroscience*, 4, 437–441.

Phillips, M. L., Medford, N., Senior, C., Bullmore, E. T., Suckling, J., Brammer, M. J., . . . David, A. S. (2001). Depersonalization disorder: Thinking without feeling. *Psychiatry Research: Neuroimaging Section*, 108, 145–160.

Piper, W. (1930/1976). *The little engine that could*. New York: Platt and Munk.

Pizzagalli, D. A., Lehmann, D., Hendrick, A. M., Regard, M., Pascual-Marqui, and Davidson, R. J. (2002). Affective judgments of faces modulate early activity (~160ms) within the fusiform gyri. *Neuroimage*, 16, 663-677.

Ploghaus, A., Narain, C., Beckmann, C. F., Clare, S., Bantick, S., Wise, R., Matthews, P.M., Nicholas, J., Rawlins, P., Tracey, I. (2001). Exacerbation of pain by anxiety is associated with activity in a hippocampal network. *Journal of Neuroscience*, 21(December), 9896–9903.

Ploghaus, A., Tracey, I., Gati, J. S., Clare, S., Menon, R. S., Matthews, P. M., Nicholas, J., and Rawlins, P. (1999). Dissociating pain from its anticipation in the human brain. *Science*, 284(5422), 1979–1981.

Porges, S. W. (1995). Orienting in a defensive world: Mammalian modifications of our evolutionary heritage. A polyvagal theory. *Psychophysiology*, 32, 301–318.

Porges, S. W. (2011). *The polyvagal theory: Neurophysiological foundations of emotions, attachment, communication, and self-regulation*. New York: Norton.

Preuessner, J. C., Dedovic, K., Khalili-Mahani, N., Engert, V., Pruessner, M., Buss, C., . . . Lupien, S. (2008). Deactivation of the limbic system during acute psychosocial stress: Evidence from positron emission tomography and functional magnetic resonance imaging studies. *Biological Psychiatry*, 63, 234–240.

Pulliam, J. V. K., Dawaghreh, A. M., Alema-Mensah, E., and Plotsky, P. M. (2010). Social defeat stress produces prolonged alterations in acoustic startle and body weight gain in male Long Evans rats. *Journal of Psychiatric Research*, 44(2), 106–111.

Putnam, F. W. (1989). *Diagnosis and treatment of multiple personality disorder*. New York: Guilford Press.

Putnam, F. W. (1992). Discussion: Are alter personalities fragments or figments? *Psychoanalytic Inquiry*, 12(1), 95–111.

Putnam, F. W. (1997). *Dissociation in children and adolescents.* New York: Guilford Press.

Putnam, F. W., Guroff, J., Silberman, E. K., Barban, L., and Post, R. M. (1986). The clinical phenomenology of MPD: Review of 100 recent cases. *Journal of Clinical Psychiatry*, 47, 285–293.

Pynoos, R. S., Frederick, C., Nader, K., Arroyo, W., Steinberg, A., Eth, S., Nunez, F., and Fairbanks, L. (1987). Life threat and posttraumatic stress in school-age children. *Archives of General Psychiatry*, 44(12), 1057–1063.

Rainville, P., Duncan, G. H., Price, B.C., and Bushnell, M. C. (1997). Pain affect encoded in human anterior cingulate but not somatosensory cortex. *Science*, 277(August), 968–971.

Raskind, M. A., Peskind, E. R., Kanter, E. D., Petrie, E. C., Radant, A., Thompson, C. E., . . . Straits-Tröster, K. (2003). Reduction of nightmares and other PTSD symptoms in combat veterans by prazosin: A placebo-controlled study. *American Journal of Psychiatry*, 160(2), 371–373.

Rauch, S. L., van der Kolk, B. A., Fisler, R. E., Alpert, N. M., Orr, S. P., Savage, C. R., . . . Pitman, R. K. (1996). A symptom provocation study of posttraumatic stress disorder using positron emission tomography and script driven imagery. *Archives of General Psychiatry*, 53, 380–387.

Reinders, A. A. T. S., Nijenhuis, E. R. S., Paans, A. M. J., Korf, J., Wilemsen, A. T. M., and den Boer, J. A. (2003). One brain, two selves. *Neuroimage*, 20, 2119–2125.

Reinders, A. A. T. S., Nijenhuis, E. R. S., Quak, J., Korf, J., Haaksma, J., Paans, A. M. J., . . . den Boer, J. A. (2006). Psychobiological characteristics of dissociative identity disorder: A symptom provocation study. *Biological Psychiatry*, 60, 730–740.

Rhudy, J. L. M., and Meagher, M. W. (2000). Fear and anxiety: Divergent effects on human pain thresholds. *Pain*, 84, 65–75.

Roesler, T. A., and Wind, T. W. (1994). Telling the secret: Adult women describe their disclosures of incest. *Journal of Interpersonal Violence*, 9, 327–338.

Ross, C. A., Heber, S., Norton, G. R., Anderson, D., Anderson, G., and Barchet, P. (1989). The dissociative disorders interview schedule: A structured interview. *DISSOCIATION*, 2, 169–189.

Ross, R. J., Ball, W. A., Sullivan, K. A., and Carof, S. N. (1989). Sleep disturbance as the hallmark of posttraumatic stress disorder. *American Journal of Psychiatry*, 146(6), 697–707.

Rothschild, B. (2000). *The body remembers: The psychophysiology of trauma and trauma treatment.* New York: Norton.

Rothstein, A. (1991). Sadomasochism in the neuroses conceived of as a pathological compromise formation. *Journal of the American Psychoanalytic Association*, 39, 363–375.

Russell, P. (1998). The role of paradox in the repetition compulsion. In J. G. Teicholz and D. Kreigman (eds.), *Trauma, repetition, and affect regulation: The work of Paul Russell* (pp. 1–22). New York: Other Press.

Ryle, A. (2001). *Cognitive analytic therapy and borderline personality disorder.* New York: Wiley.

Ryle, A. (ed.). (1999). *Cognitive analytic therapy: Developments in theory and practice.* New York: Wiley.

Rynearson, E. K. (2006). *Violent death: Resilience and intervention beyond the crisis.* New York: Routledge.

Sandler, J. (1976). Countertransference and role responsiveness. *International Review of Psychoanalysis*, 3, 43–47.

Sar, V., Tutkun, H., Alyanak, B., Bakim, B., and Baral, I. (2000). Frequency of dissociative disorders among psychiatric outpatients in Turkey. *Comprehensive Psychiatry*, 41(3), 216–222.

Sawchenko, P. E. (1983). Central connections of the sensory and motor nuclei of the vagus nerve. *Journal of the Autonomic Nervous System*, 9(1), 13–26.

Scaer, R. C. (2001). *The body bears the burden.* Binghamton, NY: Haworth Press.

Scheff, T. J., and Retzinger, S. M. (2001). *Emotions and violence: Shame and rage in destructive conflicts.* Lincoln, NE: iUniverse.

Schmahl, C. G., Vermetten, E., Elzinga, B. M., and Bremner, J. D. (2003). Magnetic resonance imaging of hippocampal and amygdala volume in women with childhood abuse and borderline personality disorder. *Neuroimaging*, 122, 193–198.

Schmithhüsen, G. (2013). "Time that no one can count, always begins anew": Thoughts concerning the function and meaning of the so-called negative therapeutic reaction from the perspective of time standing still. In L. Wurmser and H. Jarass (eds.), *Nothing good is allowed to stand: An integrative approach to the negative therapeutic reaction* (pp. 67–96). New York: Routledge.

Schore, A. N. (1994). *Affect regulation and the origin of the self: The neurobiology of emotional development.* Hillsdale, NJ: Lawrence Erlbaum.

Schore, A. N. (2003). Affect regulation and repair of the self. New York: Norton.

Schore, J. R., and Schore, A. N. (2008). Modern attachment theory: The central role of affect regulation in development and treatment. *Clinical Social Work Journal*, 36, 9–20.

Schwartz, H. L. (1994). From dissociation to negotiation: A relational psychoanalytic perspective on multiple personality disorder. *Psychoanalytic Psychology*, 11(2), 189–231.

Searles, H. (1967). The dedicated physician. In R. W. Gibson (ed.), *Crosscurrents in psychiatry and psychoanalysis* (pp. 128–143). Philadelphia: Lippincott.

Segal, H. (1979). *Klein*. London: Karnac.

Seinfeld, J. (2002). *A primer of handling the negative therapeutic reaction*. New York: Jason Aronson.

Shapiro, F. (1995). *Eye movement desensitization and reprocessing*. New York: Guilford Press.

Shaw, D. (2013). *Traumatic narcissism: Relational systems of subjugation*.New York: Routledge.

Shengold, L. (1974). The metaphor of the mirror. *Journal of the American Psychoanalytic Association*, 22, 97–115.

Sherrington, C. S. (1900). Experiments on the value of vascular and visceral factors for the genesis of emotion. *Proceedings of the Royal Society*, 66, 390–403.

Shimamura, A. P. (2007). Priming effects in amnesia: Evidence for a dissociable memory function. *Quarterly Journal of Experimental Psychology Section A: Human Experimental Psychology*, 38(4), 619-644.

Shin, L. M., and Liberzon, I. (2010). The neurocircuitry of fear, stress, and anxiety disorders. *Neuropsychopharmacology Reviews*, 35, 169–191.

Shin, L. M., Rauch, S. L., and Pitman, R. K. (2006). Amygdala, medial prefrontal cortex, and hippocampal function in PTSD. *Annals of the New York Academy of Sciences*, 1071, 67–79.

Siegel, D. J. (1999). *The developing mind: Toward a neurobiology of interpersonal experience*. New York: Guilford Press.

Sierra, M., Baker, D., Medford, N., and David, A. S. (2005). Unpacking the depersonalization syndrome: An exploratory factor analysis on the Cambridge depersonalization scale. *Psychological Medicine*, 35, 1523–1532.

Sierra, M., and Berrios, G. E. (2000). The Cambridge depersonalisation scale: A new instrument for the measurement of depersonalisation. *Psychiatry Research*, 93, 153–164.

Sierra, M., Senior, C., Dalton, J., McDonough, M., Bond, A., Phillips, M. L., . . . David, A. S. (2002). Autonomic response in depersonalization disorder. *Archives of General Psychiatry*, 59, 833-838.

Simeon, D. (2004). Depersonalizaiton disorder: A contemporary overview. *CNS Drugs*, 18(6), 343–354.

Simeon, D., and Abugel, J. (2006). *Feeling unreal: Depersonalization disorder and the loss of the self*. Oxford: Oxford University Press.

Simeon, D., Guralnik, O., Hazlett, E. A., Spiegel-Cohen, J., Hollander, E., and Buchsbaum, M. S. (2000). Feeling unreal: A PET study of depersonalization disorder. *American Journal of Psychiatry*, 157, 1782–1788.

Simeon, D., Kozin, D. S., Segal, K., Lerch, B., Dujour, R., and Giesbrecht, T. (2008). De-constructing depersonalization: Further evidence for symptom clusters. *Psychiatry Research*, 157, 303–306.

Skelton, R. (ed.). (2006). *The Edinburgh international encyclopaedia of psychoanalysis: Dissociation.* Edinburgh: Edinburgh University Press.

Solomon, J., and George, C. (1999). The place of disorganization in attachment theory. In J. Solomon and C. George (eds.), *Attachment disorganization* (pp. 3–32). New York: Guilford Press.

Solomon, M. F., and Siegel, D. J. (eds.). (2003). *Healing trauma: Attachment, mind, body, and brain.* New York: Norton.

Somer, E., and Szwarcberg, S. (2001). Variables in delayed disclosure of childhood sexual abuse. *American Journal of Orthopsychiatry*, 71(3), 332-341.

Sperry, M. (2013a). Putting our heads together: Mentalizing systems. Psychoanalytic Dialogues, 23(6), 683–699.

Sperry, M. (2013b). Response to commentaries. *Psychoanalytic Dialogues*, 23(6), 715–719.

Squire, L. R., and Kandel, E. R. (1999). *Memory: From mind to molecules.* New York: Scientific American Library.

Sroufe, L. A. (1996). *Emotional development: The organization of emotional life in the early years.* New York: Cambridge University Press.

Stechler, G. and Kaplan, S. (1980). The development of the self—A psychoanalytic perspective. *Psychoanalytic Study of the Child*, 35, 85–105.

Steele, K., van der Hart, O., and Nijenhuis, E. R. S. (2001). Dependency in the treatment of complex posttraumatic stress disorder and dissociative disorders. *Journal of Trauma and Dissociation*, 2(4), 79–116.

Steele, K., van der Hart, O., and Nijenhuis, E.R.S. (2005). Phase-oriented treatment of structural dissociation in complex traumatization: Overcoming trauma-related phobias. *Journal of Trauma & Dissociation*, 6(3), 11–53.

Stein, D. J. and Simeon, D. (2009). Cognitive-affective neuroscience of depersonalization. *CNS Spectrums*, 14(9), 467–471.

Steinberg, M. (1993). *Structured clinical interview for DSM-IV dissociative disorders.* Washington, DC: American Psychiatric Press.

Steiner, J. (2011). *Seeing and being seen: Emerging from a psychic retreat.* New York: Routledge.

Stern, D. B. (1997). *Unformulated experience: From dissociation to imagination in psychoanalysis.* Hillsdale, NJ: Analytic Press.

Stern, D. B. (2004). The eye sees itself: Dissociation, enactment, and the achievement of conflict. *Contemporary Psychoanalysis*, 40, 197–237.

Stern, D. B. (2010). *Partners in thought: Working with unformulated experience, dissociation, and enactment.* New York: Routledge.

Stern, D. N. (1985). *The interpersonal world of the infant.* New York: Basic Books.

Stickgold, R. (2005). Sleep dependent memory consolidation. *Nature,* 437(27), 1272–1278.

Strahan, E. J., Spencer, S. J., and Zanna, M.P. (2002). Subliminal priming and persuasion: Striking while the iron is hot. *Journal of Experimental Social Psychology,* 38, 556–558.

Summit, R. (1983). The child sexual abuse accommodation syndrome. *Child Abuse and Neglect,* 7, 177–193.

Suomi, S. J. (2006). Risk, resilience, and gene× environment interactions in Rhesus monkeys. *Annals of the New York Academy of Sciences,* 1094(1), 52–62.

Susani, C. V. (2010). Identity disorder and the psycho-analytical process. *Psyche,* 64, 481-504.

Szymanski, K., Sapanski, L., and Conway, F. (2011). Trauma and ADHD—Association or diagnostic confusion? A clinical perspective. *Journal of Infant, Child, and Adolescent Psychotherapy,* 10(1), 51–59.

Teicher, M. H., and Samson, J. A. (2013). Childhood maltreatment and psychopathology: A case for ecophenotypic variants as clinically and neurobiologically distinct subtypes. *American Journal of Psychiatry,* 170, 1114–1133.

Teicher, M. H., Samson, J. A., Sheu, Y.-S., Polcari, A., and McGreenery, C. E. (2010). Hurtful words: Association of exposure of peer verbal abuse with elevated psychiatric symptom scores and corpus callosum abnormalities. *American Journal of Psychiatry,* 167(12), 1464–1471.

Terr, L. C. (1979). Children of Chowchilla—A study of psychic trauma. *Psychoanalytic Study of the Child,* 34, 547–623.

Terr, L. C. (1991). Childhood traumas: An outline and overview. *American Journal of Psychiatry,* 148, 10–19.

Tomkins, S. S. (1995). Script theory. In E. V. Demos (ed.), *Exploring affect: The selected writings of Silvan S. Tomkins* (pp. 312–388). New York: Cambridge University Press.

Tomkins, S. S. (2008). *Affect, imagery, consciousness: The complete edition, Book One: Volume I: The positive affects, Volume II: The negative affects.* New York: Springer.

Tomkins, S. S., and McCarter, R. (1995). What and where are the primary affects? Some evidence for a theory. In E. V. Demos (ed.), *Exploring affect: The selected writings of Silvan S. Tomkins* (pp. 217–262). New York: Cambridge University Press.

Torem, M. S. (1990). Covert multiple personality underlying eating disorders. *American Journal of Psychotherapy*, 44(3), 357-368.

Tulving, E. (1985). Memory and consciousness. *Canadian Psychology*, 26, 1–12.

Tulving, E., Schacter, D. L., and Stark, H. A. (1982). Priming effects in word-fragment completion are indpendent of recognition memory. *Journal of Experimental Psychology: Learning, Memory, and Cognition*, 8(4), 336–342.

Turkus, J. A., and Kahler, J. A. (2006). Therapeutic interventions in the treatment of dissociative disorders. *Psychiatric Clinics of North America*, 29, 245–262.

Valenstein, A. F. (1973). On attachment to painful feelings and the negative therapeutic reaction. *Psychoanalytic Study of the Child*, 28, 365–392.

van der Hart, O., Nijenhuis, E. R. S., and Steele, K. (2006). *The haunted self: Structural dissociation and the treatment of chronic traumatization*. New York: Norton.

van der Kolk, B. A., Hostetler, A., Herron, N., and Fisler, R. E. (1994). Trauma and the development of borderline personality disorder. *Psychiatric Clinics of North America*, 17(4), 715–731.

van der Kolk, B. A., MacFarlane, A., and Weisaeth, L. (1996). *Traumatic stress*. New York: Guilford Press.

van der Kolk, B. A., Perry, J. C., and Herman, J. L. (1991). Childhood origins of self-destructive behavior. *American Journal of Psychiatry*, 148(12), 1665–1671.

Van Derbur, M. (2003). *Miss America by day: Lessons learned from ultimate betrayals and unconditional love*. Denver, CO: Oak Hill Ridge Press.

van Houdenhove, B., Neerinckx, E., Lysens, R., Vertommen, H., van Houdenhove, L., Onghena, P., . . . D'Hooghe, M.-B. (2001). Victimization in chronic fatigue syndrom and fibromylagia in tertiary care: A controlled study on prevalence and characteristics. *Psychosomatics*, 42, 21–28.

Vermetten, E., Schmahl, C., Lindner, S., Loewenstein, R. J., and Bremner, J. D. (2006). Hippocampal and amygdalar volumes in dissociative identity disorder. *American Journal of Psychiatry*, 163, 630–636.

Vermilyea, E. G. (2000). *Growing beyond survival: A self-help tool-kit for managing traumatic stress*. Baltimore: Sidran Press.

Vuilleumier, P., Richardson, M. P., Armony, J. L., Driver, J., and Dolan, R. J. (2004). Distant influences of amygdala lesion on visual cortical activation during emotional face processing. *Nature Neuroscience*, 7(11), 1271–1278.

Waelder, R. (1936). The principle of multiple function: Observations on over-determination. *Psychoanalytic Quarterly*, 5(1), 45–62.

Watkins, J. G. (1971). The affect bridge: A hypnoanalytic technique. *International Journal of Clinical and Experimental Hypnosis*, 19, 21–27.

Watkins, J. G. (1992). *Hypnoanalytic techniques*. New York: Irvington.

Watkins, J. G., and Watkins, H. (1997). *Ego states: Theory and therapy*. New York: Norton.

Way, K. G. (2006). How metaphors shape the concept and treatment of dissociation. In R. A. Chefetz (ed.), *Dissociative disorders: An expanding window into the psychobiology of the mind* (vol. 29:1, pp. 27–43). Philadelphia: Elsevier.

Weekes, C. (1969/1990). *Hope and help for your nerves*. New York: Signet.

Weinberger, J., and Westen, D. (2008). RATS, we should have used Clinton: subliminal priming in political campaigns. *Political Psychology*, 29(5), 631–651.

White, R. M. (2000). Unraveling the Tuskegee study of untreated syphilis. *Archives of Internal Medicine*, 160(5), 585–598.

Widen, S. C. (2013). Children's interpretation of facial expressions: The long path from valence-based to specific discrete categories. *Emotion Review*, 5(1), 72–77.

Widen, S. C., and Russell, J. A. (2010). The "disgust face" conveys anger to children. *Emotion*, 10(4), 455–466.

Winnicott, C. (1989). D. W. W.: A reflection. In C. Winnicott, R. Shepherd,and M. Davis (eds.), *Psychoanalytic explorations: D. W. Winnicott* (pp. 1–18). Cambridge, MA: Harvard University Press.

Winnicott, D. W. (1949/1958). Mind and its relation to the psyche-soma. In *Collected papers: Through paediatrics to psycho-analysis*. New York: Basic Books.

Winnicott, D. W. (1953). Transitional objects and transitional phenomena: A study of the first not-me possession. *International Journal of Psychoanalysis*, 34(part 2), 89–97.

Winnicott, D. W. (1960a/1965). Ego distortion in terms of true and false self. In *The maturational processes and the facilitating environment* (pp. 140–152). London: Hogarth Press and the Institute of Psycho-Analysis.

Winnicott, D. W. (1960b). The theory of the parent-infant relationship. *International Journal of Psychoanalysis*, 41, 585–595.

Wolberg, L. R. (1945). *Hypnoanalysis*. New York: Grune and Stratton.

Wolff, P. (1987). *The development of behavioral states and the expression of emotions in early infancy: New proposals for investigation*. Chicago: University of Chicago Press.

Wurmser, L. (1994). *The mask of shame*. Northvale, NJ: Jason Aronson.

Wurmser, L. (2000). *The power of the inner judge: Psychodynamic treatment of the severe neuroses*. Northvale, NJ: Jason Aronson.

Wurmser, L., and Jarass, H. (eds.). (2013a). *Nothing good is allowed to stand: An integrative view of the negative therapeutic reaction*. New York: Routledge.

Wurmser, L., and Jarass, H. (2013b). Introduction. In L. Wurmser & H. Jarass (eds.), *Nothing good is allowed to stand: An integrative view of the negative therapeutic reaction* (pp. 1-25). New York: Routledge.

Yamada, M., and Decety, J. (2009). Unconscious affective processing and empathy: An investigation of subliminal priming on the detection of painful facial expressions. *Pain*, 143, 71–75.

Yamada, Y., and Kawabe, T. (2011). Emotion colors time perception unconsciously. *Consciousness and Cognition*, 20(4), 1835–1841.

Yehuda, R. (1998). Psychoneuroendocrinology of post-traumatic stress disorder. In C. B. Nemeroff (ed.), *Psychoneuroendocrinology* (vol. 21, pp. 359–379). Philadelphia: Saunders.

Yehuda, R., and Bierer, L. M. (2009). The relevance of epigenetics to PTSD: Implications for the DSM-V. *Journal of Traumatic Stress*, 22(5), 427–434.

Yehuda, R., and LeDoux, J. (2007). Response variation following trauma: A translational neuroscience approach to understanding PTSD. *Neuron*, 56, 19–32.

Yin, Y., Jin, C., Hu, X., Duan, L., Li, Z., Song, M., . . . Li, L. (2011). Altered resting-state functional connectivity of thalamus in earthquake-induced posttraumatic stress disorder: A functional magnetic resonance imaging study. *Brain Research*, 1411, 98–107.

Zanarini, M. C. (2009). Psychotherapy of borderline personality disorder. *Acta Psychiatrica Scandinavica*, 120, 373–377.

Zanarini, M. C., Frankenburg, F. R., Jager-Hyman, S., Reich, D. B., and Fitzmaurice, G. (2008). The course of dissociation for patients with borderline personality disorder and axis II comparison subjects: A 10-year follow-up study. *Acta Psychiatrica Scandanavica*, 118, 291–296.

Index

apparently normal personality
   (ANP), 93
assertive anger, 159. *see also* anger
association
   reestablishing capacity for, 192
   tolerable, compartmental content
      and road to, 77
associative processes, 1, 133
   self-states and, 70
   waking and sleeping periods and,
      109–10
associative recall, 124
attachment, 59
   avoidant, 19, 89
   disorganized/disoriented, 19, 89,
      140
   disrupted, unleashing of fear,
      and, 178, 206
   early loss and "fading" of, 297–98
   fear, relationship, and, 206–17
   insecure, 37, 89
   secure, 19
   see also Type D attachment
attachment behavior, Strange
   Situation and, 19–20
attachment bond, bitterly painful
      emotional experiences
      originating within, 43
"attackment" relationships,
      negativity and, 287–88, 361
attention deficit hyperactivity
      disorder (ADHD), 79
attribution, false, undermining of
      reality testing, 294, 295
audio recordings of sessions
   discoveries made while listening
      to, 376
   hearing nuances of interactions
      in, 349
autobiographical knowledge,

behaviors without crucial links
   to, 52
autonomic arousal, depersonalization
   and blunting of, 203
autonomic nervous system (ANS),
   heart and respiratory rate and,
   167
avoidance strategies, left-brain, 48
avoidant attachment, 19, 89

Bardy, B., 35
BASK model, 111, 165, 197, 346
Beah, I., 179
Beck Depression Inventory,
   version II, 120, 121
bed nucleus of striaterminalis,
   nonspecific fear cues and
   activation of, 182
Beebe, B., 89
behavioral contradiction,
   dissociation and, 21
behavioral scripts
   creative curiosity required for,
      68–70
   enactive knowing and, 35
behavior(s)
   addictive, 60
   amnesia for, 122
   compartmentalization of, 60
   disremembered, 114
   dissociation and detachment of,
      from awareness, 31
   dissociative process and
      increased detachment from, 77
   emotions and activation of, 140
   three pillars of dissociative
      process and, 28
   see also action(s)
being heard, creating sense of, for
   patient, 97, 99

phobic core, harsh inner judge and,
    296
physical abuse, 40, 55, 94, 289, 293,
    301, 304, 309, 311–12, 364, 365
physiological state of patient
  becoming keen observer of, 117
  meaning and, 76
pituitary gland, 167
pleasure
  intense, speechlessness and, 46
  pain and neurobiological
    similarities with, 247
pornography, addiction to, 235
positive emotions, right fusiform
  gyrus and, 150
posthypnotic work, re-alerting
  instructions in, 149
posttraumatic stress disorder
    (PTSD), 161, 191
  complex, 58
  documentable comorbidity
    between bipolar disorder and,
    81
  DSM definition of trauma in, 190
  emotional awareness, emotional
    adaptibility, and, 159
  emotionally overmodulated
    version of, 79
  flashback of, as dissociative
    symptom, 28
  loss of hippocampal volume in
    wake of, 36
  persistence of, hypothesis for,
    184
  rat living conditions and levels
    of, 90
  reexperiencing hyperarousal
    model of, 79
  sexual activity and hyperarousal
    symptoms of, 247

sleep disturbance as hallmark of,
    109
  soldiers, deeply altered sense of
    self, and, 192
  testing for dissociation in face of,
    185
posture, 76, 169
power, mother's judgment and,
    296
powerlessness, sexual addiction,
    affect scripts, and, 229
prazosin, 103
precuneus, verbal abuse,
    developmental lag, and, 39,
    156, 289
prefrontal cortex,
    depersonalization and
    decoupling of amygdalar
    alarm functions, insular
    interoceptivity, and, 202
pretend modes of thinking, 92,
    347
primary process modes of
    thinking, 166, 166n4
priming, 124–25
privacy intrusion, 294, 295
procedure, implicit memory and,
    35
projective identification, enactment
    in treatment and, 34
pseudodelusions, 130, 193, 258
pseudohallucinations, 130
psychiatric assessments, self-
    state psychology, dissociative
    experience, and, 81
psychic equivalence
  definition of, 91–92
  in dissociative transitional space,
    347
psychic trauma, 191

right brain, dissociative process, and, 29
as stressor, according to DSM-5, 189–90
trauma-time adhesiveness, 299
trauma time issues, failure of fear extinction and, 186
treatment alliance, strong, patients catching deflective process and, 28
trichotillomania, 62–65
True Self, 73
trust, 144, 177
Turkish populations, dissociative disorders present with conversion in, 203
twitching movements, 76
two-faced replies, 3
Type D attachment, 318
  adult borderline personality disorder and, 90–91
  adult dissociation and, 20, 91, 91n3
  lack of coherence and, 44
  narrative incoherence and parents of children with, 235
  patterns typical of narratives in, 60
  preserving the good mother and, 87
  simultaneous contradictory internal working models of, 94
  Strange Situation and, 19

ultradian cycling, 80
ultra-ultra rapid cycling (UURC), 80
unexplained ownership, 114
unformulated experience, 254
unintegrated experience, 87

United States of Tara, 228
unreality, feelings of, 97
unresolved experience, lack of coherence and, 44
"unthought known" (Bolas), 36
UURC. *see* ultra-ultra rapid cycling (UURC)

vagus nerve, hypothalamus and, 167
Valenstein, A., 297, 298, 306
value conflicts, harsh inner judge and, 296, 297
vasoactive intestinal polypeptide, stress and, 167
verbal abuse
  impaired left- and right-brain communication and, 156
  internal experience of, 119, 120
  language, negativity, and, 294–97
  neuroanatomic developmental delays and, 39–40, 289
veridical memory, 252
"vertical split," 196, 325
Veterans Administration hospitals, exposure therapy less used in PTSD treatment in, 175n7
VIP. *See* vasoactive intestinal polypeptide
viscera, brain connection with, 167
visceroception, insula and, 202
visual associational cortex, depersonalization and, 203, 204
visualization, decision making and, 124
voice tone, 139
V.P., split brain procedure for epilepsy and case of, 38, 39

Also available from

THE NORTON SERIES
ON INTERPERSONAL NEUROBIOLOGY

*Love and War in Intimate Relationships: Connection,
Disconnection, and Mutual Regulation in Couple Therapy*
Marion Solomon, Stan Tatkin

The Present Moment in Psychotherapy and Everyday Life
Daniel N. Stern

The Neurobehavioral and Social-Emotional Development of Infants and Children
Ed Tronick

*The Haunted Self: Structural Dissociation and the Treatment of Chronic
Traumatization*
Onno Van Der Hart, Ellert R. S. Nijenhuis, Kathy Steele

Changing Minds in Therapy: Emotion, Attachment, Trauma, and Neurobiology
Margaret Wilkinson

For complete book details, and to order online,
please visit the Series webpage at www.tiny.cc/1zrsfw